TRESPASSES

POST-CONTEMPORARY INTERVENTIONS
Series Editors: Stanley Fish and Fredric Jameson

TRESPASSES

....

Selected Writings   MASAO MIYOSHI

Foreword by
FREDRIC JAMESON

Edited and with
an Introduction by
ERIC CAZDYN

Duke University Press   Durham and London   2010

TO NOAM CHOMSKY

As I went walking, I saw a sign there,
And on the sign it said "No Trespassing."
But on the other side it didn't say nothing,
That side was made for you and me.

WOODY GUTHRIE, "THIS LAND IS YOUR LAND"

CONTENTS

Fredric Jameson

FOREWORD
....

A new historical situation demands, if not new terms, then at least a reconceptualization of the old ones, and nowhere is this more evident than in the work and reception of Masao Miyoshi. Two old paradigms confront us here (and confront each other as well), that of intellectuals and their specializations on the one hand, and that of nations and their exiles on the other.

There are still refugees and the misery of exile, perhaps more than ever before in the history of the world, and yet the pathos of what we may call the modernist exile—from the Romantics to the Spanish Civil War—is today surcharged if not effaced by a new cosmopolitanism, in which the intellectuals of globalization write in several languages for lay publics and move freely across the invisible borders of the Internet.

As for academic fields, a Victorianist who turns into a Japanologist, a theorist of globalization who documents the structural decay of the American university system (and who is also an art critic and a distinguished photographer)—such a figure may also demand a reconceptualization more radical than what still passes for "theory" in what used to be the "poststructuralist" era.

Who is this Masao Miyoshi? Or as the popular idiom puts it so well: where is he *coming from*? He himself admits he is trespassing. Yet oddly enough, he is trespassing in Japan fully as much as in the United States. Or, if you want to think of the university as his homeland, then there he can be seen to trespass with a vengeance. Meanwhile, in his other life as a visual artist, he takes time out to trample that field too. In short, nothing is safe from him. Is it a temperamental matter or a character trait or simply a bad habit?

Indeed, Walter Benjamin once wrote a rather enigmatic article called "The Destructive Character," about the great Viennese satirist Karl Kraus; it puts the whole current discussion about negativity and critical theory in a new light: "The destructive character knows only one watchword: make room; only one activity: clearing away. His need for fresh air and open space is stronger than any hatred. The destructive character is young and cheerful. For destroying rejuvenates in clearing away the traces of our own age." And Benjamin adds: "No vision inspires the destructive character. He has few needs, and the least of them is to know what will replace what has been destroyed."

How different this is, and how bracing, from the plaintive warnings of the official "Frankfurt School" about the disappearance, the slow suffocation, the intensifying compression of a dense and positivist world without negativity. "I know what I'm against," remarked Horkheimer, "but I don't know what I'm for." Fair enough: but it is easy for the apocalyptic efface-ment of negativity and critical thinking to appear, particularly in Adorno, like the grumbling and complaining of mandarin and academic intellec-tuals in the brave new Americanized world of applied science and rampant consumerism. (We can find a healthy correction to this impression in Gilles Deleuze's celebration of just grousing—"la plainte.") This particular cri-tique of critique, or negation of negativity, generally turns into wholesale anti-intellectualism.

Miyoshi is never anti-intellectual, although there are very few specific intellectuals who escape his judgments: what he has it in for is the cor-ruption of the institutions to which these intellectuals have capitulated; above all, the university itself. So this is not one more complaint about academic intellectuals, one more nostalgic evocation of the good old days of freelance "public" intellectuals, the radicals of the epoch of critical journalism. It is a denunciation of the historical situation itself, without pious moralizing. If ecological militancy offers a worthy provisional task for intellectuals today, we must also reckon in the complacency with which Miyoshi contemplates the possible extinction of all human life from the planet (on the grounds that, after all, we would only be getting what's coming to us in the first place).

Indeed, this emphasis on the negative, critical, destructive focus of Miyoshi's work is the best way to come to terms with the otherwise seemingly heterogeneous subjects and topics across which, like the blinding light of a beacon, it relentlessly plays: radical art, the commercialization of the university, the nation-state, Japan and the West, cultural studies, subjectivity and pronouns, ecology, the state of things from Korea to the Mexican border, or from Cardinal Newman to *documenta X*—such are the seemingly heterogeneous materials united by a commitment to an implacable unification of the aesthetic and the political, of attention to art and attention to globalization, which Miyoshi's life work holds out for us like an ideal.

He is quite impartial in his practice of that attention: as between the United States and Japan no sides are taken, and Western misunderstandings of Japan are denounced without hesitation (what does "interesting" mean? why turn *Genji* into an American novel? with as a literary bonus, an account of how differently the Japanese I-novel functions); but when the critical focus shifts back to Japan itself, its own prosperity, arrogance, and provincialism—not to speak of chauvinism—are equally roundly rebuked. As in the title of his wonderful little book on the first Japanese visitors to the United States after Admiral Perry, *As We Saw Them*, the content of the pronouns, the "shifters," is unstable; it could refer to either of us, and does in turn: both critical standpoints themselves subsumed under the failing category of the nation-state and repudiated without the benefit of some liberal and tolerant multicultural world humanism beyond all national standpoints.

Nietzsche thought pessimism should be energizing and invigorating. Miyoshi's writing is just that, sparing us the obligatory and "constructive" liberal platitudes and with Brechtian cheerfulness taking a hard look at just how bad things are today. Nobody does it quite like him.

Eric Cazdyn

TRESPASSER
....

An Introduction to the Life and Work of Masao Miyoshi

Masao Miyoshi is one of those critical intellectuals who always seem to be a half-beat faster or slower than the rest of us—out of sync just enough to invariably recharge a fatiguing discussion or breathe new life into a tired trend of thinking. It is a peculiar set of speeds indeed, and one that is most impressive when viewed over the long term and in relation to some overarching problems of concern. Whether in terms of literary form, cross-cultural relations, architecture and photography, global economics or ecological effects, the problem of difference (how incommensurable qualities exist among peoples, nations, artistic forms, historical moments) and totality (how an overarching logic relates seemingly disparate entities) is always central to Miyoshi's thinking. But when we look to Miyoshi's work for a comprehensive theory of difference or totality, it is nowhere to be found. This is because his emphasis on one or the other of these terms is always inspired by specific historical imperatives—ones that shape his theoretical priorities and scholarly choices, priorities and choices that cannot be abstracted out in advance.

To take just one example, in the 1970s and 1980s Miyoshi began to emphasize difference as a strategic political act. By arguing that the Japanese prose narrative should not be so quickly identified with the Western novel (as it was so often in Japanese studies and as revealed by the obligatory blurbs on the back of so many translated Japanese works—"just like Dostoyevsky," "the next Faulkner"), Miyoshi exposed how appeals to universality were nothing more than thinly veiled rationales for domination. To delink and emphasize difference, within area and literary studies at the time, therefore, was one way to expose the violence implicit in modernization theory. By the 1990s, however, the emphasis on difference had lost its progressive edge for Miyoshi and turned into a reactionary form of humanities-based criticism, one that argues for uniqueness and radical difference in a way that meets up not only with neoliberal versions of multiculturalism but with the most insidious neonativist discourses. The problem now becomes how to think similarity and continuity (how to think totality) without forgetting the sordid history of so much universalist desire.[1] Or to put this another way: at a moment when everyone is an Orientalist (the expert who knows too much about Asia and the amateur who cannot read a street sign; the apologist who defends Asia and the basher who attacks it; the native who excessively self-identifies with his or her Asian roots and the foreigner who exoticizes Asia or could not care less about it), at a moment like this, when the Orientalist refers to everyone and to no one, we know that times have changed and that we need to rethink the usual ways by which we come to terms with that relation known as Asia and the World. Miyoshi's most current response is to turn to the planet and to rethink the role and possibilities of the contemporary university (this argument is included here as *Literary Elaborations,* and is the only piece by Miyoshi in this volume that has not previously been published).

Indeed, this rethinking exemplifies Miyoshi's incessant and perpetual movement away from the mainstream, breaking into new fields and shaking things up before others come along to smooth things over—by which time he is already somewhere else wreaking more intellectual havoc. This penchant for trespassing, for unlikely incursions and path breaks, can be traced back to his early days in Japan. Masao Miyoshi was born in 1928, the youngest of three boys, to a relatively wealthy Tokyo family. While Miyoshi's ancestry can be traced back to a premodern Samurai line, his father made his living in stocks and commodities (while seriously collecting Asian art), following the Meiji injunction ending the feudal class system. Miyoshi's youth, during the early Showa period of the late twenties and thirties, was a moment of dramatic transformation. Not only was the Taisho experiment with cultural hybridity and interest in all things non-Japanese (1912–1926) over, but capitalisms east and west were shaken to their cores by the great crash of 1929. For Japan this resulted in more state centralization, leading to a runaway militarism marked by the 1931 advance into China and the openly acknowledged empire project. Miyoshi's childhood, therefore, coincided with a social moment of censorship and acquiescence, two qualities that are never associated with his unhesitating and daring form of criticism.

From an early age Miyoshi was reading novels in English and paying a price for it. When a commitment to the English language produced politicized suspicion, in the ultranationalist Japan of the mid-1930s and early 1940s, Miyoshi was already experiencing an outsider consciousness. Like his older brother Eiji, Miyoshi attended the prestigious First Higher School (Ichiko), which had him reading everything from German idealist philosophy to the novels of Henry James. This intellectual and social formation was much more significant than his subsequent experiences at the University of Tokyo—the most famous Japanese university and most important in minting the Japanese ruling class. Miyoshi rarely attended classes there and prided himself on self-study, again mostly in English and mostly despite the misgivings of his peers. Eiji served in the Japanese military, and the experience of witnessing Eiji's trauma on the day of his induction forced Miyoshi (in however unconscious and unformulated a way) to intensify his questions about the war and the larger political mythologies of Japan. Of course, there was precious little room to express such questions and concerns, but the desire to challenge the seemingly natural and to question what most view as unquestionable has been one of Miyoshi's lasting proclivities, and one that can be traced back to these early days.

The Second World War (or the Fifteen Years War as it is called in Japan, 1931–1945) remains a central experience of Miyoshi's life, a baseline and existential source that invariably finds its way into his subsequent thinking and writing. What persists throughout Miyoshi's work, however, is not only the vast and devastating violence of Japan's aggression throughout Asia, combined with the horrific terror of the Tokyo firebombings and the effects of the two atomic bombs, but the toll the war took on individual consciousness, on the fragile subjectivities that lived through such a dreadful time—Miyoshi's own consciousness in particular. Almost forty-five years following the war, Miyoshi writes,

> My point of departure is where I am situated now: as a citizen and resident of the United States, still haunted by the memories of two past wars, and ever rankled by unceasing global crises. I try to teach and

know. My first war experience was as a Japanese subject with little knowledge of the unfolding history around me. My second, the war in Vietnam, was as a naturalized U.S. citizen acutely aware of my earlier ignorance during what is known in Japan as the Fifteen Years War. This time, I promised myself, I would learn and act—resist the State, if necessary. Did I?[2]

In 1952 Miyoshi came to the United States as a Fulbright student at Yale University, later completing a Ph.D. in English at New York University. After returning to Japan for a short stint at the Peers School (Gakushuin University), where he taught English and where the current emperor attended, Miyoshi went back to graduate studies and in 1963 he accepted a position in the English department of the University of California, Berkeley. As one of the first nonnative speakers of English to teach Victorian literature outside of their native countries (and certainly the first Japanese, although by that time he had become a U.S. citizen), Miyoshi aroused interest in colleagues and students alike. But it was his first major publication, *The Divided Self*, which was warmly received in both England and the United States.

No doubt Miyoshi associated his own radical self-questioning in the midst of war with the ways Victorian writers experienced similar tensions endemic to their times and gave expression to this in their writing. Notably, and as a precursor to so many intellectual choices to follow, Miyoshi explains in the preface to *The Divided Self* that there are generally three different ways to explore this Victorian war of the self: (1) by focusing on how such subjective disruptions express themselves (however unconsciously) in the very formal undoing of the novel; (2) by focusing on how a writer's self-awareness and knowledge of these disruptions are thematized and ideologically inscribed in the text; and (3) by tracking the biographical issues in which the life and art of an individual writer become indeterminate. Without wanting to underplay any one of these three approaches (the formal, the ideological, or the biographical), let alone their inextricability, Miyoshi prioritizes the ideological inquiry, or how the explicitly self-conscious Victorian writer faces this split self at the moment of empire and how this awareness is figured in writing. Miyoshi repeats this penchant for a wide-awake and straight-up engagement with a problem throughout his career (in the way he reads literature, criticism, and the world), as expressed in the following sentences, written decades after *The Divided Self*: "As I teach, I try to be neither nostalgic about my own past nor utopian about the world. To see what constitutes the world and to describe it without allegorization is nearly impossible, but such an impossibility is what all of us are conscribed to inhabit."[3]

This impossible but inescapable demand to represent the world is the central problem of Miyoshi's 1974 book on the modern Japanese novel, *Accomplices of Silence*. In a culture that values restraint and the perfectly executed silence, modern Japanese prose fiction writers find themselves in a perpetual state of betrayal. To write a sentence, especially in a form that is not as rule-bound as Japanese poetry, is to defy the most powerful social conventions. "To bring forth a written work to break this silence is thus often tantamount to the writer's sacrifice of himself, via defeat and exhaustion."[4] *Accomplices of Silence* struck an odd chord within literary and East Asian studies, which was partly due to Miyoshi's unusual profile. Miyoshi is a native Japanese speaker with a Japanese secondary and undergraduate education. But he was trained as a Victorian literary scholar, with an American Ph.D. and no formal training in East Asian studies. This eccentric and utterly unique composition functioned like an explosion in the field, as Miyoshi threatened many in East Asian studies, and Japanese literary studies in particular. In the early 1970s, East Asian studies in the United States still owed its formation to cold war imperatives. Most scholars in the field were either former missionaries from pre–Second World War days or former military who learned their Japanese during the U.S. occupation of Japan (1945–1952). Fluency in Japanese, a specific training at one of a handful of American universities, provided the pass key to an exclusive and somewhat ghettoized group of Japan experts—who, more often than not, were disingenuous about their political role as cold warriors, rarely had much exchange with scholarship in other disciplines, and dismissed outside challenges under the pretence that there was nothing to be learned by anyone without a specific type of training (language, modernization theory, and an anthropological instinct to essentialize ethnic difference). Six years before Edward Said's *Orientalism*, Miyoshi was well on his way to exposing the political uses and misuses of academic knowledge and the uneven power relations at stake during cross-cultural exchange.[5]

Already acting as a key faculty supporter of the free speech movement during the mid-sixties, when students at the University of California, Berkeley, insisted that the university administration lift a ban on on-campus political activities, Miyoshi became even more involved with the anti–Vietnam War protests and teach-ins that were intensifying through the late sixties and early seventies. By this time Miyoshi had become close to Noam Chomsky, organizing local antiwar actions together at Berkeley as they shared a trenchant criticism of American intellectual culture and of how academics were only too ready to serve as instruments of the state. Following the U.S. defeat in Vietnam, Miyoshi's political activity and questioning of his chosen profession were cranked up even further, now reconfigured toward the Middle East after meeting Edward Said and traveling to the West Bank (together with Fredric Jameson and Hayden White) as an independent observer of the fierce political situation there. Knowing little about the region at the time, or Palestinians and Israelis, Miyoshi was already reflecting on the structural pitfalls encountered when individuals and nations attempt to define themselves—how such a project not only consistently reduces enemies and others (often leading to violence), but how it also reduces the self in equally destructive ways—a concern that is best expressed in Miyoshi's 1979 publication of *As We Saw Them: The First Japanese Embassy to the United States (1860)* (a chapter from this book is reprinted in here).

When Miyoshi reads the travelogues and memoirs of the Japanese travelers to the United States and the documents of Americans traveling to Japan (most notably those at the time of Townsend Harris's visit in 1856), he redefines the terms and paradigms for each—for, when a single lens with a single focus is used to perceive and understand both, we usually end up seeing nothing at all. This, in fact, is what has produced so much of the confusion and misunderstanding that have infected U.S.-Japan relations all the way to the present. The encounter between "Us" and "Them," which Miyoshi leaves appropriately ambiguous in the book's title, is shot through with difference, and we must be vigilant not to understand the Japanese in Western terms and not to understand the Americans in Japanese ones. For example, Miyoshi reads the Japanese and American travelogues against the different traditions of the literary diary in the two countries, as well as in relation to different subjective experiences of time and space. The inclination toward mechanical bookkeeping of nautical coordinates and chronological events by the Japanese travelers (almost always lacking the hyperawareness and romantic individualism of the Americans, who impose meaning on events) was influenced by a distinct lack of self-consciousness and a persistent Tokugawa tendency to account for travels away from home in a strictly chronological order. By placing the incommensurable experiences of the Japanese and the Americans side by side without collapsing them into a single frame of adventure, Miyoshi breaks open a form of cultural study that neither particularizes nor generalizes. In this way *As We Saw Them* links up with Said's insistence that Orientalism is the West's understanding of the East based on the West's own terms. But by emphasizing so many structural misunderstandings, Miyoshi takes *As We Saw Them* a step beyond Orientalism, which, when translated back into U.S.-Japanese relations, means that Americans cannot even understand the Japanese based on the Japanese's own terms.

Cross-cultural understanding, therefore, is not only about getting it right through a dutiful respect for the Other and the refusal to employ self-imposed terms, but a continual tearing down of all rigid identities, however much (or especially because) such identities stem from the native self itself. Miyoshi perfectly rehearses here what has now become a required response to dominant discourses of multiculturalism and identity politics. This is not to imply, however, that Miyoshi did not take race and ethnicity seriously as categories of difference and as a foment of discrimination. Indeed, such concerns ultimately shaped his decision to leave UC Berkeley, in 1986, and become the Hajime Mori Professor of Japanese, English and Comparative Literature at the University of California, San Diego. At Berkeley, the Oriental languages department was interested in Miyoshi, especially following the excellent reviews of *Accomplices of Silence* and *As We Saw Them*, but wanted to keep him at a distance. Several students within that department, however, found his unorthodox form of criticism and decidedly wide-ranging knowledge and interests liberating, especially appreciating the way Miyoshi is neither obsequious nor superior toward Japan. When one Japanese American Ph.D. student came to Miyoshi after feeling slighted by some members of the Oriental languages department, Miyoshi investigated and came to agree that the student had been treated unjustly, and that this injustice was not totally unrelated to the student's race. Miyoshi defended the student in a highly publicized grievance and ultimately supervised his successful Ph.D. dissertation, but in the process was further alienated from those in the department (for more about this incident refer to the interview published here). The English department was still amenable to Miyoshi, but its Euro-American focus was becoming narrowly defined and less tolerable to him. These circumstances, together with an offer to be part of the literature department at UC San Diego (a more experimental program open to the non-West and interdisciplinarity) were what finally inspired Miyoshi to leave Berkeley after almost twenty-five years of service.

The move to San Diego, in 1986, coincided with a shift in the role of Japan in the world. Only forty years after the war, Japan had become an economic superpower with the world's second largest economy and a trade surplus with the United States that stood at $50 billion. From enemy to occupied nation to key American ally and bulwark against the wave of communism in East Asia, Japan was now reconfigured as the number one threat to the United States. Exacerbating these fears were best-selling non-fiction books with titles such as *The Enigma of Japanese Power* and *Trading Places: How We allowed Japan to Take the Lead*.[6] U.S. politicians appeared regularly on television denouncing the Japanese for not playing fair and for exploiting its sinister version of "Zen capitalism." But the redemonization of Japan was not complete until the Toshiba Machine Corporation scandal of 1988, when that company's sale of advanced submarine technology to the Soviet Union was uncovered: Japan had, in a span of only forty years, gone from ashes to asphalt to adversary. In an attempt to counter this trend, the Japanese Ministry of Education, large Japanese corporations such as Mitsubishi and Sumitomo, and cultural institutions such as the Japan and Sasakawa Foundations increased their investments in U.S. universities, financing chaired professorships, language programs, and student fellowships—in the hope of appeasing the animosity, if not turning it into a celebration of the Japanese model. What emerged from this was a polarization of Japanese studies in the United States that was quite different from the way the field was configured during the cold war. Miyoshi's intervention in the debate, in the form of his 1991 *Off Center: Power and Culture Relations between Japan and the United States*, not only refused to apologize for or bash Japan, but exposed the buried assumptions driving both sides—most notably by emphasizing how Capital itself is indifferent to such differences. To crack open such a position, however, required a rethinking of his previous work, especially his relation to Japanese studies.

As noted, Miyoshi was an outsider to Japanese studies and spent his youth in Japan immersed in Western literature. His interest in Japan was triggered the day Mishima Yukio (the respected novelist and celebrity in Japan) committed hara-kiri (ritualized suicide) in a public display atop the military headquarters in Tokyo in November of 1970. Only weeks earlier, the chair of Berkeley's English department asked Miyoshi what he thought about Mishima's recent book-length essay, *Sun and Steel* (*Taiyo to tetsu*). Miyoshi took this simple inquiry as an opportunity to begin thinking about Mishima and Japan, a change of focus for Miyoshi that became more earnest following Mishima's suicide. Indeed, it was this new turn that quickly led to *Accomplices of Silence*. But there was something else: Miyoshi wrote *Accomplices* and *As We Saw Them* in response to a bias he detected in Japanese studies in which, despite the scholarly interest in Japan, there was an undercurrent of assumed Western superiority in the way Japan was still judged by Western standards. To counter this, Miyoshi read the Japanese prose narrative and Japan's first diplomatic dispatch to Washington, D.C., in neutral and symmetrical terms in order to recuperate the autonomy of the Japanese objects of study. For Miyoshi, this was the critical move required by the times. By the late eighties, however, a shift was necessary that challenged the imaginary symmetry. Here is how Miyoshi describes it in his introduction to *Off Center*:

> *Off Center* is thus an attempt to restore asymmetry in our perception. It tries to see Japan's encounter with the other not from a "neutral" or "objective" (meaning Eurocentric) viewpoint, but from an oppositionist perspective. It does not pretend to be universal, inasmuch as universalism at present cannot be other than a mask for concealment and forgetfulness. It seeks to be inclusivist and categorically rejects exclusivism. It not only discards Eurocentricity and ethnocentricity, but does its best to eschew ethnicity and nationalism as well as racism and statism so that history may be read in its fullness undisturbed by borders and boundaries that have been constructed as colonialism progressed.[7]

Miyoshi still wants to emphasize radical difference between his terms (in this case Japan and the United States), but this difference is informed by the larger identity of the geopolitical system—one that is stamped by the persisting history of colonialism. Miyoshi performs this shift in the first two chapters of *Off Center*, in which he reads the Japanese prose narrative as an alternative form of the novel (now preferring to call the prose narrative by its Japanese name, the *shosetsu*, instead of by the universal category of the novel, which he still employed in *Accomplices of Silence*). By reading the formal components of the shosetsu (narrative, plot, point of view, character, texture, length, authorship) in terms of third-world literatures derived from an oral tradition, Miyoshi ultimately reads the modern Japanese prose narrative as a refusal of Western hegemony and colonialism in general and the Western novel in particular.

This problem of the difference of Japan within the totality of the world system is also the main theme of "Postmodernism and Japan," a special issue of *South Atlantic Quarterly* that Miyoshi edited with Harry Harootunian in 1988 (and which later became a book published by Duke University Press).[8] Although the Japan of futuristic marvels and sublime traditions presented itself as the ideal place to fantasize about postmodernism, in which the implosion of meaning and the atemporality of history seemed to require a trashing of so many "bad" metaphysical terms (such as "history" itself), Miyoshi and Harootunian warned how such a celebration dangerously echoed the cultural exceptionalism (*nihonjinron*) of the pre–Second World War moment: "What this reflex produced was a conception of Japan as a signified, whose uniqueness was fixed in an irreducible essence that was unchanging and unaffected by history, rather than as a signifier capable of attaching itself to a plurality of possible meanings."[9] They go on to argue: "It is this sense of a Japan as signified, unique and different from all other cultures, that is promoted by the most strident and, we should say, shrill spokesmen for Japan's postmodernity."[10] This collaboration with Harootunian (one of the most important intellectual historians working today and another progressive renegade in the Japan field) and with Tetsuo Najita, the eminent historian of Japan, dated back to the mid-1970s, when Miyoshi was a visiting professor at the University of Chicago. Indeed, the influence of *Postmodernism and Japan* and then two subsequent volumes coedited with Harootunian (*Japan in the World* and *Learning Places*) has, more than any other contribution, forced scholars of Japan to rethink their assumptions and allegiances to the role of area studies in the contemporary university.[11]

To a certain degree Miyoshi and Harootunian were too successful. The subsequent desire to "apply" Western theory to Japan was more often than not undertheorized, a gratuitous and professionalizing tactic that met up with the parochialisms of the former generation of Japan specialists. Miyoshi's response was to move away from the Japan field and begin to think about asymmetry and postmodernism in a more global context. The question of postmodernism for Miyoshi was, as it was for Fredric Jameson and David Harvey, a question of how to narrate historical change, namely how to indicate the discontinuities of the present while holding fast to the continuous logic of capitalism itself.[12] Walking this tightrope was not an easy task, especially at a moment when the rigor of poststructuralism's conception of difference began to weaken in the face of so many politically correct appropriations, especially by North American academics and university administrators. At a moment when culture was understood as a privileged realm in which to explore the peculiarities of postmodernity (relegating the economy to just another realm of specialized study), Miyoshi once again made one of his legendary turns. This time, it was to the global economy and the transforming role of the nation-state as studied in two key articles, "A Borderless World? From Colonialism to Transnationalism and the Decline of the Nation-State" (1993) (reprinted here) and "Sites of Resistance in the Global Economy" (1995). Indeed this move was already previewed in the introduction to *Off Center*, when Miyoshi wrote, "In fact, if I were to find it necessary to revise this book someday, it might begin with the task of dismantling national and regional borders and boundaries such as those between Japan and the United States, or the East and the West, substituting economic, racial, and gender differences as they relate directly to problems and events in global history."[13]

In the early 1990s the term "globalization" had rarely been spoken, and it was not until the mid- to late 1990s that globalization discourse emerged and soon dominated the academy in North America and beyond. In fact, one of the key texts of the debate was *The Cultures of Globalization* (published in 1998), edited by Miyoshi and Jameson, following the international conference at Duke University a few years earlier. Before this time, the preferred terms were "post-Fordism," "postmodernity," "flexible accumulation," "late capitalism," and "transnationalism." One of the casualties of the discursive dominance of "globalization" was the deemphasis of the economic dimension, the key concern of Miyoshi's intervention.

After recounting the history of colonialism and the emergence of the modern nation-state, Miyoshi argues for a key shift from the multinational corporation to the transnational one, where national identification decreases and corporate self-interest increases. Employing both journalistic and academic sources, Miyoshi painstakingly describes this transition in terms of the remarkable transfer of wealth from the poor to the rich (always emphasizing that the process is ongoing and that the logic of the transnational corporation is more a future destination than a present reality). In "A Borderless World?" Miyoshi has little nostalgia for the nation-state (however much the question mark at the end of the title indicates ambivalence), but is more concerned with the detrimental effects of transnational corporatism. Can profit-driven transnational corporations perform the welfare duties of nation-states? Who will take care of the health and living conditions of the mobile working class as its members follow the trail of global capital? What about environmental destruction? And where is academia in this transition—only too ready to cooperate with transnational corporatism? Back when most in the humanities were content to focus on the globalization of culture (novels and films about diasporas or consumerism; the world consolidation of the culture industry), Miyoshi already anticipated the central questions of our present moment. He writes, "What we need is rigorous political and economic scrutiny rather than a gesture of pedagogic expediency. We should not be satisfied with recognizing the different subject-positions from different regions and diverse backgrounds. We need to find reasons for such differences—at least in the political and economic aspects—and to propose ways to erase such 'differences,' by which I mean political and economic inequalities."[14]

"Sites of Resistance" further described how the vast inequities in the world persisted, giving the lie to the "utopia" trumpeted by many media blowhards. In this piece, Miyoshi's style is blunt and direct, relying on an array of mainstream sources, such as newspapers, magazines, and U.S. government reports. Losing patience with the academic fashion of over-qualified sentences and the intricate rehearsal of subtle theoretical problems, Miyoshi became more declarative in his proposals to reclaim the state, cultivate a fully empowered representative interstate organization, intensify grass-roots activities, and reorganize transnational labor unions. In a final passionate bid, Miyoshi challenges himself and his colleagues with the following provocation:

> We can break out of the vicious circle of mutual reference and mutual endorsement among scholars. We can, in a small way, revitalize our knowledge and learning during these interim years by redirecting argument, by ignoring rote history, by finding new contexts, by replacing references and bibliographies, by bringing praxis closer to home, by setting aside antecedents, by discarding autocratic requirements, by upsetting professionalism, by stripping academic respectability, by shunting gibberish, by encouraging idiosyncratic students, by reshaping the scales of excellence, by dissecting the deadening effects of institutionalism, in short, by being scrupulously intellectual and remaining staunchly skeptical about scholarly journals, books, and conferences, as well as university regulations and department rules on intellectual matters— even when we discuss postmodernism, multiculturalism, postcolonialism, feminism, or identity politics.[15]

The near absence of cultural objects in these two articles is quite conspicuous. Of course, such a lack is to be expected by those writing about the world system from the social sciences, but for a literary scholar not to begin or end an analysis with culture (whether seen as utopian, dystopian, or flat-out irrelevant) is quite rare. Yet Miyoshi's omission was anything but a dismissal of culture; rather, it was an appeal to a different sort of intellectual activity—one that did not rest on expertise but that risked learning something new and actually saying something about it. To not cover and compensate for this amateurism with a sophisticated cultural analysis, therefore, was a way for Miyoshi to seriously respond to his own challenge of upsetting professionalism.

When Miyoshi did write about culture in the mid- to late 1990s, he did so with an eye on how to make, criticize, and experience art within the situation of transnational corporatism. Without wanting to endorse an older modernism that held its distance (however critically) from the social, Miyoshi refused to celebrate the total integration of so much postmodern art. After Oe Kenzaburo won the Nobel Prize for Literature in 1994, Miyoshi wondered whether Oe's relentlessly reflexive and historically fraught work still mattered at a moment when younger Japanese writers such as Yoshimoto Banana and Murakami Haruki were becoming world-famous for hollowed-out sentences that formally mirrored the commodity culture out of which their work was born.[16] After attending the 1995 *Anywise* conference in Seoul, Miyoshi refocused this question about contemporary artistic production in terms of architecture. Responding to Peter Eisenman's argument to "move architecture away from itself," Miyoshi writes, "I think of a more literal and less cerebral eradication of architecture: to bring architecture around to the material context, to the outside space where ordinary workers live and work with little participation in the language, texts, and discourse of architecture."[17]

In a dialogue with architect Rem Koolhaas, Miyoshi compliments Koolhaas for wanting to deal with the ugliness of the material context, but asks how he protects himself from turning ugly—meaning how not to totally surrender to transnational corporatism.[18] Both Miyoshi and Koolhaas agree that this negotiation is the most important issue each faces as artist, critic, and citizen. In "Outside Architecture" (reprinted here) Miyoshi offers the following provisional answer, "Perhaps, instead of building guilty conscience into aesthetically, theoretically, intellectually admirable but useless shapes and forms, we might stroll in the streets . . . and learn how people live in the 'filthy' and 'uninviting' places. There may be more life there than in architecture's patronage houses, where the patrons are not always more satisfied or more comfortable than the residents of these streets."[19]

In a 1997 *New Left Review* piece (reprinted here) on *documenta X* (one of the world's most important exhibitions of contemporary art, held every five years in Kassel, Germany), Miyoshi takes issue with the overwhelming negative response to the event and the harsh criticism of its radical and uncompromising director, Catherine David. Miyoshi admired David's personal professional risk, her refusal to pander to the art industry and media, her pursuit of an intellectual vision that unapologetically emphasized the persistent links between culture and politics. Such a spectacle is easy to criticize (especially for radical artists and critics, not to mention so many leftist academics), but Miyoshi implores us to reflect on the larger stakes:

"If the opponents of bourgeois art acquiesce over dX, there may not be another opportunity for a long time to fight for a culture that makes sense."[20]

Ten years later Miyoshi does imply that the opportunity has passed—that the space has been effectively snuffed out for art to recuperate the crisis of global inequality. The novel, for example, is always conceived in relation to its sales to readers and, therefore, today it invariably becomes a demographic problem that merges with advertising and a larger consumerist ethos. Of course, criticism is just as susceptible to this late capitalist logic. Miyoshi, whose photographs have been published in recent years, does wonder if there might not be something different about photography. When reflecting upon his own photographic practice, he states:

> Of course photography is very much a part of consumerism, but I think there is a way of taking photographs that does not connect to it. A photograph can exist without a viewer. You can take pictures without thinking about the viewer at all. Whereas the novel is impossible to write without thinking about a reader. Once I start thinking about the reader it turns into consumerism. If I don't, I can't do it; but a photograph gives you some freedom to take pictures without thinking about viewers, it's just about me and the subject matter.[21]

Despite this lamentable situation of criticism and culture, Miyoshi does find one overarching topic that currently occupies his attention and requires another rethinking of his former commitments. This is the environment. Although we can detect a concern for ecology even back in Miyoshi's early writing, it is not until "Literary Elaborations" that it becomes full-blown—now bringing together his interest in the university and the global economy (not to mention his interest in pushing—or elaborating—literature beyond itself) in relation to what has become the rock-bottom issue of our time. "No one can escape from the environmental crisis, and no segment of life can be free from it (even though the rich will try to survive longer than the poor, of course)."[22] In a world where everyone is equally at risk, asymmetry is now turned back into symmetry and difference back into similarity—not in order to reduce difference or to pretend that it does not exist, but to bracket it at a moment when to do anything less is to imperil the species.

"Literary Elaborations" is divided into three sections. The first concerns the contemporary university and how a corporate logic based on efficiency and utility heightens academic professionalism and careerism. Miyoshi has little nostalgia for the decline of such "useless" disciplines as literary studies, while at the same time he is not cheerful about some of the newer alternatives, such as identity, area, and cultural studies. This section is followed by a detailed history of modern academia, returning to its premodern roots in the early medieval university. By tracking patronage and funding sources over centuries, Miyoshi is able to contextualize the way the market appropriates higher education today and how the contemporary research university is geared toward information and technology rather than critical examination. The final section offers Miyoshi's almost unthinkable solution: a uniquely transdisciplinary and global environmental protection studies that would radically reconfigure the various academic disciplines and merge the humanities, social, and hard sciences:

> I would like all courses in every discipline to be saturated with environmental and social consciousness. The administration of the university may well hesitate or even disapprove, but it is a comparatively easy restraint to break down, since individual instructors can choose course contents, somehow undercutting their official oversight. Individual instructors must take the initiative and responsibility, as they did with feminism and ethnic studies a few decades ago—until these concerns were acknowledged, and then gradually spread, and finally accepted and established in the mainstream curricula.[23]

Literature, history, political science, and other disciplines would not simply tinker around their canonical edges (bringing an already established rigor to ecological problems), but allow the perspective of ecological protection to transform the traditional disciplines themselves. For Miyoshi, and not surprisingly, economics is most in need of reorganization, especially around the concepts of pricing and production—a reorganization that requires the transformation of social relations and a serious reflection on what we are working and living for. "But that is exactly what the study of ecology ultimately requires."[24]

In a final provocation, Miyoshi argues that environmental protection is about the protection not only of human life but of the planet itself—even if human extinction is a very real possibility. Of course we must reflect on our act of collective murder, which would bring philosophical concerns to the forefront of environmental studies. But it is at the very end of "Literary Elaborations" where Miyoshi, meditating upon what other life-forms may exist after the end of humans and before the end of the planet, makes another one of his unexpected turns, this time into the future itself: "For now, a new kind of environmental studies will need to decide whether human extinction is worth thinking about. . . . At this time of very little hope all around, we can at least look forward to ongoing life on earth. And as long as we entertain any hope, we will manage to find the courage to keep trying."[25]

This nightmare combined with a fantasy is actually more modest and more realistic than it at first appears. Miyoshi experiences a tension between wanting to analyze the university (its past, present, and future) and wanting to analyze the larger social and ecological situation. He then shows how these two are inextricable and inescapable for those in the university. He realizes that there is much to be done outside of the university (whether this will entail revolution is not really his concern), but those connected to the university have to start somewhere—and reconfiguring the university and its curricula is a better place to start than writing so many *New York Times* op-ed pieces or participating on so many governmental panels. Despite its dramatic tone and radical vision, "Literary Elaborations" is, in fact, one of the more practical, reasonable, and provocative pieces of writing today.

One constant in this overview of Miyoshi's life and work is that when faced with what appears to be an unavoidable choice between two options, he somehow manages to break into an unexpected (and, for most, unthinkable) alternative. But this is not achieved by simply splitting the difference between extremes and taking comfort in moderation. Rather, Miyoshi criticizes and recuperates both positions (East and West, theory and antitheory, intellectual and artist, native and foreigner, environmentalist and excessive consumer, literature and economics) only to end up somewhere else by the sheer force of his engagement, which almost always entails the scrupulous and fearless study of a new field. Miyoshi not only forecasts the temperature of a specific moment with uncanny accuracy, but influences the currents and sea changes to come.

And yet it is not only the changing content that marks Miyoshi's risky critical practice, but also the formal changes and methodological reverse-courses he enacts along the way. Beginning with symmetrical similarities when analyzing the divided self within the singular modernity inhabited by Victorian writers, to emphasizing symmetrical differences (between East and West in *As We Saw Them* and *Accomplices of Silence*), to asymmetrical differences (as North and South gets added to the equation in *Off Center*), to asymmetrical similarities (as global inequalities are described in "A Border-less World" and "Sites of Resistance"), before returning to symmetrical similarities (in the shared ecological dangers depicted in "Literary Elabora-tions"), Miyoshi's uncompromising moves resemble less a tightening circle than an expanding one that inexorably breaks into the world as well as the future. Miyoshi has demonstrated that to be truly engaged in the world means facing it as squarely as possible, not being afraid to move into its unknown, relying less on past achievements or repeated solutions than on fresh risks, and finding ways to engage even its most miserable and hopeless aspects. But just as so much wishful thinking in response to the brutality of our present moment is often depressing and paralyzing, leaning into and staring right back at the reality of our world could be oddly encouraging—an encouraging criticism or critical encouragement that, after a half-century of on-the-money interventions, Miyoshi's work still performs.

As this book was on the brink of publication Miyoshi was diagnosed with a terminal illness. Facing such a diagnosis invariably means facing the medical establishment. The over-specialization, turf warfare, and compro-mising influence of business interests for which Miyoshi criticized the contemporary university, is currently the driving characteristics of medical care. Rich and poor alike are vulnerable to the system's vicious logic—which terrorizes us either by blocking access to care or by administering too much care. In the middle of his personal struggle, Miyoshi cannot help but find himself once again playing the role of the trespasser, this time into the medical realm—bringing with him his off-center questions as he fol-lows the threads that tie contemporary medical practice to the seemingly disparate details of everyday life, from culture to politics to our most subtle existential experiences. It is difficult to say what Miyoshi's fully formed analysis of medical culture would be. But what is certain is that it would be scrupulous in research, capacious in scope, and "enlivening" to all those inside and outside the discourse. It is for this reason why along with the name "trespasser" we might also call Miyoshi the "enlivenor," not just breathing new life into the various fields he breaks into, but enlivening the various people he meets along the way. There is something about his critical style, from his crisp sentences to his extemporaneous wit, which makes it simply impossible to be disheartened or uninspired around him. Miyoshi enlivens. And I can think of no other more important quality, both as an intellectual and as a friend, to share with others and the world.

. . . . .

MASAO MIYOSHI DIED ON OCTOBER 1, 2009.

LITERARY ELABORATIONS

....

"Literary Elaborations" was explicitly written for Trespasses. *Bringing together research on the history of the university and contemporary ecological thought and practices, Miyoshi proposes a radical vision for the contemporary university —one that calls on those in the various disciplines to surrender their protected academic turf and prioritize a transdisciplinary approach to the current ecological situation.*—ED.

We can surely destroy ourselves, and take many other species with us, but we can barely dent bacterial diversity and will surely not remove many million species of insects and mites. On geological scales, our planet will take good care of itself and let time clear the impact of any human malfeasance.

STEPHEN JAY GOULD, "THE GOLDEN RULE: A PROPER SCALE FOR OUR ENVIRONMENTAL CRISIS," *EIGHT LITTLE PIGGIES* (1993)

In the Western world, the university began as a guild of teachers and students in the Middle Ages, and even now the faculty help and promote each other as if in a labor union. The university's role in society, on the other hand, has been shifting—at first gradually, but since the nineteenth century rapidly, within the framework of the nation-state and industrial capitalism. I begin with an examination of today's faculty and intellectuals in higher education—in conjunction with teaching, specialization, and public utility. I will go on to question the ascendancy and perceptible dissolution of the humanities, considering especially the decline of literature including its newer subjects. In this connection, I will look back to the beginning of the university, tracing conspicuous major changes, both academic and social, and then return to the current crisis in commodified higher education and culture in general. The widely shared sense of exigency is here regarded as a convergence of crises in the deterioration of the environment both physical and social. In the vacuum remaining after the humanities debacle, therefore, environmental studies is proposed as we continue our search for hope, not for the life of the university, but for human existence itself. There will be three sections in this essay: "Today's University," "The University in History," and "Environmental Studies and Human Extinction."

Today's University

Those of us who have long inhabited academia are likely to believe that we could look out at the world at any time with nothing obstructing or distorting our sight. We are sure of our training and knowledge and simply assume that our view is accurate and comprehensive. Although we are increasingly expected to specialize in a limited field, we are still sure of our own general academic and intellectual standing—especially in literature and the humanities at large. The public outside the university reinforces our belief in ourselves, and, for various reasons, makes us feel at ease with our own sense of authority. The mainstream media, such as the *New York Times* or the BBC, mention and quote us, treating academics as perhaps the most reliable sources of information and opinion. Is our claim to authority legitimate?

Our acceptance of authority has several causes—each with a different consequence for society and for ourselves. To begin with, most of us received our certification from reputable institutions. Next, we are all teachers. We are supposed to know better than our students, and as we face students in the classroom, they are usually supportive rather than adversarial. They like to believe that they are getting proper education. If we like to teach, it's not just because a captive audience is a treat, but also because teaching builds our self-confidence. We feel we know a great deal, we are articulate, we are thoughtful. "Professor" is still a revered title, although it has a somewhat ridiculous ring, evoking disconnected dreamers or self-satisfied bores. As mainstays of the academic bureaucracy, we are prominent and indispensable on campuses. As we walk around our campus, we believe that it belongs to us and we are a pillar of the institution. The comfort of bureaucracy is seductive, and loyalty grows. And we seldom meet those who have not been to college; thus we live safely in a gated community. Of course we grumble about our schools all the time, but in the end we identify with them. Reviews of the books we write are more often than not courteous and complimentary. As insiders, we have to help each other. We are all of us poised to turn into "public intellectuals," and we wait for the media to seek us out whenever something breaks out in any place with the remotest connection to our fields. With increasing frequency, as a matter of fact, some of us are called on to serve clients more specific and consequential than the media—governmental agencies and private corporations. When academics enter a contractual relationship with an external institution, our authority—reinforced by the presumed independence and integrity of learning—is not necessarily compromised at once. The advice offered by academics can be genuinely mediative. The Intergovernmental Panel on Climate Change, to take a prominent recent example, has served to intercede with clarity and decisiveness among many conflicting concerns.[1] It is undeniable, however, that academic endeavors are often placed under heavy pressure by special interests. In other words, our vision of the world can be affected by a predisposition.

These pedagogic, institutional, public, and consultative roles are interlinked to promote our authority. The categories are neither cumulative nor hierarchical: teaching does not enhance a teacher's standing in the institution; campus privilege does not extend beyond the university; and media access does not always result in consultancies. And yet the classroom is the foundation of this whole enterprise, and everything else emanates from it and contributes back to it—whether research publications, public pronouncements, or specialized consultations. Of course this is true, in fact far truer than we are willing to admit. But the problem is that we don't let ourselves fully acknowledge it.[2] Our minds have been occupied elsewhere, and the university has been deeply involved in several serious developments.

One, the idea of authority has been replaced by that of expertise. Despite the general respect the public still seems to hold for academia and also despite our own confidence in ourselves as intellectuals, we are now experts rather than authorities. This difference is hardly trivial: an authority knows not only her/his specialty but also understands its place in the scheme of learning. An expert, on the other hand, is trained only in the field of specialization, and refuses to take even a step beyond it. Two, professionalism has come to dominate academia. Scholars are now professionals to whom what's professional and what's not is crystal clear. And the disciplined experts do not transgress, discarding a vast portion of learning as amateurism.[3] Knowledge must be certifiable and transmittable. As the authority-expert contrast is in the area of knowledge, the amateur-professional polarity is in the area of vocation. Three, careerism has grown alongside professionalism. Now that scholarship is a profession, professors feel no embarrassment in admitting success to be their goal. They aim not only at climbing up the social ladder, but also at success in specific projects ranging from the books they write to the honors and prizes they seek. Curiosity and learning are no longer crucial, success and recognition are. The avocation of teaching, once presumed modest, has been thoroughly converted to an openly competitive occupation where students, professors, and administrators alike are dead serious about grades, ranks, and finances.

To take an instance of this all-too-familiar change in higher education, teaching is now considered a contractual transmission. Before a term begins, professors unambiguously spell out the objects of transference for the benefit of students. The course syllabus is unalterably promised, and sample questions from finals are published to avoid surprises later. Bibliographies are not idiosyncratic but standardized, so nearly all professors and graduate students share identical references and citations, names and titles. Standardization, in short, functions as quality control. The teachers describe their standards for grades: they want the leased knowledge back with no dent or loss in the transaction. During the whole process, deviation is disallowed, whether from students or graduate assistants or professors. After the final exams, students are in turn expected to grade teachers for their quality of service in packaging and delivery—more important than the contents of the packages. In this contractual transaction, preparation and class work are calculated as investments and the grades as profits by both students and teachers. Institutions are ranked by the number of applicants they attract, the number of degrees they produce, their placements at graduation, and—as proof of their scholarly excellence—the number of Nobel, Booker, Pritzker, Pulitzer, MacArthur, Guggenheim, and other worthy honor and prize winners. Degrees from top institutions obviously guarantee a rise in market value and reputation. Neither teachers nor students expect much from what transpires in the classroom any more.

What's important for them both is the fact of their having been there, the ownership of a share in the brand name. In this commercial enterprise, the faculty—we—are full participants. Is our outlook on the world invulnerable to these commercial relations?

Most will agree that this is an ominous aberration in educational history. Many of us have been appalled by it, and demoralization has been observed among some instructors and graduate students, though less among administrators. The prominence of specialization, professionalism, and careerism in higher education began to be talked about several decades ago, as world trade became transnational with the decline of the cold war and the intensification of capitalism. The "global" economy may not be solely responsible for the educational aberration—what caused the global economy, to begin with?—but we should reflect on its several features if we are to think seriously about "intellectuals" in higher education. For the question before us now is: Can those in the humanities—we—deal with the force of "globalization" and keep our vision of the outside world straight? What features of "globalization" have affected the humanities?

First, efficiency. The "global" economy is driven by the search for maximum efficiency (i.e., profit) and expansion (i.e., power). The cheapest labor with the fewest regulations is the goal of offshore transfer. Trainable labor is abundant everywhere. A few experts with high-tech tools can easily replace a horde of expensive workers abroad and at home. We professional experts set up such employment schemes and are thus adversarial to the workers. Manufacturers and moneylenders move their currencies, investment, technology, and production all over the world. In fact, financial speculations of all kinds have replaced manufacture as the main means of accumulating money, vastly shifting wealth to a few. We are often advisors and participants in the projects of foundations and nongovernmental organizations (NGOs). They claim to be nonprofit and altruistic, but often they are not. Academics circle the globe at a nearly matching pace. Our traveling is not just physical, either. We help erase geographical differences. Regardless of regional differences, we speak and teach the same language, that of efficiency. Closer at hand, an example of "efficient education" is the invention of the virtual university and the storefront university, where a handful of experts control a host of uncertified, minimally paid instructors. As we know too well, in our research universities it is graduate students who carry the burden of undergraduate education.[4] In what way do we resist the force of "globalized" exploitation? More important, how do we know that our worldview can remain unwarped by our own complicity in exploitation?

Second, transnationalism. Players in the "global" economy disregard the boundaries and unities of the nation-state. We are less bound by the state and freer to challenge legal and political restrictions. Loosening of national affinity may be beneficial in challenging the state power and control that wreaked havoc in so many places in the last century. It should be recalled here that the humanities have evolved over several centuries in order to legitimize modern states, and, if not quite in the name of patriotism, the disciplines have been complicit in many state projects. The decline of the humanities may be, therefore, not entirely deplorable. Transnationalization, however, weakens the whole range of social imagination and sensibility that has produced modern arts and academic disciplines, which in fact contributed in the past to the promotion of public service and communal networks. The replacement of public service and social networks with self-interest and private profit has been disastrous. Social fragmentation and isolation, in addition to the widening gap between wealth and poverty, are among the obvious consequences. The "globalized" academics are among culprits here rather than victims.

Third, utilitarianism. Humanities disciplines—literature, arts, philosophy, history, and other subjects—are traditionally not supposed to be utilitarian but devoted to the general betterment of learning and understanding. They took pride, at least until the mid-twentieth century, in being useless to bourgeois society.[5] That's why public intellectuals were historically born and bred in the humanities. That has dramatically changed: the humanities is now expected to be of use to society, or rather to those on top of society, and must legitimize its existence in neoliberal universities. Thus the professors' achievements are evaluated quantitatively as well as qualitatively. Terms like "productivity," "efficiency," "publicity," "market," and "management," once rarely heard in the academy, are now part of the basic vocabulary in "brand name" universities. Specialization and professionalism are attempts on the part of those in the humanities to justify their presence in the global economy. But that is not all. Their careerism, too, is officially encouraged in the name of efficiency. Can academic disinterestedness be maintained, and commitment to justice be kept unwavering, and more important, can "justice" actually be found, in the middle of the constant jostling for utility and success?

Will the humanities survive in the neoliberal university? One answer would be simply, no: vanishing is more likely. Disappearance in the near future is quite possible. Most likely, however, the humanities will live on for a while longer in one form or another. Even conventional studies of canonic works by a few writers may persist in a few colleges and universities. In the service of elitism and snobbery, some students may still listen to teachers and study their age-old book lists and class notes. But the formal analyses of dominant literary work that filled academia from the 1940s up to, say, 1980—here I speak mainly of literature, although it can be said of other disciplines more broadly—are scarcely being written any more, and read even less. While we were paying scant attention, a large section called literary criticism vanished from both bookstores and university press catalogues.

Alternative humanities have certainly emerged. First, works by so far neglected female writers and minority writers came to the rescue. The reform was extremely important at the beginning, contributing politically to the establishment of ethnic and gender equity. But this substitution now looks less promising than it once seemed. The reason is obvious. Studies in gender and minority literatures, arts, history, and so on almost always lead to tautology and identity exceptionalism. ("Japanese literature is Japanese," and "Japanese literature—which is unique—can be understood only by the Japanese.") Identity politics, whether male or female, gay or straight, white or colored, national or regional, invariably extends beyond self-confidence only to become deadlocked and tautological. This stifling academic identitarianism should not be confused with the political struggle for racial and gender equality in the world, which is infinitely liberating, much as racism and gender bias are unceasing, ubiquitous, and multifarious. Political activism against discrimination and segregation aims at the elimination of inequity and class division, thus its goal of universal equality can be universally shared, while ethnic and gender studies almost always seek to maintain, and even reinforce, the uniqueness and integrity of each group. No group, however, can remain totalized for long, and can never be "pure." Once identified, a group breaks up into differences. Factionalism erupts, as it has among feminist and ethnic cliques, asserting different aspects of an identity and forming separate subgroups. Begun as a resistance movement, identity politics ends up being territorialism. Although identity studies have made important contributions toward ending the Eurocentric, male-dominated, and homophobic age, their future in providing a zone of political freedom and commitment as well as intellectual curiosity seems limited.

Second, far more dubious than identity studies is "area studies." Once notorious for complicity with Second World War and cold war policies, area specialists are creeping back again—this time to partake in transnational corporations' depredations. Area studies experts have two pretexts for the salvage of waning humanities. One, local knowledge is obviously useful to the "global" expansionists. Although English is nearly the lingua franca of our time (at least until it gets replaced, probably by Chinese, in the late twenty-first century), still the exploiters need to communicate with the natives in order to exploit them. Experts can expedite. By segmenting the world into distinct places, they can conceal the grand project of global imperialism. Two, area experts claim interdisciplinarity. This time the need for interdisciplinary studies is greater: the universities, torn asunder by the professionalism and territorialism of their departments, want some appearance of reintegration. Administrators, who understand the nearly autonomous power of departments and don't like to see their own power dispersed, agree with the undergraduates who prefer general education to specialized fragments. Administrators everywhere want to encourage interdisciplinary approaches, although they do not dare challenge the departmental structure. The problem here is that area studies cannot be interdisciplinary in the age of specialization. Experts who study the same area in different departments seldom mix with each other, especially when learning the language of an obscure region and its culture is too demanding in time and energy to allow for the study of anything else. Thus Sinomusicologists have no inclination to share their ideas with experts on the Chinese economy. What would they talk about? They may get together at a center, an institute, or a seminar, but eventually go home to their several departments, where the all-important business of hiring, firing, and promotion takes place. Interdisciplinarity is not transdisciplinarity. Area studies will not offer a zone for free investigation. Place remains place without intellectually extending to space and environment.[6]

Finally, if the humanities cannot hope to survive by conversion into identity studies, and if area studies offers no hope of interdisciplinarity, can it look for any other form of learning from which to see the world, unwarped by profit or domination? The most popular program is "cultural studies," now at least as widespread as conventional, ethnic, or area studies disciplines. Housed usually in history, literature, sociology, and anthropology departments, it has so far eluded attempts to define itself.

To the extent that cultural studies takes for its texts any event and situation, from cultural artifact to political development, this seems to be a promising direction to take for escaping atrophy and redundancy.

But then, what is culture?

We might as well begin with Matthew Arnold, who strategically deployed the word in *Culture and Anarchy* in the mid-nineteenth century. As Frederic Harrison, a radical of the time, lampooned it and as Arnold agreed in gleeful response, the idea was "fiddlestick or moonshine." Not only because the word was a new import from German, but also because the double roles "culture" played in the book were fundamentally unclear.[7] On the one hand, Arnold meant by the word "the best that has been known and thought," that is, "excellence"[8] in literature, arts, and in the conduct of life. On the other hand, he insisted that culture was neutral to classes, but without ever using the word to mean a "way of living" as in the sociological usage. Most readers forget that the book's subtitle is "An Essay in Political and Social Criticism." In the context of the time of its publication (1866–1869), "anarchy" referred to the social unrest represented by the industrial workers' riots on the brink of a revolution. "Monster processions in the streets and forcible irruptions into the parks, even in professed support of this good design, ought to be unflinchingly forbidden and repressed. . . . Because a State in which law is authoritative and sovereign, a firm and settled course of public order, is requisite. . . . Thus, in our eyes, the very framework and exterior of the State, whoever may administer the State, is sacred."[9] Culture, as Arnold saw it, was a tool for the state, to combat revolution.

Although the aristocracy ("Barbarians") and the middle class ("Philistines") despised each other, the fusion of privilege and money was inevitable. By the end of the nineteenth century, the industrial and financial class triumphed over the aristocracy within the frame of the nation-state, which was now the agent of national and international politics and economy. In this new age, what place did the poets and artists occupy? Standing apart from those in power, many thought of themselves as romantic rebels and critics. They took pride in being independent and isolated. As Arnold saw, in the scheme of British culture and anarchy the state belonged with the upper classes and not the lower orders ("Populace"). The artists were ambivalent toward the imperial capitalist state. Men of culture knew, however, that, despite their criticism of and reservations about the middle class, they had to sell their art and poetry to those who could appreciate and afford it. In this split between their contempt and their need for money and honor, in this schizophrenia, modern art and literature were born and grew.

Every poet and artist has played out this schizophrenia in his or her own way. Some imagined themselves as aristocrats in sympathy with peasantry; others joined the Communist Party but participated in no revolution. There were many who abandoned high culture, secretly despising themselves for the concession. Always there were a few who refused compromise and remained faithful to high art, frequently depoliticizing its source and use by focusing on form and structure. On it went—throughout the Gilded Age, the fin de siècle, the Roaring Twenties, the Depression era, the ascendance of fascism, the Second World War, and the postwar affluence. There was a constant debate on the role of art and culture throughout. For example, between Adorno, who believed in the authenticity of art, and Benjamin, who embraced at least film, a new mechanized art form. Marcel Duchamp and the Dadaists made fun of high art. Later, Raymond Williams and Stuart Hall on the one hand and the populists on the other continued the debate. Still, the place of high culture was kept intact as some sacrosanct space. Then, in the 1960s, something happened.

The sixties was indeed an extraordinary decade. Although the Second World War was a real enough crisis, the conflict, once over, was found to have done little to shake the fundamentals of Western civilization. If anything, the war reaffirmed them. It was in the sixties that crises converged from unexpected sources, so numerous and interlocked that I know I am suggesting here only a few obvious junctions.

Eisenhower began to aid the French colony in Vietnam only a few months after the end of the Korean War, in 1953. Early in his administration, Kennedy sent "advisors" to Southeast Asia, and by November 1961, there were already sixteen thousand troops in Vietnam. Nineteen sixty-one was, of course, the year of the Bay of Pigs disaster. The escalation in Vietnam continued throughout the sixties from Kennedy to Johnson to Nixon to Ford and ended at last in a decisive defeat, in 1975. The final defeat had a profound effect on the American psyche, as we can never forget. Decolonization continued to spread throughout the world. The perceived liberation of long-oppressed peoples may well be one of the central motivating forces of the turbulent sixties. The student rebellion of the sixties was in no sense revolutionary, but the civil rights protests, merging with the antiwar, university reform, feminist, and third-world movements, seriously challenged the bourgeois assumptions of the fifties. Authority that had been traditionally vested in the government, university, police, church, museum, journalism, and other social and cultural establishments was fundamentally questioned. When Martin Luther King defied the laws of Alabama, he was also asking Americans if racism was America's only dysfunction. The students who intended to help with voter registration in the South returned home to the North only to face the arbitrary rules of the universities, the perverted uses of the law, the patriarchic suppression of women in all corners of society, the inequity in the distribution of wealth, and of course the destruction of Vietnamese and American lives. How fundamental the change was is not easy to assess even now. (After all, the war in Iraq still continues.) Nevertheless, people could no longer be sanguine about the way they related to the power structure. And this was not limited to the United States or the West, but was nearly worldwide, as we saw in the student rebellions everywhere in 1968.[10]

What is fascinating about the sixties, however, is that those supposedly "radical" students and youths, who no doubt tried to resist the culture of their affluent parents, were not so clear about where they were heading. There were alternatives: a search for peace and the health of all on the planet, as shown by King, Rachel Carson (*Silent Spring*, 1962), and the *Whole Earth Catalog* (1968), and a path toward self-realization as revealed by Timothy Leary, Abbie Hoffman, and Jerry Rubin, and their followers. These alternatives were not far apart. Both were against Arnoldian "culture" as a means of guarding and administering the state. The erosion of authority in the sixties extended far beyond the political counterculture, into literary, artistic, and academic territory. Likewise, the division between popular culture and high culture was rapidly being dissolved with the emergence of figures like Andy Warhol, the Beatles, and Amiri Baraka, who even high-art devotees had to acknowledge were undismissible. Their appeal was powerful, to antiestablishment critics and students. Soon an expanding number of sophisticates began to accept their work, while elite artists retreated further and further to a reduced audience of experts and connoisseurs in museums and academia. Something oddly new was taking place in this reconfiguration of culture and counterculture. By 1970, even high culture did not belong to the few, and the new culture was widely spread, sold, and bought.

The Woodstock concert of 1969 may offer an example of this explosive energy of fusing politics and pleasure in that decade. Two young men fresh out of college staked millions of inherited dollars for an antiwar extravaganza. Their intention wasn't clear to themselves. A counterculture party, a bacchanalian celebration of sex, rock, and drugs, a reckless grab for bucks, as well as a peace protest. As a newspaper then described it, yesterday's flower children had become the leading businessmen of the moment. Even the sober antiwar activists couldn't dismiss a gathering of 400,000 as trivial, although some of them in fact tried to laugh it off. The combination of folk and rock as represented by Joan Baez, Arlo Guthrie, Ravi Shankar, Janis Joplin, Jefferson Airplane, The Who, and Jimi Hendrix, among many others, was not just a familiar popular music happening. To discuss the pop music of Woodstock, the polarities of classical and popular music, or culture and counterculture, were useless. In the Dionysian ecstasy of mass demonstration, symbolic of the exploding world population (as we will see), even trained classical musicians discerned the power of new sounds, which belonged to the people—like pre-Renaissance music, and unlike the music of the modern age, which alienated a majority of listeners. The Woodstock festival was a cultural event in other ways, too. In choosing the Catskills farmland, the festival expressed a yearning for green woods and open fields. Further, while it was a countercultural celebration, it was not antibusiness, antimoney. Woodstock was one of the earliest demonstrations of counterculture turning itself into a money-making commodification.

During the decade, in short, high culture was merged with pop culture (which functioned as a new version of avant-gardism). The emergent culture rejected exclusivity and elitism. It was full of energy and appeal. It was unafraid of vulgarity, that is, of being inerudite and plebeian. At the same time this new culture did not distinguish itself from consumption. To fit into the new structure of political economy, consumption was raised to the level of a craft, of style, which transnational megacorporations promoted with the meticulous use of art and science. All branches of culture, from music (concerts and recordings) to arts (design), from literature (best sellers) to theater (shows), from history (spectacle) to geography (tourism), were for sale, enmeshed with consumption in a new way, that is, with spending and profiting. People were retrained to find in consumption fun, fulfillment, and public service. So people spent, but only a very few profited. Within decades the discrepancy produced unprecedented inequity in wealth and income all over the world, both within nations and internationally. As everybody knows by now, in the United States real wealth is concentrated in the top 1 percent—or even the top 0.1 percent—of the population. In 1998, 225 of the world's richest individuals had assets totaling $1 trillion, equal to the collective annual income of the poorest 47 percent of the human population. In March 2007, *Fortune* magazine reported that there were now 946 billionaires in the world, and their combined net worth was $3.5 trillion. Even Lawrence Summers recognizes that "the trend toward increased inequality is continuing and may even be accelerating."[11] Wealth is gathered from five-sixths of the world population, leaving out the bottom billion.[12] All profits seem to be sucked up to the top, while producing an insatiable debauchery of consumerism that now fills the whole space of culture. Arnold might well now name his book "Consumption and Anarchy."[13]

Of course, cultural apologists will dismiss such pessimism. For them great literature and art can still open the mind and enable general criticism to rise to political activism for reform. They may be right: there was a time when the mark of high culture was seen as opposition to power and as compassion for all. And even now some cultural products might inspire individuals and lead them to self-negation and commitment to justice. Further, the condition and configuration of culture in society might change again depending on the political economy of the world. But for now, culture as a historical force is inexorably absorbed by consumerism.

Where does the discipline of cultural studies stand in this consumerism?

The university that houses cultural studies is in the middle of this maelstrom of buying and selling driven by the transnational megacorporate structure, and, as I have already described, it is now devoted to specialization, professionalization, and careerism. Within the discipline of cultural studies, we are expected to speak about all-inclusive culture—with authority that may or may not be legitimately ours. I am not at all sure whether the discipline of cultural studies can escape the anarchic situation of which it is itself a part, and which it supposedly investigates. Can it escape from the seductive illogic of disregarding its own relationship to the failures it diagnoses? Isn't the same cultural studies that investigates general commodification and consumerism *itself* a commodity, just like antiart art?[14] A consumer may pretend not to be consuming, or to be doing something else, but a student of cultural studies cannot critique consumerism from a disinterested perspective while the discipline itself is deeply engaged in consumerism. And my own study is obviously not exempt from this requirement. It needs to place the university, consumerism—and culture—in the scale of things in the world.

In this nearly hopeless intellectual situation, I see one zone of studies and criticism that might be able to claim political and economic independence, which is environmental justice studies. When all academic efforts—including environmental management and sustainability technologies—are finally reducible to consumerism under the sway of transnational capitalism, ecological protection based on universal social justice should be able to stand on its own, aloof to corporate and state power altogether. By now life on the planet as endangered needs no explanation.[15] And the planet is integral to all—rich or poor, male or female, urban or rural, industrial or nomadic. No one can escape from the environmental crisis, and no segment of life can be free from it (even though the rich will try to survive longer than the poor, of course). Environmentalism is, therefore, uniquely transdisciplinary and global. Environmental justice studies thus ought to have a central, indispensable place in the university. Even the most fanatic defender of competitive capitalism needs to understand that capitalism could not continue to expand in the changing environment. And all other branches of knowledge—from economics to history, from art history to physics—ought to be reformulated in relation to it. Here the logic of argument is absolutely compelling, or should be absolutely compelling. But it is not. It still has to face the unintelligent self-concern that is capable of dismissing the uncontestable crisis as just one theory, an improbable fantasy. If the head of the richest and mightiest nation on earth is allowed to give mere lip service to the need for environmental protection, while pursuing business interests, blindly or knowingly, then the whole of environmental concern could be disregarded. Man's self-destructive will seems unfathomably tenacious.[16] I will discuss later a possible way of making environmentalism central to our national and planetary life.

If ecology is not allowed to reorganize or replace the humanities, nothing else can. Without a critical, evaluative discipline—the anchor for learning —the university will be reduced to a training school only for workers and professionals, which in fact it is rapidly becoming. Can the university survive merely as a training place for skills? The answer will have to be no in the context of the modern university. What appears to us an aberration now was, however, once the perfectly normal mode of education. Here we need to take a somewhat longish detour and look at how the modern university has evolved.

The University in History

Higher learning goes back to antiquity, or millennia before, in Egypt, Mesopotamia, India, China, and elsewhere. Institutionally, however, today's university traces its roots to the European medieval church schools. By the eleventh century, order was restored out of the chaos that had resulted from the collapse of the Roman Empire. Europeans were learning from the Muslim civilization and Byzantine Empire that had absorbed Greco-Roman learning.[17] Monasteries and churches offered teaching in schools established in cathedral towns. The economic and social life of the Middle Ages was growing complex enough to require the service of institutionally trained lawyers, physicians, and theologians, so cathedral schools rapidly spread. Among these, Paris and Bologna stood out. In Paris students and masters gathered at a *studium* where a renowned scholar attracted students. Masters organized themselves into guilds, very much like contemporary cobblers' and weavers' craft guilds and today's labor unions. The guilds jealously guarded their monopoly rights to grant licenses and degrees, a tradition that has lasted to this day. Groups called "nations" were formed in accordance with their geographic places of origin. The subjects in the arts faculty consisted of trivium (grammar, rhetoric, and dialectic) and quadrivium (arithmetic, music, geometry, and astronomy), while teachers of theology, law, and medicine were in separate faculties. The courses offered by the arts faculty were viewed as "lower," because they were considered preparatory for the "higher" courses that specialized in theology, law, and medicine. The structure is similar to today's distinction between the undergraduate and graduate faculties. Among the higher faculties, the studies of civil and canon law were the most popular, followed by medicine. Theology was the least attractive to the students. The medieval university even had a program in secretarial and notarial arts in one branch of the rhetoric course, resembling today's paralegal training.[18] The universities, in other words, were primarily for training civil and ecclesiastic administrators and practitioners, not philosophers, pure scientists, or arts scholars. Of course, in a world where faith and reason had complex and pervasive relationships, the choice of monastic contemplation for a vocation, for instance, cannot be dismissed as unscholarly and careerist, nor did the medieval universities fail to produce some of the greatest minds in human history, such as Abelard, Albertus Magnus, Bonaventura, and Thomas Aquinas, whose *Summa* systematically synthesized Aristotelian philosophy and Christian theology to provide a new perspective. But the university as an institution was much like today's professional school, although ecclesiastical life was far more inclusive in the medieval world than any single profession today. The teachers in the faculty of arts were, like today's graduate assistants, themselves students enrolled in programs for advanced degrees. Each nation was headed by an elected "rector" or "proctor." The faculty regularly met at various levels such as the arts faculty, the executive council, or the university senate. And from the beginning of the university, rivalries and fractures within and among the nations and faculties were ceaseless.[19]

The early medieval universities had no physical campus. That meant that the masters could move their teaching site to another town fairly freely in search of better living and learning conditions. For the students, too, travel and moving presented no problems of communication, as they all shared Latin as the language of their education, thus readily conversing with masters and students of other regions. Students from other towns and provinces needed lodgings, which evolved into hospices and dormitories, and then into colleges by the fourteenth century. The students not only lived together in colleges, but were placed under the protection and supervision of university officials. At Oxford and Cambridge, residential colleges were semiautonomous corporations offering instruction of their own.

In Bologna, nations were not masters' guilds, but students'. First, foreign students formed a fraternity association, against often abusive local officials. Students of law, who were mostly mature foreigners, first formed their own regionally separate nations for protection from landlords and municipal-tax and military-service requirements. Eventually they merged with other students to form two or three larger groups. The municipal authorities of Bologna and Paris at times challenged these student nations. The students, however, played off the local authorities against the principalities, monarchs, or the Holy Roman Empire to protect and advance their own interests. They also took direct action such as staying away from Paris or Bologna en masse, thereby denying the city considerable business revenues. They also employed strategies such as strikes or boycotts, at times against their masters. The students at Bologna gained control over nearly all aspects of the university, including hiring and firing of the faculty, fixing their pay, granting or denying them leaves of absence, finally reducing the masters to a position of subservience. The masters had to keep themselves in the good graces of their students, who were, indeed, able to manipulate and bully their teachers.[20]

There were other conflicts, too, between local and central authorities, in ecclesiastical as well as secular matters. The masters and the students, or the university as a whole, had to learn the art of power struggle in order to survive. These were also the days when Europe was ravaged by the Black Death, which reduced the European and Asian population by 30 to 40 percent, and when the Hundred Years War raged between England and France. Despite such horrors and catastrophes, many more universities were founded during the thirteenth and fourteenth centuries from Italy to Scandinavia, from England to Bohemia. By the end of the fourteenth century, there were seventy-nine universities in Europe.[21] Because of the mediatory role the university learned to play among diverse power centers, it was able to avoid head-on collisions with authorities to a surprising extent. There were few instances of repression and persecution of dissenters, unlike in the following centuries, when the waves of neohumanism, Protestant reformation, and Catholic Counter-Reformation swept over Europe, tearing apart the academic world that coexisted with the papacy in the Middle Ages, however tenuous the relation might have been.[22] In spite of occasional disruptions, the principles of *Lehrfreiheit* (freedom of teaching) and *Lernfreiheit* (freedom of learning) were largely maintained by masters and students as well as by outsiders, but this independence was more like monopoly labor rights than "academic freedom" in the modern sense.[23] The domination of the church was unquestioned. The student body was still small, and it was mostly from the burgher class, uncritically aspiring for a place in the state or church hierarchy. Students did not come from the upper echelons of society (princes, army generals, or landowners), for whom university learning offered little of use.

Neohumanism rapidly spread in fifteenth-century Italy among the men and women who found liberation in classical literature. While they pursued the pleasures of secular and worldly learning—Greek and Latin literature, poetry, history, Platonic philosophy, Hebrew, oratory—the universities remained largely hostile and closed to the new learning. Higher education was functional and vocational, and scholastic learning and traditional trivium and quadrivium dominated. The bulk of the university's budget was allocated for legal and medical studies then—as now. Bologna was renowned for its law, as Padua was famous for its medical faculty. Aristotelian philosophy was selectively read so that it could provide medieval scholarship with a theoretical basis. But the university was aloof to serious studies of secular humane letters. Absolutes were held, but no universals were allowed. An increasing number of enthusiastic humanists had to find a place for studies outside the university. That is how "academies" came into existence. Neither teaching nor degree-granting institutions, the academies were voluntary and informal associations of scholars with a shared interest in literary and exegetical studies. The learned amateurs met regularly at private residences to converse on literary and intellectual topics. Unencumbered by rigid rules, restrictive theology, or guild monopoly, humanist academies played an important role in the intellectual life of fifteenth- and sixteenth-century Europe.

In France and Germany, the situation was more or less the same as in Italy. Scholastic training for the clergy remained the central mission of the university, and the conservative faculty of arts continued to prepare the students for law and medicine in addition to theology. The University of Paris was the center of opposition to neohumanism, and the German universities, too, were fiercely opposed to the new learning. Conservative scholars were threatened by the unfamiliar and impractical curriculum; Greek suggested paganism to them, while Hebrew was repugnant to the anti-Semitic masters. Besides, the German scholars hated Italy. By the sixteenth century, however, the newly established Collège de France founded chairs for Greek, Latin, Hebrew, French, and philosophy, and the new learning slowly spread through northern Europe.

England was kindlier to the new learning. Although traditional scholarship remained in control and most masters and students were hostile, the chancellor at Cambridge invited Erasmus in the early sixteenth century to teach Greek. King Henry VIII, who had broken with Rome over his divorce and was suspicious about the old scholastic teaching, created the Regis Professorships at Oxford and Cambridge for divinity, civil law, physics, Hebrew, and Greek. Around this time, the student body of Oxford and Cambridge began to change from burghers' sons dedicated to vocational training to aristocratic and princely students who wanted "polite learning" as a requisite for becoming "gentlemen" in elegant society. This helped the dissemination of neohumanism, or liberal education. When the newly created Corpus Christi College at Oxford came under an attack from students of other colleges for its humanist studies, King Henry VIII ordered the dons to cease intimidation, and Thomas More, a friend of Erasmus, condemned the antihumanist masters. In the course of the sixteenth century, the new learning gradually took root in Europe as a whole, introducing a less mnemonic learning that would encourage the personal growth of individual elite students rather than promote civil and ecclesiastical careers. The idea of liberal arts thus began—to form in time the foundation of today's liberal arts, or general, education.

During the Reformation, university men were active throughout Europe. Ulrich Zwingli studied at the universities of Vienna and Basel and later organized a university in Zurich, and John Calvin studied at the Sorbonne, then wandered from city to city, at last settling in Geneva where he continued to revise the *Institutes of the Christian Religion*, perhaps the most influential document in the development of Protestantism. He also recodified the Genevan laws and constitution. Unlike Martin Luther, who sought a return to primitive simplicity, Calvin accepted capitalism and encouraged trade and production, although he also opposed exploitation and self-indulgence. The University of Geneva became the model for Protestant universities like Leiden in the Netherlands, Edinburgh in Scotland, and Harvard in New England.

In England, where Henry VIII established the Church of England, the Reformation was at first a matter of policy, not doctrine. The anti-Rome stance of the Anglican Church was in time elaborated. Under Henry VIII, Edward VI, Elizabeth, James I, Charles, Oliver Cromwell, Charles II, and William and Mary, England was seen widely swaying between the two polar positions of pro-Rome, Counter-Reformation, and anti-Puritan on the one hand, and anti-Rome, pro-Reformation, and Puritan on the other. Of course, some believed the Anglican Church to be more truly apostolic than Rome and thus more authentically Catholic than the papacy, and, finally, via media, neither Catholic nor Puritan. As the Church of England swung widely from one extreme to another in rapid succession, not only episcopal teachings but also university instruction had to conform. Canon law, once a coveted preparatory course toward careers of ecclesiastic preferment, was eliminated from the Protestant university curriculum. The king of England being the supreme head of the Anglican Church, a crime against the crown was both treason and apostasy. Threats of censorship and prosecution were everywhere, and the rules and regulations were tightened by acts of parliament such as the Uniformity Act of 1552, the Act of Supremacy of 1554, the Treasons Act of 1554, and the Clarendon Codes of 1562–1565, which excluded non-Anglicans from Oxford and Cambridge. The Thirty Years War raged in Germany, and in France the bloody Huguenot Wars lasted for more than thirty years. Members of the university community were forced to swing back and forth between the Catholic and Protestant forces, and, more crucially, they were forced to stand guard against the constant surveillance emanating from both church and state in the minutest details of university life.

The conflict was not just between Protestants and Catholics, but also among Lutherans, Calvinists, and Zwinglians. What's more, even within the Lutheran—or Calvinist—sect, fierce internecine disputes were ceaseless. These factions tore up what little there was of the medieval community of scholars and students. As one group gained power, it was liable to suppress the others, as the Roman Church had for centuries. The duke of Saxony, who was converted by Luther, dismissed all the University of Leipzig professors who resisted Lutheranism. At Catholic Vienna, on the other hand, all theology professors had to adhere to Catholic orthodoxy. The spirit of intolerance and inquisition persisted. And on both the Catholic and Protestant sides, many scholars were victims of prosecution: Thomas More, Kepler, Galileo, and Giordano Bruno, to name only the most conspicuous.

The rise of empirical science in the sixteenth and seventeenth centuries was not registered in European universities. Discoveries by Tycho Brahe, Galileo, Kepler, and Newton were not taught in most of them, nor were new inquiries like Bacon's *Novum Organum* (1620) and Descartes's *Discourse on Method* (1637). In the late seventeenth and eighteenth centuries, intellectuals gradually assembled in academies outside the universities, such as the Royal Society of London, the Berlin Academy, the Academy of Sciences in Paris, and the Lyncean Academy in Rome. Much as when humanist learning had spread among European men of letters a century earlier, established university scholars were still too inflexible in their theological doctrines and sectarian struggles, which were becoming increasingly irrelevant to the rapidly emerging modern world. Earlier, it had been the aristocratic class that sought for a new learning to establish its place in the evolving society. This time, the driving force originated in the growing needs of the state and trade, as they expanded. But university men were once again frightened of new knowledge and methods that threatened their training and expertise. The long period between the late fifteenth century and the end of the eighteenth century was a nadir for the European universities.[24] Thus from Montaigne to Bacon, from Voltaire to Gibbon, great minds of the time expressed contempt for the vacuous pedantry of the university faculties. In fact, of Spinoza, Descartes, Pascal, and Montaigne (and later, in the seventeenth and eighteenth centuries, Leibnitz, Montesquieu, Hume, Rousseau, and Diderot) none taught at universities. The inability of the university to keep up with society is shown in both the law and medical faculties. The increasing number of real estate transactions in the fourteenth century created a need for lay practitioners of common law, which the universities could not supply. This led to the establishment of the Inns of Court in London. The first lay institution of higher education, the Inns supplied a professional training not available in the universities. Surgery fared worse.

The traditional faculty of medicine was strictly devoted to book learning based on Hippocrates, Galen, Aristotle, and other ancient authorities. Surgery, on the other hand, was viewed, at least in England, as a manual skill not deserving a place in the university. As is well known, the surgeons could not receive a charter recognizing their profession. They thus received guild status only by affiliating with barbers and founding the Company of Barber-Surgeons in 1540, which lasted as long as two centuries after that.[25] Even William Harvey's discovery of the function of the heart in 1724 was not generally accepted in England for a century. Outside England, the situation was better by then: in France and Italy especially, teaching in the flourishing medical schools was based on observations made in practice.

Even in these years there were a few universities where the new learning was eagerly embraced. German universities like Halle and Göttingen, the Dutch universities of Leyden and Utrecht, Scottish universities like Edinburgh and Glasgow were all receptive to new science and, later on, to the spirit of the Enlightenment. Even at Oxford and Cambridge, there were a few men who tried to introduce some experimental and technical education. And yet the universities as a whole failed to establish their mission as the centers of intellectual life. Despite efforts to keep their monopoly of higher learning intact, scientific teaching in England drifted away after the late seventeenth century to the royal laboratory in St. James Palace and the Royal Society in London, and to numerous nonconformist academies in provincial towns. The Schism Act of 1714 tried to crush such diffusion of education, but the national and industrial need for applied technology slowly overcame the rear guard resistance. Scholars capable of criticizing their age were kept outside the classrooms where, as Bishop Butler said, lectures were "lifeless and unintelligent."[26]

In other parts of Europe, conditions were not much better. The idea of the modern university was already in circulation by the time Immanuel Kant published his last book, *The Conflict of the Faculties*, in 1798, the tail end of the age of Enlightenment. Polemical and engaged, the tract defended the "lower" faculty of philosophy, critical investigation, against the "higher" faculties of theology, law, and medicine that were controlled by both church and state. Kant used the medieval terms without comment, which seems to indicate that they were still very much in currency in the eighteenth-century German university, as if the intervening centuries had not passed. Church and state interference in higher learning was nothing new then, as it is not for us, even today.

Kant's purpose was to challenge the anti-Enlightenment censorship of Prussia under Fredrick William II. He insisted:

> It is absolutely essential that the learned community at the university also contain a faculty [of philosophy] that is independent of the government's command with regard to its teachings; one that, having no commands to give, is free to evaluate everything, and concerns itself with the interests of the sciences, that is, with truth: one in which reason is authorized to speak out publicly.[27]

The principal concern of *The Conflict of the Faculties* was thus with the primacy of free and open examination and the public's right to the free use of its reason. Although the faculties, or disciplines, in the university have immensely increased in range and number since Kant wrote, his remarks on the university demonstrate how unchanged the institution has remained during the intervening two hundred years. As a public institution, it dealt with the entire content of learning by "mass [*fabrikenmässig*] production." The university operated by a "division of labor [*Vertheilung der Arbeiten*]" where every branch of the sciences had a professor or specialist, headed by a dean. These public teachers together formed a "kind of learned community called a university," which would have certain autonomy "since only scholars can pass judgment on scholars as such." It had its own authority to grant degrees and create doctors (*Conflict of the Faculties*, 23) in accord with the tradition of the university.

Kant was wary about the presence of professors within the university who were willing to compromise with the censoring government, calling them "businessmen or technicians of learning," and "tools of government." On the other hand, Kant was also well aware of "scholars at large, who do not belong to the university but simply work on part of the great content of learning, either forming independent organizations, like various workshops (called academies or scientific societies), or living . . . as an amateur" (25). For Kant, as for academicians before and after, institutional autonomy was a vitally important matter. He is a modernist in punctiliously demanding philosophical freedom while granting the state the right to intervene in the matters that concern it—theology, law, and medicine. What makes

Kant's treatise strategic here is its intermediate position between the traditional university and the modern university, linked by the same terminology and problematics. While the Kantian insistence on untrammeled free inquiry places him in modernism, the vocational structure of the university had changed little since the Middle Ages, and in fact did not change until recent years. The university as an institution had long been far more uninquiring, conservative, and unchanging than we are accustomed to imagining it.[28]

Like everything else in history, the emergence of the modern university did not occur in isolation. It is an outcome of webs of details of personal, public, regional, national, and international developments in all aspects of life. I am not interested here in identifying the probable causes of the emergence of the modern university, but find it useful to locate a number of conspicuous concurrent events so that we can better reflect on the later stage of the university that has evolved in proximity to these parallel happenings. Adjacent circumstances, whether cause or effect, are obviously interrelated, each determining and adapting to the courses of the others. At any rate, the circumstances that would strike anyone as closely related to the rise of the modern university would be: the accelerating growth of the human population; the Enlightenment; the American and French Revolutions; the establishment of the nation-state; the growth of capitalism; the rise of democracy and individualism; urbanization and the Industrial Revolution; the widening gap between the rich and the poor; acceleration of colonialism and imperialism alongside the evolution of the nation-state; and formation of the idea and project of culture and civilization. With the establishment of the modern university and its aftermaths in our time as the focal point, I would like to pursue just one of these circumstances, population increase, in detail, as it becomes crucial to the purpose of this essay.

In the same year as Kant published *The Conflict of the Faculties*, 1798, Thomas Malthus published *An Essay on the Principle of Population*. A refutation of William Godwin's and the marquis de Condorcet's idea of progress and human perfectibility, the tract was a conservative reaction to the French Revolution and its aftermath. One of the earliest discussions of the rise in human population and its implications, his analysis of population is not so much an empirical exercise in demography as a statement of an ideological policy against the Poor Laws that had been implied in the writings of antecedent economists including David Hume, Robert Wallace, and Adam Smith. But for these thinkers the population increase was a sign of prosperity, not the unqualified disaster it was to Malthus. His thesis of geometrical increase of population and arithmetical growth of food supplies proved wrong even during his lifetime. He believed nonetheless that to prevent the otherwise inevitable catastrophe that would result from such an imbalance, the population (meaning the poor) must be held down to a zero increase. There are "checks to population," according to Malthus, which he summarized as "misery and vice." In a not immediately comprehensible taxonomy, Malthus further divided such "checks" into "preventive" and "positive." The preventive checks correspond to modern family planning by delayed marriage and premarital sexual restraint, while the positive checks mean the rise in mortality resulting from population growth and dire poverty—malnutrition, hard labor, unwholesome habitations among the lower classes, plus their "vicious customs with respect to women, great cities, unwholesome manufactures, luxury, pestilence, and war."[29] On the basis of quasi-scientific evidence, Malthus forcefully gave support to the antirelief opinions then dominant in England. The "lower classes" in this view "seem always to live from hand to mouth . . . and they seldom think of the future. . . . All that is beyond their present necessities goes . . . to the ale-house" (chap. 5). Thus the Poor Laws that supposedly assured a comfortable life for the lower classes that did not labor to deserve it merely encouraged idleness and incompetence and "weaken[ed] one of the strongest incentives to sobriety and industry, and consequently happiness." He advocated that public relief be denied to those married poor who made no provisions for their children. They should depend solely on private charity, their hardship thus serving as a lesson to other paupers. The Poor Laws did nothing but deprive the rich of the fruit of their hard work. The "evils" attendant on the Poor Laws were "irremediable" (chap. 5). He even went as far as to say that "no child born from any marriage . . . should ever be entitled to parish assistance."[30]

His antirelief proposal is startlingly harsh and mean-spirited even to recent readers who are fully accustomed to similar attacks on public welfare by Ronald Reagan, Margaret Thatcher, and others since the 1980s. Malthus offered a powerful boost to the anti-Jacobin rulers and establishment economists of his day, and thus despite the vehement protests from social reformers and humanitarians like William Cobbett, S. T. Coleridge, William Hazlitt, Thomas Carlyle, Charles Dickens, and Marx and Engels, his influence extended to the leading politicians of the day like the younger Pitt, to the mainstream clergymen of the established church, to the liberal *Edinburgh Review* circle, James and John Stuart Mill, and of course Charles Darwin. It might be added here that as if to prove Kant's point about the professors who are "tools of the government," Malthus was the first professor of history and political economy in England when he taught at the college "established by the East India Company for the education of its servants."[31]

Why population growth and the relief program triggered so much penurious resentment just at that time is a question interesting enough to be further considered. First, the French Revolution aroused fear among the British rulers and they were prepared to view the "lower classes"—or the masses—as at least potentially dangerous and subversive. They were to be suppressed, if not eliminated. Second, the enclosure of the village commons that had begun centuries earlier and continued on and off ever since had a final crescendo in the late eighteenth century and in the earlier nineteenth. Those driven out of their villages were vagrants—the "homeless" of our time—roaming on the streets of cities and rising industrial centers. Third, Poor Law relief was beginning to cost an alarming amount, and rulers and political economists were anxious to cut down the expenditures. Fourth, although the statistics in the Malthusian essay were not based on a verifiable calculation,[32] the population was indeed increasing rapidly not only in England, but also in the world. This pace of population increase, unprecedented in human history, needs more comments at this point.

It is widely believed that the world population was rising very slowly until the beginning of the eighteenth century, but the intensity of acceleration thereafter is not widely appreciated even now. The world population around 1700 is estimated as 680 million, an increase of less than 100 million since 1600, a century earlier. The eighteenth century saw a sharp rise: 771 million in 1750 and 954 million in 1800. In 1850, half a century later, it rose to 1.2 billion, and in 1900 it climbed to 1.6 billion. In 1950, just after the Second World War—and a mere half century ago—the world population was 2.5 billion, a little less than a billion more since 1900. The population, however, more than doubled in the half-century after 1950, to reach more than 6.6 billion in 2007.[33] To fully understand the changing rate of the increase, let me suggest a graph that shows the years along the horizontal axis, and the population figures along the vertical. Since the species *Homo sapiens* came into existence 250,000 years ago, population growth was imperceptible till the beginning of human civilization several centuries B.C.[34] In the year 1, most demographers agree, the population was somewhere around 250 million. On the graph, the curve showing the population barely rises from the horizontal axis, if one billion in population is marked vertically by a centimeter. Let's indicate one century horizontally also by a centimeter. In this reversed L-shaped graph, the upward curve begins to depart from the base at the point three centimeters away from the vertical axis, leaping six centimeters and higher, merging with the vertical line (which represents the present). Almost the entire rise, in short, takes place in the three centimeters at the extreme right. How about the precivilization era that extends anywhere from ten thousand to two million years? The horizontal line that expresses one century by one centimeter extends to the left from one to two hundred meters.

Of course, the growth rate varies from continent to continent, from region to region, from locality to locality. Between 200 A.D. and 600 A.D., for example, Asia, Europe, and Africa lost population, while the Americas gained; between 1700 and 1800 most continents gained substantially, as has already been mentioned, but Africa saw a decrease. Between 1750 and 1850, the English population nearly tripled, from 5.7 million to 16.5 million, while the German equivalent less than doubled, from 15 million to 27 million. And the French population increased by merely 40 percent, from 25 to 35.8 million.[35] Between 1950 and 2000, however, the population of every continent, and nearly every country, grew immense, even though the rate of growth was not uniform. Much of what takes place in various aspects of recent human life, including the development of the modern university, should be considered in connection with this demographic history.

If the horizontal crawl means the continuity of slow change, the sharp vertical rise means abrupt transformations. Especially in the last fifty years, five millimeters in the graph, the population increase has been far faster and far more widespread than ever before. (The momentum still continues: according to the National Census Bureau, the world population as of August 2008 is over 6.8 billion, three-quarters of a billion increase since 2000.) And quantity affects quality. Of course, let me repeat, regional and local variance remains large. Rural areas as well as inner cities are being hollowed out and inland areas lose more and more to coastal zones. Developed nations not only increase at a slower rate, but are leveling off or even losing absolutely. Thus the major portions of the increase are taking place in the developing nations, and especially around their urban centers.[36] And yet it is safe to say that for nearly everyone, being alive in the twenty-first century means facing an unprecedented congestion of people—with all the unanticipated consequences.

Malthus's calculation was hopelessly wrong, to begin with, and his fear of the ultimate shortage of food supply has not materialized. The advance in agricultural technology has been—so far—sufficient to stave off starvation in nearly every place on earth. If there are still famines and malnutrition—even in industrialized nations—they are usually due to failures in the distribution, not in the production (which was what Malthus had predicted) of food.[37] And his skewed idea about the Poor Laws is, although still in circulation, fortunately not dominant. The final chapter on food production, however, has not yet been written, and humanity may well have to face eventually the ultimate consequences of the overuse of fertilizers, insecticides, and other chemicals, which contaminate the earth's supply of surface water and the ocean as well as food. Climate change and growing demands may deplete our aquifers.[38] Genetically modified seeds still have an unknown future. More interestingly, the imbalance between population increase and production growth is working in exactly the opposite direction to Malthus's prediction: between 1950 and 2000, the economy expanded sevenfold. That means a phenomenal growth in consumption and waste, producing problems at least as critical as those of population expansion, if not more so.[39]

A rapid increase in population and migration has generated these and other visible consequences: crowding in cities with inadequate infrastructure—no housing, no fair employment, no urban planning, no police, no schools, no sanitation, no medicine, no labor laws, no drinking water, no sewage, no rational transportation system, no clean air, no energy, and no light. And yet the rich run riot with insane luxuries in a period that even the owner of Yves Saint Laurent and Gucci calls "the age of irrationality."[40] The invisible effects are at least as overwhelming: the general uncertainty about what is to come, the feeling of being alone and adrift in a space cut off from history and geography, family and fellow beings, and a sense of the inadequacy of received wisdom and previously accepted authorities. If learning used to be organized in the past around the experience of history, now it often has to be constructed from abstract speculation and analysis. Family, community, and tribe—such agents of the transmission of information, knowledge, and learning no longer prevail. To meet the challenge, an institution organized for the purpose of coping with such changes has to be invented. Can the ever slow and conservative university meet this challenge?

Before we turn to the modern university at the start of the twentieth century, the universities in the American colonies, our antecedents, must be briefly recalled here. That the first institution of higher education in North America was built in 1636 meant that the American transplant was destined to carry the religious and institutional turmoil then roiling Oxford and Cambridge. Emmanuel College, Cambridge, was one of the largest Puritan colleges in the two English universities at the time, and as Stuart control of the reform movement tightened, its graduates decided that the time had come "to establish a new England overseas; and new England must include a new Emmanuel." Thus, of the 130 English university men who migrated to New England before 1646, 35 had attended Emmanuel.[41] What the founder of Emmanuel at Cambridge said of its mission applied to the goal of Harvard College as well: to educate preachers "at once learned and zealous, instructed in all that scholars should know, but trained to use their learning in the service of the reformed faith."[42] Puritan zeal was likely disseminated in the informal collegiate living of the small school, where teachers were few (the president and two or three tutors), and the students, too, numbering around a dozen altogether. As far as classroom teaching was concerned, the curriculum was described as the conventional trivium and quadrivium, modified by humanist learning, in Hebrew and Greek for instance, and the Puritan Reformation, but there were no "higher faculties" of theology, medicine, and law.[43]

The split between learning and faith, knowledge and belief, is seldom bridged smoothly anywhere in the world, and throughout the history of education it is displayed in a myriad of forms and intensities. There were, however, fundamental differences in the unfolding of the American universities from their European counterparts in this respect. In America, there never was a central church comparable to the Roman Catholic Church of medieval Europe, the Anglican Church of England, or even the Lutheran Church in parts of northern Europe. During the colonial period, there was not even a central intercolonial government, and the British monarchy (also head of the Anglican Church) remained generally passive and distant. Even if there had been a unified colonial authority, however, the established church would not have emerged in North America, where the separation of church and state was implicit and inherent in the making of the colonies. Thus the nine universities founded before the American Revolution were diverse in their denominational affiliations. While Harvard was Puritan, and Yale was reformed Puritan, William and Mary and Columbia[44] were Anglican, Brown was Baptist, Dartmouth was Congregationalist, Princeton was Presbyterian, Rutgers was Dutch Reformed Church, and Pennsylvania was nondenominational.[45] Such plurality in denominational affiliation was a reflection of America as a decentralized colony. Religious control could be locally harsh, even bigoted (as in Massachusetts, for example), but the conflict was limited to a local site, not over a whole territory. This undoubtedly imposed the practice of tolerance in the long run, while helping to neutralize religion from a totalizing cohesive force into a function of private life, further reinforcing the separation of church and state in the United States to a degree never seen in Europe.

There were other reasons for mutual religious tolerance among the universities. If the dissenters sought religious havens in the New World, they still had to establish themselves as settlers first. There was acute need of practical knowledge, and ecclesiastical disputes could wait until material conditions improved. Besides, religious diversity among the colonies prevented any one denomination from maintaining control for long over any college it may have founded. Although Calvinists and Anglicans and Baptists vied with one another, no university could have required a religious test for admission or graduation or faculty appointment, as did Oxford and Cambridge until 1877. They had more immediate business to attend to. They had to sow, harvest, produce, and profit. There were native Indians to fight off, slaves to exploit, and vast territories to explore. The gap between the rich and the poor was spreading. Virginia had scores of immensely rich families amassing a total fortune of over fifty thousand pounds each, who lived off slaves and servants. The English king granted a proprietor the right of total control over the Maryland colony. In the 1660s John Locke wrote the constitutions for the Carolinas, which prescribed a feudalistic aristocracy where eight barons would own 40 percent of the land. Earlier, in 1630, John Winthrop, the governor of the Massachusetts Bay Colony, projected the class system in the New World: "in all times some must be rich, some poore, some highe and eminent in power and dignitie; others meane and in subjection."[46] Social necessity for the formation and maintenance of an elite class loomed larger than the nurturing of sectarian faiths. One of the Harvard commencement speakers earnestly remarked, in the 1670s, "[Without Harvard] the ruling class would have been subjected to mechanics, cobblers, and tailors, the gentry would have been overwhelmed by lewd fellows of the baser sort, the sewage of Rome, the dregs which judgeth much from emotion, little from truth. . . . Nor would we have rights, honors or magisterial ordinance worthy of preservation, but plebiscites, appeals to base passions, and revolutionary rumblings."[47]

The university was not a major social institution during the earlier colonial period. As we have already glimpsed, the size of the university was miniscule at first. In the entire seventeenth century, fewer than 600 students were enrolled at Harvard, of whom 465 graduated. Also, before the eighteenth century there was only one college other than Harvard, William and Mary, established in 1693. A third institution, Yale, or the Collegiate School in Connecticut, was founded in 1701. In 1710, Harvard had 123 students enrolled, while Yale had only 36; in 1770, sixty years later, Harvard enrolled 413, and Yale, 338. Six other prerevolutionary institutions were opened much later, between 1746 (Princeton) and 1769 (Dartmouth). "It is estimated that probably no more than one in every thousand colonists attended any of the colleges in existence before 1776, and fewer still completed a bachelor of arts degree."[48] Neither universities nor their graduates had a sufficient critical mass to affect the course of colonial or early nineteenth-century history. Because of institutional poverty and political isolation, the American universities had to wait more than one full century before they began to grow into a serious presence. There is no known record of the number of BAS or higher degrees in 1776. There were 9,372 degrees granted in 1870, of which one was a doctorate.[49] Although the construction and maintenance of an elite class was undoubtedly among the urgent objectives of the colonial universities from the earliest days, those few who attended them were mostly sons of clergymen, followed by the sons of magistrates, attorneys, shopkeepers, and rich farmers. There were also a number of students from the families of artisans, servants, and the poor. The colonial elite did not send their sons to college at all.[50]

Another significant difference between the beginnings of the American and the European universities was the economic structure of the institutions. As we have seen, the medieval universities were outgrowths of cathedral schools, later subsidized by church or state. And the entry of market forces onto the academic scene did not commence until the late nineteenth century. In America, on the other hand, by the time the universities opened, the market economy was fully operational, well before the nation-state of America was formed. Although the federal and state governments were to play crucial roles later, the colonial governments did not provide colleges and universities with stable and dependable funds. The General Court of the Massachusetts Bay Company, for instance, promised the sum of 400 pounds to a college it had chartered but was not able to fulfill the promise. The college was named after John Harvard, assistant to a pastor, who bequeathed his land, a half of his estate (799 pounds), and a library of 320 volumes.[51] In the case of Yale, Cotton Mather, who had wanted to be the president but failed to receive the office at the Collegiate School of Connecticut, asked one Elihu Yale for contributions, promising that the school would be named after him. Yale, a wealthy Anglican merchant in London, had worked for the British East India Company before his appointment as governor of Fort Saint George at Madras, from which position he was dismissed because of business scandals. Nicholas Brown, for whom the Rhode Island College was renamed, was a successful slave trader as well as a manufacturer and philanthropist.

An expert on the sociology of higher education differentiates the American universities from their British counterparts in five aspects. Here I will take up just his first point, on which I have already touched: "In America, the market preceded the society and its institutions of higher education."[52]

Whether the relative absence of support from the church and the state was cause or effect, the American universities had to seek for funds from all possible sources. As we have already seen, the charitable contributions generated by colonial abuse or slavery touched no moral sensitivity whatever; money was money, as history has always reaffirmed since then.[53] The multiple sources included student tuition and fees, alumni contributions, investments, donations from rich benefactors, institutions, foundations, corporations, as well as the church and the state. Such diversity in funding sources results in the university administration's preoccupation with the "needs and interests of this varied support community." If such a wide range of activities hurts higher education by diffusing its objective, it at the same time helps to assure the "relative autonomy of our colleges and universities, even formally 'public' institutions, from direct control and management by agents of state or central government."[54]

That the American university needs to be sensitive to the demands of multiple funding sources is unquestionable. The specific ways of its satisfying those demands, however, are varied, and contingent on the social roles of sources and institutions. To start with tuition and fees, the students and their parents are no doubt consumers and customers insofar as they choose to pay for the service of the institutions. A student's admission and enrollment are, however, not identical with the purchase of merchandise. The payment of tuition and fees does not complete a transaction; it only provides the student with opportunities for investment and speculation. The final commodity is never guaranteed by the institution, nor is such a guarantee expected. The student is as much a producer here as the institution of which he/she is a client. To the extent that the students render support to the operation of their university as well as the wages of their faculty, the faculty do have an obligation to attend to the needs of the students, although the faculty now no longer serve the demands of the student body as directly as at Bologna centuries ago. The precise nature of the students' needs is neither uniform nor definable.

Does the diversity of funding sources encourage the independence and autonomy of colleges and universities? A university established and supported by the state seldom gains the strength and independence to insist on unrestricted freedom to criticize fundamentally the policies and performances of that state. Such a university usually supports state policy uncritically—although there may be a few individual members who choose to be defiant. We have witnessed examples of the complete surrender of the university in Nazi Germany and in fascist Japan during the Second World War. Such a development was not an abrupt shift. In Germany, Hegel's metaphysical devotion to the German state, Johann Gottlieb Fichte's patriotic defense against Napoleon in his *Addresses to the German Nation* (1807–1808), and Wilhelm von Humboldt's nationalist reorganization of the university (much admired by Arnold) were all precursors of Martin Heidegger's collaboration with Hitler.[55] In fact, even Nietzsche insisted in his tract on the university that the current university was a betrayal of true German culture, of which his ideal version of the university would be a staunch protector.[56] In this sense, the failure of George Washington's dream of building a national university for the United States is to be celebrated rather than regretted. Even in the United States, the seduction of higher education by the central government is far from minimal.

What is more pertinent here, however, is not the danger of appropriation of higher education by the state, but by the market. Without force or even pressure, business can gather willing, eager collaborators around itself. So far as business is perceived to be one of many and diverse funding sources, there is little reason for serious concern. Furthermore, when the role of the university was insignificant, as in seventeenth- and eighteenth-century America, the orientation of the college and university meant, indeed, very little to the welfare of its society. However, the research university now plays a dominant role in both information and technology. Outside colleges and universities, sites of independent learning, such as "academies" in the early modern age through the nineteenth century, have become scarce. Some of the NGOs and foundations may come close to being neutral and research-devoted institutions that attract academic scholars. At the same time, one recalls that many NGOs are sponsored by states and corporations, even if this fact is not in itself a proof of bias and indoctrination. And when the economy becomes the all-embracing agency— guiding university administrators, legislators, alumni, media conglomerates, religious leaders, students, and finally, the faculty themselves—there is hardly any space left for critical examination of higher education and corporate practice.

Environmental Studies and Human Extinction

Toward the end of the first section, I suggested environmental justice studies as the only discipline that could replace the now enervated humanities. The environmental crisis is borderless, and the discipline could be kept committed to justice. The ecological program, however, is not yet established academically and institutionally, although by now nearly every institution has some version of such a discipline. It is still in a state of flux, dependent on the interests of faculty members who happen to be on the campus. By now some of the core sciences, such as geophysics, biology, urban studies, earth sciences, marine biology, and engineering, have at least a few scholars interested in ecology, but economics, law, political science, and other branches are unpredictably represented. It is largely transdisciplinary, rather than firmly departmental. And that is its strength.

Still, there are two common features I have noted in several university catalogs. One, in nearly every program, ecological concerns are pursued from the perspectives of the traditional disciplines. Thus marine biology offers observations regarding meteorological changes. This is obviously a natural course of academic development, and little to be unhappy about. What I would like to propose, however, is the reverse: that is, what the perspective of ecological protection will teach the traditional disciplines. Doesn't that open a new way of thinking about the world? Two, the programs devoted to environment and sustainability simply take for granted that civilization will continue to exist. The environmental catastrophe remains a fantasy, or dream, as far as academic studies are concerned. In traditional disciplines, the assumption of continuity is both logical and expected. But in environmental justice studies, shouldn't we identify the status of this fear and "crisis"? If the extinction of life on the planet is just an apocalyptic fantasy, shouldn't it be fully considered as such in our ecological policy and plans? What is the rationale of environmental sustainability?

While environmental studies has not been established as an independent discipline, there are by now a great number of specialists and experts in its numerous branches. This is also a usual course of development. As water, oil, or food supplies are threatened, as waste, pollutants, and pathogens increase, and as drought, flood, and extreme climate change transpire, the need for those knowledgeable and trained in the specific problems becomes urgent. There is even a specialist in environmental education, whose intention—if not thesis—has points of resemblance with my ideas.[57] I am neither interested in, nor capable of, covering developments in all such branches of knowledge and skill. To the extent that environmental justice is proposed as the alternative to the humanities, however, some fundamental outline of studies must be discussed here. I will return to the subject of extinction later.

In 2003 and 2004, a surprising number of books—nine I have surveyed—were published in English on the ecological crisis. One of the reasons for the bumper years is perhaps the publication in 2001 of the *Third Assessment Report* of the Intergovernmental Panel on Climate Change (organized by WMO and UNEP), a widely acclaimed study by thousands of scholars from more than 130 countries, which began in 1988, if not earlier. The report was extremely judicious, and yet it categorically asserted that climate warming was anthropogenic. Reactions were striking, as we will see. Some of the books on the crisis are more passionate than others; some are well documented, detailed, broad-based, and substantial, others are not. And yet they nearly all conform to the same format. Spencer Weart's excellent *The Discovery of Global Warming* (2003) makes full use of the IPCC reports of 1990, 1995, and 2001, and after discussing the skeptical responses to the reports by the administrations of George H. W. Bush and George W. Bush (and Clinton's lukewarm support of environment protection generally), he concludes that "it is very likely that significant global warming is coming in our lifetimes. . . . We have had a warning in time—although just barely in time" (199).

David Goodstein's *Out of Gas: The End of the Age of Oil* (2004) predicts that we will be out of gas in forty years (according to a figure released by BP), and concludes that "Civilization as we know it will come to an end sometime in this century unless we can find a way to live without fossil fuels" (123). *The End of Oil: On the Edge of a Perilous New World* (2004) deals with the same subject, but Paul Roberts discusses the future of all energy sources, not just oil. Natural gas, hybrid engines, hydrogen, nuclear, solar energy, wind farms, biofuel. They are all promising, but none is problem-free. While the demand for energy continues to climb, dependence on fossil fuel only rises. The power of coal and oil lobbies is overwhelming in the United States, but consumer resistance to switching to cleaner, though more expensive, energy sources is almost equally to blame. In the meantime, carbon dioxide concentrations are perilously high. Roberts might have given a little more weight, however, to possible innovations in solar and wind technology.

Another 2004 book, *Boiling Point: How Politicians, Big Oil and Coal, Journalists, and Activists Are Fueling the Climate Crisis—and What We Can Do to Avert Disaster*, by Ross Gelbspan, is a passionate book that denounces the failures of those listed in the subtitle. It includes an amazing story of a conspiracy by the Bush-Cheney White House and the Competitive Enterprise Institute. "The White House secretly requested the private, right-wing CEI to sue it—the White House—in order to have the national assessment withdrawn" (57). This U.S. National Assessment of Climate Change had been drafted by the Clinton-appointed head of the U.S. Global Change Research Program in 2002, after Bush-Cheney gained power. After making three proposals for ameliorating the deterioration—a new energy subsidy policy, energy technology transfer to developing countries, and international emissions trading—Gelbspan concludes, "One way or the other, this world we inhabit will not long continue on its historical trajectory. Like it or not, we are facing a massive and inevitable discontinuity." "It is just possible . . . [to restore] peace between people and nature" (205).

Mark Lynas's *High Tide: The Truth about Our Climate Crisis* is a travel report from Britain through Alaska, China, Peru, and so on, rather than an analysis. His parting words are: "Time is of the essence. . . . It may already be too late" (298). *Limits to Growth: The 30-Year Update* is an updated version of a 1972 publication of the same title by Donella Meadows, Jorgen Randers, and Dennis Meadows. A humane book, it covers the basics and avoids pedantry. The tools they propose for the "sustainability revolution" are "visioning, networking, truth-telling, learning, and loving" (271). James Gustave Speth's *Red Sky at Morning: America and The Crisis of The Global Environment: A Citizen's Agenda for Action* is a typically academic (that is, cautious and liberal) book. It opens with the promise *"there are solutions"* (xiii). So after surveying the "drivers of environmental deterioration," he remains optimistic. He sees hopeful signs in eight areas of transition: smaller world population, decrease in mass poverty, benign technologies, honest prices, sustainable consumption, knowledge and learning, (potential?) "good governance," and culture and consciousness (209–28). They may all be, admittedly, great goals to aim at. But are these "hopeful signs" already achieved and visible now? Do these "solutions" exist? If not, where and when do we begin to achieve the goals?

Unconvincing as these books all are in their hopefulness, Paul and Anne Ehrlich's *One with Nineveh: Politics, Consumption, and the Human Future* stands out even among them. Experts in prophecy, the Ehrlichs are unafraid of telling us our future. The human failures they list are all by now familiar: human domination on the planet, abusive consumption, wrong technology, inequitable distribution of wealth, poor governance, wrong culture, and so on. The problem I find here is that the Erlichs seem to believe their recognition of predicaments is sufficient by itself as an environmental strategy. For each problem they of course have a proper answer, which in their argument serves as a resolution. Thus in the penultimate chapter, the authors—like all the other authors discussed, and I am not forgetting myself here—propose the "difficult, but far from impossible" task of "reforming American democracy." The democratization program entails reducing the powers of special interests, electing officials not beholden to special interests, "leashing the media," reforming regulatory bodies, and finally "creation of . . . new institutions . . . to deal with novel environmental and social problems" (293ff), as if no one had ever dreamed about, or even tried, such projects before. And an even more facile observation closes the book: "In the face of pervasive injustice and massive environmental need, idealism can be realism" (334).[58]

As against all these books, *Our Final Hour: A Scientist's Warning: How Terror, Error, and Environmental Disaster Threaten Humankind's Future in This Century—On Earth and Beyond* by Martin Rees opens with the warning "The odds are no better than fifty-fifty that our present civilization on Earth will survive to the end of the present [twenty-first] century."[59] A strength of the book is the author's capacity to imagine beyond and outside humanity. Being a professor of cosmology and an astrophysicist, Rees can readily think of the rest of the universe, vastly distant from the planet on which we live. Obviously, he does not describe what this extrahuman world is like. But unlike the other ecologists whose imagination stops at the moment they mention the end of humanity, Rees begins with this possibility of our extinction, enlarging the limits of our ecological imagination. He can, for example, dream about the possibility of transforming the entire surface of Mars to make it habitable. He suggests that Mars could be warmed by greenhouse gas injection or by covering the Martian surface with soot or powdered basalt. To his credit, he does not forget ethical dangers involved in the fantasized colonization of Mars: it could contaminate Martian life (if there is any), and human colonization would be accompanied by the age-old problems of colonization, the Wild West struggle among the settlers themselves (178).

Rees is also temporally imaginative. Although he does not write the history of the future, he ponders the longevity of the earth before the sun burns it down. The cosmic context, in his view, is not entirely irrelevant to the fate of humans. Whereas earlier I placed the history of human civilization in the species' time-scale, Rees compares human existence with the solar system's: "If our solar system's entire lifecycle . . . were to be viewed 'fast forward' in a single year, then all recorded history would flash past in a third of a second" (186). However, ecological failure is itself a consequence of the acceleration within this brief human civilization.

Humans now have the capability of affecting the future of humans. If they could have millions or even billions of years, their technological achievement would no doubt be sufficient to deal with all ecological problems (182). And yet, looking away into a far distant future, Rees makes what strikes me as an irremediable and appalling error: the failure to address political problems in our everyday life. He insists, for example, that universal police surveillance—for the sake of protecting ourselves from terrorist attack—is perfectly acceptable (66). He also concludes that new risks of "bio" or "cyber" terror or error cannot be eliminated from our increasingly interconnected world. To safeguard against them, however, he seems to believe that we need to encroach "on some cherished personal freedoms" (186). The idea that environmental concerns can coexist with the divestment of civil rights must be unequivocally dismissed. The preservation of the environment *is* a civil right, and any position that fails to recognize this is self-contradictory and incompatible with environmentalism.

Like Martin Rees, James Lovelock rejects anthropocentricity. Unlike Rees, who observes the integrity of cosmology and astrophysics, Lovelock denies the disciplinary division between geophysics and biology, calling his Gaia theory "geophysiology."[60] In fact, Lovelock ignores many other scholarly conventions such as "specialization," "professionalism, and "career-ism." He calls himself a scientist who has been approved by journalists like Simon Winchester and Bill McKibben, but also by professional scientists and engineers. In sharp contrast to Martin Rees, who has received the highest honors for a scientist—in addition to being named Astronomer Royal of England, master of Trinity College, Cambridge, and president of the Royal Society in 2005—Lovelock is an eccentric hermit-scientist. He works in a farmhouse in Devonshire, has no academic affiliation, and hates the peer review process as a "self-imposed inquisition" (*The Ages of Gaia*, xvii). Lovelock's skepticism about the modern university is unimpeachable. Does he exemplify the idea of a new kind of independent scholar who learns in his own space?

The planet, according to Lovelock, is a living organism that has remained hospitable to life for billions of years despite the rise in the temperature of the sun. This homeostasis is a result of the balancing of many factors in the universe, which Lovelock attributes to the benevolence of Gaia, the meta-phoric goddess of the whole universe. Gaia is the deity of a totality of which humanity is only a small part. Gaia is not antihuman, but what is crucial to humans is trivial in Gaia's view. Thus Lovelock believes that if humans persist in disrupting the global environment, Gaia could replace humans with another species. The attraction of Lovelock's theory is this critical view of environmentalism as overly human-centered, concerned as it is with the future supplies and resources of sustainable industrial expansion. At the same time, Lovelock is not as much concerned with ecological crises (such as climate warming) as the other environmentalists, since Gaia—that is, the universe—is self-regulating and the world is homeostatic. (This idea is, of course, vulnerable to exploitation at the hands of the energy industry and the Bush-Cheney administration, because of Lovelock's conviction that homeostasis guarantees the endurance of the ecological balance, thereby dispensing with the need for regulation and intervention, as we will see.) At least in *The Ages of Gaia*, written in the 1980s and reissued in 1995, and even in *Homage to Gaia*, his autobiography, published as late as 2000, Lovelock trusts Gaia, who is expected to reduce carbon dioxide emissions and restore the earth's balance.

The Revenge of Gaia: Earth's Climate Crisis and the Fate of Humanity (2006) abruptly changes all this. In a chapter called "The Life History of Gaia,"

Lovelock says that he began to notice serious changes in the environment that he hadn't before. "Why does Gaia not resist this adverse change?" (43). "As a scientist I know that Gaia theory is provisional and likely to be displaced by a larger and more complete view of the Earth" (139). "I was so wrong" (147). Thus Gaia, after all these forty years—and several books—is killed off by her votary. In fact, as the book closes, Gaia is entirely forgotten. Instead, a prosaic explanation replaces her, rambling on about what is happening to the environment and what we humans should be doing now.

Lovelock had always insisted that the idea of Gaia was not a poetic myth, but a scientific theory. Why did he change his mind between 2000 and 2006? Was there any monumental event in the world? What took place in Lovelock's and Gaia's life, it seems, is that he read the IPCC Third Assessment Report (49–65) and other scientific work, like Martin Rees's *Our Final Hour* (147), for the first time. (The two documents, which he had never mentioned earlier, make their appearances in *The Revenge*.) Till then, in other words, environmental degradation had not been really a serious development for him, but merely an incident that would have corrected itself in time. Lovelock now brushes off his metaphor as only metaphor, and accepts science as a newly found truth. In the process he makes several stunning remarks. One, the lovely Devon countryside where he lives was the "face of Gaia" (151), that is, keeping his own farmland pastoral was his environmentalism. Two, his demographic ideal is "a stabilized population of about half to one billion" in "prosperous societies" (141)—like Malthus, but more like Les Knight's nihilistically utopian VHEMT (the Voluntary Human Extinction Movement).[61]

Three, we may not perish all at once, but we should consider the possibility of gradually intensifying disaster in climate change. A few will survive the catastrophe for a while by escaping to the Arctic: "One thing we can do to lessen the consequences of catastrophe is to write a guidebook for our survivors to help them rebuild civilization without repeating too many of our mistakes" (157). "No such book exists." "What we need is a book of knowledge written so well as to constitute literature in its own right. . . . It would be a primer of philosophy and science. . . . It would also be the survival manual for our successors." And finally, "what we need is a book written on durable paper with long-lasting print" (157–58). In this three-page-long prescription for a guidebook, Lovelock is totally oblivious of his goddess friend. What surprises me most is his confidence that the survivors will want to waste their time reading a manual written by those who ruined human civilization and couldn't save even themselves. Lovelock's at times loveable fairytale of over forty years collapses in a complete shambles of incoherent fragments that offer nothing to our efforts to fight ecological degradation.

I might have written too much on a worthless fantasy of hope and despair, but Lovelock is not atypical of the environmentalist discourse.

So the human race might not survive the twenty-first century. But apocalyptic eschatology offers nothing, unless we are addicted to prayers. The fundamentalists are eager to exploit the ecological crisis for evangelizing, with their vision of doomsday: "For the remaining brief span of your life, give all you have to us, the only true Church, and be counted among the select faithful for whom eternal life begins with the Second Coming." Fortunately, the fanatic desperadoes and their opportunistic handlers are not so dominant yet. Besides, we may indeed acquire the technology to regulate the environment and human behavior in time to save ourselves. The problem is how should humans be living their everyday lives now in the face of this uncertainty? Are we doing enough? Most scientists, as we have seen, doubt it. Personal energy-saving and emission-reduction gestures such as driving a hybrid car, turning off lights and air-conditioners, installing solar panels, and eating and drinking with utmost caution are, of course, important, and since 2007 the rising price of gas has been discouraging the addiction to driving in the United States, but that will not change the direction of climate deterioration. We will be stepping irreversibly toward the tipping point. If the change is ever to occur, it will have to be structural, locally and globally.

The IPCC Fourth Assessment Working Group II Report, *Climate Change 2007: Impacts, Adaptation, and Vulnerability*, was released in the spring of 2007. Chapter 19, dealing with "Assessing Key Vulnerabilities and the Risk from Climate Change," has meticulous and comprehensive lists of vulnerabilities (19.3) divided into categories such as social systems (19.3.2), regional vulnerabilities (19.3.3), ecosystems and biodiversities (19.3.4), geophysical systems (19.3.5), extreme events (19.3.6), and an update on "Reasons for Concern" (19.3.7), as well as a list of "response strategies to avoid key vulnerabilities" (19.4). I am fairly certain that even a glance at this chapter—or even the one-page-long "executive summary" of the chapter—alone would get the most confirmed antienvironmentalist at least interested in the environmental problem. The report as a whole predicts "some large-scale climate events have the potential to cause very large impacts, especially after the 21st century," and further that "impacts . . . are very likely to impose net annual costs which will increase over time as global temperatures increase" ("Summary for Policymakers," 11). Interestingly enough, the Working Group III Report, *Climate Change 2007: Mitigation of Climate Change*, argues that there are various options in climate change mitigation, and the more we try, the smaller impacts will be. More significantly, such ecological efforts will not materially alter the growth of GDP: citing the Energy Information Administration analysis of 1998, it states that "the real GDP loss . . . is reduced to 0.3% by 2020 when recycling benefits are taken into account" (11.4.3.1).[62]

People everywhere are worried, and they correctly believe that the United States is the primary obstacle to any significant change. But those in power in the United States are not listening to the people's fear, despite pretensions to democracy. Or maybe I am wrong: most Americans, led by the Bush-Cheney administration as well as by corporate interests, are ignorant even today of ecological conditions and insist on driving for their pleasure and fulfillment. From the largest corporations like BP, Wal-Mart, and DuPont to neighborhood stores and fast-food chains, all advertise their environmental conscience. We all know that this is entirely greenwash for the purpose of keeping business as usual. We also know that journalism matches business in greed and indifference. And yet we don't know how we can change our course in terms of the economy and ecology? How can we begin to restrain capitalism? Change our leaders? Do we need an armed revolution? All the ecologists discussed above—without a single exception —dream about changes in consciousness, culture, consumption, politics, and so on, but on the one important subject, how to initiate these changes, they are completely silent.[63]

Earlier, I talked about environmental studies as the only possible discipline—or way of seeing—that can remain free from the culture of consumption, and can reunite university studies. Here I am proposing it no longer as the salvation of the university, but as the only means to reverse our disastrous course toward the end of human civilization. And we have in our hands the means of spreading the news. Not efficient, but this is what we are trained, or constrained, to do. What we *can* do—even at the semi-defunct university. As we try to install an enlightened government in the United States and try to regulate business, we can continue to teach, and teach well. I would like all courses in every discipline to be saturated with environmental and social consciousness. The administration of the university may well hesitate or even disapprove, but it is a comparatively easy restraint to break down, since individual instructors can choose course contents, somehow undercutting their official oversight.[64] Individual instructors must take the initiative and responsibility, as they did with feminism and ethnic studies a few decades ago—until these concerns were acknowledged, and then gradually spread, and were finally accepted and established in the mainstream curricula. Gender and ethnic equity is yet far from actualized. Reform activism is more social than academic, as I have argued earlier. Compared with a mere several decades ago, however, the changes are distinctly notable, and the contributions by academics are—especially at the earlier stages—impossible to ignore.

Ecologically revised literature—that is easy enough, although I would insist on making the alteration more fundamental than just discussing ecology in Romantic writing.[65] History ought to add precivilizational periods, including the preceding five extinctions in the planet's history. Peter D. Ward's and Donald Brownlees's *The Life and Death of Planet Earth: How the New Science of Astrobiology Charts the Ultimate Fate of Our World*, among many others, is useful in articulating the rarity of human life in the universe. It also clarifies the difference between the end of the planet and the end of humans.[66] Political science obviously needs to include the politics of capitalism and ecological violence in history as well as current global relations and ecology. Emission trading alone should easily provide a lively topic for this exhausted discipline.

I could go on, but the most important discipline that ought to be reorganized in environmental terms is economics. Reexaminations of supply and demand, wealth and poverty, accumulation and distribution, necessity and luxury, for instance, continue to be urgently needed. But more broadly, the two concepts that need to be crucially revised are pricing and production. The price of an automobile as well as of gasoline, for example, at present excludes the cost of building and maintaining roads as well as the cost of cleaning polluted air. Economics was formed after the triumph of capitalism to serve the corporations by carefully making the public pay for the "externals." And exactly at that moment serious environmental destruction commenced. Therefore, a new economics must reexamine the assumption of the line that divides what is inside from what is outside the pricing structure, that is, the internal and external to the "economy," or, more generally, what capital pays (and charges) and what capital should pay (and evades). The basis of a price is, as the economy is constituted now, a fiction, a deception. The reconsideration of prices, in other words, requires the transformation of social relations. Taxation is one means for the reorganization of pricing, and it must be fully utilized. But the internalization of the externals merely sustains the conditions of capitalism that depends on the growth of production, that is, consumption. Second, the meaning of production needs radical reexamination. At present, any circulation of money is thought of as production. A corrupt politician is charged, say, with bribery and conspiracy. He will retain lawyers and spend a huge amount on fees, which are added on to the GDP as production. A woman is overworked and requires therapy and medication—the costs of her cure are of course added to the GDP. In other words, much of what is being "produced" can and should be avoided—together with our increased production of landfills: the politician should not have committed the crime; the woman wouldn't have been stressed in a slower-paced society; we should see what we acquire for what it is. Much of what fills the industrialized household is unused and only takes up space. To contain these useless goods, people build larger and larger homes, all the while working harder and believing that they are producing more. A new economics must define exactly what production is and what consumption, or waste, is. Does our "production" improve our civilization? Of course, such reflection will finally lead to the question of what we are "working" for, or, in fact, what we live for. But that is exactly what the study of ecology ultimately requires. The expansion of our material acquisition is at the bottom of our misery today, and our shameful legacy to our children and their children.

Finally, however, I would like to add one more subject to the new, expanded ecology program. All my arguments—like those by the environmental scientists I discussed above—have been based on the assumption that human life will go on with no end. My proposal here is the addition of a topic, the sixth extinction. The end of humans.[67] What does the species' end mean? Is there any meaning in studying that eventuality? We personally live our lives with full knowledge that we will die sooner or later. And yet in our daily life we are oblivious of the death that ends it—until death descends on us, usually without much warning. The death of humanity—if it is imaginable—is no analogy to personal death, of course. As we ignore climate change and possibly accelerate our termination, we are not just dying, but also murdering our children and their children. Shouldn't we reflect on the connection between our consumption and our act of murder? In one sense, the species' extinction and personal death share a feature, the existence of survivors. As we die, younger generations will fill our personally vacated space; as our species perishes, other species will take over. And we keep our hope because of their presence after we vanish.

Aside from environmental collapse, there are other possible causes of human extinction—nuclear mishaps or violent pathogens, to take obvious examples. Whatever the cause, however, humans will not vanish all at once. The speeds and stages of depredation are unknowable, but it is certain that some—likely the poor—will die earlier than others, most probably the rich. The early deaths may be small in number, or huge, nearing a majority, hundreds of thousands, millions, or even billions. The point is when a catastrophe of global proportion hits us, how is it going to be managed by survivors? Imagine Hurricane Katrina or the 1998 Bangladesh floods that inundated two-thirds of the land and endangered more than twenty million people, and multiply the intensity a hundred- or thousand-fold. Who would be in a position to guide the survivors? We recall FEMA's utter incompetence in New Orleans, but then think about a global disaster in a world that has no organization whatever. Facing the calamity with no consciousness of ethics or social rules, would survivors suddenly be neighborly to each other? Or warring for their own personal survival, thereby accelerating the destruction? This picture alone should justify the introduction of the topic of human extinction into our course of general studies. Environmentalism cannot exist without social justice, but social justice cannot be expected to prevail without ecological consciousness.

The death of humans is not the end of the planet. The earth, too, will ultimately end, like all other planets in the universe. But that has nothing to do with ecological problems. Planetary destruction requires a totally different kind of force. And as long as there is a physical earth, there will be other kinds of life on the planet—microbes, ants, rats, cockroaches, or whatever. And as long as life goes on, there will be other cycles of evolution. That is, after the end of humans, there will be life, other kinds of life that will evolve to produce their own civilizations. A new posthuman species will have its own life cycles. Of course, it may end up producing its own Bush-Cheney management. But that will take a great many millions, if not billions, of years. For now, a new kind of ecological studies will need to decide whether human extinction is worth thinking about. If it is, what about the cycles that will commence after ours is completed? At this time of very little hope all around, we can at least look forward to ongoing life on earth. And as long as we entertain any hope, we will manage to find the courage to keep trying.

....

This is an excerpt from chapter 3, "Minds," of Miyoshi's book, As We Saw Them *(1979). Miyoshi analyzes the travelogues written by the members of the first Japanese mission to the United States in 1860—only seven years after Commodore Perry's own mission that "opened" Japan. A close, formal reading of the travelogues, as well as the travelogue genre itself, enables Miyoshi to draw qualitative distinctions between Tokugawa and American subjectivities. This work anticipates developments in literary studies by granting a careful literary reading to non-literary texts and also Japanese and cross-cultural studies by challenging the universalization of cultural value.*—ED.

The extant travelogues and memoirs left by members of the 1860 Embassy proper and the *Kanrin Maru* escort group number about forty altogether. Although one of them, Hirose Kakuzo Kaneaki's *Kankai koro nikki* (The Diary across the Oceans), appeared in print shortly after the adventure in 1862, for the most part the travelogues were not intended for immediate publication. The decade of the 1860s, especially its first half, was a dangerous and bloody period both for foreign residents and those Japanese who had dealings with them. Any diarist trying to publish such a manuscript would do so only at great risk. Having applied to the authorities for a permit to publish his travelogue, a member of the 1862 Mission to Europe soon withdrew his request in fear of retaliation.[1] Hirose's travelogue was an exception and seems to have made no visible impact.[2]

The absence of contemporary printing does not mean, however, that these manuscripts were not read. Most works existed in several copies: as many as thirty or more remain, for example, of Tamamushi's journal.[3] His specific instructions, "Not to be read by anyone," on the cover of book 8 (of the copy transcribed by him) seem to imply that other sections of that copy plus all other copies (all of which omit the subversive book 8) were indeed for circulation. Furthermore, most of the surviving copies in the authors' own hands had clearly been rewritten and revised after the journey was over. In fact, only a very few works were left in the initial diary form showing day-by-day entries during the voyage.[4] It certainly appears then that the writers were interested in showing their records to others and not merely in copying them as a mnemonic exercise. There are instances where the author either lectured or dictated, from memory and notes, to an interested audience (as in the case of Kato Somo and Kimura Tetsuta).[5] In short, the manuscripts were read quietly but eagerly despite the general hostility toward everything Western.

Among the documents, a few were simply intended to serve as technical logs and account books: Midshipman Akamatsu Daisaburo's *Amerika yuki kokai nikki* (Diary of the Voyage to America) and Kosugi Masanoshin's *Akoku joge sonohokanikki* (Diary of North and South America . . .) diligently record navigational operations aboard the *Kanrin Maru* to the exclusion of everything else; likewise, Chief Treasurer Morita Kiyoyuki's several volumes register expenditures and official memoranda. There is also a huge unpublished official record of the Embassy in six volumes.[6] Still others, like Katsu's and Fukuzawa's, look back from a safe distance of several decades after the fact to view the experience as a nostalgic episode of their youth. Finally, the work left by the chief ambassador, Shimmi Buzen-no-Kami Masaoki, is a series of *waka* (short poems) in the convention of *uta nikki* (poetic diary) intended more as a literary effort than a travel record.

It should be emphatically stated here, however, that the great majority are essentially personal travelogues, the writers' reports of their encounters with a strange people aimed at an audience who knew little about either the people or the country.

Most of the works are now available in print, the few that are still in manuscript form being of small interest. The most important modern collections are the first two volumes of the *Kengai shisetsu nikki sanshu* (KSNS) (Selection of Embassy diaries) and the seven-volume set *Man'en gannen ken-Bei shisetsu shiryo shusei* (SS) (Collection of the Historical Materials of the 1860 Embassy to the United States). Some, like Muragaki's *Ken-Bei-shi nikki* (Diary of the Ambassadors to the United States) and Yanagawa

Masakiyo's *Kokai nikki* (Diary of the Voyage), have been translated into English, but these renderings are quite unreliable, being inaccurate and unidiomatic throughout, as well as deceptive. (Apparently the translators—who all seem to have been motivated by some program or other for promoting "friendship" between the United States and Japan—simply laundered out any comments they felt might prove insulting to Americans, thus making the travelers appear markedly banal and unsophisticated.) Aside from the question of editions, a number of identical phrases and descriptions recur among the works. I have already remarked on several cases, and there is no doubt that some writers, eager to leave a memorial, but having little original to say for themselves, in certain situations simply lifted whole passages from their colleagues. One unidentified writer complains that more than a few diaries were copied from various records, especially from the single most important source, Tamamushi's *Ko-Bei nichiroku* (Chronicle of the Voyage to America), which indeed shares a considerable number of phrases and descriptions with many of the journals.[7] However, this does not discount the possibility that Tamamushi and others may have had common sources of information rather than intending to plagiarize.[8]

Finally, these documents written by such a diverse assembly of men from all stations of life—from high Tokugawa bureaucrats like Shimmi and Muragaki and brilliant minds trained in Dutch learning like Fukuzawa and Katsu to members of "outside" domains like Tamamushi, even down to nonsamurai menials like Kahachi—project a good representation of the Tokugawa mind as it encountered the mysterious West, just at the dawn of modern Japan. Being so convinced, I would like to examine the form and style of the travelogues, with the hope of more closely observing the contours of that mind.

One of the most striking features of the 1860 Embassy travelogues is the uniformity among them in both substance and form, that is, in what they wrote and how they wrote. Of course, some degree of stylistic difference and divergence of opinion does exist as we have already seen. And yet, in perceptual and formal aspects—the way they observed and commented, the style of their entries, the degree of abstraction or specificity, the personal involvement or disengagement from their own experience, even regarding the realm of opinion and attitude, and the subject matter they typically chose to write about—their uniformity is as palpable as is the diversity prevailing among, say, the travelogues left by contemporary Western visitors to Japan, such as Ivan Goncharov and Wassly Michaelovitsch Golownin, Townsend Harris and Henry Heusken, Rutherford Alcock, Sherard Osborn, and Laurence Oliphant.

I would first like to discuss the documents as *travelogues*, mainly focusing on the spatial sense revealed in the accounts. Obviously, both the ship's passage and the Embassy's tour through the states are essential to the narrative progression of the travelogues, which progress as the travelers voyage forth. And yet travelogues often seem characterized by a tension between the descriptive impulse to follow closely the route itself and the imaginative energy to reorganize the mere facts of the voyage into a more personal meaning. In the course of narration a tourist's actual itinerary, the basis of his travelogue, is continually mediated by such energy. Thus, the travelogue as a form always vacillates between a close account of the trip and an imaginative interpretation of it, which in the extreme case amounts to fiction. When this happens, the actual itinerary recedes to function as mere metaphor; on the other hand, when a travelogue tries to eliminate this fiction altogether, it becomes a record serving some purpose other than simply telling a story. Most travelogues, in other words, fall somewhere between *Gulliver's Travels*, *Pilgrim's Progress*, and the picaresque novel at one extreme and a mechanical naval log or routine flight record at the other.

By the normative travelogue I do not mean only literary travelogues such as Goethe's *Travel to Italy*, Dickens's *American Notes*, James's *The American Scenes*, and Lawrence's *Twilight in Italy*, but also the nonliterary travelogues of C. Pemberton Hodgson, J. R. Black, Lieutenant James D. Johnston, and George Henry Preble, as well as those of the now familiar Heusken and Harris, and Goncharov and Oliphant. I likewise refer to the long tradition of literary travelogue-diaries (*tabi-nikki* and *kiko bun*) descending from the Heian period to the Tokugawa, including *Tosa nikki* (935), *Kaidoki* (1223), *Tokan kiko* (1242), *Izayoi nikki* (1282), and *Towazugatari* (1306), down to Basho's masterpieces like *Oku no hosomichi* (1702) and *Oi no kobumi* (1709). Even in the more purely documentary travelogues—such as Ennin's ninth-century chronicle of his travels in T'ang China—the organizing impulse is often discernible to a degree scarcely evident in most of the 1860 accounts, which sometimes perilously approach the form of the log.[9]

Where does this inclination toward mechanical bookkeeping come from?

Why is there so little evidence in most of these records of any will to interpret, or impose any imaginative structure on raw experience? Let us take one of the most common types of entry in the 1860 documents. While at sea, almost every voyager seems fascinated with the ship's changing location, which is recorded daily in a great majority of the travelogues. In many journals, a single notation marking the ship's latitude and longitude—plus at times a brief mention of weather or temperature—constitutes the entire record for a given day. To take just one example:

> The 14th day, the fifth month; clear, rain in the afternoon; thermometer 70°. Day's run (from two yesterday to noon today) 181 *ri*.
> Latitude N. 40°0′ Longitude W. 70°0′[10]

One is curious also why the ship's position was so important to them. Were nautical details always so interesting, especially to the ambassadorial members on the *Powhatan*? Did they really feel it essential that their readers know their geographical coordinates on a given day? Was there nothing more provocative to write about aboard the *Powhatan* and the *Kanrin Maru*, where they were after all living at close quarters with the barbarians for the first time? Answers to such questions must necessarily be fairly detailed.

For the Japanese, landlocked for generations in their island country, the ocean vastness without landmarks and bounded only by the horizon on all sides was a totally new environment. Back in Japan, by contrast, the space they inhabited was always distinctly defined in terms of fiefs and domains. The ordinary samurai dwelt either in his lord's castle-town (*joka-machi*) or in Edo, where the Shogunate law of hostages (*sankin kotai*) required that the lord reside every other half year. The direct Tokugawa vassal (*hatamoto*), too, lived either in Edo, in a provincial Tokugawa territory (*tenryo*), or in his own domain assigned by the Shogunate. The common people—farmers, artisans, and merchants—also ventured out of their native towns and villages occasionally for purposes of pilgrimage, peddling, or recreation. When they did, however, they—everyone—had to secure a passport, for along the major highways there were checkpoints (*sekisho*) controlled either by the central Tokugawa regime or the local fief government to prohibit unauthorized movement. Thus, despite increasing traffic along the highways during this period, any individual's whereabouts was still a jealously watched aspect of feudal life.[11] People were always expected to account for being out anywhere away from home. A geographic curfew of this sort nonetheless produced compensating benefits, enabling samurai and lords alike to experience a deeper relationship to the immediate environment. Each person had his own niche in the local space. It appears that the neo-Confucian insistence on identifying lord-vassal loyalty (*chu*) with filial piety (*ko*) played a significant role here, for we see that the fief, or political space, was identified with the familial space. In addition, everywhere in this small island country, local historical and poetic associations (*utama-kura*, poetic pillow) abounded, and there were numerous scenic places and historical sites (*meisho*) familiar to all since earliest childhood.

As a result, the space persons occupied at home was a world bound by the nexus of values and myths, where people and the immediate locale had real meaning and relationship within a religious and psychological scheme. For most Japanese at the time, their country (*kuni*) meant their fief (*han*) and not Japan as a whole; to the extent that Japan as a nation amounted to anything at all—as it must have to these first international travelers—it did so in an extension of the tribal and familial concept (as did their fief); in other words, it was only a larger unit presided over by the Tokugawa Shogunate (or, increasingly in the last Tokugawa years, by the emperor above him).[12] Whether referring to the fief in particular or the "divine country" (*shinshu*, or *shinkoku*) as a whole, this space was a mythical territory such as Mircea Eliade has called the "sacred space."[13]

The sea, however, was "outside space," annihilating all such meaning and myth as it does all local boundaries. As much as half a century later, even a serious student and teacher of English, Natsume Soseki, sailing to England for a two-year stay, felt the same power of the sea as it threatened to wash over all the familiar distinctions and meanings. He wrote a long essay in his somewhat eccentric but charming English about the "nothing-ness" of the ocean, and of life itself, as though using the foreign language would somehow talismanically restore his confidence:

The sea is lazily calm and I am dull to the core, lying in my long chair on deck. The leaden sky overhead seems as devoid of life as the dark expanse of waters around, blending their dullness together beyond the distant horizon as if in sympathetic stolidity. While I gaze at them, I gradually lose myself in the lifeless tranquility which surrounds me and seem to grow out of myself on the wings of contemplation to be conveyed to a realm of *vision* which is neither aethereal nor earthly, with no houses, trees, birds, and human beings. Neither heaven nor hell, nor that intermediate stage of human existence which is called by the name of *this* world, but of vacancy, of nothingness where infinity and eternity seem to swallow one in the oneness of existence, and defies in its vastness any attempt of description.[14]

The samurai of 1860 knew much less of course about such ways of responding to this experience of "outside space," and they must have found the American navigators' provision of a daily announcement of the ship's coordinates comforting. By its clarity, regularity, and authority, they were in a way redeemed each day from floating nameless, unlocated, and without discernible destination in a sea of what Eliade calls "profane space."[15]

It is true that one could find the log-like form in a few documentary diary-travelogues of Tokugawa Japan. *Hokuyuki* (1807), written by two Mito samurai about their intelligence tour in Hokkaido, is a good example.[16] And yet, in Kaibara Ekken's *Kisoji no ki* (1685), Shiba Kokan's *Saiyu nikki* (1815), Motoori Norinaga's *Sugegasa nikki* (1772), Tachibana Nankei's *Toyuki, Seiyuki* (1795–1805), or Kiyokawa Hachiro's *Saiyuso* (1855), the entries are—though often impersonal and unspeculative—structured, detailed, and informed with the sense of ease and intimacy with the spaces visited. In the 1860 records, on the other hand, the writers do not seem fully able to comprehend what they see and experience, the log-like entry of the ship's position being one instance of this general attitude toward profane space. Thus, they tend to describe geographic movement only, and that often in unadorned numerical terms: today we left Washington and came to Baltimore; today we left Baltimore and traveled ninety-eight miles to Philadelphia, stayed at a hotel called the Continental with seven stories occupying about a hundred *ken* square of land, having crossed on the way three rivers, two of which had iron bridges with railroad tracks on them.

Only in a few exceptional cases is there an apparent desire to encompass and schematize this alien space rather than just paratactically run on in it. Tateishi Tokujuro, Sano Kanae, and Tamamushi divide their travelogues into separate units, each devoted to a city, in which they discuss in turn "geography," "people and culture" (*fuzoku*), "weather," "agriculture," "animals," "currency," and "commodity prices." Although their way of looking at each city as a separate territory derives partly from their long-accustomed view of fiefs as autonomous demarcated spaces, their format also reflects a borrowing from geography textbooks read before their departure (or after their return).[17] In fact, Sano and Tateishi explicitly state that their general surveys of cities are based on geography books (*chirishi, chirisho, chiri jiten*, and so on). While these few diaries do show an effort on the part of the writers to structure and interpret unfamiliar environments so as to make some sense of them, this is a rare phenomenon, most of the diarists almost hypnotically yielding to the rolling expanse which bears them forward.

It is similar with landscape description. From the Heian period to the Tokugawa, travelogues are not distinguished by elaborate verbal descriptiveness. For instance, the creative energy of even the major literary travelogues seems to find expression mainly in the composition of poems as the foci of the works, and any meditative or observational impulses that surface are held in check by various restrictive conventions. In short, one might say that the traveler's imagination is always redirected away from the actual landscape by poetic memory and association (*utamakura*). In works like *Sarashina nikki*, *Towazugatari*, and *Oku no hosomichi*, however, there are occasional passages which sensitively portray nature. Hills and trees, birds and flowers, ripples on the surface of a lake, the shadows of clouds moving across a meadow, the flash of sunlight in the distance—such particularized scenes, though carefully ensconced in an elaborate convention, take the reader quite by surprise with their sensuous immediacy. In the Embassy records as a whole, there is much evidence of the writers' wonder at the beauty of the places they visit, but they seem unconcerned with verbalizing their observations in detail. Take, for example, the two most descriptive accounts of San Francisco Bay, a splendor which all the members of the Embassy seem to have admired, and compare them with Heusken's exhilaration when sighting Mount Fuji. Here is Muragaki on San Francisco Bay:

> As the smoke from the guns drifted away, there emerged from behind it, a lively city, with houses stretching along the foot of the hills, and the dock crowded with men and women. The city was far superior to the Sandwich Islands, and the houses, built four or five stories high, looked beautiful.

After a short while, the *Powhatan* weighed anchor, and slowly steamed into the Bay, which, from four to five miles across at the entrance, became narrower, surrounded by smoothly outlined hills on both sides. There were no woods in sight, but herds of cattle or sheep grazing on the hillside, looking as small as so many black ants. The presence of curiously shaped rocks in the Bay, some of reddish hues and others black, made the scenery quite beautiful.[18]

And Morita, the chief finance officer:

I was told this place was San Francisco. In the morning we sailed over the rough waters between two protruding hills. There was a battery with two cannons. There were many brick buildings with four or five stories. Their chimneys were as high as the watch-towers in Edo, towering over the house roofs. On both sides of the ship, all the hills bore the colors of spring, and the blue grass and green trees were as in a painting. Sheep and cattle and horses were idling on the hillsides. The hills jutting out into the waters were faintly visible, and the reflections of the distant sailboats were as quiet as though sitting on the surface of the water. There were mountains in the rain, there were mountains in the sun, and the beauty of the scene was amazing to see.[19]

And here is Heusken, Harris's interpreter, on Mount Fuji:

As we near the valley and emerge from the clouds that hover over the summit of Amagi, the countryside begins to unfold; valleys of ravishing beauty upon which the sun casts a gentle glow appear before our eyes. Rounding a mountain, I sight through the foliage of a few pine trees a white peak that gleams in the sun. In an instant I realize that I am looking at Fujiyama. Never in my life will I forget the sight of that mountain as I saw it today for the first time, and I don't think anything in the world will ever equal its beauty. There are mountains three times higher than Fuji; the glaciers of Switzerland are, no doubt, impressive and magnificent; the summit of the Himalayas, the sublime Dawala-quiri, raises its venerable brow to immeasurable heights, but one cannot see it until one has climbed other mountains that hide it from sight in the plains; one sees but ice and glaciers; snows surround you wherever you may turn your eyes. But here, in the midst of a smiling countryside covered with abundant crops—with pine groves and giant camphor trees that seem to vie in longevity with the very soil where they were born, making shade with their majestic foliage for some *miya* or chapel, dedicated to the ancient Gods of the Empire, and as a backdrop for this theatre of plenty and serenity—the pure outline of the unique Fujiyama rises like two symmetrical lines toward the sky, whose pale blue seemed dark, compared to the immaculate snows of the mountain that reflected, like another Kohinoor, the rays of the setting sun.

In spite of myself I pulled the reins of my horse and, carried away by an outburst of enthusiasm, I took off my hat and cried: "Great, glorious Fujiyama!" Glory forever to the mountain of mountains of the Pacific Sea, which alone raises its venerable brow covered with eternal snow amidst the verdant countryside of Nippon! Jealous of its beauty, it will not suffer a rival which might lessen its splendor. Its crown of snow stands out alone above the highest mountains of Nippon, and Amagi, which we have just passed after a most difficult day, seems only a small hill, hardly worth mentioning.

Ah! Why don't I have about twenty of the friends of my younger days around me! The surrounding hills would soon repeat the echo of a thrice-repeated *hip, hip, hip, hurrah* in honor of the sublime Fujiyama.[20]

Heusken's description is not only detailed and comparative, but he insists that he himself be a dramatic character in the scene. He is placed stage center in the space he is viewing: Mount Fuji and the boyishly exuberant Heusken stand face to face, as it were. On the other hand, Muragaki and Morita hover like pale shadows in the wings; their San Francisco Bay sketches are detached and the observers themselves distant—if not absent altogether. The numerous conventional terms (mainly *kambun* epithets and phrases) that abound in the imagery remind one of some modest scrolls. Comparative references are, naturally, limited: as against Heusken's Alps, Himalayas, and Dhaulagiri, Morita offers the homely "Edo watchtowers." Heusken is relaxed, fully absorbed in discovering the grandeur of Fuji, while Muragaki and Morita are aloof to an unfamiliar loveliness. And as if to avoid the challenge of the unknown, they seek protection in cliches and numbers and measurements ("four or five stories," "four to five miles," "two cannons"). The Japanese travelers clearly feel out of place, and dare not allow themselves to be at ease with nature in America.

Another way of looking at this perceptual and formal passivity is to think of it in temporal terms. Read as diaries, the 1860 Embassy records reveal certain significant features. In the sense that practically all of them have a day-to-day format, they are diaries. But again these particular diaries do not have narrative characteristics of the form as are generally understood. Following the pattern of my discussion of the travelogue form, I would like to place the 1860 documents in the contexts of both literary and nonliterary *diary* traditions of Japan and the West.

The diary by definition follows the days and months in the natural flow of time, and yet most diaries reveal a counterimpulse at work to transcend the temporal determination, very much as we saw was typical of the travelogue form. In real life, things happen all the time one after another; in a diary, the recordings are bound to be selective, and arranged in a sequence to yield projected meaning. One might readily think of Western literary diaries—like Samuel Pepys's *Diary* or Defoe's *The Journal of the Plague-Year*—to see how these "diurnal" records radically approach being works of art. Or, take Thoreau's *Walden*, a diary account of the writer's stay near Walden Pond for two years, two months, and two days. The diary is basically a redemptive form beginning with the winter of spiritual death and ending with the spring of resurrection. So organized, it turns into an interpretation, or fiction. As with *The Pilgrim's Progress* and *Gulliver's Travels* for the travelogue, so with *Wuthering Heights* and *The Sorrows of Young Werther* for the diary, where, despite the fact that these works have a carefully wrought temporal delineation, the fictive imagination breaks chronometric events into a new arrangement which is in itself a shape, or meaning.

Works in the Japanese literary tradition of the *nikki*, too, are almost always battlegrounds between the habit of staying in step and the impulse to mold the sequential experiences into some significance. Take the numerous "search for the way" (*gudo*) and "pilgrimage record" (*sankeiki*) type travelogue-diaries—*Kaidoki, Tokan kiko, Tsukushi-michi no ki*, and so on and on—where the actual chronology is universally adjusted to a conventional calendar: the seekers always leave home in the fall, for instance. Likewise in the great poet Basho's travelogue-diaries, the facts or surface events of his trips are continually pitted against the interior, poetic journey through an imaginary time-space strictly defined by the conventions.

As against these literary diaries, one must of course mention here the immense and unbroken tradition of the documentary diary born before the ninth century and still alive in our own time. First written in Chinese characters (*kambun*), these journals were basically court chronicles. Unlike the literary diaries written in the Japanese syllabary (*kana*) by women, these chronicles merely recorded the public events and court ceremonies on a daily basis often with no personal comments at all. Some of them, written by extraordinarily determined men, spanned several decades: Fujiwara Michinaga's *Mido Kampaku-ki*, for instance, was written over twenty years (998–1021), *Gyokuyo* by Kujo Kanezane over thirty years (1164–1200), and Sanjonishi Sanetaka's diary, *Sanetaka-ko-ki*, continued for a full sixty years (1474–1535).[21] In such massive diaries, control of the overall shape would obviously have been impossible. As their authors lived, grew old, and died, these works began, continued, and ended. The diaries were coauthored, as it were, by individual men and by time itself.

By the Tokugawa period, most documentary diaries were no longer written in Chinese characters, nor were they so uniform in style, tone, and subject matter. Although many of the old conventions still survived (brief, public, impersonal entries; compulsive attention to the weather; general lack of interest in overall form), there were signs of greater diversity. If Arai Hakuseki's entries (1693–1717) were brief (the famous Chushingura—the Forty-Seven Ronin—vendetta receives a mere three lines!), Umezu Masakage's (1612–1633) were comparatively long. While public, official diaries still flourished in this period, those by Yamashina Kototsune (1576–1601), Matsudaira Ietada (1577–1594), or Kawai Koume (1849–1885), to take random examples, were private and personal. Also, whereas many were *either* private *or* official, Matsuzaki Kodo's *Kodo nichireki* (1823–1844) contained a mixture of personal experiences, social events, lecture notes, and comments on books. And Motoori Norinaga left many diaries each quite different from the others: his 1763–1767 entries are no more than page after page of daily weather reports, while his *Zai-Kyo nikki* (1752–1757) shifts from a brief and Chinese-character style to an elaborate record written in the Japanese syllabary. In short, the early conventions were loosened enough by this time to allow wide divergence in format. And there is no reason to believe that the 1860 Embassy members had only one model in mind while composing their daily entries.

Unlike those extremely long diaries, however, the 1860 Embassy documents detail a single trip of relatively short duration. As such they could readily have been molded into narrative form, had the writers felt any desire to impose some interpretation on their experience. Yet one finds among the forty-odd records not one with a narrative framework. Almost without exception, the 1860 diaries fall under the complete sway of the day-to-day progress of time. Many begin with the first day of the trip and close with the last, between which all descriptions and comments are ascribed to definite dates in some cases without the omission of a single day. That is, the travelers do not organize experience into a structure that counteracts or supplements the flow of time. As they live through time, their accounts of their experiences, like the minutes of a committee meeting, follow a chronometric sequence, and this seems to provide adequate expression for them. What I wish to argue here is that these diaries assumed a daily log form, not because the writers felt more natural clinging to the old official diary convention but because they were for some reason inhibited from interpreting their unique experiences. As the trip begins, the diary begins; the travel ends, and so concludes the diary. The trip *is* in itself the whole meaning of the writing.

Now to compare the 1860 Embassy diaries with the documentary, non-literary accounts of voyages to Japan by contemporary Westerners: first of all, there are very few Western works left in the form of diaries—Townsend Harris's, George Henry Preble's, Edward Yorke McCauley's, Samuel Wells Williams's, and Dr. James Morrow's. Of these five, the last four, which record the Perry expedition, were forced to remain in the (unpublished) diary form by the commodore's ban on keeping any private record of the adventure. (Heusken's journal does not belong with these, since his unexpected death gave him no chance to consider its possible final form, nor does Hawks's *Narrative of the Expedition*, which is an official chronicle written by a third party.) All the rest—by J. W. Spalding, Edward De Fonblanque, Robert Fortune, Sherard Osborn, James D. Johnston, and Bayard Taylor, as well as Alcock, Ernest Satow, C. Pemberton Hodgson, Golownin, Oliphant, and Goncharov—are set in a narrative mode with a beginning, a middle, and an end, consequentiality, and structure. To point out this difference is not simply to refer to the relative socioliterary roles the diary form plays in the two cultures. The difference is quite important. Western travelers, unwilling to leave everyday events discrete and uninterpreted in the flow of time, were determined to impose some meaning by lifting them out of the strictly chronological order. Second, individual entries in diaries by Harris and others show a continual struggle against all-powerful time. They seldom let stand a mere account of activities without analysis; they reminisce, compare, speculate, generalize, and dramatize, to an extent nowhere evident in the 1860 diaries. We shall see more on this later, when an extended comparison is made between Harris's style and Muragaki's.

This impression that the writers simply allowed the force of time to carry them along is reinforced by the circumstance that written Japanese at the time had no paragraph structure, or even a distinct sentence form. A sentence typically runs on and on, until a new sentence imperceptibly materializes, growing out of the previous one. Descriptions and comments continue without a break until a new subject is introduced or a new date entered. The absence of punctuation and paragraphing alerts one to the fact that ideas are not propositional. That is, the will to organize perceptions into words, words into sentences, and sentences into arguments is weakened by the passive acceptance of the diurnal and nocturnal cycle which, in controlling so much about the shape and contents of the diaries, apparently satisfies the writer's need for form.

Even the calendar used on the voyage posed a minor dilemma. The Japanese of those years used a lunar calendar which was not abandoned until 1873. Thus, while aboard American ships and in the United States, whenever they discussed their plans or itinerary with the Americans, their chronometric system had to be adjusted to an alien time scheme. For example, one of the ambassadorial letters written in English in Washington, D.C., to the secretary of state is dated "the 25th day of the second-thirth [sic; intercalary third] month of seventh year of Ansei,"[22] which translated means May 14, 1860. The hours of the day, too, were numbered off differently. The result was that a sort of capsule of time, a protective bubble, was formed around the Japanese travelers, as though they were carrying a bit of Japan along, a sacred time-space precluding their being plunked directly into the middle of the American reality.

In this respect, Western travelers in Japan fared quite differently. While they could not readily participate in the time of their strange environment either, they had the white man's confidence that their chronometric system was nearly universal in the world outside this eccentric island. In their view, Japanese time was a quaint and inconvenient residue from the past, whereas theirs flowed throughout the world.

If the Japanese ambassadors were both spatially and temporally alienated —unable to feel at ease in American places or to refer freely forward and backward during their tour—it may be interesting to surmise their attitude toward their own experience. How did they see and relate to their actions and observations? This question brings us to the second, and perhaps most important, feature of the diary as a form: the first-person narrator whose daily experience presumably provides the basis for the narration. The diary as understood in the modern West is by definition a record of one's personal experience/observation, intended in some cases to remain closed to all but the author himself, but in others to be made public while retaining the appearance of privacy. Either way, the form is fundamentally first-person. What is remarkable about the 1860 Embassy records—and the ancient and extensive Japanese diary tradition as a whole—is the general absence of the first-person narrative feature.

Granted, there are a few among them that employ the first-person narrative voice as well as various first-person pronouns. Let me, however, concern myself at present with the overwhelming majority that are narrated throughout with hardly any first-person pronouns, leaving those exceptional works for later discussion.

The lack of first-person pronouns in a Japanese narrative does not by itself indicate a third-person narrative, since the Japanese sentence regularly omits the pronouns, especially in the nominative case, unless clarification is particularly needed. In addition, the verb conjugation has no reference to the person of the subject and thus no bearing on the determination of the narrative person. To be sure, the system of honorifics, defining as it does the relative status positions of narrator, reference, and listener, helps clarify the identity of the omitted subject. And there are other grammatical features that suggest the narrative voice. Still, many sentences remain quite unclear as regards the identity of the narrator and the omitted subject. The Japanese equivalent of "took a walk around nine o'clock" can, theoretically, be in either the first, second, or third person, depending on the narrative context.[23]

There is also the case of "ambiguous" pronouns that might be construed as either first- or third-person. Take an example from *Ikoku no koto no ha*, written by Kahachi, the humble stokers' foreman on the *Kanrin Maru*. Throughout, the dominant pronominal term he uses is *ichido*, "altogether," which can mean all of us, all of you, or all of them. While the context clearly rejects the second person, it is sometimes impossible to determine whether Kahachi numbers himself as one in the "altogether" (thus marking the narration as first-person) or not (thus marking it as third-person). In fact, the overwhelming impression is that Kahachi, like many others, did not much care whether the story he told included himself or not. It is only on the basis of the content and context of the narrative along with various grammatical features that one can ascribe the third person to most of the 1860 Embassy accounts, and that only in a very general sense. The diaries by Murayama, Masuzu, Namura, Morita, Nonomura, Sano, Fukushirna, Kosugi, Yoshioka, Hirose, Kato, Kimura, and Ono, and *Amerika tokai nikki* (Diary of the Voyage to America), by an unidentified writer, all belong in this category, the first-person pronominal terms (such as singular *yo*, *ware*, *sessha*, *boku*; and plural *warera*, *bokura*) occurring but rarely in these documents.

Confronting something so totally new as these men were, why was it, then, that they didn't talk about it in the terms of *personal* experience? Why were they only interested in describing people, events, and things, like faucets and call bells, horse carriages and fire engines external to themselves? What is the meaning of such thorough impersonality? First, we can say that as, by and large, second- and lower-echelon officers, they were in no position to make any important choices or decisions—particularly during the voyage. This meant that they were necessarily quite passive as regards action and movement. While they did not figure much in the picture, what was seen and heard did, and had to be recorded. Second, and concomitant with the first point, their sense of self was different from the Western, which tends to particularize and individualize any experience. Kahachi's report is a good example of this, but others, too, demonstrate indifference to their own feeling and response, even to their personal condition.

Take, for instance, a section of Murayama Hakugen's *Hoshi nichiroku*

(The Embassy Chronicle). His entries from February 15 through 18 (according to the envoys' lunar calendar, the twenty-fourth through the twenty-seventh day of the first month) read as follows:

> 24th. Fine, cloudy, windy. [My] countrymen were without exception seasick; some vomited; fortunately, I did not go so far as to throw up; but felt nauseated and lay in bed eating nothing all day.
> 25th. Fine, cloudy.
> 26th. Fine.
> 27th. Drizzled. Stormy; great waves; [my] countrymen all took to bed and could not walk around; the ship rocking greatly; could not get to sleep throughout the night; [an] American voyaging for twenty years says [he has] never encountered a storm like this; [my] countrymen quite exhausted.[24]

He does talk about his own seasickness once, referring to himself as *yo*; but any interest in talking about his own condition is continually deflected so as to describe it in terms of the group (*hojin*, countrymen) of whom he is only one member. The analysis here might have to be slightly qualified by the fact that Murayama was a physician attached to the Embassy and his interest in others might thus be interpreted as appropriately professional. But such is not the case, this being but one of many examples and chosen simply for its brevity.

Nonomura Tadazane's entry for March 29 (in the lunar system the eighth day of the third month) likewise deemphasizes his presence in the scene:

> The 8th day, third month. Between three (half past eight [Japanese time]) and four (seven [Japanese time]) this dawn the heaven in the direction of the north shone like a flame; [my] countryman [countrymen?] saw this, and says [said?] land must be near, [it] must be a brush-fire; and [he? I? they? we?] asked an American; [the American answered that he had] seen this before, but [he] didn't know the reason; [a] Dutch book explains it merely as the northern light; southeastern wind; the ship sailed in the oxtiger [northeastern] direction; thermometer 60 degrees; before noon 270 *ri*.
> Latitude N. 36°57'25"
> Longitude W. 135°26'14"[25]

To Murayama, his own experience is not of vital interest; and as for Nonomura, whether he personally saw the "northern light" (aurora borealis) is not at all clear and is insignificant as well. In both entries, one has the impression that things happen to them all, and these shared experiences *are* what interest them individually.

In fact, this sighting of the "northern light" is also reported in the works of Kato, Sano, Kimura Tetsuta, Hirose, and Tamamushi.[26] But with the exception of Tamamushi's *Ko-Bei nichiroku*, no book specifies the narrator as having the experience by the unmistakable "I saw" or "we saw." Only by the context—detailed description, illustration, declarative tone—can the reader surmise that the writers were most probably among those witnessing the phenomenon, but it is still perfectly possible to argue on the other hand that they may indeed not have seen it personally.

Related to this ambiguity of perspective is the curious fact that it is impossible to establish authorship of several of the 1860 journals. True, there is nothing surprising about people leaving their diaries anonymous: some writers felt no reason to sign manuscripts while they were being privately circulated. At the same time, what is odd is that some, like *Kanrin Maru ko-Bei nisshi* (Chronicle of the Voyage of the *Kanrin Maru* to America) or *Amerika tokai nikki* (Diary of the Voyage to America), can pretty well be attributed to one man or one of a few (on the basis of external evidence and the content and style of the remarks themselves), and yet these diary authors describe (what is probably their own) actions without once relating the writer to the self written about. Here again, the official documents— say, the minutes of a committee meeting—could be said to have the same impersonal style. But the 1860 Embassy diaries are, as I have established earlier, *not* official records. Further, they are hardly devoid of signs of the authors' involvement. Indeed, anonymous diarists' personal responses— contempt, dissatisfaction, admiration—are just as freely expressed (or unexpressed) as in other, author-identified diaries of the group. It appears that the interest in the *who*, who viewed, did, and felt, is characteristically ignored for the *what*, what was viewed, done, and sensed, as though personality were of little importance to either reader or writer.

Now for the few exceptional travelogue-diaries that do make fairly regular use of I-pronouns. The most conspicuous is Vice Ambassador Muragaki's work. Surely his being the second in command of the group must have required the "I." Although quite passive as a diplomat, still he could not evade the authority vested in his office. His inferiors looked to him for leadership; the chief ambassador asked his counsel; and the Americans talked to him and expected discussion, planning, decisions. Thus, when making diary entries, he could not easily avoid the first-person singular pronoun (*onore*, self, is the word he chose probably for its slightly tough, mock-boorish connotation, rather than *yo*, the neutral, dignified pronoun most commonly used in the 1860 records). Psychologically, too, Muragaki was, as we have seen, rather a self-important man. He always considered himself a cut above his subordinates, and this attitude is quite salient in his diary. (He calls them *gesu*, menials, rascals.) Muragaki seems then to view America from a separate individual perspective, and not from a position of group identities. At the same time, his encounter was finally not at all personal. There is little engagement of his personality, sense and emotion, thought and feeling, as we will examine in greater length later on. If this sounds somewhat paradoxical, one should recall that his isolation was itself part of the hierarchic structure, and his consciousness thus largely socially defined.

Kimura Settsu-no-Kami Yoshitake, commodore of the *Kanrin Maru*, was very much in the same position. As leader of the escort group he had to assume authority and responsibility, and consequently his *Hoshi Meriken kiko* (The Ambassadorial Travel to America) inevitably contains many first-person sentences. Kimura, however, was a naval administrator trained by Dutch officers, and his officers in turn were mostly cadets educated at the Nagasaki Naval School. Further, he was for some time associated with his American counterparts at the Mare Island Naval Shipyard. Finding himself in this way among a congenial professional group, he was more relaxed with Americans than diplomats like Muragaki, and, as we have seen, there seems to have been a genuine exchange of visiting and friendship between the Americans and Kimura's crew. Reflecting this, his writing, too, is far less guarded and dislocated than Muragaki's. Just as Midshipman Ishikawa's navigational log is matter-of-fact and unselfconscious, so is Commodore Kimura's. His is an objective and unobtrusive "I," a merely functional and descriptive "I," inserted there because his position required a separation of the "I" from the others. While discrete, this "I" experiences no hierarchic alienation from his inferiors or from the Americans as is evident in Muragaki's writing. Nor does he seem concerned with his own particular experience. Somehow one cannot help seeing here an early example of that important by-product of technology; achievement, by circumventing and supplanting ordinary language and personality, of a smooth and efficient intercultural "communication" by professional and technical experts, not rivaled by diplomatic and cultural representatives.

The record of the head of the Embassy, Shimmi Buzen-no-Kami Masaoki, similarly employs the first-person pronouns. It is unique in consisting of a series of poems (waka) in the convention of the poetic diary (uta nikki). It begins with waka commemorating the departure and ends with those celebrating the return. Its literary value is not impressive. Highly imitative, the poems are no more than the expression of social refinement, what must have passed among the Tokugawa samurai for a measure of taste and sophistication. In Hawaii, for instance, he exchanged a series of playful poems with an officer in his retinue, expressing a mock-attachment to an American woman he chanced to see. One of them, a self-admitted imitation of Ki no Tsurayuki's famous waka, reads like this:

To pick a flower
From the shadow on the water.
Gaze and gaze in vain.
Mizu no moni, utsuru hana o oru gotoku,
Itazura ni nomi, miru zo haka naki.[27]

He also wrote several verses toying with puns on the names of the queen of Hawaii and President Buchanan's niece. If he shows any talent, it is for social manners, not poetry. Transcribed after his return, the poetic diary is nonetheless striking inasmuch as it reveals the ambassador as totally poised, not at all ruffled by the exposure to the strange and the unaccustomed.

Tamamushi, who habitually employs an "I" pronoun (yo in this case) in his *Ko-Bei nichiroku*, is different. Ambassador Shimmi's manservant during the voyage, Tamamushi was born to a low-ranking samurai family in the Sendai domain in the north. During his early years, he was a brilliant student at the clan's official school. After running away to Edo, he worked for a time as a laborer for Hayashi Daigaku-no-Kami Fukusai (or Tosho), the hereditary lord rector of the official Tokugawa college, the Shoheiko Institute (comparable to, say, Oxford in its early days). Once recognized for his gifts, Tamamushi was quickly promoted to head tutor (*jukucho*) at the school. It happened that Hayashi was the chief negotiator for the Commodore Perry talks in 1854, and Tamamushi's joining the Embassy was no doubt traceable to his master's influence. In fact, on their departure from Japan, it was no other than Iwase Tadanari, one of the initial planners of the Embassy back in 1858, who wrote Tamamushi a farewell poem in classical Chinese.[28] Now, while Tamamushi's scholarship was truly distinguished, there was nothing in his background to suggest any substantial exposure to "Dutch learning." The curriculum of the Shoheiko school was solidly Neo-Confucian and quite orthodox, and Hayashi was, if anything, known for his contempt for the newfangled Western learning.[29] Tamamushi had toured in the North, and discussed the nature of the Russian threat in a nine-volume geographical study (which may have given him the opportunity to ponder the international situation of the time), and, as we have already noted, he had read *Kaikoku zushi* and other books on the West. But still, at the time of his departure from Japan, he was as dead set against the barbarians as anybody else in the Embassy.[30] Once, while on board the *Powhatan*, Tamamushi heard the crude men of the West playing musical instruments, and was profoundly irritated. And being constantly subjected, in such claustrophobic quarters, to the harsh, unfamiliar American gabble only further grated upon the aide's ragged nerves. Therefore, when visiting with a Chinese emigré in Honolulu, he declared himself a "dedicated student of the Way of the Sages [*seikyo*, or *seido*, Confucianism], unlike many others on the Mission trained in Western learning."[31]

And yet Tamamushi was always fair, giving recognition where due. On the stormy crossing, it was not only his Japanese colleagues who offered him assistance and encouragement; several American sailors made clear, across the language barrier, that they were concerned with their passengers' welfare and comfort. He also appreciated the American officers' genuine camaraderie with their men, in marked contrast to their rank-conscious Japanese counterparts. Little by little, Tamamushi's evaluation of the Americans began to change. And as we saw earlier, his good feelings toward America gradually became more authentic than anyone else's on the Mission. As he mulled over the questions raised by America and its people, he had to disengage himself from the others, and use the first-person singular.

Unlike Vice-Ambassador Muragaki's "I" necessitated by external authority, Tamamushi's developed as he assumed critical authority and intellectual responsibility for himself. His exceptional insight and commentary demanded that the first-person singular pronoun not be left implied, but made fully explicit. Thus, the subject of his sentences must be isolated from the generalized "we-they" by the singular, unambiguous, and explicit "I."

The Muragaki-Tamamushi contrast is intriguing. Both had been contemptuous toward the United States at first. However, Muragaki's attitudes remained essentially unaltered. If he did come to concede to the West's superiority in weapons development and health care, his evaluation of America as an inferior and barbarous country never wavered. The voyage, then, was little more than a necessary aspect of his career in the Tokugawa regime, and the reward on his return—audiences with the shogun, a promotion, and gifts such as an elaborately wrought hilt, fifty pieces of gold, four seasonal dresses, and 1,500 bushels of rice a year (300 *koku*)—was the acme of achievement he had all along striven for.[32] The rhetoric of the summary, toward his diary's end, reveals Muragaki as close-minded as ever, as though he had never taken any time off from his bureaucratic routine.

Tamamushi, on the other hand, underwent a serious reexamination of his beliefs. Intellectually caught short, he was nonetheless honest and alert to all he experienced, not allowing the inertia of prior convictions to interfere with personal observation. If there was any early sign of modern awareness in the 1860 Embassy records, it was surely most visible in Tamamushi's, whose first-person singular pronoun is a sign of the exceptional mind that harbored no fear of keeping one's distance from the others. It is noteworthy that this critically uncompromising book by Tamamushi was the one more modeled after and copied from than that of any other writer in the group, and it has survived in far more copies today than anyone else's.

In the first chapter of my book on the Embassy, *As We Saw Them*, I mentioned that the kind of information gathered by the Japanese travelers in 1860 was disconcertingly mechanical and uncoordinated, and pointed out two external factors contributing to such poor performance: linguistic incompetence and the severe restriction on personal movement. Here I would like to discuss what information meant in the context of Japanese intellectual life, and relate it back to the perceptual and formal features of the travelogues, especially to the absence of self-consciousness.

Many Western visitors to Japan in the 1850s recorded the puzzling and frustrating experience of not getting the simplest questions answered by officials. That master ironist Goncharov put it this way:

> "What is the population of Nagasaki?" I once asked Baba Gorozaemon—through an interpreter, of course. He repeated the question in Japanese and looked at a second colleague, who looked at a third, who in turn looked at a junior *baniosi*; the junior *baniosi* looked at an interpreter, and so the question and the look came back to Baba again, though without an answer.
>
> "Sometimes there are fewer," said Sadagora at last, "and sometimes there are more."
>
> "Are all your houses one-storeyed, or do they sometimes have two storeys?" asked Pos'et.
>
> "They sometimes have two storeys," said Kichibe and looked at L'oda.
>
> "And sometimes three," said L'oda, looking at Sadagora.
>
> "There are sometimes even five," said Sadagora.
>
> We began to laugh.
>
> "Do you often have earthquakes?" asked Pos'et.
>
> "Yes, we do," answered Sadagora, looking at L'oda.
>
> "How often? Once in ten years or once in twenty years?"
>
> "We have them once in ten years and once in twenty years," said L'oda, glancing at Kichibe and at Sadagora.
>
> "The mountains crack and the houses fall down," added Sadagora. And the whole conversation continued in this fashion.[33]

Townsend Harris's complaint is exasperated and humorless. Transmitting the U.S. Patent Office's request for information about Japanese cotton, he received next to no reply:

> It is a beautiful specimen of Japanese craft, cunning and falsehood. Their great object appears to be to permit as little to be learned about their country as possible; and, to that end, all fraud, deceit, falsehood and even violence, is justifiable in their eyes. It is true that this is the most difficult country in the world to get information; no statistics exist; no publications are made on any subject connected with industry.[34]

There is no question that the functionaries were under strictest command not to reveal any information whatever about Japan to foreigners. But where, we ask, did this policy of noncommunication and secretiveness originate? A paranoiac worry over national security? A totalitarian structure depending for survival on rigid adherence to an official line? Of course. But underlying these in turn was a philosophical attitude toward knowledge which requires some explanation.

First of all, while the Japanese declined to answer the foreigners, that is not to say they kept their mouths shut or their minds closed. They asked numerous questions about the West, as has been mentioned by nearly every foreigner who came in contact with them around that time. Similarly, Harris's frustration and Goncharov's lampooning notwithstanding, the Japanese were not unacquainted with the system of keeping records. On the contrary, the records stored by the Tokugawa and domainal governments, towns, villages, and families are so immense that they now serve historians as a treasure house perhaps unparalleled in the world. There were also continual experimentation and innovation in agricultural skills and financial management.[35] When the Tokugawa officials faced Westerners, however, they were unwilling to share the knowledge with strangers. Information had to remain within the tribe.

Second, when the Japanese faced Westerners, they wanted only a particular kind of information. Very early on, Arai Hakuseki (1657–1725), an eminent Neo-Confucian scholar and high-ranking advisor to the Shogun, divided the realm of knowledge between the "metaphysical" (keijijo) and the "physical" (keijika), conceding to the West superiority in practical and technological knowledge while making no qualification whatever for the moral excellence of the Neo-Confucian worldview.[36]Despite his considerable curiosity about the West, he peremptorily dismissed, for instance, Christianity as "irrational" and "immoral." Arai Hakuseki wanted to learn technology from the West, but not what had contributed to produce it, that is, the assumptions and values that had formed the whole culture. His attitude was more or less typical of the succeeding "Dutch scholars'" toward the Westerners: learn practical knowledge but, as for moral and other values, preserve what is already there—the indigenous Japanese, the earlier imports from China, and some Buddhism, however the blend may have been defined by individuals.

Quite obviously, the Tokugawa period was intellectually far from dormant over its two and a half centuries. From the very beginning, the Chu Hsi worldview was challenged by Kaibara Ekken (1630–1714), Arai Hakuseki himself, Ogyu Sorai (1666–1728), and many others. Miura Baien (1723–1789), one of the greatest skeptics of Tokugawa Japan, for instance, raises in epistemological treatises such as *Taga Bokkyo kun ni kotaeru sho*, 1777 (In Answer to Taga Bokkyo) fundamental questions concerning the ground for belief. What is interesting about these extremely difficult but fascinating books is, however, that Miura does not persist in calling *all* into doubt; instead, he questions the doubting self itself. Instead of finding the thinking self as the proof of being, Miura Baien eventually leaps back to the security of community, the Neo-Confucian political absolute as embodied in the Tokugawa structure.[37] And as for the ultimate acceptance of the Confucian categories of *chu* (loyalty), *ko* (filial piety), *jin* (charity), and *rei* (hierarchic distinction), even scholars in the Oyomei (Wang Yangming) school, critical of the Tokugawa administration, such as Nakae Toju (1608–1648) and Kumazawa Banzan (1619–1691), strayed very little indeed.[38]

Even later "Dutch scholars" like Hiraga Gennai (1728–1779), Sugita Gempaku (1733–1817), Honda Toshiaki (1743–1820), or Sakuma Shozan (1811–1864) were quite aloof to what we might call the "humanistic" aspects of Western culture, which they might well have come across in their perusal of Western books and documents. As a matter of fact, even those ideologue activists in the mid-nineteenth century who were practically agitators for insurrection against the Shogunate—like Yoshida Shoin and Hashimoto Sanai—never thought of putting their Western knowledge to use for reexamining these traditional hierarchic values. They desired Western knowledge only because they considered it helpful to fell the Tokugawa House (though not the hierarchic structure itself), and paradoxically to expel the Westerners themselves. Sakuma Shozan's slogan "Eastern morality, Western technology" (*Toyo no dotoku, seiyo no geijutsu*), was soon slightly abbreviated to "Japanese soul and Western technology" (*Wakon yosai*), and this new version was to survive well into Meiji Japan and even, in several aspects, into present days.[39]

Their determination to keep the "metaphysical" (read moral, or cultural) tradition undisturbed was shared not only by ideologues, but also by actual rebels and rioters of the time who attempted armed rebellions against the authorities. Oshio Heihachiro (1793–1837), who attacked the magistrate of Osaka on behalf of the starved populace, nonetheless took it for granted that the direct imperial rule would cure the Tokugawa ills, in his *Gekibun* (Summons to Insurrection, 1837).[40] Miura Meisuke, a leader in the great peasant riot of 1853, asked his relatives to remain loyal to their good lord in his prison letters.[41] In short, before the 1867 Restoration, there were extremely few men who were willing to seek, or even felt any need for, alternatives to the traditional principles of *chu*, *ko*, *jin*, and *rei*.[42] For scholars and activists alike, knowledge still responded to the calls of an insular society requiring ever-renewed affirmation of inherited values, not systematic information for adapting to a new philosophy, nor a universalist perspective on the world mediated by an individual's unabridged life experience.

The information the 1860 Embassy members collected was certainly not of a type to spark any comprehensive "humanistic" confrontation with the tradition. So much of it consisted of separate (and more often than not, trivial) facts and data, and so little was organized toward any "theoretical" understanding of the new experience. Admittedly, the Western counterparts were not much better. Alcock's construction of Japanese grammar, Oliphant's pastoral myth built after a two-weeks' sojourn, and George Smith's theological verdict on the Japanese are all preposterous misunderstandings of Japanese culture as we conceive it now. Yet, in these wrongheaded books there is an awareness that facts and nonfacts, data and nondata must be evaluated, selected, and coordinated before they are acceptable. With the exception of Tamamushi and Fukuzawa (whose memoir was written decades later), the Japanese diarists of 1860 were satisfied with accumulating large amounts of unrelated materials that would not significantly shake their convictions about the world outside.

To put it differently, of these three main obstacles to information gathering, the first two were shared by visiting Westerners of the time as well; they could not speak the language of the host country, and their movement, too, was seriously limited (though in their case by the host government). And yet Alcock and Siebold, Hodgson and McCauley were all—whether aware of it or not—children of Copernicus and Descartes, Hamlet and Faust. Not only were they curious about their surroundings, but curiosity propelled their lives. They were adept—as the Japanese chose not to be—in modifying or simply abandoning established beliefs and dogmas in the face of new discoveries. The reader of an Occidental travelogue would at once be impressed by the qualitative difference between the texture and density of its analytic observation and that of its Japanese counterpart. What separates the two is their differing attitudes toward information and knowledge, insight and understanding, and, closely related to this, their essential difference in attitude toward the self.

Before modern analytic thinking emerged, the Westerner had to acquire the habit of speaking in the isolated first person, as did Descartes in his *Discourse*. Dependence on an implied first person and the resulting ambiguous subject in Japanese did not encourage a similar development. The "I" tended not to detach itself from the other "I's" and thus stayed immersed in the world. There was neither the joy nor the misery of the lonely self; instead, with the ambiguity of the subject allowing his action and being to be collective, man in Japan retained the security of community, however temporally and spatially circumscribed he may have been by the tribal mythology. If Maruyama Masao is right, as I believe he is, in diagnosing the conspicuous absence of the speculative habit (*shiso*) in the whole Japanese tradition, it is a price the culture has been willing to pay. It has chosen to forego universalist knowledge, skeptical observation, and individual reflection in order to sustain a close and coherent community inherited from the long past.[43]

For all its inclinations and preferences, Confucianism was by no means a deterrent to other kinds of learning. If it was not exactly charged with the humanistic spirit, it nonetheless taught a reverence for learning in general; if free inquiry was not the first principle of Confucian learning, it allowed the student to interpret the Way of the Sages as *he* saw it; and if group consciousness was dominant, it yet encouraged vigorous competition within the group. Besides, theirs was a largely pragmatic version of Confucianism. Thus was the Tokugawa mind prepared with a context of learning that would readily allow a new influence to begin its work. For instance, once the information brought back by the 1860 Mission was found to be overly random and mostly useless, this inadequacy was efficiently corrected. The next Tokugawa embassy, the 1862 Mission to Europe, was more pragmatically organized in accordance with that realization.[44] Actually, this ability to absorb vigorously what was only very recently encountered would be unthinkable without the system of basic education provided by the long Confucian tradition and the bureaucratic structure deeply rooted in it.

THE TALE OF GENJI

....

Translation as Interpretation

In this short review of Edward Seidensticker's 1978 translation of The Tale of
Genji *(originally published in 1979 in the* Journal of Asian Studies*), Miyoshi
reverses the common concern of translation studies (i.e., how to render the
classic text readable to a contemporary and foreign audience) by asking how the
original text itself can influence the language of the translation. By highlighting
the untranslatable aspect of* Genji, *Miyoshi argues that it is precisely in the
desire to engage this impossibility where true cultural exchange occurs.*—ED.

Tardy reviewers are punished even before they begin their assignments.
Punctual and conscientious scholars have preempted salient topics, while
most readers, having read the work itself by this time, are likely to have
made up their own minds. In the case of Edward G. Seidensticker's translation of *The Tale of Genji*,[1] one of the most significant recent publications
in the Japanese field, several excellent reviews are already in print: Earl
Miner's incisive discussion of the formal features (*Times Literary Supplement*): Edwin Cranston's careful examination of the details, especially the
rhythm, the names, and *waka* (*Journal of Japanese Studies*); and Marian
Ury's meticulous comparison of this new translation with Waley's (*Harvard
Journal of Asiatic Studies*). A laggard reviewer is trapped: he must parrot
what is by now standard: that Mr. Seidensticker's achievement is indeed
splendid; that his work, at the same time, does not superannuate Waley's
masterpiece (as the translator is the first to acknowledge); that the new
English *Genji* is not only complete but is more accurate than its antecedent,
through its use of the annotated modern editions and modern renditions in

Japanese now available; that the introduction and notes are less copious than one would like; that some of the remarks made in them are rather astonishing ("[the rhythm of the original] is brisker and more laconic, more economical of words and less given to elaboration [than Waley's]"); and that some translations of the names of the characters are unfortunate, although others are felicitous. The reviewers are not in unison on all points, of course, nor am I in agreement with everything they say. (To take only one example, Mrs. Ury's description of *The Tale of Genji* as a "novel" is open to dispute. See, for example, Nomura Seiichi's *Genji monogatari buntai ron josetsu*.) Still, there seem to be unusually numerous agreements among reviewers.

One such point that would perhaps bear further consideration is Mr. Seidensticker's prose, which is uniquely *his*, obviously reflecting *his* interpretation of the work. Urbane, lucid, and sharp, his text reads well. Perhaps too well, and herein lies a question that is inevitably raised. In what sense is this translation an attempt "to imitate the original in all important matters"? While I am fully aware of the impossibility of locating precise equivalents between Japanese and English, I cannot help pondering the words of another eminent translator, Vladimir Nabokov: "Any translation that does *not* sound like a translation is bound to be inexact upon inspection; while, on the other hand, the only virtue of a good translation is faithfulness and completeness. Whether it reads smoothly or not, depends on the model, not on the mimic." Mr. Seidensticker, too, notes in his introduction that "[Waley] tidies things up by cutting, and therefore 'improves.'" What about his own work? Does his version retain the texture of Lady Murasaki's Japanese? Does it successfully avoid improving and editing the original?

I will try to restrain my urge to repeat what has already been done so well by Professors Cranston and Ury in comparing the original and the translations, and remark instead on a few points that occurred to me as I was comparing the texts word by word and sentence by sentence. Mr. Seidensticker's *Genji* is as thoroughly English as, say, *Pride and Prejudice*, despite the conspicuous Japanese references. By this I mean that he defines syntactic units, clarifies the narrative voice, and lessens ambivalences and ambiguities. And, above all, irony is stressed. Anyone who has had a chance to read *Genji* in an older text (or its modern reproduction or reprint, such as the Aobyoshibon photo-reproduction by Yamagishi Tokuhei and Imai Gen'ei, or the Kochibon edition by Akiyama Ken and Ikeda Toshio) would note, as Tamagami Takuya has been strenuously arguing over the years and as Mr. Seidensticker surely knows, that *Tale of Genji*, as a *monogatari* is essentially a verbal flow scarcely marked by punctuation or paragraphing, that is, by a spatially structural concern. Words follow upon words, as endlessly varied in tones and shades as undulating *gagaku* music. As readers accustomed to the novel, however, we are continually pressured by our own expectations and biases to fit the contours of *Genji* into the shape of a modern fiction. Readers of the Nihon koten Bungaku Taikei or Shogakkan edition of *Genji monogatari* are forced to decipher the tale, rather than allowed to experience it. For to consult with these abundant and helpful notes and comments is to seek *the* meaning the editors assign to a given word or passage. Even punctuation is an act of interpretation. Tamagami's own unpunctuated Kadokawa edition is better. But even this version—despite his numerous caveats and avoidance of all punctuation except commas—leads the reader to assume that *Genji* has phrasal and clausal units and paragraphic sections. In addition, Tamagami's modern rendition contradicts his theory of the *Genji*'s structure. In accord with his theory (rather than his practice), I believe that *Genji* is not at all a novel, a modern narrative form that weaves its incidents into a plot and presents autonomous and discrete characters that supposedly refer to imagined individualities. The Aristotelian concept of the beginning, middle, and end hardly applies to *Genji*; nor does the clarity of modern ironic vision which Mr. Seidensticker seems so eager to recognize in Murasaki Shikibu's art.

The point is that the reader of the original doesn't know precisely where, for instance, a quotation begins or ends, and I suspect no Heian reader really cared. Mr. Seidensticker's version cleanses all such ambiguities, and turns the tale into a modern Western novel (or romance), unavoidably changing the nature of the Heian sensibility. We see in it an ironic drama or, as one awestruck and wrong-headed reviewer finds it, a quasi-Victorian moral didacticism.

In the Heian tale, plot and character, together with syntax, fuse into an all-embracing time flow which affords the reader an occasion to feel and reflect on his being and nonbeing in life (which may be at the same time non-life). Mr. Seidensticker's rendition tends to convert these shadowy palaces, temples, and hamlets inhabited by princes, princesses, and hermits into well-lit salons crowded by modern Western ladies and gentlemen.

Let me offer just one passage as an example, hoping this will not be a summerstock production of Professors Cranston's and Ury's performances. Here is Seidensticker's version of the opening passage of the second chapter, "Hahakigi" (The Broom Tree):

> "The shining *Genji*": it was almost too grand a name. Yet he did not escape criticism for numerous little adventures. It seemed indeed that his indiscretions might give him a name for frivolity, and he did what he could to hide them. But his most secret affairs (such is the malicious work of the gossips) became common talk. If, on the other hand, he were to go through life concerned only for his name and avoid all these interesting and amusing little affairs, then he would be laughed to shame by the likes of the lieutenant of Katano.

And here is my experiment:

> The Radiant *Genji*, in the name alone, so grand, could be extinguished, having so many faults, indeed, these risqué affairs, might be proclaimed, to later ages, and float a name for frivolity, so worried, kept certain affairs hidden, even these were talked about by someone, what a malicious gossip, and quite cautious about people, trying to remain sober, there was nothing romantic, would have been scoffed at by Katano no Shosho . . . .

Obviously, this is not English, nor am I suggesting here that anyone should be mad enough to try to publish an unreadable, non-English *Genji*. Furthermore, even this Japanese-English rendition is too English because of its added articles, number, and person, its loss of honorifics, and so on. The point is, though, that the concepts of accuracy and precision are meaningless as long as one is concerned only with the correspondence with and the departure from the annotated, decoded modern texts that seem designed to fly at the single "correct" meaning. The original *Genji*, I repeat, flows and drifts. At every turn, the stream of narrative opens up an unexpected perspective which also revises what has come before. The subject of a verb is often unknown, then is revealed, then is lost again; the narrator blends with characters, who also subtly intermingle with each other and with their environments. Such, it seems to me, is the world where the Radiant Prince of *Genji* and Princess Aoi, Prince Kaoru, and Princess Oigimi, flow with time.

Can this world be recreated in the modern English language with its fixed syntactic expectations? Maybe not. Virginia Woolf once said that "the sentence is not fit for a woman; it was invented by a man." Woolf, of course, knew Arthur Waley well, and she even wrote a review of his *Genji* when the first volume appeared in 1925. It so happens that Woolf's language, especially after *Mrs. Dalloway* (1925) and *To the Lighthouse* (1927), has features uncannily like those of Lady Murasaki's as I read the two women writers from two vastly different traditions and times. One need only remember here that, beginning with the second decade of this century, Woolf and many others worked hard to free the prose narrative from the dominance of the modern individual consciousness. The experiment with stream of consciousness is one such attempt; depersonalizing of the narrative voice, disembodying of characters, loosening of the point of view, immersing of the spatial structure of the novel in the flow of time are all similar endeavors. One idly dreams what might have happened had Woolf learned to read Japanese, or, better still, had she translated *The Tale of Genji*! ← *OMFG*

Modern English is so firmly established today that it resists accommodating unidiomatic translations, Nabokov notwithstanding. Commercial publishers, I have been told, often go so far as to hire a rewrite person who knows no Japanese to clean up a clumsy translation of a Japanese novel. Japanese attitudes toward translation are in sharp contrast. In the past one hundred years, the Japanese, in their eagerness to know the world outside, have become a people addicted to translation, and consequently the translation style has been invented. And as everybody knows, even their daily speech has been profoundly affected by what they understand to be Western languages. The influence is evident not only in vocabulary, but in syntax as well. Such change, or confusion, if you will, in idiomatic Japanese, is the price they have been willing to pay for knowing the West, and themselves. Of course, this kind of change and confusion occurs frequently in the history of any language; the changes in English during the eleventh century, following the Norman conquest, are a familiar example. A language absorbs, grows, or declines. Can the original text of *Genji* influence today's English? The question sounds absurd. Can another writer render *Genji* into the style of a Virginia Woolf? The question seems less absurd. In short, a translation which interprets in greater fidelity to the spirit and style of the Heian masterpiece remains a possibility. And it is in *trying* to fulfill such possibilities that true cultural exchange occurs. In some sense, Mr. Seidensticker's translation was meant to be such an attempt.

WHO DECIDES, AND WHO SPEAKS?

....

Shutaisei and the West in Postwar Japan

Published in Miyoshi's Off Center *(1991), this essay focuses on the problem of* shutaisei *(subjectivity) as it was questioned and produced in Japan immediately following the Second World War. Here we see Miyoshi critical of Japanese forms of subjectivity (and Japanese forms of theorizing subjectivity) that function to cultivate depoliticized citizens, while at the same time refusing to measure these deficiencies against Western standards.*—ED.

My point of departure is where I am situated now: as a citizen and resident of the United States, still haunted by the memories of two past wars, and ever rankled by unceasing global crises. I try to teach, and know. My first war experience was as a Japanese subject with little knowledge of the unfolding history around me. My second, the war in Vietnam, was as a naturalized U.S. citizen acutely aware of my earlier ignorance during what is known in Japan as the Fifteen Years War. This time, I promised myself, I would learn and act—resist the state, if necessary. Did I?

As I teach, I try to be neither nostalgic about my own past nor utopian about the world. To see what constitutes the world and to describe it without allegorization is nearly impossible, but such an impossibility is what all of us are conscribed to inhabit.

Shutaisei, according to Kenkyusha's *New Japanese-English Dictionary*, is "subjectivity; subjecthood; independence; identity." All four words are pertinent, but none of them exactly corresponds to the Japanese term. The absence of an English equivalent underscores that *shutaisei* is a native invention. Initially coined by the Kyoto *philosophes*,[1] it is a word widely used after 1945 to fill a perceived gap in the Japanese language. The Japanese thought they saw the concept they named *shutaisei* everywhere in Western intellectual discourse: individualism, democracy, liberalism, libertarianism, subject, subjectship, subjectivism, and libertinism flourished without bound. A compound of *shu* (subject, subjective, sovereign, main), *tai* (body, substance, situation), and *sei* (quality, feature), the word means inclusively the agent of action, the subject of speculation or speech act, the identity of existence, and the rule of individualism.[2]

Dealing with the idea of shutaisei as it was deployed comprehensively in the immediate postwar years in political and institutional programs, in intellectual exchanges, and in literary works, this essay will examine the role played by the West in the form either of the ruling Allied Powers or of a generalized intellectual and cultural model. Throughout, self-definition in terms of the individual or the nation as a whole is its concern. The context is specific as to time and place; the argument, however, which concerns power, knowledge, and art, is obviously not localized.

Supreme Commander

No Japanese knew what to expect in the summer of 1945. The fate of the vanquished is in the victor's hand; the victor knows it, the vanquished does not. The Potsdam Declaration merely suggested the general outline of Japan's future. The innermost circle of the ruling class who participated in the surrender proceedings expected and hoped for the best, that is, that the status quo would be maintained. They believed the coming changes to be only minor adjustments.[3] Ordinary people, on the other hand, were anxious, and retribution was taken for granted.

Not that the Japanese were wholly ignorant of the outside world. Newspaper and news agency correspondents were stationed in neutral and friendly cities such as Stockholm, Zurich, Berlin, and Lisbon, and some diplomats in Moscow and Bern were trying to communicate and negotiate with the Allied Powers.[4] Thus they knew a little about the intentions of the Allies and even about the early signs of strain in U.S.-Soviet relations before the spring of 1945. Still, the continual quarrels among the war leaders in Japan made analysis of news and reports extremely difficult and their transmission to the public nearly impossible. In addition to the harshest information control, there was a shortage of paper, limiting the daily newspapers to two pages, with minimal tidbits of hard news and proportionately ample propaganda.[5] People were of course told of the latest lost battles but were repeatedly assured of the final victory; and they tried their best to believe the unbelievable.

The initial conflict between the Japanese rulers' hope for continuity and the conquerors' zeal for fundamental alteration of the enemy state was easy to understand. What no one knew then, and what we could see only retrospectively, was the great freedom with which the occupation policy was formulated and executed at the early stage by General Douglas MacArthur, the Supreme Commander of the Allied Powers (SCAP). How was one officer allowed such latitude in decision making? And what constrained him later?

First, the basic documents setting forth the U.S. occupation policy—several working papers issued by the State-War-Navy Coordinating Committee after December 1944, the Potsdam Declaration, and the Basic Initial Post-Surrender Directive of August 29, 1945—were all written in too general and broad terms to serve as adequate guidelines for SCAP's particular problems. While the August 29, 1945, Directive cautioned that it was "not the responsibility of the Allied Powers to impose upon Japan any form of government not supported by the freely expressed will of the people,"[6] it stipulated nonetheless a number of principles on matters such as freedom of religion, democratization, and various reforms (part 3, section 3). Literally interpreted, the document could have permitted the overthrow of the Japanese government with no interference from the occupation authorities. Second, the highest office in the occupation structure was to be the Far Eastern Commission in Washington, D.C., which would be represented in Tokyo by the Allied Council for Japan. Because of the deteriorating relationship between the United States and the Soviet Union, however, the commission, composed of the fifteen nations that had warred with Japan, was not established until later, and even then was never allowed to function fully by the United States. China was too weak to be considered seriously as a great power; the influence of Great Britain was being phased out of the Pacific region; France's participation in the war with Japan had been minimal; and the Soviet Union was to be the target of containment. As far as the United States was concerned, the occupation was, unlike in Germany, "allied" in name only, and the actual administration was solely in the hands of the supreme commander's headquarters. General MacArthur, for instance, virtually ignored the Allied Council meeting. Third, the general's relationship with his home government was hardly cordial. Of course, no war hero is expected to conform to the rules meant for ordinary bureaucrats. MacArthur was not even an ordinary hero; he was a living myth aspiring to become a living god, replacing the emperor himself. Under the circumstances, he was apt to ignore communications emanating from the likes of President Truman or Secretary of State George Marshall. George Kennan, one of several State Department officials dispatched to Japan to investigate the general's intentions and activities in 1948, later recalled his mission as "nothing more than that of an envoy charged with opening up communications and arranging the establishment of diplomatic relations with a hostile and suspicious foreign government."[7]

Perhaps more fundamentally, however, there was the marked degeneration in U.S.-Soviet relations. Even before the Yalta Conference, there had been ominous exchanges.[8] In subsequent texts such as Churchill's Fulton speech in March 1946, Truman's joint Congress speech in March 1947, Marshall's June 1947 Harvard speech, and Kerman's "X" article in July 1947, one sees the unmistakable steps of acceleration in rhetoric and intensification of measures in the name of national security. There were internal critics like Henry Wallace and Walter Lippmann, but the Truman administration steadily worked to maintain the global hegemony of the United States bequeathed by Great Britain at the demise of its empire. Henceforth, any regional conflict and local problem had to be assessed in terms of the grand scheme of "world peace." There is a startlingly blunt statement made by George Kennan, widely hailed as one of the most lucid and humane of the Washington policy makers, that "we have about 50 percent of the world's wealth, but only 6.3 percent of its population:

> In this situation, we cannot fail to be the object of envy and resentment. Our real task in the coming period is to devise a pattern of relationships which will permit us to maintain this position of disparity without positive detriment to our national security. To do so, we will have to dispense with all sentimentality and daydreaming; and our attention will have to be concentrated everywhere on our immediate national objectives. We need not deceive ourselves that we can afford today the

luxury of altruism and world-benefaction. . . . We should cease to talk about vague and—for the Far East—unreal objectives such as human rights, the raising of the living standards, and democratization. The day is not far off when we are going to have to deal in straight power concepts. The less we are then hampered by idealistic slogans, the better.[9]

The Soviet Union responded in kind, and paranoia became a settled condition of world diplomacy.

MacArthur's policy changes reflected this widening global rift. At first the Government Section of the General Staff, composed of former New Dealers impatient to democratize the Japanese state, was in ascendancy, initiating a rapid series of sweeping reforms ranging from full-scale revision of the Constitution to land redistribution, dissolution of trust and combines, revamping of the educational system, purging of over 200,000 war leaders and functionaries, establishment of labor unions and organizations, the establishment of individual civil rights, the guarantee of free speech, free press, and academic freedom, a step toward equal rights for men and women, and the redistribution of wealth through taxation. Even the war-fatigued apathetic Japanese were astonished by the radicalism of such reforms. Communist Party leaders hailed the American occupation troops as the liberators of Japan. The news reached Washington and began to trouble the policy makers as they pondered the economic and industrial potential of Japan in the context of the cold war. As Washington now saw it, Japan ought to be incorporated with the Western alliance rather than being left in isolation in abject defeat. MacArthur's experimentation must be halted, and his reformers must be restrained. Before the end of 1946, the Intelligence Section of the General Staff, headed by a German-born general (a Franco admirer who "looked like, and sometimes thought like, Hermann Göring"),[10] led the management of the occupation. By the summer of 1948 MacArthur's initial dream of converting Japan into a Switzerland was over; Japan was now a friend of the United States, an ally in arms if at all possible, as suggested first by Secretary of War Kenneth C. Royall in January 1948 and spelled out in the National Security Council resolution 13-2 of October 1948.[11] The MacArthur–dictated Constitution had to be either rewritten or reinterpreted to enable such a transformation.

What is significant in this barest summary of the occupation is, first, the irrelevance of MacArthur's basic policy to Japan's own interest, and, second, the absence of events and actions initiated by the Japanese in these immediate postwar years. It should at once be admitted that the military occupation of a defeated nation in a total war inevitably leads to its integration with the victor nation's own political and economic objectives. In such a situation very little can be institutionally carried out by the defeated nation. In Japan's case, exhaustion after a fifteen-year war and inexperience in defeat—among other things—drove people into an acute spell of dejection. In response to each of these reform proposals or orders, Japanese officials were passive and dependent, and citizens were uncritical and docile. Inertia indeed engulfed the whole population.

Even under the most adverse circumstances, however, people do survive, and survival requires maneuvering. They needed food, shelter, and clothing; and they had to get used to the imposed changes. In the process they learned what they had not learned before and would not have learned had they won the war: domestic privacy. The newly found privacy in Japan was not part of the integrated whole, as it might be in an established liberal bourgeois society. It constituted a dialectic opposition to the all-invading, hitherto largely unchallenged state. For the first time the Japanese encountered a space outside collective existence. This autonomy of the private might be expected to grow into a full political consciousness with individual rights guaranteed by the state, but Japanese political history is more circuitous. The discovery of privacy was effectively incorporated into the economic pattern of production and consumption with the dazzling economic success of the sixties, bypassing political individualism. At any rate, the phenomenon was not recognized for what it was even when the postwar writers were engrossed with the existential problems involving shutaisei.

Several developments in the public sphere demonstrated all was not prostration and acceptance. The labor movement gathered momentum far exceeding SCAP's encouragement or expectation. Assisted by the intensifying food and employment crisis throughout 1946 and spearheaded by Korean and other non-Japanese residents, unions were organized on an immense scale and prepared a united front for a general strike in February 1947. Although it began with SCAP's blessing and ended with SCAP's alarmed intervention, still it was as close as Japan ever came to a workers' revolution. A second development was the performance of Prime Minister Yoshida Shigeru. Unlike the previous three prime ministers, Yoshida, a conservative/liberal prewar diplomat, was not intimidated by either Mac-Arthur or his lieutenants. He was aware of the U.S.-Soviet disharmony and sensitive to schisms at the headquarters, which he manipulated so that he, a conservative, might stem the tide of reformism. After his third administration especially, Yoshida was skillful enough not only to stall American zeal but at times even to slow the "reverse course" of American policy to the advantage of Japan as he saw it.[12] When John Foster Dulles tried to force Japan to rearm in the face of Mao Zedong's victory, for example, Yoshida was adamant in resisting the pressure. Disliked by the intelligentsia, Yoshida was no doubt committed to the interests of power and money, and his contributions to the reconstruction of Japan are far from indisputable. In view of the other Japanese leaders overwhelmed by the conqueror, however, Yoshida's insight into the cold war and his use of such knowledge stand out as marks of independence and autonomy. Does this mean that MacArthur and Yoshida, who were portrayed together in Richard Nixon's Leaders,[13] recognized each other, a megalomaniac American warrior meeting an autocratic Japanese conservative to play the game of remaking a country? Hardly. Yet the Second World War was perhaps the last war in which one could entertain a romance of oversized heroes. Multinational corporatism thereafter would enmesh the world too closely to allow room for the invention of heroism. Yoshida was one such personage it was Japan's turn to produce.

Finally, one must mention the enormous activity in literature and in ideological discourse that burst onto the scene soon after the end of the war. As if to make up for lost time during the preceding fifteen years or more, writers expressed and exchanged views that had been anathema. The texts published then are interesting in themselves; in context of shutaisei, they also illuminate the nature of Japanese political thought.

Critics and Intellectuals

Beginning in the winter of 1945–1946, numerous journals and periodicals were inaugurated, and others were resurrected. Older luminaries were awakened from hibernation, and new talents were recruited. Those crudely printed and bound publications—under titles such as Sekai (World), Nin-

gen (Humanity), *Chisei* (Intellect), *Tembo* (Prospect), *Shinsei* (New birth), *Kindai Bungaku* (Modern literature), and *Shin Nihon Bungaku* (New Japanese literature)—were full of desperate hopes mixed with gnawing uncertainties. They were exuberant over the suspension of censorship and "thought control," although the relief was far from unqualified, as SCAP at once initiated a censorship system of its own.[14] Quite naturally, liberation by foreigners from the long oppression by native leaders made writers question what had brought them to where they were. The agonized reassessment of the past history, the present situation, and the future course engaged every intellectual who had lived through the hostilities since the thirties.

One circumstance may have helped to focus such questions on the issue of war responsibility: Prince Higashikuni Naruhiko, who was the first prime minister after the surrender, emphasized the need for "general penitence on the part of the entire population" (*zen kokumin so zange*)[15] as the first step in the reconstruction of Japan. Although the recommended wholesale penitence was for losing the war rather than for waging it, his intention was clearly to preempt the inquiry into war responsibilities and to diffuse it, as if such a strategy might satisfy the Potsdam Declaration provisions concerning war crime retribution. Higashikuni was swiftly disabused of his self-serving interpretation of history. SCAP ordered the arrest of principal wartime leaders soon thereafter.

As the novel idea of war crime gradually sank into the minds of the Japanese, several writers began to express their own views about the writers' involvement in the war. It is ironic that the whole issue of shutaisei— encompassing responsibility, autonomy, independence, individuality, and self-identity—emerged at least partly as a response to the American demand that war criminals be named and punished.

A series of interrelated questions was raised. Why was Japan defeated? What went wrong? The questions surrounding the destruction of the empire were at once replaced by those regarding the commencement of hostilities. Why did the Japanese invade China and attack Pearl Harbor? At whose instigation? Didn't they, people and rulers alike, know that Japan's resources were extremely meager? If not, what blinded them to this and other obvious facts? Such questions in turn led to those about the political makeup of the country. What made people accept the decisions of their leaders? Who were these leaders? How did Japan's decision-making process systematically exclude the populace at large? Or did the people participate? If yes, was the entire population to blame after all? Was the Japanese form of governance intrinsically inoperable and iniquitous? And, finally, is there something uniquely wrong about Japan? What are the "essential" features of the Japanese people?

These are all enormous questions, none of which was readily answerable. In nearly every article published in these postwar journals, however, the discussion inevitably touched on shutaisei, whether it began as an inquiry into Marxist historiography, into the junction of ideology and literature, or into the development of scientism in Japan. The Japanese were surrounded by curious eyes; they had to know themselves. The war years were now presented as a period of general stupor during which people followed orders and suggestions like automatons. How to regain or, more precisely, to nurture shutaisei was a principal topic of Japanese intellectuals as they exchanged views and opinions in these bleak months.

In the March 1946 issue of *Ningen* magazine, Shiina Rinzo begins his "Significance of Postwar Literature": "Postwar literature has revealed the individual's determination to take responsibility for being human. . . . In postwar literature what is not true in the individual's own terms is no longer seriously considered, and one stakes oneself on the subjective truth. To be strongly subjective is what differentiates today's literature from that of the past years."[16] But what is individuality? As Shiina sees it, suffering alone is unique to an individual, and thus suffering confirms individuality. Suffering, however, must not be allowed to become self-sufficient, nor should it be permitted to degenerate into nihilism. How does one prevent such degeneration? Shiina seems entirely satisfied with setting forth his answer in moral and psychological terms. One ought to suffer, one ought to try the impossible, one ought to love humanity, one ought to seek happiness. . . . Shiina's advocacy of shutaisei is just that, an advocacy. How does one, or Japan as a nation, begin to achieve it? How can the impossible be made possible? The Japanese suffered during the war, but nothing happened. How can anything happen now only because they suffer? Shiina seems to be implying that the defeat at the hands of Western nations automatically confers on the Japanese a new ability to "return to one's own shutaisei." Is Shiina suggesting that the Japanese can discover self-identity and self-will by fiat? His sense of urgency is unquestionable, but his indifference to history and the current political situation causes the article to fall far short of being germane.

In "A Second Adolescence" ("Daini no Seishun," February 1946), Ara Masahito compares the Japanese people of 1945 to the Dostoyevsky of 1848, sentenced to execution and then reprieved at the very last moment. Now that Ara, like Dostoyevsky, has been saved from doom, he might as well think through the ideals of his first adolescence, which had proved nearly fatal. His earlier inspiration sprang from Christianity and altruism (*hyumanizumu*), both of which, when examined closely, revealed an underlying egoism. He was repulsed by this self-centeredness, but as he shed his youthful egoism, he also lost his adolescence to the war and with it his hope for humanity. The only way he could have kept his youth intact was by getting involved in subversive activities or by exiling himself abroad. Now given this second chance, he would rather confront the fundamental selfishness. Rigorously pursued to its limits, this philosophy of egoism might eventually prove to be a higher form of humanism. People who gave up their adolescence to the war must now embark on a journey to happiness, even if the pilgrimage should strike them as sordid and vulgar.

Ara's regret for having missed out on his first spring might win sympathy, and his resolve to be true to himself—which he insists on calling "egoism"—might be an honest enough strategy for life. Very much like Shiina's proposal, "A Second Adolescence" attributes the loss of his youth merely to a personal, psychological mischoice, as if the war that embroiled millions of people had little to do with it. Follow the right principle—"subjectivity" for Shiina and "egoism" for Ara—and history as well as your personal life will be amended.

In response to Ara, Kato Shuichi attacks egoism as too limiting to be a satisfactorily comprehensive vision. Humanism can never be founded on egoism, according to Kato, because it is "too bourgeois, too inert."[17] Kato, however, is not totally negative about Ara's idea of egoism. Insofar as egoism is defined as a purely formal proposal for the establishment of shutaisei in Japanese literature, Ara is on the right track; Japanese literature must be first rooted in a consciousness of self before it can aspire to transcendental and universal humanism. If Kato is distinct from Ara and Shiina in asserting the need for humanism, he is very much like them in setting up an undifferentiated notion of general humanity. History—which might be expected to particularize—is ultimately subordinate to this universal (i.e., Eurocentric) humanity. Japan lost the war, and it should rejoin the rest of the world, which would presumably embrace all nations including Japan without prejudice or discrimination.

Odagiri Hideo's "The Creation of New Literature: Toward a New Step" ("Shinbungaku sozo no shutai: Atarashii dankai no tameni," June 1946) also celebrates the freedom he and others have enjoyed in recent months. To secure the pleasure of liberation, Odagiri argues, writers ought to be creating truly distinguished works, which, however, are nowhere to be seen. The essay, remarkable for its tortured zigzag argument, progresses in this fashion: How do they get around to writing great works? By having the right worldview. But simply having the right view is not enough. Art needs real feelings. But feelings alone won't suffice either. Don't forget the world view, but heighten it with one's own felt experience. When the essay finally comes around to close the circle, it leaves the reader with a recommendation of something like "reality as it relates to one's own raw experience" (*jibun to no kanren ni okeru genjitsu*).[18] In concrete terms, the "reality" seems to mean the writer's own personal history of the last ten years, that is, the history of acquiescence and collaboration with war efforts. According to Odagiri, the writer's betrayal of his social responsibility is everybody's problem. In fact, unless all writers seriously examine their spiritual stigmata, there will be no new start in Japanese literature.

Odagiri does not explain what exactly constitutes wartime apostasy. Which failures are serious crimes, on the scale ranging from subversion of war aims by violence (which practically no single writer was willing to commit) to aggressive leadership in war planning (which likewise hardly anyone was guilty of)? Most writers, including the twenty-five whom Odagiri named as war criminals in another article, fell in the gray area between the two extremes. They were guilty because they acquiesced and cooperated; but they were also innocent because they were not informed and were under duress. Thus despite Odagiri's efforts to designate specific criminals, most discussion about war responsibility was likely to be deflected to collective guilt, although the "general penitence" that Prince Higashikuni had recommended was clearly inadequate.

Maruyama Masao's article "The Logic and Psychology of Ultra-Nationalism" ("Cho-kokkashugi no ronri to shinri," May 1946) succinctly describes this situation of murky guilt and innocence as unique to Japan. He insists that the European state structure is neutral to cultural values, whereas in the Japanese state, constructed on the emperor system, emperor worship fills private as well as public space. The lack of neutrality in the state structure makes possible the governmental control and subjugation of people's privacy and individuality. Maruyama believes that even the emperor himself lacks final authority, since unlike the European monarch he is held accountable to the authority of his ancestral succession.

Maruyama's analysis of the emperor system and its effects on Japan's intellectual and political history is astute, and his observation of the general absence of shutaisei in Japanese thought and action can be ignored only at a serious risk. His comparison of Japanese ultranationalism with German fascism, however, reveals an inexplicable predisposition toward Germany. According to Maruyama, German officials were fully conscious of their decisions and purpose and so were clearly responsible for their acts, while Japanese leaders such as General Tojo Hideki were merely following the dictates of their superiors in the hierarchy emanating from the authority of the emperor. Thus, at the war tribunals, Maruyama says, "a Tsuchiya turned pale, a Furushima cried, and a Göring roared in laughter," pointing to the intellectual superiority of the latter.[19] Does this mean that the Germans, who rationally and consciously committed the act of genocide, were somehow more intellectual, more enlightened, than the Japanese, who remained unselfconscious—that is, lacking in shutaisei? Exactly what is German "rationality"? Isn't Maruyama guilty here of a blind acceptance of the West, not uncommon among the elites of "less advanced" nations? Unlike the spokesmen of the newly liberated colonies such as Mao, Frantz Fanon, or Aimé Césaire, Maruyama is indifferent to the moral pitfalls of the West, having been bedazzled by its predominance in artistic, intellectual, and technical achievements. Isn't there a serious ideological failure in not recognizing an utter loss of sanity and humanity in what he calls German "rationality"? This purblindness is rather extraordinary for an agile and sophisticated mind like Maruyama's, especially because in the very same article he makes the pertinent suggestion that Japan's adventurism is "a modest attempt to follow the example of Western imperialism."[20] Yet he is all too satisfied to view Japan as uniquely irrational, as guilty of special kind of ultranationalism that robs its subjects of clarity and choice.

The shutaisei controversy is cognate if not identical with the issue of war responsibility. And the writers' nervousness was widely visible in Japan. As Maruyama called it much later, a "community of penitence" (*kyodo kaikontai*) seems to have taken over the late forties intellectual scene.[21] The one group that stood outside this embarrassed crowd was a small number of communists who had firmly resisted the militarists, risking years of imprisonment or exile. Although even they did not go to the extent of bearing arms against the Japanese state, they were nonetheless heroic resistance fighters in the eyes of the liberal apostates as well as the general public. The prestige of Marxism in the postwar shutaisei discourse was at least in part due to the prominence enjoyed by Tokuda Kyuichi, Shiga Yoshio, Nosaka Sanzo, and Miyamoto Yuriko and her husband Miyamoto Kenji, for having remained uncontaminated. In addition to their personal presences as moral exemplars, the Marxists contributed to the shutaisei exchange by proposing a defense of free will and choice in the dialectic of historical inevitability. Umemoto Katsumi, for example, argued that freedom was a historical product, and insofar as human freedom allowed choice, people must do all they can to remove the source of moral evil and social injustice. The acceptance of historical inevitability was perceived to constitute a ground for moral intervention. This essentially liberal humanist revisionism conducted on such a high level of abstraction eventually became undistinguishable from all others. The Marxists' euphoria with the American liberators and their ignorance of the cold war helped to sustain their argument as abstract, metaphysical, and, ironically, unpolitical.[22]

A number of people who were worried about the blurred boundaries of war responsibility decided to join the morally pure Communist Party, thereby purging their guilty consciences. By the time they made up their minds to join the party, however, MacArthur had already begun to alter his earlier policy toward the revolutionary movement. As became painfully clear later on, not a few of them had to reverse themselves once again as the unpredicted prosperity of the sixties alongside the intensification of the East-West conflict made their party membership less than an association with glamorous heroism.

If the objective of this postwar soul-searching was to inquire into the conduct of the Japanese state in relation to its neighboring nations, it might as well have been directed to the larger context of international aggression and colonialism during the last century. Are not aggressive nations equally guilty? All individuals? Should there be distinctions among them in accordance with the severity of the crimes? What is the general war crime above and beyond specific acts of brutality and atrocity condemned by the Geneva Conventions? Is it a moral sin or legal crime? According to whose law? Are the Hiroshima and Nagasaki bombings justified? If the Allies, too, are guilty on specific counts, why are they not being tried? If they are guilty but not to be brought to trial, what is the status of the Tokyo Tribunal? Was the cause of the Allies wholly guiltless? Isn't it perfectly possible to argue, as did Takagi Yasaka earlier and Noam Chomsky later on, that Japan was following the precedent established by Great Britain and the United States, and was exercising its own Monroe Doctrine and realizing its own Manifest Destiny?[23] And if the Japanese version of Manifest Destiny is distinguishable from its acts of aggression and atrocity, how should the two be articulated? This type of fundamental inquiry was not attempted by most Japanese critics and historians either before or after the end of the occupation in 1951. The writers seem simply to have presumed that war crimes had been committed by the Japanese, without asking about the precise charges.

There were several reasons for the Japanese reluctance to scrutinize the West's record. First was fear of occupation censorship. In retrospect, one sees how arbitrary, ineffective, or even absurd the practice of censorship was in this—as in any other—case. But in the forties, when the occupation forces were still hailed as Japan's liberators, the censor's moral authority and disciplinary power were very much revered and dreaded. The Japanese would do anything to avoid incurring SCAP's wrath, including keeping mum about the role of Western imperialism in the history of Japan's aggressive war. The silence was of course ironic in view of the self-examination that the Japanese were supposedly undergoing at the time. The abstruse philosophers who talked about the Kantian, Hegelian, and Marxian notions of shutaisei never took full cognizance of the moral and intellectual discrepancies that lay between the freedom they discovered in the abstract and the restrictions they accepted in actuality. In the course of investigating their past moral failure, they were once again failing to face up to the ongoing abuse of power. One cannot leave out, at the same time, the hypocrisy of those U.S. missionaries of democracy who as a matter of course banned the exercise of democratic principles once their own interests were involved.

Second was the discrediting of Pan-Asianism. Had fear of censorship been the sole reason for this silence, it would have ended with the conclusion of the peace treaty in 1951. Such was not the case. Even though the issue of war responsibility was kept alive after that date, Western hegemonism was not discussed except by a few sober critics such as Takeuchi Yoshimi and several right-wing revisionists such as Hayashi Fusao.[24] In order to understand this hesitation, one should recall that Pan-Asianism, which proposed the liberation of Asia from Western imperialists, had been thoroughly appropriated by the militarists during the war. Thus in those early postwar years few reputable writers would want to be associated with it. To be identified as revisionist was as serious a disgrace as being classified with war criminals. In 1955, for instance, Yoshimoto Takaaki wrote "The Poets of the Previous Generation" ("Zen sedai no shijintachi"), raising anew the question of war responsibility. In the essay Yoshimoto assails Odagiri and others for passing for resisters while they were actually collaborators. Yoshimoto is quick to point out contradictions between their wartime poems and their postwar statements. According to him, most of the writers who claim to have fought against the militarists are in fact hypocrites and opportunists, "quasi-fascist agitators earlier, and quasi-democratic sentimentalists now."[25] Yoshimoto is fierce and unrelenting in this essay, as always. But his disapproval seems limited to the domestic versions of hypocrisy, without considering them in the historical international context.

The third factor involved in this silence about Western responsibility was the International Military Tribunal for the Far East, which was, and was then perceived to be, totally arbitrary and farcical. The concept of the war crime tribunal, like the idea of the crime against peace or the crime of war conspiracy, was a Second World War invention with no legal precedent. But the Japanese were forced to accept the verdict of the tribunal in accord with the terms of surrender. In the course of prosecution, moreover, the clearly innocent were punished while the manifestly guilty were left alone. The most obvious among the latter, the one who might best fit the description of war criminal, was Emperor Hirohito. If not directly responsible for the planning and execution of the war itself, he indisputably presided over the martial rites and ceremonies that moved and guided his loyal subjects. And yet, whether because of his supposed influence over his subjects or his prior understanding with the United States, he was safely placed under the supreme commander's protection. If he was innocent, no militarist leader could have been condemned. In this, as in other matters, the predictable verdict of the Tokyo Tribunal intensified the sense of moral futility. As the Japanese viewed it, justice was as usual one-sided. Radhabinod Pal, the only dissenting judge at the tribunal, mentioned the need to remember the general context of the alleged crime:

> To appreciate what happened, it is only just to see the events by putting them in their proper perspective. We should not avoid examining the whole of the circumstances, political and economic, that led up to these events. This is why I had to refer to matters like the Britainocentric economic world order, the diplomatic maneuvers at Washington, the development of communism and the world opinion of the Soviet policy, the internal condition of China, the China policy and practice of other nations and the internal condition of Japan from time to time.[26]

Hardly a full-scale inquiry into Western expansionism, Pal's argument was indeed a mild protest. Yet he and the Japanese defense lawyers were summarily dismissed, and others did not dare speak up against the blatant travesty of justice. In this act of silence, the Japanese reexperienced the history of compromise and acquiescence.

Fourth was the longstanding deference to the West. Ever since the Tokugawa isolation was shattered by the encroachment of the Western fleet, the Japanese had been fearful of the advanced technology and vast wealth of Western powers. As they learned about its civilization, they were similarly awed by its philosophy and literature, music and arts. The West was to be the center and the norm; and the non-West, peripheral and marginal. The early advocates of enlightenment urged their compatriots to abandon the ranks of Asia and join the West. Thereafter the Japanese, like most other colonized non-Westerners at that stage, had to cope with their own sense of insecurity. In its own people's eyes, Japan was a minor nation overwhelmed by the superior force and culture of the West. They were to "catch up" with the West, to model themselves after the more "advanced" culture on the monolinear scale of progress. Japan's xenophobic ultranationalism was merely the mirror image of this West-worship, which alone can explain the amazingly smooth transition in 1945 from the resolve to fight to the last soldier to the determination to build a peaceful nation.

At the same time, Japan was also one of the very few non-Western nations that had managed to keep itself unoccupied and unsubjugated until 1945. Hence, its pride and sensitivity about its supposed status as a "first-rate" world power, and its traditional exclusivism that often surfaced as outright contempt for the former colonies of the West. In fact, Japan's own colonialism had to be more brutal than the Western versions because they knew how much they had in common culturally and racially with their victims; in order to convince themselves, not to say their victims, of their superiority, they had to resort to naked force. Looking askance at the rest of the third world, the Japanese considered themselves civilized and advanced. When they faced the West, they knew they did not quite belong. Racism is nothing but a form of self-illusion.

Postwar Fiction

With the resurgence of publications, fiction writers, too, were reactivated. Not that they were jubilant over the passage of a dark period. Attentive to the details of daily life by the nature of their work, they were even more bewildered than critics and commentators. But self-examination was urgent for them also. Their works offer further testimony to the postwar crisis of Japanese identity.

Old masters like Nagai Kafu, Tanizaki Junichiro, and Kawabata Yasunari resumed their disrupted work. The war seems to have left relatively few scars on them. Tanizaki completed *Silent Snow* in 1947 (*Sasameyuki*; translated as *The Makioka Sisters*). If the work's apparent lack of interest in the war is a mark of the author's resistance, its indifference to the postwar years may also point to a criticism of the occupation-imposed reforms.[27] Nagai Kafu, too, published works that had been written earlier. The fact that he could print after the war what he had written under quite different circumstances says something about his perception of the war. As for Kawabata, he had made several contributions to the war effort, about which he remained rather taciturn. Does this suggest his unconcern with the matters of war and peace in particular, or with public affairs in general? What constitutes

Kawabata's identity as a writer? How does he relate to the world surrounding him? These are no easy questions to answer. Kawabata completed *Snow Country* (*Yukiguni*) in 1948. The newly added parts do not betray any experience of the devastating war and defeat.[28]

The younger writers' involvement with the war was far more traumatic. During their formative years the war had expanded and intensified from Manchuria to China, then to the Pacific. Some had already started to write at the earlier stage of the war, while others began their careers after the surrender. They were impatient to speak up, although not always equipped with an interpretive will or confidence. Many writers seemed to find consolation in merely recording their not readily decipherable experience. One group of writers who were most conspicuous in 1946 were the Marxists, who had engaged in some form of resistance activity in the preceding years. Of these, Noma Hiroshi and Shiina Rinzo will have to be noted.

Noma's "Dark Paintings" ("Kurai e") appeared in 1946. It describes a young student's search for his place among revolutionary friends in the midwar years. The story is temporally unstable: at several points the hero reflects on the narrated time from a postwar vantage point. Nothing happens in the story itself, although it is told that several revolutionists were arrested for subversive activities and died in prison later. Various attitudes toward the revolutionary program are introduced, and the protagonist, characteristically, broods over his possible choices:

> There is no possible way of living for him except finding a way to pursue self-perfection in Japan. For Japan has not yet established individuality, and the establishment of individuality is a serious question awaiting a solution. This idea derives from a conviction about the need of achieving bourgeois democracy, but [he] thought of it in terms of engraving on his flesh the scars of continual efforts in pursuit of self-perfection.[29]

How this bourgeois self-reliance relates to his friendships with the revolutionists is not made clear, nor is Noma's postwar view of this earlier adolescent self-search. His heavy-handed prose is literal and unironic, demonstrating the postwar Noma to be still undistanced from the midwar resolve of noncommitment. The protagonist, a likely spokesman for the intellectual Noma Hiroshi, is quite smug toward his father and other working-class adults, without whose support and money young revolutionaries like himself are not likely to survive even for a day. Noma's indifference to the economics of daily life, coupled with the insistently arbitrary reading of Brueghel's paintings of the title, make this initiation story depressingly self-centered and sophomoric.

Shiina Rinzo's "Midnight Feast" ("Shinya no utage," 1946) is a story of unmitigated despair. The first-person narrator lives in a shoddy apartment house in a burned-out Tokyo street. All the residents in the building are misfits from the lower depths, making do from day to day on little nothings picked up from the city rubble. Most characters, including the hero, are sick and dying. Among those dejected castaways, the only vigorous one is the hero's uncle, who owns this prison-like apartment house. He is heartless, ugly, and lame. The hero and his next-door neighbor, who happens to be a young prostitute, are both about to be evicted by the ruthless uncle. As the two prepare for homelessness, they mumble to each other, "Really, it's a miserable life. Besides, nothing can possibly happen."[30] As the girl pats him like a child, his hair falls out in strands.

Once again, nothing happens in the story. The hero lives by a creed of endurance: "Simply by endurance I become freed from all heavy burdens. To endure is, for me, to be alive." No one is in control, and those few who have any power over the others are vicious and ugly. Like the unceasing rainfall in the story, life never lets up. And yet the "I" refuses to give up hope. He must endure the unendurable. Shiina's *Ningen* article must be recalled in this light. One must not be nihilistic, one must endure. His idea of shutaisei proves to be a stoic determination to live on despite poverty and iniquity. In Shiina's view, then, there is finally no difference between war and peace, domination and surrender, justice and injustice, for evil is a condition of life. Shutaisei is, paradoxically, always attainable depending on one's fortitude. Shiina may be persuasive as a transcendental moralist, but as a Marxist historian of the intellectual and political conditions of Japan he is nearly useless.

Unlike Noma and Shiina, who both went through an activist stage, the members of the *Buraiha* (vagabond) group—Oda Sakunosuke, Tamura Taijiro, Sakaguchi Ango, and Dazai Osamu—are not closely associated with Marxist ideology. Tamura was arrested once, and so was Dazai, both in alleged violation of the Peace Maintenance Act. But the four are chiefly remembered for their so-called decadence manifestoes rather than their political creeds. The notion of decadence suggests sensuality and freedom, and hence independence and autonomy. Tamura's "The Gate of Flesh" ("Nikutai no mon") was a sensational success at the time of its publication in March 1947. The story describes a group of street girls who seek shelter in the basement of a burned-out building. In a world where the old order has crumbled and nothing has taken its place, the young prostitutes form a tribe for self-protection. They have one strict taboo: no sex except for money. The plot was even then a cliché: A young man shot by the police while committing an armed robbery joins the group. One of the girls falls in love with him and has an orgasm for the first time. As she is being punished by torture, she awakens to the pleasures of flesh. Her "body, encircled by a pale white halo, was resplendent like the prophet on the cross."[31]

The reference to Jesus, too, is quite a cliché (see Ishikawa Jun's "Jesus in the Tokyo Ruins" ["Yakeato no Iesu"], Dazai Osamu's *The Setting Sun* [*Shayo*], or Ooka Shohei's *Fires on the Plain* [*Nobi*] among others); there is no clear sense why Christianity suddenly becomes relevant—unless any *deus ex machina* will do.[32] At any rate, this sadomasochistic depiction of convulsive female limbs seems to offer a new expression of vigor and energy rarely seen in war-ravaged Tokyo. Flesh is honest, even mysterious. Against the wartime libidinal suppression, what was felt to be brute sexuality seems to have reaffirmed the actuality of existence. When reread many years later, however, the story shows itself as full of fantasies and delusions. The warm camaraderie among the misfits, the cleanliness of underground communal living, the male power to endow women with purpose as well as pleasure—Tamura's idealizing of the illicit and fantasizing of male dominion are unrestrained. Rather than a witness to individual emancipation through sexual liberation, "The Gate of Flesh" is a paean to control and discipline, the only new departure being the sexist exploitation that has replaced military subordination. Sexuality may be a gate of flesh and may indeed serve as an opening to selfhood, but as it is depicted in this story, it is hopelessly bonded to the exercise of power.

Oda Sakunosuke is preoccupied in "Today's Scenes" ("Seso," April 1946) with the verbal surface that makes clear his affinity with Edo *gesaku* writers. And just as the works of the *gesaku* writers were heavily mediated by textuality rather than directly faced with raw experience, so is Oda's writing always distanced from carnal drives. The story is, typically, about a writer who is looking for subjects for his story. It takes the form of a string of episodes, some describing the narrator's encounters with people, and others repeating the stories told him by these people. The story is set in actual places in Osaka, and the time, too, is specific, consequently lowering the barrier between fiction and nonfiction. The representational level of storytelling is continually coalesced with that of the story told; an "Oda Sakunosuke" makes his appearance as a character, as is often the case with Oda's work.

Ostensibly, "Today's Scenes" depicts the changed—that is, degraded—scenes of contemporary Japan. Thus the protagonist wanders among the denizens of Osaka, collecting sleazy episodes for the story that the author is in the process of writing under the title of "Today's Scenes." This complicated structure notwithstanding, there is a sort of core episode that concerns the notorious real-life murderess Osada, who killed her lover in the middle of lovemaking, severing his genitals as a token of their love. (This event forms the central plot of Oshima Nagisa's well-known film *In the Realm of the Senses*.) The narrator receives a copy of the court transcript of her trial that provides him with another episode. The owner of the Osada papers, his old friend who comes in and out of the story, is now intimate with the madame of the Café Dice, but as the story comes to its end, the man's past relationship with Osada herself is disclosed. The name "Dice" suggests Oda's philosophy of composition, namely that the narrative ought to remain without closure, with all its elements left to chance and accident. (In another story, "Soredemo watashi wa yuku," the plot unfolds as the protagonist throws a dice at every decisive moment, thus turning the final work into a collection of characters and events barely connected in one integral unit.) Oda believes in the chance form, rejecting the authorial interpretive will that imposes its control on the work. Whether Oda's accidentalism is successful or not is not an issue here. His idea of "accidental fiction" (*guzen shosetsu*) is fascinating either way in view of the general emphasis placed on shutaisei at the time. In Oda's view and actually in his work, the author's authority, control, and responsibility are deliberately minimized. As though all such determination were finally trivial, Oda reverts to eighteenth-century conventions and locates Japan's contemporary scenes in that older context. It is indeed ironic that Oda—remembered for his willful decadence and demimonde licentiousness, qualities judged to be components of the shutaisei movement—should turn out to be a self-effaced occasionalist for whom randomness, not willed control, moves the world.

In his use of himself as a central persona, Dazai Osamu resembles Oda. Of course, all "I-fictionists"—in fact, most Japanese fiction writers—are alike in this regard. But it is further in the concealment of their privacy under the masks of humor and irony that the two resembled each other. If other I-fiction writers exude the heated air of sincerity and honesty, Oda and Dazai are ostentatious in their studied insouciance. The two also depend on the accidentals of their real life for the plot of their work, not because these events are intrinsically important but because they are uncontrolled. They let accidents propel their story lines in random directions. Thus the verbal surface that deflects and refracts and the whimsical turn of events together work to effect open-endedness, ironically undermining the ostensible program for self-discovery.

One thing that keeps the two apart is Dazai's unashamed preoccupation with aristocracy. In *The Setting Sun* (1947) certainly, but also in many other works, Dazai keeps returning to recuperate and define the distinction of nobility.[33] He often insists that his is a moral and spiritual meritocracy, not a hereditary rank. But in Dazai's mind, aristocracy by birth and aristocracy by merit (a suspect category to begin with) keep merging. Especially after the legal institution of aristocracy (*kazoku*) was abolished and several sensational scandals involving ex-royals and ex-nobles were reported by the press in 1947, the decline of the once-glamorous group powerfully excited Dazai, who had always hankered after the rank of distinction. This sentimental attachment, very much like celebrity worship, was shared by other middle-class writers like Mishima Yukio. They all craved a mixture of exclusiveness, cosmopolitanism, affluence, and dandyism, using class terms to express their own claims to superiority.

Sakaguchi Ango, notorious in the immediate postwar years for his philosophy of "depravity," finally may not be radically different from Dazai or Mishima in snobbery, but he, at least, avoids class metaphors, as does Oda. In "On Depravity" ("Daraku ron," April 1946), Sakaguchi confronts Japan's changes since the previous summer. All that was prohibited is now permitted; those who were about to die for the emperor's glory are very much alive, earning their living on the black market. The intense beauty in the face of death and destruction is all gone. What is left now is the pain of survival, the routines of being alive day to day. "We fall not because we were defeated. We are degraded because we are human beings. . . . But we are too weak to keep falling forever. . . . Sooner or later we end degradation and find the way of the *samurai* or emperor worship. . . . By falling to the utter limits of degradation, we must find ourselves, our salvation."[34] Sakaguchi privileges degradation because his strategy for the recovery of shutaisei is the acceptance of decay as the necessary condition of life: letting go, instead of choice. Soon the ascent will begin. By accepting the vulgar and low, the individual will be relieved of the worries of the bourgeoisie.

A few months after "On Depravity," Sakaguchi wrote a story called "An Idiot" ("Hakuchi"). Set in the Tokyo of 1945, the story describes a seedy neighborhood where the protagonist lives. One day a schizophrenic neighbor's imbecile wife strays into the hero's house. He lets her stay and as the air raid becomes a regular event in Tokyo, they begin to sleep together. One night the whole neighborhood goes up in flame in an air raid. As the man takes the idiot woman along to escape from the fire, he wonders what it means to be with her. "Is the sun going to shine on me and on the pig who is standing by my side?"[35] The story was intended to exemplify the argument of "On Depravity." By reaching the bottom of degradation one can find the path of ascent. It is difficult, however, to apply Sakaguchi's decadence principle to this story. The protagonist is a thoughtful man throughout, and there is little in his act that can be called degraded. Is having sex with the idiot woman a depraved act, because a part of him can think of her only as a "pig"? Possibly. But as Sakaguchi tells the story, he sleeps with her out of kindness and responsibility rather than exploitation and brutalization. As a matter of fact, even the essay "On Depravity" itself does not fully explain what is meant by "depravity." Whatever is illustrated in the essay does not correspond to what is usually understood by the word. Sakaguchi describes a mild derring-do of bourgeois dimensions neither shocking nor even reprehensible by the most level-headed standards. Since his sin fails to reach the depth of degradation, his salvation, too, promises to be no more than a tiresome minor attainment. In Sakaguchi's world the self is not allowed to venture far in either its fall or rise. Sakaguchi closes another essay by saying "I just want to live for myself."[36] But even that perfectly reasonable wish, which he must express in a gesture of defiance, seems somewhat beyond Sakaguchi's reach.

Shiina, Noma, Tamura, Oda, Dazai, and Sakaguchi were all spokesmen for the darkest period of Japan in the late forties. But these writers who intended to mark the return of peace reveal no signs of individual freedom. Selfhood is inextricably woven into the fabric of Japanese society. The individual clamors for autonomy and independence are audible, but the voices seem drowned out by the tribal chorus of the fallen empire

These writers are also all practitioners of "I-fiction" (*shishosetsu*). Aren't I-fiction writers supposed to be autobiographical—that is, concentrated on the shaping of the self? Despite their self-preoccupation, none of the six writers is seriously critical about the core of selfhood. Shiina is too eager to flee from the self in transcendental affirmation; Noma's criticism is indulgent and incomplete; Tamura is bonded to the cliché; Oda surrenders the self to the accidental and uncontrollable; Dazai nervously performs to an audience; Sakaguchi, too, is bound by the dictates of his society. Thus despite their apparent defiance and independence, the I-fictionists are once again confirming society's unloosened control of their beings. Mishima's *Confessions of a Mask* (1949), too, is a timorous exhibition of a middle-class prig's breach of his society's normal expectations. The more they gaze at themselves, the more they see the shadows of their tribe instead.

The best way to approach this aspect of I-fiction, which might also throw light on shutaisei, is to read the work not as the author's moral and spiritual confession, but as a literal recording of the composition process. It has always been important for the Japanese writer to document the circumstances in which a poem was conceived, written, and read. Beginning with the oldest of the poetic collections, the *Manyoshu*, with its prefatory notes, the convention is alive throughout Japan's literary history, appearing in all the poetic anthologies, *zuihitsu* essays, and Basho's travelogue-diaries. Obviously the performative quality of Japanese literature requires discussion on its own. What is interesting here is that I-fiction can be looked at not as evidence of shutaisei (self-search, self-determination, self-identity) but as exactly the opposite, the public disclosure of the circumstance of the work's composition. Of the six works mentioned here, "Dark Paintings," "Today's Scenes," and *The Setting Sun* are clearly performative: they write themselves. As for Shiina, Tamura, and Sakaguchi, they wrote numerous works that have their texts themselves as their references. In the postwar years, when the individual's identity crisis was profound, fiction writers were not exploring the ground of the modern self so much as following the long-established habit of tracing the circumstances of their writing. The unprecedented circumstance of defeat and humiliation may have driven these writers into the abyss of self-doubt. But to see that is also to understand that the novelty of the circumstance made them retrogress even more compulsively to the process of writing. So viewed, postwar I-fiction is not new in any significant sense. Similarly, it is not shutaisei but its absence that is fascinating about Japan's orthodox fictional form.

Choices

Postwar actions and inactions, exchanges of ideas, and literary configurations form an intriguing picture of shutaisei. As the intellectuals eagerly assented to SCAP's dictates, they concealed their surrender by means of ungrounded abstractions or stylized sensationalisms. The program of shutaisei was from the beginning deliberately, and hopelessly, severed from the world they in fact inhabit.

WHY SHUTAISEI?

Most intellectuals of Japan, whether before, during, or after the war, seem to agree that shutaisei is not their conspicuous trait, and that its full development is desirable as a universal modern value. There seems to be little question that individuality in personality, autonomy in action, and freedom in thought and expression are not characteristic of modern Japanese society. The legal and political system of pre-1945 Japan testifies to it; the absence of resistance and the pattern of conformity throughout the war years provide further evidence; and the I-fiction as I have redefined it is also a witness. The postwar refusal to discuss seriously the history of Western hegemonism also adds credence to this proposition. Socially and psychologically, collectivism still prevails. Shutaisei, or subjectivity/subjecthood/independence/individuality, however, is of course not a universal value. Were it universal, Japan—like any other society—would have developed it on its own as a crucial cultural factor. It is of course no less historical and culture-specific than feudalism, Protestantism, or any other socio-psychological category. Shutaisei arose in the West in the modern period in response to specific events and developments, and if Japan has retained its collectivism despite its "modern" enlightenment and technology, it may well have its own reasons.

The world today certainly does not present a pretty picture. The cold war between the so-called democratic West and Soviet East may indeed be over; yet hopelessly sundered between the rich North and poor South, the world is continually threatened with conflicts and miseries, if not with the eruption of the nuclear armageddon. Races and tribes battle—formerly in the context of the West-East confrontation and now more frequently in the name of economic expansionism or reactive fundamentalism—in the Middle East, the Americas, Asia, Europe, and Africa; factions and sects contend everywhere. Internal competition also fragments societies. Do nations, races, classes, sexes, and groups benefit from the unceasing assertion of individual interests and self-concerns? Doesn't brute power always lurk behind the rule of shutaisei?

Even history seems to require revision. As we reread Shakespeare's *Tempest*, Defoe's *Robinson Crusoe*, and Conrad's *Heart of Darkness*, we are gazing straight into the records of expansionism and colonialism. Once we fix our thought on the West, however, our speculation immediately turns to the nightmare of Japanese imperialism, which, too, hauled millions and millions to their graves. Japan's aggression may have been the one self-assertive act that Japan has "successfully" managed to learn from the Western model. If aggression is indeed inseparable from shutaisei, does Japan—or do we all—need shutaisei? Can we now afford shutaisei?

For Japanese intellectuals as well as for Westerners, the job may well be to see the absence of shutaisei in Japanese society for what it is, and to recognize how it operates in various areas. After all is said and done, the uncritical pursuit of shutaisei in Japan may be still one more example of Japan's gestures toward Westernization, and thus ironically proof of its lack of shutaisei. Conversely, the West may learn from Japan not just management techniques, but a model for truly civilized behavior as it studies Japan's longstanding avoidance of individualism. Isn't it possible after all to reject shutaisei without at once falling into the suffocating regimentation of conformism and collectivism?

In the West, on the other hand, the death of the subject is very much talked about. According to Fredric Jameson, for instance,

> Such terms [as the "alienation" and "fragmentation" of the self] inevitably recall one of the more fashionable themes in contemporary theory —that of the "death" of the subject itself—the end of the autonomous bourgeois monad or ego or individual—and the accompanying stress, whether as some new moral ideal or as empirical description, on the *decentering* of that formerly centered subject or psyche. (Of the two possible formulations of this notion—the historicist one, that a once-existing centred subject, in the period of classical capitalism and the nuclear family, has today in the world of organizational bureaucracy dissolved; and the more radical poststructuralist position for which such a subject never existed in the first place but constituted something like an ideological mirage—I obviously incline towards the former; the latter must in any case take into account something like a "reality of the appearance.")[37]

LOST

Japan's extraordinary economic success has been, up to now, largely unaccompanied by a spirit of self-criticism. Of course, there are occasional critiques by writers and scholars of the nuclear threat, cultural vulgarization, and environmental destruction, but they are sporadic and fragmentary. A general system of criticism is yet to be revealed.

Above all, Japan's immense economic power is exercised in conjunction with global corporate expansionism and the relentless consumerization of individuals. Systematically dehistoricized, the collective nonindividuals of Japan seem to be leading the whole pack of peoples and nations, in both the West and the Rest, to a fantastic dystopia of self-emptied, idea-vacated, and purpose-lost production, consumption, and daydreaming.

All-encompassing consumerism is, ironically, a version of shutaisei, since it is sensual, bodily, and systematic. If intellectuals of the immediate postwar period—such as Maruyama Masao, Otsuka Hisao, or Umemoto Katsumi—meant by shutaisei a kind of modern, Western, liberal individualism, Japan's present may have indeed fulfilled such a program, or at least realized what was implied by such an ideology: an ultraintensified and superaccelerated form of "rational" (controlled) capitalism. By overleaping the modern age of Hegel and Marx, Kierkegaard and Nietchze, Sartre and Chomsky, Japan may have already arrived at an empire of signifiers without a single signified—all advertising signs and trademarks, and no meaning. Isn't that the world of Tanaka Yasuo's *Nantonaku Kurisutaru*, the ultimate consumerist vacuity in which the act of buying alone serves as the confirmation and reassurance of individual beings?

THE INVENTION OF ENGLISH LITERATURE IN JAPAN

....

This essay was originally published in 1991 in the journal boundary 2 *and later appeared in* Japan in the World *(1993), edited by Miyoshi and H. D. Harootunian. Here Miyoshi turns his critique to the idiosyncratic character of English literary and language studies throughout the history of modern Japan— an idiosyncrasy that enfeebles the scholarship and effectively severs it from English studies conducted outside the country. This culturally contingent and parochial development leads Miyoshi to question the nation-state as the central organizing principle for literary and language studies.*—ED.

English is a huge business in Japan today. Practically everyone in this country of 120 million people goes to high school, where English is taught several hours weekly for as many as six years; nearly half of all high school graduates go on to colleges and universities which, as of now, continue to require English.[1] What all this means is both a massive dose of English for everyone and an immense pool of English faculty and instructional re- sources, that is to say, a thriving multibillion-dollar industry. Nearly every- body is exposed to so much school-taught English for so long that this alien language practically serves as a second language for the Japanese. Under such circumstances, it is intriguing indeed to find the studies in Japan of English literature and the English language to be so idiosyncratically coordinated and so markedly divergent from what is understood to be English studies outside of the country. Although this discussion is con- cerned mainly with the specific nature of the study of English literature in Japan, it seems both necessary and profitable to consider the wider context within which the discipline has evolved and is practiced.

General English Education

Let me begin with a brief survey of institutions involved in English studies in Japan today, focusing on how they operate, rather than on how they are officially and bureaucratically organized. There are three main institutional English programs: (1) high school English, in conjunction with the cram school (*jukenjuku* or *yobiko*) version, which is largely targeted to the collegiate entrance examination; (2) academic studies in English literature (including the collegiate general education English); and (3) "conversation" school (*kaiwa gakko*) and business English. Although they all seek to teach/study English, they remain discrete with hardly any interchange among them.[2]

First, high school English, together with cram school English, is modular and formulaic, just as basic foreign-language teaching tends to be everywhere. From the long history of collegiate exams, a list of certain sentence constructions has been compiled, and the students are expected to master them for they are the likeliest questions to be asked on the exams. Thus, they memorize "No sooner . . . than . . . ," or "It is . . . that . . . ," filling the blank spaces with appropriate words.[3] Likewise, a standard vocabulary and a set of grammar questions have been developed, and such specimens are learned by heart. The rigor of memorization, it goes without saying, is merciless. At times a teacher offers a canonic text, such as one of Hawthorne's short stories or a Keats poem, but the text for the occasion is tamed and standardized in the sense that it is dissected into component sentence and phrase units. Reorganization of such modular units back into an integral text or speech act is hardly ever anticipated. Thus, when a high school graduate passes the difficult college entrance exam in English, the competence falls within the agreed-upon territory of "exam English" (*juken eigo*), which has very little to do with English as it is spoken in the United States, England, or any other place where English is commonly spoken. This does not mean the language is not understood, because it obviously is. The point, however, is the particular object and mode of understanding that results from the curricula as organized in Japan. I will discuss this further later on, but let me just point out here that the successful college entrant is unlikely to be able to speak or write easily understood English.

Since most students consider what they learn at their schools inadequate for the tough entrance exams, they spend after-school hours at cram schools, where English and math are the most urgent subjects. The cram school is a profit-driven institution once considered irregular or even sleazy. Because of the democratic and demographic trends that make admission to a prestigious college formidably competitive, however, high-performance cram schools are quickly rising in social esteem as well as commercial value. Nowadays there are even hard entrance examinations for the *yobiko* themselves. As cram schools display spectacular success rates (55 percent are admitted to Tokyo University, 60 percent to Kyoto University, etc.), they come to enjoy prestige, and with the prestige comes influence. It is no overstatement to say that one of the clues to the state of formal English instruction in Japan lies in the practice at cram schools. The learning process is single-mindedly channeled to winning in the competition, thus radically turning English acquisition into a means to a specific career strategy. The critical and cultural speculations that might at times accompany the knowledge of a foreign language are not only irrelevant, but they may, if ever contemplated, even be a distraction.[4]

As to the second category of institutional English programs, let a few words suffice here, since I will be elaborating on it below. The high school graduates who continue to the college level are faced with more of the same practice. They will read, that is, parse and translate, the canonic work word by word, sentence by sentence. Equivalency is always assumed between the two languages, with the tacit understanding that the balancing of the two sets of vocabulary is all there is to English studies. The controlling idea is thus "accuracy": once an idea is "accurately" transferred from one language context to another, the job is done. Spoken English, which presupposes greater movement within the system of English itself, is relegated to trivial status. Reading is all-important in the world of university English. English in this sense is very much like Latin, or more exactly, *kanbun*, Chinese texts read and pronounced as Japanese.

In fact, throughout the typical student's career in English, the training is predominantly in written documents. Thus, some students feel that they must supplement this written learning with oral practice, and to satisfy this need they enroll at "conversation" schools set up for that purpose. Unfortunately, conversation schools remain by and large commercial enterprises under little academic supervision. Although the number of students who attend such schools is small, it is rapidly increasing. These institutions devoted to lessons in oral English have several interesting features. First, the "conversation" taught in such schools is also formulaic. "How are you, Mr. Smith?" "Fine, thank you, Mr. Tanaka. And how are you?" Thus goes the "conversation," and the minute the teacher—who is often an American or English baccalaureate or undergraduate, and not necessarily in English —tries to conduct an unstructured talk, the effort is met with embarrassed silence. At these schools the student also expects to be taught the substance of conversation, topics and opinions, feelings and attitudes, as well as the sound and shape of English.[5] Second, proper pronunciation is ineffectually attended to. If the notorious confusion of liquids, *l*s and *r*s, is very much talked about, for instance, the rest—from vocalic values to specific consonants, not to mention accent and intonation—receive less emphasis, usually because of the oversized enrollment. Still, those who attend the conversation schools at least hear "real" English sounds,[6] which is not at all the case in most regular schools, where teachers have learned the sounds from their teachers, who learned from their teachers, who . . . for several generations with little exposure to non-Japanese English. Third, however undisciplined they may be, it may well be in such conversation and business-oriented institutions that Japan's encounter with the outside English world can finally commence. Here, at least, the exchange is unmediated by the long accumulation of the naturalized English, which seems far too autonomous, introspective, and uncommunicable.

These three institutions are discrete, with very little in common. They are staffed by different kinds of instructors trained in different curricula with very little exchange among them. Likewise, they have different clienteles: the high school/college axis, together with the cram school, is more or less limited to the young population at large, whereas the conversation school offers a sort of continuing education mainly directed to youngish adults both in and out of business. Spoken English does not receive respect in the mainstream institutions, where the English phonemes are in fact taught through written phonetic signs (the International Phonetic Alphabet, or IPA) that stand in for pronounced sounds. At times one encounters a Japanese scholar with extensive and accurate knowledge of IPA representations who is at the same time neither willing nor able to sound them out. Thus, oral *Ei-kaiwa* (English conversation) is out, while literate forms of *Ei-*

go (English reading), *Ei-bunpo* (English grammar), and *Ei-sakubun* (English composition) constitute the principal field of study. Of course, oral and literate categories can be combined, but they rarely are. At the center are the college and university English departments which, as the clearinghouse of literary and linguistic researches, ought to guide the whole English-learning industry. Do they? If so, how do they guide it?

The Beginnings of Studies in English Literature

Japan's mid-nineteenth-century encounter with the outside world was largely involuntary. To the extent that it could not be resisted, the rendezvous was one-sided; it was, in fact, nearly an invasion. The recognition of this helplessness led Japan to both adore and reject the West at the same time. When studies of English were at last acknowledged to be a necessity by the Tokugawa government in 1856, the program was first placed at the Institute for Research on the Barbarian Books (Bansho Shirabe Dokoro). After many protests from Western diplomats, the name was changed seven years later to Kaiseisho, or the Institute for Open Development. Using shipwrecked sailors, interpreters in Dutch, and Chinese books on the geography and language of the West, the institute tutored the young samurai gathered from all parts of Japan. It was a government school from the beginning, and after it grew to be the University of Tokyo, it was placed under the jurisdiction of the Ministry of Education. English studies, in short, arose in response to the needs of the state.[7]

Earlier, the teachers were recruited from foreigners attracted to the typical colonial situation and the generous compensations. All courses, regardless of the subject, were taught in English, and every student had to study English (language and literature) as well. The tenure of the faculty was temporary. At the same time, they were left alone in their conduct of courses by the ministry. The reasons for the foreign teachers' freedom were several. First, the need to learn from the West was so urgent for both the Tokugawa and Meiji governments that they were in no position to interfere. Second, general thought control was relatively relaxed in the earliest years of the Meiji era, although the government tightened its hold soon thereafter. Third, the educational bureaucrats were determined to emulate Britain and eagerly sought to find or create parity and equivalence between the two nations. Thus, although the government was ever on guard against the dangers of alien teachings, the acceptance and importation of much of alien thought and customs was considered desirable and inevitable.

This climate did not last long, however. The Meiji oligarchy was sufficiently alarmed by the rising oppositionist movement, and the Imperial Precept on Education was issued in 1890 to set the course of the Ministry of Education and all the institutions under its jurisdiction along the line of emperorism, which enabled wide-ranging control and centralization. The Sino-Japanese War of 1894–1895 intensified the wariness of the state officials. Japan was well on its way to Asian domination. The ministry gradually phased out the system of foreign teachers as it sought to tighten its rein over the faculty and curricula and to reduce the costs of education. Japanese faculty trained abroad were to replace the foreign teachers and it was under such circumstances that Lafcadio Hearn's contract was not renewed and Natsume Soseki (who later became Japan's best-known novelist) filled the vacancy around the turn of the century. Thereafter, foreign teachers became supplementary luxuries, not fundamental players, in Japan's educational structure. This could be considered the first step in nationalizing education, the teaching of English literature in particular.[8] Of course, the disappearance of the English-speaking faculty meant the silencing of foreign sounds as well as alien opinions. "De-oralization" of English in Japan could be said to have commenced at this point.

Easy to recognize but hard to comprehend fully is the remoteness of the Japanese and English languages from one another. In the late 1850s and early 1860s, the need for word books, or interlanguage dictionaries, was quite urgent. The two sets of vocabulary were far from parallel, however; too often, objects and ideas in one society were absent in the other. The invention of equivalences was thus the first critical step in an arduous process of translating English words into Japanese.

The assumption of equivalence between two languages at least implies equivalence between the two cultures. The relations between Japan and England were overwhelmingly characterized by differences rather than similarities, however, and such an idea of equivalence was hard to accept and nearly impossible to realize in the practice of translation. Nevertheless, the Japanese felt that it was strategically vital and politically crucial to insist on equivalence and symmetry. The idea of cultural comparability was inextricable from the basic quid pro quo principle of international diplomacy.

The fact that an English text could be translated into Japanese, and vice versa, was seen at least partially as an act of demonstrating Japan's cultural compatibility with Britain at a time when the British Empire ruled the world. Further, the Japanese aspiration to stand side by side with the British may well have been more than just a quest for cultural legitimacy. Its own imperial agenda did not lag long behind its confrontation with the Western threats in the mid-nineteenth century: Japan was to be the Britain of at least the Far East.

The difficulty in actually translating from English to Japanese was immense. When John Stuart Mill's *On Liberty* was translated in 1871, the translator had to diverge from the tract into a summary of Mill's life, as he was unable to naturalize the exotic political text. Shakespeare's plays were "translated" into *kabuki* productions in the 1870s via Charles and Mary Lamb's *Tales*, a rendition of the plays designed for children. Thus, it was a remarkable feat that by Soseki's time, merely a generation later, Shakespeare's texts had been "Japanized" together with many canonic works including eighteenth-century, Romantic, and Victorian poems and novels. Whether or not such textual transformations into Japanese were "accurate" requires a different study in a different context. What matters here is that the task was carried out and that it contributed to the formation of a bourgeois culture, and along with it, "literature."

The Japanese word for literature, *bungaku*, had been in use for many centuries. Earlier it had meant "studies" in general, or "textual commentaries," and not (1) literary productions, a category of aesthetic writing and performance considered distinct from others such as rituals, ceremonies, science, religion, history, and philosophy; or (2) organized studies thereof, an institutionalized discipline. This newer formulation arose in the West at the end of the eighteenth century. Historically, it was implicated in the development of national/regional consciousness at the time when Christianity was losing its hold on Europe and secularization was on the rise. Literature emerged as nationalism began to require the unifying myth for a nation-state for governance, especially at the time when Europe encountered the non-West in its program of colonial expansion. English literature, for example, was organized by colonial administrators in India earlier than in England, according to a recent study, as Britain faced the need to explain itself to the Indian subjects.[9] Literature was also useful as the ruling class was confronted with the proletariat displaced by the expansion of industrial capitalism. Together with "culture," an even more diffuse idea, literature was to provide a sense of agreement and community among the disparate groups of a nation. The Meiji enlightenment leaders found a similar need for "literature" in Japanese society and used the word *bungaku* in the new sense that had spread by Soseki's time among writers and scholars. In short, by 1900 literature seems to have taken root in Japan with all its problematic contours intact.

People knew what was meant by several compound words of *bungaku*: *bungakusha* (men of letters), *bungaku-shumi* (arty taste), *bungaku seinen* (arty adolescent), and *bungakkai* (literary world). The specific application of the word—what belonged to literature and what didn't—however, was far from clear. The line between literature and history, or between literature and popular conventions, for instance, was blurred. It took decades to reach the vaguest agreement as to the circumference of literary work and performance.

Even less understood was the newly institutionalized discipline of literary studies, *bungaku* in the second sense. Even in the West, where "literature" has a longer history, the definition of literature has never been resolved, as those in academia well know vis-à-vis the conflicts among old New Criticism, new New Criticism, criticisms of difference, cultural studies, and "conventional" scholarship. The situation in nineteenth-century Japan was certainly no better.[10] As a matter of fact, the general uncertainty surrounding the nature of literature as a discipline was manifest in its academic organization itself. The University of Tokyo in the second half of the nineteenth century was in a constant flux. It changed its name and structure practically every year. In 1877 it established the School of Letters (Bungakubu), together with the School of Science and the School of Law, but the School of Letters was not a purely "literary" school. It comprised departments of philosophy, history, and political economy in the First Division (Dai-ikka) and a Department of Japanese and Chinese Literatures in the Second Division (Dai-nika). Courses in the English language and English literature were taught in all the departments in both divisions, but English literature as a discipline was not formed into a separate institutional unit until 1887.[11] When Soseki entered the university in 1890 and graduated from the Department of English three years later, the program had been pretty much established as a curriculum. What then did Soseki study, and how did he feel about his studies?

Natsume Soseki as an English Scholar

By the time Natsume Soseki succeeded Lafcadio Hearn as a lecturer in the English department at the Imperial University of Tokyo in 1903, most of the problems with English studies in Japan had already surfaced. The linguistic distance between the two languages, the uncertainties surrounding the discipline of literature, and the weight of nationalism that hung heavy on the studies of foreign literature at the height of imperialism—these issues confronted scholars at every stage in the newly evolving discipline of English literature in Japan, though they were only infrequently articulated.

There had been a succession of British and American teachers for nearly thirty years at the university. None of them before Lafcadio Hearn's arrival in 1892 was a distinguished scholar, and they automatically introduced in their courses the canon of English literature that was being established in their own home countries.[12] Thus, Soseki learned English literature from one James Main Dixon, a graduate of St. Andrew's at Edinburgh, who later taught at the University of Washington and the University of Southern California. Soseki recalled his teacher afterward before an audience of college students:

> [Dixon] told me to recite a poem or a sentence, or to write in English. He scolded me when I mispronounced a word or omitted an article. He asked in exams when Wordsworth was born or died, or how many Shakespearean folios were extant, and told us to list Scott's works chronologically. You young people would know whether these facts could enable us to understand what English literature is. No one had any idea from this what even literature could mean, not to say English Literature.[13]

Most teachers seem to have simply recycled what they had learned at their colleges, dutifully covering the eras and genres, filling mechanically the dates and facts of biographical and other events, and drilling in prosody and rhetoric. They gave little thought to what memorizing dates and names meant. There were a few among the foreign teachers who had been trained in philology in Germany, and they no doubt taught the most recent grammatic and scientific theories. They were not, nor could they have been, distracted by the idea of a possible difference between English literature in Japan and English literature in Britain or the United States. Nor were they concerned with what literature could mean in the context of Japanese society then. What was good in their home countries was of course good enough for their Japanese students. Facts were unchallengeable as long as they were facts. Whether such "universalism" and "positivism" deserve commendation or condemnation, the Japanese students were expected to swallow the teachings whole, without being told what it was that they were ingesting. There were very few students like Soseki who kept their nagging doubts alive.

Soseki's career in the English field lasted well beyond his student days. For over a decade he tried to accept the discipline as it was then practiced. As a student, he wrote on Whitman's poetry or the Romantic ideas of nature. After graduating from the university, he went on to teach and then in 1900 was ordered by the Ministry of Education to study in England for the purpose of learning English literature firsthand so that he might transplant it upon his return. Thus began the most miserable two years of his life. He attended W. P. Ker's lectures at London University, and finding them too elementary, had tutorials with W. J. Craig. Craig, however, was too preoccupied with his Arden Shakespeare Edition and, besides, could not take a Japanese scholar of English very seriously. Soseki had no one to talk to and was desperately lonely. He persisted nevertheless in pondering what literary studies meant and, what was more important for him, what it could mean for a Japanese to study English literature. He read, wrote, and collected books in nearly total isolation until he had a severe nervous breakdown.

The notes he kept in London were later organized into three essays, two of which are theoretical attempts to discover "universal literary forms" that would enable every scholar to approach literary works regardless of national borders. While *Theory of Form in English Literature* (*Eibungaku keishiki ron*, 1903) and *Theory of Literature* (*Bungaku ron*, 1907) are obvious failures, they nonetheless clearly display serious misgivings with academic criticism and scholarship as well as a determination to examine the validity of (foreign) literary studies to its logical end. *Literary Criticism* (*Bungaku hyoron*, 1909), on the other hand, is a more conventional literary history of eighteenth-century English literature.[14] This book is impressive in its range of information and shrewdness of judgment. Remarkable documents as they all are, Soseki's dissatisfaction with himself as a critic and a scholar is undisguised. He may not be accurate in calling his own works "corpses of failed attempts, or worse, corpses of deformed children,"[15] but his verdict on his own critical procedures as lacking in "clarity," "originality," and "methodology" emanating from a "confused mind" [16] will have to be accepted. A Japanese scholar of English literature, as Soseki saw it, had to either imitate what an English scholar had already said or make do with casual and arbitrary impressions, and thus he/she could not have the confidence of being a genuine scholar. The possibility of a Japanese scholar shaping a new opinion from his/her own perspective never seems to have occurred to Soseki. "If you want to be a scholar," he advised, "you should choose a universal subject. English literature will be a thankless task: in Japan or in England, you'll never be able to hold up your head. It's a good lesson for a presumptuous man like me. Study physics."[17] He gave up English soon thereafter and devoted himself to writing fiction. In fiction he could at least feel he was "true to himself" (*jiko honi*).[18]

Around the turn of the century, on the other hand, three Japanese published books in English that would represent Japanese culture and society from their own viewpoints. Uchimura Kanzo's *How I Became a Christian: Out of My Diary* (1895); Niitobe Inazo's *Bushido: The Soul of Japan* (1899), and Okakura Kakuzo's *The Ideals of Japan* (1903), *The Awakening of Japan* (1904), and *The Book of Tea* (1906) are all essentialist books pleading for the uniqueness of Japanese culture. Although their aspiration for situating Japanese culture among the ranks of world civilizations in its own terms is perfectly understandable, their placement of Japan in Asia as its leader is—even in the light of the turbulent years between the Sino-Japanese and Russo-Japanese Wars—dangerously prophetic of its disastrous adventures half a century later. It is notable, however, that by writing these texts in the language of the dominant other, the three men were seeking to make Japan available to the indifferent outside world and thereby to lessen Japan's marginality. Had they received a proper response from the Western intellectuals in a dialogue that would help them place Japanese culture and society in the world, the course of the modern Japan might have been different. They were, however, more or less ignored except by a very few, such as Ernest Fenollosa, who, though an "Orientalist," took an active interest in Japanese literature. Also, the sort of energy that had propelled these three ran out, and the disappearance of foreign teachers exacerbated the trend. The number of works in English by Japanese writers has been minimal ever since, and Japan's isolation has deepened.

The critical issues Soseki confronted were never vigorously discussed but rather were deliberately avoided, and institutionalization of English literature continued on. *Eigo seinen* (literally, English-language youths, translated as *The Rising Generation*) was launched in 1898 to serve—despite its ghastly title—as the central organizing paper of the English establishment of Japan to this day. A massive number of translation projects began to render most canonic texts of Britain and the United States available at a brisk pace. The founding fathers of English studies in Japan established their patriarchy in the 1920s, compiling dictionaries and publishing historical surveys and biographical accounts. A sizeable series of annotated texts was published in the 1920s as well, some of which still serve as the standard texts for students. Such productions lasted until the early 1940s when the intensifying Fifteen Years War silenced the students of enemy literature for several years.

Recent Studies

With the U.S. occupation after the Second World War, English studies revived and newer Anglo-American names were energetically introduced for several decades. Nevertheless, during the century and a quarter of English studies, the scholarly orientation has been remarkably consistent. Works and writers were usually mediated and contextualized by the totalizing historical narrative of English (and American) literature. Such history was segmented into *literary* histories and biographies. Theoretical studies of any kind were rarely attempted, and the long-tested interpretation and appreciation via annotations, impressions, and comments were substituted for scholarly investigations. What has prevailed then, is the ongoing doctrine of equivalence, which by emphasizing identification minimizes the significance of difference. The problems of English literature as they are faced in England are transplanted to become the problems of the Japanese study of English literature. There is nearly total indifference to the Japanese context in which such naturalization of alien perspectives must continually occur. Thus, Shakespeare studies by L. C. Knights and Frank Kermode—authoritarian and ethnocentric as they are—are accepted by Japan's scholars as authentic and, therefore, authoritative. In fact, it seems the more ethnically exclusive a critic is, the greater the respect proffered him/her. Take the nearly universal and unabated worship of T. S. Eliot in Japan. His Eurocentricity and Anglo-Catholicism are not only tolerated but in fact revered as the unassailable truth, as if the colonial attraction to the metropolitan and imperial center were the desirable and inevitable gesture of a cultured sophisticate. Eliot's *Idea of a Christian Society* and *Notes toward the Definition of Culture* are taken at face value as *the* textbooks for understanding culture. Thus, Aimé Césaire, George Lamming, and Ngugi wa Thiong'o, who might propose to them alternative arts and views, are by and large unread by the non-Western Japanese. Edward Said's *Orientalism* has been read principally as a part of the Middle East discourse and is viewed as having little to do with Japan or cultural understanding generally.

Younger scholars continue to take note of new theoretical developments in Europe and the United States. New names are again becoming familiar to the Japanese scholars and students. As never before, new works—by Derrida, Foucault, feminists, Jameson and Frankfurt theorists, Eagleton, and lately, so-called New Historicists—are being introduced and translated. Although enthusiasm with the new in the West is considerably less visible now than it was in the late 1940s through the 1960s, the English studies business seems far from bankrupt. Thus, the April 1991 issue of *Eigo seinen* (*The Rising Generation*) is devoted to "Rereadings of Literary History." One scholar writes about the Marxist perspective, efficiently and intelligently summarizing Jameson, Eagleton, and Benedict Anderson and touching on some other issues such as the *Tempest* criticism in recent days. Another discusses "New Historicism" as he criticizes Stephen Greenblatt and his company (Louis Montrose, Don Wayne, and Catherine Gallagher are on his list). Still another scholar introduces feminist criticism, briefly mentioning Lillian Robinson, Showalter, Gubar and Gilbert, Toril Moi, Irigaray, and many others. Although the writing is not acute or insightful, it does well the job of listing active names. All are indeed good introductory essays, useful to curious beginners. What is absent in all of the articles, however, is any indication of the awareness of the meaning of these critics and theorists in the context of both English studies in Japan and Japanese society/culture itself. Whatever New Historicism may mean in the United States (is it the white man's—or the humanist's—last hope?), can it mean the same thing in Japan? Do these critics in Japan also believe in the hermetic autonomy of history that will enclose (or foreclose) the possibility of resistance and opposition? How does the Japanese scholar situate New Historicism in Japan's own social and historical context? Shouldn't there be a new generation of Sosekis? There is no indication of new Sosekis gnawed by similar doubts. Instead, there is only the old acceptance of the authority of the West—even when a Western critic questions the authority of the West![19] Despite the newness of the names now being cited in Japan, it is the continuity and persistence of the old habit, rather than the freshness and originality of an unfamiliar evolution, that are striking at present.

The most authoritative survey of English studies in Japan is a collection of essays by leading scholars in the field that examines the hundred years since 1868 (*Nihon no Eigaku hyaku-nen*). As is to be expected of works by Japanese scholars nowadays, it is comprehensive and informative. What is most striking about the publication, however, is the nearly complete absence in it of historically interpretive speculation. Japan's contact with the West in the nineteenth century was a moment of heightened self-consciousness of Japan in the world, as has been discussed above. The writers and students of the time were alerted to the difference of the self from the other, and this shock of discovery brought all habits of thought into an unprecedented crisis. The Japanese accepted the challenge to undertake monumental reforms and adaptations in a struggle against perceived colonial subjugation. Understanding English was a part of this program. Their task was carried out, and they survived the crisis. Yet the centenary project neither interprets nor evaluates the historical development as a whole or individual scholars and their works specifically. As if in fear of possibly desecrating the memories of their ancestors, they refrain from the job of criticism and merely celebrate in reverence. A critical analysis of the mid-nineteenth-century crisis is yet to be undertaken.

More recently, the Pacific War placed English studies in a singular circumstance. Scholars were, according to an article in the hundred-year history, "devoted" to the literature of England,[20] and yet were prohibited from pursuing it further by the leaders of their country. The author of the article says that research and teaching were entirely suspended, although speculation continued in agonized silence throughout the wartime crisis. After the summer of 1945, they reflected on the war experience, and tried to make sense of English studies in Japan. The article is a deeply personal account of the war experience, and it contains the potential for important questions. What is remarkable about the article, however, is that there is no intellectual engagement in it concerning the question of Japan in the world, the Japanese imperialist ambition interlocked with Western hegemonism, of which the studies of English in Japan have been a part. It remains mum even about the nature of the particular difficulties faced by the scholars of English. Did they approve of the war? Did they oppose and resist? If they did not, why not? If they did, how? If they were bewildered and disabled, where did this paralysis and impotence come from? Power and literature, literature and culture, politics and culture, economy and academia—such issues are simply ignored in the ongoing studies of English, as the author of the article and other scholars reflect on the critical war years in peaceful retrospection. Even now, several decades after the so-called postwar period, at this safe distance of time, there has been no significant statement concerning the crisis of scholarship as it was implicated in the devastating militarism of domination, aggression, and suppression. All the familiar repetitions of modular annotations, timely introductions, arbitrary impressions, and self-serving reminiscences ("I met Northrop Frye" and "when I had my last talk with Samuel Beckett") fill the intellectual vacuity of academia. However accurate, clever, or sensitive, such undertakings are trivial, or worse. Instead of modular segmentations and random fragmentations, all critical notes need to be aligned. English and Chinese literatures, literature and arts, culture and politics, economy and academia, the state and intellectuals—all must be reconnected and reexamined.

The situation of literary scholarship in other parts of the world might not be much better.[21] Cynicism and quietism are certainly not limited to Japan. Nevertheless, questions are being raised by a few nearly everywhere in the world as to the efficacy of the nation-state as the form of governance or as a space for study, or as to literature as a discrete discipline, or even concerning "culture" as a viable concept. National literature as it existed in the late nineteenth century, or even as late as the 1960s, is now very much in doubt in a good many places. For "literature" to be alive, it may require a different organization in a different context. Shouldn't the problem be unambiguously acknowledged and confronted in Japan as well, so that the vigor of critical speculation can be restored?[22] There are scholars outside of Japan who are eager to hear from their Japanese colleagues how they read, interpret, organize, and reorganize English—or any other—literature.

A BORDERLESS WORLD?

....

From Colonialism to Transnationalism and the Decline of the Nation-State

First published in Critical Inquiry *in 1993, this influential essay about the transforming role of the nation-state became one of the early and essential contributions to the debate about globalization. The piece also marks a crucial de-emphasis of literary and cultural analysis by Miyoshi as he stresses the necessity for humanities-based scholars to study and intervene within political and economic debates usually reserved for social scientists.*—ED.

Discourse and practice are interdependent. Practice follows discourse, while discourse is generated by practice. As for the discourse on colonialism, there has been a long lineage of engagements with the history of colonialism. One recalls essays by practioners like John Locke, Edmund Burke, James Mill, and Thomas Macaulay early on, and critiques of the practice by Hobson, Lenin, Luxemburg, and Schumpeter, among many others, since the height of imperialism. Numerous metropolitan fiction writers are darkly obsessed by the presence of remote colonies, from Melville and Flaubert, to Conrad and André Gide. Actually, hardly any Western writer, from Jane Austen to Thomas Mann, from Balzac to D. H. Lawrence, could manage to escape from the spell of modern expansionism. The modern West depends on its colonies for self-definition, as Edward Said's book, *Culture and Imperialism* (1993), argues.

In the area of literary theory and criticism, however, the discourse on colonialism has a surprisingly brief history. One needs to remember that writers of the negritude movement and other third-world writers like Aimé Cesaire, C. L. R. James, Frantz Fanon, and George Lamming[1] began to voice their views from the oppositionist perspective soon after the end of the Second World War.[2] And yet, it was only fifteen years ago—well after the disappearance of administrative colonialization from most regions of the world—that the discourse on colonialism entered the mainstream of Western theory and criticism.[3] Examining history from the perspective of personal commitment to resistance, Said's *Orientalism* dramatically heightened the consciousness of power and culture relations in 1978, vitally affecting segments of disciplines in the humanities.[4] In other words, it was not until years after the end of formal colonialism between 1945 and 1970 that theory was enabled to negotiate issues of colonialism as an admissible factor in criticism. The time gap of a good many decades in literary history here is interesting enough if only it demonstrates the discipline's habitual unease and disinclination in recent times to engage with extratextual matters, especially those concerning the imminent transfer of powers and resources. The history of decolonization and the memory of administrative and occupational colonialism, dangerously verging on nostalgia at times, are the base on which colonial and minority discourses have been built in recent years.[5]

The circumstances surrounding this process of "liberation" and "independence," however, have no widely accepted narrative as yet. Does colonialism survive today only in a few places, such as Israel, South Africa, Macao, Ireland, and Hong Kong? Does the rest of the world enjoy the freedom of postcoloniality? The problem we face now is how to understand today's global configuration of power and culture, which is both similar and different vis-à-vis the historical metropolitan-colonial paradigm. This essay is concerned with such transformation and persistence in the neocolonial practice of displacement and ascendancy, and with its specular engagements in discourse. The current academic preoccupation with "postcoloniality" and "multiculturalism" looks suspiciously like another alibi to conceal the actuality of global politics. This essay argues that colonialism is even more active now in the form of transnational corporatism.

We might begin with the beginning of the decolonization process.[6] The end of the cold war in 1989 has enabled us to look back at the history of the past half-century—or an even longer period—from a less inertial perspective. We are, for instance, once again reassessing the end of the Second World War, which radically altered the world system. The destruction of

German and Japanese aggressions did not result in the full resuscitation of the hegemony of the European industrial states. The West European nations, especially Britain and France, were too seriously injured to be able simultaneously to rebuild their domestic industrial bases and to sustain their military forces to dominate over their colonies. In retrospect, the Soviet Union kept up the front of a military superpower while disastrously wrecking its production and distribution systems. Although the avowed war objective of Germany and Japan—liberation and decolonization through the "New World Order" (*die neue Ordnung* and *sekai shin chitsujo* in Axis slogans)—was a total sham, the colonized of the world that had sided with their master states in the Second World War seized the day and would not settle for less than independence and autonomy. Liberation was demanded and allowed to take place over the several subsequent decades, albeit under varying circumstances.

After the Second World War, independence appeared to mark the end of a period of humiliating and exploitive colonial domination that had lasted anywhere from decades to centuries over at least 85 percent of the earth's land surface. And yet freedom and self-rule—for which the colonized had bitterly struggled often at the cost of immense sacrifice—were unexpectedly elusive. Decolonization did not realize emancipation and equality, nor did it provide new wealth or peace. Instead, suffering and misery continued nearly everywhere in an altered form, in the hands of a different agency. Old compradors took over, and it was far from rare that they went on to protect their old masters' interest in exchange for compensation. Thus the welfare of the general population saw little improvement; in fact, in recent years it has worsened in many old colonies with the possible exceptions of the East Asian newly industrialized economies (NIES) and the Association of Southeast Asian Nations (ASEAN).[7] The "postcolonial" deterioration which Basil Davidson recently called "the black man's burden"[8] was a result of double processes of colonization and decolonization, which were inextricably intermeshed. We are all familiar with the earlier stage. As the colonizers drew borders at will, inscribing their appropriations on a map, tribes were joined together or fragmented apart. Those who were encircled by a more or less arbitrary cartographic form were inducted into servitude on behalf of the distant and unseen metropolis. Western culture was to be the normative civilization, and the indigenous cultures were banished as premodern and marginal. And although subaltern resistance proved far more resilient than then believed, and colonial programs were never really fulfilled anywhere, the victor's presence was powerful enough in most places to maintain a semblance of control and order despite unceasing resistance and opposition.

With the removal of formal colonialism after the Second World War, the cartographic unit that constituted a colony was now perceived by both the departing colonizers and the newly freed to be a historically autonomous territory, that is to say a modern nation-state, with a national history, national language, national culture, national coherence, and finally the state apparatus of its own as symbolized by the national anthem, flag, museum, and map. The entity was, however, no more than a counterfeit reproduction of, and by, its former conqueror in many places, having neither a discrete history nor logic that would convince the newly independent citizens of its legitimacy or authenticity. Earlier, while struggling against the oppressors, self-definition was not difficult to obtain: oppositionism articulated their identity. Once the Europeans were gone, however, the residents of a colonial territory were thrown back on their old disrupted site, which had in the precolonial days operated on a logic and history altogether different. The liberated citizens of a colony now had to renegotiate the conditions of a nation-state in which they were to reside thereafter. Retroversion to nativism might have been an option, but third-worldism was now found to be fraught with inequalities and contradictions among various religions, tribes, regions, classes, genders, and ethnicities that had been thrown together in any given colonial territory. And the inefficiency in production and distribution was often horrendous. The golden age of memory proved to be neither pure nor just, nor even available, but a utopian dream often turned into a bloody nightmare. The hatred of the oppressors was enough to mobilize toward the liberation struggle, but was inadequate for the management of an independent state. As Fanon predicted earlier in the game, attempts at nativism have indeed ended in disastrous corruption and self-destruction, and they are still ongoing events in many parts of the world today. Once absorbed into the chronopolitics of the secular West, colonized space cannot reclaim autonomy and seclusion; once dragged out of their precoloniality, the indigenes of peripheries have to deal with the knowledge of the outside world, irrespective of their own wishes and inclinations. And yet the conditions of the modern nation-state are not available to most former colonies.[9]

One recalls that Western industrialized nations had the luxury of several centuries—however bloody—to resolve civil strifes, religious wars, and rural/urban or agricultural/industrial contradictions. Former colonies had far less time to work them out, and they were under the domination of alien powers. Thus most former colonies have yet to agree on the logic and objective of a geographic and demographic unit. The will to fragmentation battles with the will to totalization. One cannot forget that there were countless cases of overt and covert interventions by the United States and other colonial powers through economic, political, and military means. And peaceful progress has been structurally denied to them. Alliances among third-world states against first-world domination such as the Bandung Conference (1955), the Organization of Petroleum Exporting Countries (OPEC, 1960), United Nations Conference on Trade and Development (UNCTAD, 1964), and the New International Economic Order (NIEO, 1974) have all performed poorly, ultimately surrendering to the Breton Woods system, which the victorious West established in 1944 for the postwar management of the ruined world with the World Bank, International Monetary Fund (IMF), and General Agreement on Tariffs and Trade (GATT) as the three central economic instruments.

It is widely agreed that the nation-state is a modern Western construction. It can be further argued that the gradual ascendancy of nation-statism around 1800 in the West was a function of colonialism. Earlier, at the beginning of the modern period, the European monarchs sponsored adventurist projects, which were further propelled thereafter by the bourgeoisie's greater need for markets and resources to form a policy of colonial expansion. About the same time, as the industrial revolution increased production efficiency, urban areas received the influx of a large percentage of agricultural labor, creating a pool of surplus population.[10] These potentially rebellious unemployed and displaced workers needed to be depressurized in the margins of the labor market. Toward that end, the organizers of colonialism had to persuade their recruits and foot soldiers about the profitability as well as the nobility of their mission. Voyaging into distant and savage regions of the world was frightening enough, and the prospects of sharing the loot were far from assured. Above all, bourgeois leaders had to conceal their class interests, which sharply conflicted with the interests of the populace at large. They needed crusaders and supporters who trusted their good faith, believed in the morality of their mission, and hoped for the eventual wealth promised for them. Thus the myth of nation-statism (i.e., the belief in the shared community ruled by a representative government) and the myth of *mission civilisatrice* (i.e., the racial superiority of the voyagers over the heathen barbarians) were perceived as complementary and indispensable. In such an "imagined [or manufactured] community,"[11] the citizens were bound by "kinship and communality"; they were "in it together." In the very idea of nation-statism, the colonialists found a politico-economical as well as moral-mythical foundation on which to build their policy and apology.

Thus the development of Western colonialism from the sixteenth to the mid-twentieth century coincides with the rise and fall of nation-statism. The fate of nation-statism in recent years, however, is not synonymous with the "Rise and Fall of the Great Powers," as Paul Kennedy argues.[12] The bourgeois capitals in the industrialized world are now as powerful, or even far more powerful, than before. But the logic they employ, the clients they serve, the tools available to them, the sites they occupy, and finally their identities have all changed. They no longer wholly depend on the nation-state of their origin for protection and facilitation. They still make use of the nation-state structure, of course, but their power and energy reside in a different locus, as I will argue later on.

Even before 1945, Winston Churchill sensed that Britain had to yield its imperial scepter to the United States. If not at the Yalta Conference, by the time he was voted out of Downing Street, he knew the management of the world was now in the hands of the United States. He was of course right. The colonial history since 1945 thus converges with U.S. history. At the end of the Second World War, the United States economy was finally free from all scars of the Depression. With the coming of the peace, however, the prospects were far from rosy. To downscale the wartime economy would mean a drastic rise in the unemployment figure (that had stood at a miniscule 1.2 percent in 1942) as well as an absolute plunge in production and consumption, resurrecting the nightmare of 1930. There were a series of labor strikes (steel, coal, rail, and port) in 1946; President Truman's veto of the Taft-Hartley Labor Act curbing strikes was overturned by the Congress in 1947. It was under such circumstances of economic tension and unease that the president decided to contain "communist terrorism" in Greece and Turkey in 1947, and the Marshall Plan was inaugurated to aid European reconstruction. The GNP that sank ominously by 19.04 percent in 1946 leapt back to a minus 2.75 percent in 1947; and if it remained at a stagnant 0.02 percent in 1949, the Korean War (whose origins are not as yet unambiguously determined)[13] saved the day: it rose by as much as 8.54 percent in 1950 and 10.34 percent in 1951.[14] Similarly, just about the time the Peace Treaty with North Korea was signed in 1953 (and resulted in a minor recession), the United States began to aid the French government in its anti-insurgency war in Southeast Asia, shouldering three-quarters of the costs; and the training of South Vietnamese troops commenced in 1955 after the catastrophic defeat of the French army at Dienbienphu in 1954. When President Eisenhower warned Americans against the "potential for the disastrous rise of misplaced power" in the hands of the "military-industrial complex" and the "scientific-technological elite,"[15] the security state system had already been firmly—perhaps irretrievably—established in the United States. (One notes that this was the decade in which the universities expanded to absorb the returned GIs, lowering the male-female college attendance rate well below the 1920s' level.[16] And in literary theory and practice, conservative ideology and formalist aestheticism of course dominated.)

The cold war, regularly reinforced by hot "anticommunist" skirmishes, then, was a pretty dependable instrument for U.S. economy to organize its revenues and expenditures, and to maintain a certain level of production and distribution. One notes in this connection that "in every year from 1951 to 1990, the Defense Department budget has exceeded the combined net profits of all American corporations." Although the U.S. Constitution does not accord the president the top economic power, "subordinate to the President/C.E.O. are the managers of 35,000 prime contracting firms and about 100,000 subcontractors. The Pentagon uses 500,000 people in its own Central Administrative Office acquisition network."[17] The Pentagon, in short, is the U.S. equivalent of Japan's Ministry of International Trade and Industry (MITI): it plans and executes a centrally organized economic policy. Thus it is more accurate to say that the national security questions were essentially economic in nature rather than the other way around: the

U.S. economy guided world relations rather than uncontrollable foreign threats determined the conditions of the U.S. economy.

Soon after the recession in 1957–1958, the Kennedy administration sought to expand international trade by lowering European Community tariffs through the GATT Kennedy Round. The so-called liberalization of trade in the early 1960s restored the integrated world market and encouraged direct foreign investment with the result of a marked rise in European investment by American enterprises. Such an expansion in international trade led to a rapid development of "multinational enterprises" and "transnational corporations," that is, giant companies that not only import and export raw and manufactured goods, but transfer capitals, factories, and sales outlets across the national borders, as will be explained more fully later on. And this history of economic organizations needs to be recalled here in the context of global "decolonization."

The fracture of the British Empire was accelerating throughout the 1960s with the loss of innumerable colonies, one after another—from Cyprus, Nigeria, and Kenya to Jamaica, Malaysia, and Singapore.[18] Having lost Indochina and other colonies in the 1950s, France, too, finally yielded Algeria in 1962. At the same time, the U.S. GNP increased at a brisk pace of 7 to 9 percent with fairly low inflation and unemployment rates. Economically and militarily invincible, the United States was ready to protect capitalist interests everywhere, but especially in Vietnam. If President Johnson tried to win support for his "Great Society" and "War on Poverty" programs by offering a Southeast Asian expedition to the conservative oppositions, his gamble was calamitous. As no one can easily forget, protests raged across the country, splitting the nation into doves and hawks, Clintons and Gores. On the antiwar demonstrators' enemy list, the names of defense-related corporations were conspicuous: General Motors, General Electric, DuPont, and Dow Chemical, to name a few. And it is many of these corporations that began during the sixties to set the pattern of systematic transfer of capitals and factories overseas. There were other factors, too: technological innovations in automation, synthetic chemistry, and electronic engineering, which produced an enormous accumulation of capitals and a remarkable improvement in communication and transportation as well. The U.S. policy of liberal trade as touched on earlier was both a response and an instigation of such a development.

In the late 1960s, the global domination of U.S. multinational corporations was unchallengeable. Mainly centered in the western hemisphere, and less in Africa and Asia, the U.S. foreign direct investment (FDI) amounted to a half of all the cross-border investments worldwide, far surpassing the British FDI, which stood at 20 percent, and the French FDI, at less than 10 percent.[19] Transnational corporations (TNC) meant U.S. transnationals then, and this pattern remained unchanged until the mid-1970s. The concentration of U.S. investments in Western Europe can be explained by high interest rates in Europe, the emergence of the European Economic Community, U.S. tax laws favorable to overseas profits, and comparatively low costs of skilled labor in Europe. The serious task of controlling the world order for the West was still assigned to the U.S. government that was charged with military and political programs of aid and intervention.[20]

Around 1970, European and Japanese TNCs emerged rapidly to compete with the U.S. counterparts, and their main target was none other than the advanced manufacturing industries in the United States itself. This bold move is explainable by several economic developments. First, the U.S. dollar was devalued after the Nixon administration froze wages and prices and suspended conversion of dollars into gold in 1971, making the U.S. attractive for foreign investment. Second, the U.S. market also recovered attractiveness after the political instability and unpredictability in the rest of the world as a result of the fourth Middle East war of 1973 and its consequent oil embargo. Third, the European and Japanese industrial recovery was strong enough to wage a vigorous investment campaign in the United States. Finally, the trade friction intensified in time, and European and Japanese manufacturers saw an advantage in building plants inside the U.S. market. The U.S. share of TNCs was still overwhelming, but in the 1980s it fell to one-third as against Britain at 18 percent, West Germany at 10 percent, and Japan at 8 percent.

In 1985 the United States negotiated a depreciation of the dollar at the G5 meeting in New York. The Plaza Agreement forced the dollar down by one half against the yen, raising Japan's currency value by 100 percent. Though aimed at an increase of U.S. exports to Japan and a decrease of Japan's exports to the United States, the measure was not really effective. Before long, moreover, Japanese TNCs realized the power of the strengthened yen, with which they proceeded to stage an aggressive campaign of investment, while cutting prices as much as they could to maintain their market share. What characterizes this stage of multinational development is, in addition to continued investment in the United States, a general concentration on four regional targets: tax havens (e.g., Curaçao in the Dutch Carribean); OPEC nations; Asian NIES (South Korea, Taiwan, Hong Kong, and Singapore); and ASEAN countries (Thailand, Malaysia, Indonesia, the Philippines, Singapore, and Borneo). Many of these nations were ruled by authoritarian governments that banned labor unions and opposition parties, thus achieving political "stability"—a minimal requirement for a large-scale TNC commitment. There has also been a gradual development of TNCs among the OPEC, NIES, Mexico, and India, and others, investing in each other as well as the United States. Also, smaller corporations (i.e., those with capital outlays of between 100 and 500 million dollars) in both industrialized and less industrialized nations were active in transnationalizing their operations. And this coexistence of TNCs of various origins (including joint ventures) is what makes the analysis of economic hegemony so complicated and difficult.

What emerges from this is an increasingly tightly woven network of multinational investments among European Community, North American, and East Asian countries, gradually transforming the *multi*national corporations into *trans*national corporations. The distinction between the two corporate categories is certainly problematic: the terms are frequently used interchangeably. If there are differences, they are more or less in the degrees of alienation from the countries of origin. The range of international trading might be explained developmentally as follows. First, simple export/import activities of domestic companies, linking up with local dealers. Then, the companies take over overseas distribution and carry out their manufacturing, marketing, and sales overseas. Finally, the transnational corporations denationalize their operations by moving the whole business system including capital, personnel, and research and development. This final stage is reached when a corporation promotes loyalty to itself among shareholders, employees, and clients rather than to its country of origin or host countries. Thus, a "multinational" corporation (MNC) is one that is centrally headquartered in a nation, operating in a multiple number of countries from it. Its high-echelon personnel largely consists of the nationals of the country of origin, and the corporate loyalty is, though increasingly autonomous, finally tied with the home nation. A truly "transnational" corporation, on the other hand, might no longer be closely tied to its nation of origin, but is adrift and mobile, ready to settle anywhere and exploit any state including its own, as long as the affiliation serves its own interest.[21]

Let me repeat here that a sharp distinction between TNC and MNC is impossible, since the precise extent of denationalization of a corporation is not readily determinable. There is, for instance, no systematic study of the TNC tax obligations as against the MNC counterparts, or of the comparararative patterns of foreign direct investment between the two forms. MNCs are as self-regarding as TNCS. However, a recent tendency toward lesser national identification and greater corporate self-interest is nonetheless discernible. In other words, despite the ongoing dependence on the state apparatus (e.g., the military when needed), multinational corporations are in the process of *de*nationalization and *trans*nationalization.

There are still relatively few corporations that completely fit the TNC specification, but there are examples—such as Asea Brown Bovari among large-scale companies and Yaohan among smaller specimens. Starting in Sweden, Asea Brown Bovari, with annual revenues of over 25 billion dollars, has no geographic center.[22] Yaohan began as a Japanese grocery-store chain, which severed its Japanese tie, moving first to Brazil and then resettling—for now—in Hong Kong. It should be noted here that the corporate tax in Japan was 49.98 percent, whereas the Hong Kong counterpart stood at 16.5 percent in 1989.[23] Its chairman declares that his real target is the one billion Chinese in the twenty-first century.[24] Many MNCs on the other hand are on the alert between their home countries and host countries as they map out their strategies for maximizing profits.

TNCS of this type became more visible in the 1980s, although the loss of national sovereignty to the multinational companies had been discussed since the 1960s, or even earlier.[25] That this development should take place in the eighties was no accident. After President Carter's stagflation in the late seventies, President Reagan had a clearly defined program to promote private interests, supposedly with the conviction that strong private sectors would necessarily benefit the populace as a whole (but, in all likelihood, by simply following the cue cards handed over by the corporate designers of the policy). It is during this decade that the transfer of wealth from the poor to the rich was carried out with remarkable efficiency. Corporate taxes were cut. Public services such as education, welfare, and medicine were reduced in the name of efficiency, resulting in a marked reliance on private enterprises such as Federal Express and private security services instead of "inefficient" public institutions such as the U.S. Postal Service or municipal police departments. There has even been talk of privatizing penal systems and public universities.[26] This decade also witnessed the reduction of the income tax rates for the higher brackets: the top tax on wages in 1945 was 94 percent, and in the 1950s through 1970s it was in the 87 to 70 percent range, while with President Reagan's arrival the top tax on wages fell to 50 percent, and in 1991 under the Bush administration it stood at 28 percent.[27] Thus the top one percent of Americans received 60 percent of the after-tax income gains between 1977 and 1989, while the bottom 40 percent of families had actual declines in income. According to the May 6, 1991, *Business Week* cover story, "Are CEOs Paid Too Much?," the typical CEO pay was more than eighty-five times that of a typical manufacturing worker's pay in the United States, while the comparable ratio in Japan was only seventeen times.[28] Kevin Phillips reports in "Down and Out: Can the Middle Class Rise Again?," however, that "the pay of top corporate executives . . . soared to 130 to 140 times that of average workers, even while real or inflation-adjusted wages continued their 1980's decline" (*New York Times Sunday Magazine*, January 10, 1993, 20). Examples of illicit and semi-illicit business practice are too many to be enumerated here—from dubious mergers and appropriations, junk bond scams, to the savings and loans scandal. The number of poor in 1991 soared to 35.7 million, that is, 14.2 percent of the total population, which is the highest figure since 1964.[29] In such an atmosphere of intensified self-regard and self-interest, corporate managers took it for granted that their business was to maximize profits— nearly regardless of consequences. They would go wherever there were lower taxes and greater profits.

It should be emphasized here that this move toward transnationalization was not just American, but global. Leslie Sklair's *Sociology of the Global System* (1991), one of the most comprehensive studies of TNCs (from a Gramscian and feminist perspective), points out that "while there is no convincing evidence that the TNCs can bring salvation to the Third World, in many poor countries the TNCs are seen as responsible for the only bright spots in the economy and society. . . . [TNCs] are very widely sought after and they carry high prestige."[30] As mentioned earlier, not only industrialized nations but NIEs and other economies also produce corporations that would maximize profits by freely crossing national borders. However one may view the TNC practice, TNCs are not beholden to any nation-states, but seek their own interests and profits globally. They represent neither their home countries nor their host nations, but simply their own corporate selves.

There are of course many other contributing factors. TNCs are immensely powerful. According to a World Bank report, 64 out of 120 countries had a gross domestic product of less than ten billion dollars in 1986, while in the same year sixty-eight TNCs in mining and manufacturing had annual sales over ten billion dollars, and all the top fifty banks, the top twenty security firms, and the top twenty-nine insurance companies had net assets in excess of ten billion. That is, of the largest one hundred economic units, more than fifty are TNCs.[31] Because of the rapid development in sophisticated computer technology—often justifiably called the third industrial revolution—in communication, transportation as well as manufacturing, the transfer of capitals, products, facilities, and personnel has been unprecedentedly efficient. Private funds—to the amount of billions of dollars at one transaction —flow from one industrial center to another, totalling every business day nearly one trillion dollars at the Clearing House Interbank Payment System in New York City alone.[32] It goes without saying that this development weakens the interventionary power of central national banks such as the Bundes Bank of Germany, Nihon Ginko of Japan, and the Federal Reserve of the United States.

Post-Fordist production methods enable TNCs to move their factories to any sites that can offer trained and trainable cheap labor forces—as long as there are political stability, tax inducements, adequate infrastructure, and relaxed environmental protections rules. Low civil rights consciousness, too, including underdeveloped unionism and feminism is crucial: although female labor is abused everywhere, the wage difference between the sexes is still greater in the third world—the target area for TNCs.[33] Global transportation is so efficient that the division of labor across national borders is now a given. Parts are produced in many places to be assembled— depending on particular tariffs, labor conditions, and other factors—at a locale strategically close to the targeted market.[34] There are innumerable joint ventures such as GM and Toyota, or GE, RCA, and Thomson SA. Banks and other financial institutions also move across borders with increasingly fewer impediments.

In this MNC/TNC operation, at any rate, manufactured products are advertised and distributed globally, being identified only with the brand-names, not the countries of origin. In fact, the "country of origin" is itself becoming more and more meaningless. The "Buy American" drive is increasingly a hollow battle plan: Honda Accord is manufactured in Ohio from 75 percent U.S. parts, while Dodge Stealth is made in Japan by Mitsubishi.[35] Or in the new Boeing 777 program, the Boeing Company makes only the wings, nose structure, and engine nacelles. "The rest of the wide-body airplane will come from hundreds of subcontractors in North America, Japan, and Europe." Almost no TV sets are wholly domestic products. "Zenith Electronics Corp., the last U.S.-owned television company, is moving final assembly of all of its large-screen sets to Mexico."[36] A TNC selects the place of operation, in short, solely by a fine calculus of costs and profits, involving the entire process of research, development, production, distribution, advertising, marketing, financing, and tax obligations.

TNCs are faced with the task of recruiting workers thoroughly familiar with local rules and customs as well as the specific corporate policies for worldwide operation. For that purpose, their workers usually involve various nationalities and ethnicities. This aspect is significant in several ways. First, TNCs will increasingly require from all workers loyalty to the corporate identities rather than to their national identities. Second, the employees of various nationalities and ethnicities must be able to communicate with each other. In that sense, TNCs are at least officially and superficially trained to be color-blind and multicultural.[37] Despite the persistent recurrence of violent racist events in the United States, it should be remarked, its immigration regulations were radically changed in 1965 to reject the ethnically defined quota system as set out by the 1952 McCarran-Walter Act. In the revised Immigration Reform and Control Act of 1986 and the November 1990 reform bill, priorities are given to skills rather than ethnicities: TNCs, especially, are allowed to claim a quota from the category of forty thousand aliens with special abilities in addition to the general category of skilled experts and professionals.[38] Third, the need of a huge pool of such skilled workers creates a transnational class of professionals who can live and travel globally, while freely conversing with their colleagues in English, the lingua franca of the TNC era. The formation of the transnational class, or what Robert B. Reich calls "symbolic analysts" in his *The Work of Nations*, is itself a development that calls for further study, especially as this exclusive and privileged class relates—or not—to those kept outside: the unemployed, the underemployed, the displaced, and the homeless.[39] The third industrial revolution, very much like the earlier two, creates an immense semiskilled and unskilled surplus of labor, causing a huge demographic movement across the world and feeding into the mass underclass of in every industrialized region.

Reich has little to say about the fate that awaits those who won't be able to move up to the class of privilege. The question remains, then, as to how the new elite managers compare to the professional class of modern industrial society and how it relates to those left marginalized and abandoned in the TNC structure. Earlier, as traditional society transformed itself into bourgeois capitalist society in the West, intellectuals and professionals who served in the planning and execution of the capitalist agenda were led to think of themselves as free and conscientious critics and interpreters. In the age of TNCs, they are even more shielded and mediated by the complexity and sophistication of the situation itself because transnational corporatism is by definition unprovincial and global, that is, supposedly free from insular and idiosyncratic constrictions. If clear of national and ethnic blinders, the TNC class is not free of a new version of "ideology-less" ideology that is bent on the efficient management of global production and consumption, hence of world culture itself. Are the intellectuals of the world willing to participate in transnational corporatism and be its apologists? How to situate oneself in this neo–Daniel Bell configuration of transnational power and culture without being trapped by exitless nativism seems to be the most important question that faces every critic and theorist the world over at this moment, to which I will return later.

The decline of nation-statism has been accelerated by the end of the cold war. War activates nationalism and patriotism inasmuch as hostility deepens the chasm that cuts "them" off from "us." The binary alignment that was present in all foreign relations during the cold war was abruptly removed in 1989. With the demise of authoritarian socialist states, bourgeois capitalism looked as if it had triumphed over all rivals. Whether such a reading is correct or wrong, the disappearance of "the other side," together with the end of administrative colonialism, has placed the nation-state in a vacant space that is ideologically uncontested and militarily constabulized. The choreographed display of high-tech force of destruction by the United States during the Gulf War could not conceal the lack of objective and meaning in that astounding military exercise. The Gulf War is the war of ultimate snobbery, all style, to demonstrate power for the sake of power in a world after the cold war. It expressed the contempt of the rich against the poor, just as the military and political force was being replaced in importance by the economic and industrial power. The single superpower, the United States, executed the war, of course, but as the "sharing" of the military expenses among the "allied nations" demonstrates, the war was fought on behalf of the dominant corporate structure rather than the United States, which served after all as no more than a mercenary. Does this mean that from now on the armed forces of the United States are in service to the corporate alliance with little regard for its own people's interest? Is the state apparatus being even more sharply cut off from the welfare of the people than before? Wealth that generates right and might seems to have overwhelmed power that creates wealth.[40]

Against the effective operation of TNCs, the nation-states more and more look undefined and inoperable. Although the end of the cold war also loosened the ties that bound nation-states such as the former Soviet Union and Yugoslavia while encouraging separatist movements in Scotland, Spain, India, Canada, and many other places,[41] these are expressions of ethnicism, not nationalism. To quote from *The New International Economy* by Makler, Martinelli, and Smelser, these independence movements are "a kind of mirrored reflection of the decline of the viability of nationalism as a politically unifying force, a decline occasioned moreover, by the economic and political internationalization."[42]

Admittedly, it is more customary nowadays to regard as "nationalistic" the "ethnic cleansing" of the Serbs, the Muslim and Hindu antagonism in India, or Islamic fundamentalism, but it seems at least as sensible to think of such neorevivalism, neoracism, and neoethnicism in conjunction with the decline of nation-statism. The fragmenting and fragmented units in these sites of contestation in the world are not newly awakened agents for the construction of autonomous nations, but for the abandonment of the expectations and responsibilities of the the politicoeconomic national projects. Ethnicity and raciality are being brandished as the refuge from the predicaments of the integrated political and economic body. As globalization intensifies, neoethnicism appeals because of its brute simplicity and reductivism—in this rapidly altering and bewilderingly complex age. But over all the separatist aspirations—from Czechoslovakia, Yugoslavia, India, and Myanmar—hover the dark shadows of economic anxieties which none of these "nationalist" units have sufficiently taken cognizance of as they are inflamed into the rush toward independence and purification. It is as if the inadequacy of the nation-state is now fully realized, and the provincial strongmen are all trying to grab a piece of real estate for keeps before all is incorporated and appropriated by transnational corporatism.

Those who have thought of the nation-state as a historical bourgeois invention for the sake of protecting national economy from the threats of free democracy might hail the negative effects of transnationalism on the nation-state. To the extent that war was an unavoidable product of national economy, as argued by Marx in his 1848 *Communist Manifesto*, there is something exhilarating about the demise of nation-statism. At the same time, the state did, and still does, perform certain functions, for which there is as of now no substitute agency. It defines citizenship, controls currency, imposes law, protects public health, provides general education, maintains security, and, more important, guides national economy (though little acknowledged in the United States, as I have pointed out earlier), all with revenues raised through taxation. In enumerating these fuctions, however, it becomes indisputably clear that the list is not a list of achievements, but of failures. In all these items, the state as a political authority seems biased and compromised. It is not the nation as an integrated whole, but certain classes, the privileged in it, that receive a major portion of benefits from the state performing these tasks. The state fails to satisfy most of its sectors; on the contrary, it leaves most of its citizenry resentful. Thus, there is a palpable aversion to taxation among all segments of population, rich or poor, although everyone knows that tax is the glue that keeps the nation-state coherent. The nation-state, in this sense, no longer works; it is thoroughly appropriated by transnational corporations. Thus for some, it is a sheer annoyance, but for a vast majority it serves as a nostalgic and sentimental myth that offers an illusion of a classless organic community of which everyone is an equal member. Such an illusion of national community stubbornly persists.

Let me take one more example of the use of nation-statism. The transnationalization of industrial production and distribution in a highly complex web across national borders largely invalidates disputes concerning import/export surplus/deficit. Robert Reich is right in arguing that wealth is accumulated at the site where research and development is carried out and managers and technicians reside, not where the corporations or manufactured goods originate.[43] As I mentioned above, the identification of the countries of origin of manufactured goods is increasingly becoming impossible, and parts of a product come from all over. The "local content" regulations are nearly impossible to enforce. Of all the U.S. imports, as much as 30 percent is from the U.S. transplants overseas, for instance, that have been established over the last several decades.[44] Further, MNCs and TNCs are indifferent as they create regions of poverty in the middle of their own countries of origin, such as the United States and Britain. It is quite possible to argue that the trade protectionists such as so-called revisionists in the U.S.-Japan trade discourse are conscious or unconscious participants in a patriotic scam to conceal the class interests involved in the bilateral trade friction. Protectionism benefits certain sectors of industry and hurts others, just as does free trade. In other words, protectionism and free trade grant favors to different portions of industry in the short run, although protectionism invariably hurts the consumers. Only when the coherence of a total nation-state is unswervingly desired and maintained, can the practice of protectionism persuade the population at large. In the present world, however, there is no example of such unquestioned national coherence—not even the notorious Japan, Inc. The "revisionists" merely stir the residual patriotic sentiment so that they can keep the illusion of national unity a while longer.[45]

TNCs are obviously no agents of progress for humanity. First, since the raison d'être of TNCs is in the maximization of profits, the welfare of the people they leave behind, or even the people in the area where they operate, is of little or no concern to them. The host governments that are eager to invite TNCs cannot be expected to be particular about the workers' employment conditions or the general citizens' public welfare. The framework of nation-state is deteriorating also in the host nations that are often controlled by dictators and oligarchs. All TNCs are finally in alliance, though competitive in several basic aspects.[46] The transnational class is self-concerned, though aggressively extroverted in cross-border movement. The labor union, which might be expected to offer assistance to workers, on the other hand, still operates within the framework of national economy. It is at present simply unthinkable that transnational labor unions will take joint actions across national borders, equalizing their wages and working conditions with their cross-border brothers and sisters. Imagine United Automobile Workers officials meeting with Mexican union representatives to negotiate together a contract with the GM management in a maquila plant![47] TNCs might raise GNP or even per capita income, but it does not guarantee a better living for all citizens. So who finally protects the workers inside the United States or outside? The TNCs are far more transnational than the labor unions, generating the unemployed and underemployed everywhere, from Detroit to Manila, from Taipei to San Diego. There is little to be expected as of now from the residual nation-state or its alternatives in the way of protecting these people. What we have heard so far in relation to the North American Free Trade Agreement from the Bush administration, the Clinton transition group, or U.S. university experts promise very little indeed.[48] As Leslie Sklair summarizes, "The choice is more likely to be between more or less efficient foreign exploitative transnational corporations and highly protected and perhaps corrupt local, state, parastatal or private firms."[49]

Second, the rapid formation of the transnational class is likely to develop a certain homogeneity among its members. Even without the formation of TNCs, the world has been turning toward all-powerful consumerism in which brand names command recognition and attraction. Everywhere commodities are invented, transported, promoted, daydreamed over, sold, purchased, consumed, and discarded. And they are the cultural products of the transnational class. The member of such a class is the leader, the role model, of the 1990s and beyond, whose one gift is, needs to be, an ability to converse and communicate with each other. Cultural eccentricities are to be avoided, if not banned altogether. National history and culture are not to intrude, or not to be asserted oppositionally or even dialectically. They are merely variants of one "universal"—as in a giant theme park or shopping mall. Culture will be museumized, and the museums, exhibitions, and theatrical performances will be swiftly appropriated by tourism and other forms of commercialism. No matter how subversive at the beginning, variants will be appropriated aggressively by branches of consumerism such as entertainment and tourism, as were rap music, graffiti art, or even classical music and high arts. Cable TV and MTV absolutely dominate the world. Entertainment and tourism are huge transnational industries by themselves. The return to "authenticity," as has been mentioned earlier, is a closed route. There is nothing of the sort extant any longer in much of the world. How then to balance the transnationalization of economy and politics with the survival of local culture and history—without mummifying them in tourism and museumization—is *the* crucial question, for which, however, no answer has yet been found.[50]

Third, workers in search of jobs all over the world are changing global demography in this third industrial revolution, as mentioned earlier. They come, legally or illegally, from everywhere to every industrial center, in either industrialized or developing nations. TNCs are in need of them, though they are unwilling to provide them with adequate pay or care. Cut off from their homes, migrant workers disappear into huge urban slums without the protection of a traditional rural mutual dependence system. The struggle for survival does not allow any leisure in which to enjoy their pastoral memory. For those exploited alien workers in inner cities, consumerism alone seems to offer solace, if they are fortunate enough to have money for paltry pleasures. In Mexico City or Seoul, in Berlin or Chicago, migrants mix and compromise alongside other aliens from other regions. Neither nativism nor pluralism is in their thought. Survival is. "Multiculturalism" is a luxury largely irrelevant to those who live under the most wretched conditions. It is merely an "import strategy" of the TNC managers, as Mike Davis calls it.[51] In fact, it may very well turn out to be the other side of the coin of neoethnicism and neoracism.

Fourth, environmental destruction is vitally involved in the development of TNCs. Since one of the central reasons for cross-border move is to escape from stringent environmental regulations, the host government is not likely to enforce the pollution control rules. The effects of the damage caused in the industrialized areas as well as NIES and third-world regions, however, is not confined to these specific localities. The proposal made by

Lawrence Summers of Harvard and the World Bank to shift polluting industries from developed countries to the "underpolluted" third world is as foolish as it is invidious.[52] Far more truly transnational and universal than even the TNCs, the effects of enviromental violence inescapably visit everyone, everywhere. Air pollution, ozone layer depletion, acid rain, the greenhouse effect, ocean contamination, and a disrupted ecosystem are finally unavoidable no matter where the damage originates. The TNCs might escape from the regulators, but we are all—with no exception—victims. Who is there to control the environmental performance of TNCs globally? Are we to rely on the good sense of corporate planners to fight off catastrophy? Can we trust the fugitives from law to protect the law?[53]

Finally, academia, the institution that might play the principal role in investigating transnational corporatism and its implications for humanity, seems all too ready to cooperate rather than deliberate. The technical complexity of TNC mechanisms requires academic expertise in sophisticated research, explanation, and management of immense information data. Those in economics, political science, sociology, and anthropology as well as business administration and international relations are not expected to be harsh critics of the TNC practice, being all too compliant at least to be its explicators and apologists. Critics and theorists in the humanities, too, are not unsusceptible to the attraction of global exchange, as I will argue once more before I close.

TNCs continue colonialism. Like the pre-1945 colonialism, they operate over distance. While they homogenize regions, they remain aliens and outsiders in each place, faithful only to the exclusive clubs of which they are members. True, old colonialism was operated in the name of nations, ethnicities, and races, and transnational corporatism tends toward nationlessness. But as I have already mentioned, even the historical nation-state was actually an enabling institution for international enterprises. British colonialism made possible the East India Company, just as the U.S. government made possible the domination of the United Fruit Company in Central America. Colonialism never benefited the whole population of an adventurist nation. As J. A. Hobson argued nearly a century ago and as has been confirmed by scholars since,[54] colonialism enriched the rich and powerful of the home country and the compradors—at the expense of the populace at large. The trickle-down theory of the 1980s was, as it is always, a wishful fantasy or, or more likely, an unadulterated con game. It is indeed sobering to remember that the war in Vietnam cost a huge amount to the United States as a whole, which of course gained nothing from that old, exhausted Southeast Asian colony of France. And yet there were a good number of stockholders, executives, entrepreneurs, and employees of the U.S. defense industry who amassed fortunes over the millions of dead and wounded bodies and impoverished souls, both Vietnamese and American. Japanese industrial recovery, too, owes a great deal to the Korean and Vietnam Wars.

TNCs are unencumbered with the nationalist baggage. Their profit motives are unconcealed. They globally travel, communicate, and transfer people and plants, information and technology, money and resources. TNCs rationalize and execute the objectives of colonialism with greater efficiency and rationalism. And they are, unlike imperial invaders, welcomed by the leaders of developing nations. In order to exploit the different economic and political conditions among the current nation-states, they ignore the borders to their own advantages. When the need arises, however, they can still ask for the aid of the armed forces of their home/host states. And in the process patriotic rhetoric can be resurrected to conceal the true state of affairs, as the Gulf War clearly demonstrated. The military, in the meantime, is increasingly assuming the form of a TNC itself—being nearly nation-free! TNC employees, too, are satisfied with their locally higher wages. And yet there is no evidence that the whole population of a host country enjoys an improvement in welfare: let me repeat, a higher GNP or per capita income does not mean an equally enjoyed increase in wealth. As the host government represses labor organization and urban industrial centers generate surplus labor, wages can be lowered and inequality can intensify, at least for now.[55] Authoritarianism is unlikely to diminish. Oppression and exploitation continue. Ours, I submit, is not an age of *post*colonialism, but of intensified colonialism, even though it is under an unfamiliar guise.[56]

I am raising these issues as a participant in the discourse on colonialism. I have myself participated in a number of workshops and conferences on the subject. It is curious, however, how quickly "colonial" discourse has been replaced by "*post*colonial" discourse. There was a conference in Berkeley called "Beyond 'Orientalism'" in the spring of 1992. Soon thereafter, there was another at Santa Cruz, this time entitled "After Orientalism." During the subsequent fall, there were at least two more, one at Scripps College, called "Writing the Postcolonial," and another, though slightly different in orientation, at Santa Barbara entitled "Translating Cultures: The Future of Multiculturalism?" And above all there is a three-year project on Minority Discourse at the Humanities Research Institute, at University of California, Irvine. These are all recent Californian events, but there are many meetings and conferences on the subject everywhere, converting academics—us—into frequent fliers and globe-trotters. And there is, of course, an outpouring of articles in scholarly publications.[57]

Such activities are presumably politically engaged intellectual exercises. But if practice follows discourse, discourse must follow practice. Very much like studies in New Historicism, these are efforts once again to distance political actuality from direct examination. Once again, we are sanitizing our academic discourse on the ongoing political conditions—this time, around TNCs and their eager host governments. We might even be masking a secret nostalgia, as we devote our scholarly attention to "postcoloniality," a condition in history that is safely distant and inert, instead of seeking for alternatives in this age after the supposed "end of history." Similarly, multiculturalism looks suspiciously like a disguise of transnational corporatism that causes, of necessity, havoc with a huge mass of displaced workers helplessly seeking jobs and sustenance. Los Angeles and New York, Tokyo and Hong Kong, Berlin and London are all teeming with "strange-looking" people. And the U.S. academia quite properly studies them as a plurality of presences. But before we look distantly at them and give them over to their specialists, we need to know why they are where they are. What are the forces driving them, how do they relate to our everyday life? Who is behind all this drifting? The plurality of cultures is a given of human life: "our own tradition" is a fabrication as it has always been, everywhere. It is impossible not to study cultures of the others; the American curricula must include "alien" histories. But that is merely a beginning. In the recent rise in cultural studies and multiculturalism among cultural traders and academic administrators, inquiry stops as soon as it begins. What we need is a rigorous political and economical scrutiny rather than a gesture of pedagogic expediency. We should not be satisfied with recognizing the different subject-positions from different regions and diverse backgrounds. We need to find reasons for such differences—at least in the political and economic aspects

—and to propose ways to erase such "differences," by which I mean, political and economic inequalities. To the extent that cultural studies and multiculturalism provide students and scholars with an alibi for their complicity in the TNC version of neocolonialism, they are serving, once again, just as one more device to conceal liberal self-deception. By allowing ourselves to get absorbed into the discourse on postcoloniality or even post-Marxism, we are fully collaborating with the hegemonic ideology, which looks, as usual, as if it were no ideology at all.

OUTSIDE ARCHITECTURE

....

This essay originally appeared in 1996 in Anywise, *one of the several* Any *volumes that brought together architects and other thinkers to engage specific architectural ideas.* Anywise *was first held as a conference in Seoul in 1995 where Miyoshi criticized contemporary architecture for ignoring the everyday needs of most urban inhabitants. Critical of both modern architecture's utopianisms and the postmodern abandonment of utopian projects, Miyoshi urges architects to move outside their discipline in order to gain perspective on how their interests coordinate with the interests of global capital.*—ED.

Last year I was in Tokyo for a few days. After a stay at a midtown hotel that is monumental, elegant, cheerless, and exorbitant—but my favorite hotel nevertheless, with windows from which I could look down on the emperor's palace, the official residences of the prime minister and the chairmen of both houses of the parliament, the Supreme Court, and numerous corporate headquarters—I moved to the adjacent city of Yokohama for a conference. The highway between the cities is raised, and from the taxi I could see miles and miles of densely built homes that were small, drab, gray, and graced with hardly any parks, plazas, or even trees. I remembered that when George Bernard Shaw visited Tokyo early in the century, he called it an endless sprawl of slums. Tokyo in the first decades of this century was far more amenable than it is now, and still it failed to escape Shaw's bad-mouthing.

Several months ago I went to Taipei. Soon after my return home to California I read an article in the *New York Times* that called Taipei "filthy, arguably the least inviting city in Southeast Asia."[1] My Taiwanese friend later told me that at about the same time a German newspaper called Taipei a "pigsty." (He cheerfully added that his friends back home found the characterization both accurate and humorous.) As I recall walking the streets of Taipei and Keelung, a port city north of Taipei, I admit that I stopped many times to look and to wonder what it might be like to live inside one of those congested and decaying apartment buildings with no yard. Dozens of children were merrily playing in the streets, which were packed with noisy cars and motor scooters. To my eyes, thoroughly spoiled by Southern California's sunny, beachy, sterilized suburbia (which Herbert Marcuse once called "another Goddamn Paradise"), it was a startling sight, one that forced me to recall what it may have been like when I was a child in the streets of Tokyo, a time and place that I now seem continually to pastoralize in my memory. These Tokyo/Kawasaki streets and Taipei/Keelung apartments are, I should note, by no means slums abandoned by real-estate interests and city administrators but solid middle- and working-class neighborhoods where ordinary citizens live their ordinary lives.

I am not so concerned with the drabness of these residential districts as with how people live in these places without much thought to the absence of what might be considered necessary amenities and attractions in many European and North American cities and suburbs. The center of Tokyo is increasingly ornamented by spectacular architecture and the efforts of urban planners. Taipei, too, has spectacular buildings, such as the unavoidable Grand Hotel, a dynastic red elephant built to the specifications of Madame Chiang Kai-shek. One residence into which I was invited can only be compared to Kublai Khan's palace on several hills of Xanadu. But if buildings such as these constitute autonomous texts in the metropolitan center, the drab streets are still their contexts. How, then, do text and context relate to one another geographically (spatially), historically (temporally), economically (politically), and aesthetically (socially)? To address some of these questions, we need to examine the basic status of architecture and city planning.

Architectural discourse, like that of city planning, is inescapably utopian. Possibly because a completed building no longer belongs to its architect but rather to its buyers and users, architecture is only fully itself while it is a blueprint under construction and thus still addressing a future condition. In this state we discuss architecture in terms of its expectation and intention, rather than its execution and performance. This future most preoccupies us during phases of violent cultural change. How can an urban building relate to the changing demands of a city? How can a city respond to its "globalized" economic needs? Such questions occupy a major portion of the architect's and city planner's thoughts. Yet the future of a building and/or a city is necessarily negotiated with the dominant powers, those who manage and administer as well as own and dictate. The dreams of those who organize and direct are increasingly transnational and corporate.

Today architecture and urbanism are also utopian because they are imaginable only to a few. Once there were many more onlookers. Ordinary citizens like Dickens or Baudelaire could stroll up and down the streets and lanes of London or Paris, and only a short time ago Roland Barthes could still enjoy a leisurely walk in Tokyo. With intensified urbanization, however, professionals gradually tightened their reins. The city gazers changed; so did the sites of observation. It is no longer people on the streets but the skyscraper builders who examine their cities—from new heights. Now the towering edifices define a city as well as economically duplicate congested space, as Rem Koolhaas argues.[2] Executive officers, too, look down from their towers to oversee their operations, and architects and planners mingle with them to calculate, design, and realize the future, even mapping it out globally. Thus built space belongs more and more to these utopian professionals who increasingly deploy tourists, the new flaneurs, or sociologists and anthropologists to explain their works. Ordinary citizens have fewer opportunities to enter these autonomous texts. Of course residents and workers can climb up to see their cities, too, but only on holidays and in regulated movements. Buildings and cities are distinct only in the minds of specialists; for the rest, the cityscape fuses with their shelters and workplaces, even though they may work inside the high-rises and even though buildings and cities are glamorized in photographs and movies on their behalf. In the United States, especially, urban geography is increasingly fragmented in a permanent design of fortification and incarceration along the borders of wealth and race, which might be another version of utopia—at least for those who are safely barricaded.

The rejection of modernist utopianism around 1970 was probably unavoidable. In the past two decades in particular, the social contradictions built into bourgeois capitalism were too brutal to contemplate in a single, seamless context. For culture industry employees, the choice was either to convert these contradictions into disjunctive fragments or to dissolve the materiality of the contradictions into linguistic games. The best example of the former strategy is the sharp division of all knowledge into disciplines and professions so that no one can gain an inkling of totality. Each sector is mandated to develop exclusive terms and methodologies as if it could successfully seal its autonomy. ("Totalization" is perhaps now the dirtiest word in the academia of industrialized countries.) An example of the latter strategy is a reassertion of linguistic and discursive priority where material obstructions such as poverty, suppression, and resistance are decomposed and erased in abstract blurs and blobs. (Hence, the popularity of terms like "hybridity" and "discourse.") Both are gestures of surrender and homage to the dominant in the hope that culture employees might be granted a share of the corporate profits. So-called global capitalism is a supremely exclusive version of utopia, to which "intellectuals" ache to belong.[3] Actually, global economy is merely a maximum use of world resources via maximum exclusion. The areas that do not promise great profits are ruthlessly ignored as, for instance, in Africa, into which a mere 2 percent of the world capital trickles. The gap between the rich and the poor is steadily widening everywhere, including the United States, South Korea, and Singapore. It is startling to learn that the ratio between the richest 20 percent and the poorest 20 percent in annual income worldwide is 140 to one and that the 358 billionaires in the world have among them a net worth of 760 billion dollars, that is, 45 percent of the net worth of the entire human race, which numbers 2.5 billion people.[4] Architecture and city planning are vitally implicated in this global inequality.

In cities, especially in what Saskia Sassen calls "global cities," the extreme consolidation of economic activities works for the production of specialized services, financial innovations, global control, and management and also markets such products. The consequence of such developments is the polarization of wealth as revealed in the sharp division between pockets of fantastic luxury and vast areas of growing poverty—a contrast fully developed in New York, London, Los Angeles, and now Tokyo as well.[5] When the feature of what Manuel Castells calls "dual cities" becomes distinct, the conflict of crime and anticrime begins to consume urban resources, demolishing the aesthetic and social intentions of architects and city planners. The contradictions of capitalism are more emphatically manifest in global cities.[6]

In retrospect, postmodernism was as inevitable as the radical transnationalization of capital since the 1960s. The end of administrative colonialism led to a need to adapt overseas resources to a changed mode of exploitation. The massive transfer of capital, labor, and production, combined with the steady maintenance of the cold war, was the central economic policy and proved immensely profitable to executives while nearly annihilating domestic labor everywhere. This led to the organized familiarization of all civilizations and societies (multiculturalism) and the retraction of national history, culture, and economy, which had been newly constructed at the dawn of colonialism and industrialism around 1800. Henceforth, the nation-state is to be disassembled or replaced by an alliance of transnational corporate bodies. Modernism was a product of the earlier European-international alliance, which insisted on the transferability overseas of antihistorical functionalism. Postmodernism, on the other hand, consciously replaces sober concentration with irony, humor, and alluring dispersal. In response to global economic mobility, postmodern architecture is not only accessible to various cultures but makes various cultures accessible. The random use of "icons" and "quotations" in postmodern architecture thus shallows out history and geography, as homogenization and standardization increase in market products and culture industries. As capitalist contradictions intensify, postmodernism strategically covers up the gulf between philosophical equality and economic freedom, which simply means material injustice and impoverishment for most people on earth.

One fundamental event in postwar architecture was learning from the Las Vegas vernacular. We find now, however, that Las Vegas, too, has undergone a crucial learning process: transnationalization and Hollywoodification. The new Las Vegas is a colossal conglomeration where world civilizations are reconstructed in casino-hotels such as Luxor, Excalibur, and the MGM Grand. Bugsy Siegel sleaze is reinterpreted in hyperreal sensuality because money no longer needs an apology. Billboards are overwhelmed by the Stratosphere, the highest tower in the United States. Economy is eros, as eros is economy, and gigantism is everything.[7] We are now told that as

Hollywood and the Disney Corporation abandon Los Angeles and migrate to Las Vegas and Florida in search of cleaner air, lower crime rates, and more money, Disney is implanting a gigantic hyperreal supersign consisting of hotel, entertainment, and retail complex right in the middle of Times Square in New York City: the "meteor moments after the crash."[8] To stay on friendly terms with its future neighbor perhaps, the *New York Times* enthusiastically reports that Miami-based Arquitectonica's project effectively evokes chaos, as did Laurinda Spear's earlier backdrops for the slick violence of *Miami Vice*. Is architecture now learning from Hollywood?

Postmodern responses to transnational corporatism however, betray a number of serious absences as well. Peter Eisenman has argued the need to "move architecture away from itself" to a concern with "the presence of the absence,"[9] that is, to do away—as I see it—with the utopian displacement that architecture is always doomed to enforce. Eisenman and others like Bernard Tschumi propose an architecture that is against itself, an architecture that manages, among other things, to free itself from power and wealth. As Manfredo Tafuri shrewdly detects, however, the " 'pleasure' that derives from the reading of the works of [John] Hejduk, Eisenman, and [Robert] Venturi is all intellectual."[10] I think of a more literal and less cerebral eradication of architecture: to bring architecture around to the material context, to the outside space where ordinary workers live and work with little participation in the language texts and discourse of architecture.

Modernism—with all of its ills—was at least mindful of those left outside architecture. Urban workers had their housing projects, though ugly, unlivable, and finally useless. Today's industrial cities eliminate those rational monstrosities and, with them, homes for vast numbers of people. Las Vegas has a steadily increasing population of homeless people, but no one remembers to mention them. In the streets of Kawasaki and Keelung, on the other hand, there are still homes and apartments, however hideous. Whether they are inhabitable or not should not be too hastily decided—especially by those who do not live there.

We cannot return to modernism. We do, however, need to think about shelter and workplaces for anyone, anywhere, and indeed "anywise." How we live is finally not that important; that we live is. Architecture is a tragic art/discipline/profession/industry/business because it doesn't know its own identity. Perhaps, instead of building guilty conscience into aesthetically, theoretically, intellectually admirable but useless shapes and forms, we might stroll in the streets of Kawasaki, Keelung, and Puchon (west of Seoul) and learn how people live in these "filthy" and "uninviting" places. There may be more life there than in architecture's patronage houses, where the patrons are not always more satisfied or more comfortable than the residents of these streets.

"BUNBURYING" IN THE JAPAN FIELD

A Reply to Jeff Humphries

This review was published in 1997 in New Literary History *as a reply to Jeff Humphries's essay "Japan in Theory," which criticized Miyoshi's and Harootunian's* Postmodernism and Japan *(1989), and also the various other scholars identified with that project. Here we see Miyoshi at his most trenchant; arguing, most seriously, that Humphries's piece is a worrisome symptom of a larger shift in North American academia in which a growing professionalization encourages self-serving and sterile attacks.*—ED.

Jeff[erson] Humphries's "Japan in Theory" has so many things wrong and hardly anything worth critical or scholarly scrutiny. A rebuttal to an essay like this will be—of necessity—tiresome to write, and perhaps even worse to read. In order to answer it fairly, a respondent needs to descend to its level. For unlike Humphries, who concludes the essay by denying the connection between a study and its stated object—of which more later—I fully intend to ground this response on the text of "Japan in Theory," however muddy and muddled it may be. It's not easy, I repeat, because Humphries's essay is malicious, ignorant, inaccurate, irresponsible, dishonest, fraudulent, lazy, sloppy, unhistorical, and incoherent. These are adjectives one seldom encounters in a scholarly publication, not because they violate the code of academic decorum, but because a professional journal ordinarily rejects lamentable chaff like this essay, obviating the need for such words. Somehow this piece squeaked through. To list all of his errors and misrepresentations, however, might be a little too extreme, since the list alone, *sans commentaries*, will have to be as long as Humphries's essay itself. Let me thus focus on several crucial points.

Exclusivism

Right on the first page, Humphries introduces the "coloniz[ers]" of Japanese studies in America. "Many of them [are] Japanese immigrants, others defectors from the conservative scholasticism of their 'missionary' (literal or figurative) parents." He identifies this group of "theoretically-minded scholars" who split the "Japanese studies community" as the "contributors to Miyoshi's edited volume *Postmodernism and Japan*," "Miyoshi and all the others," "the Japanese and expatriate Japanese contributors to this book," and "this volume and all professional conclaves." These are indeed vague terms, and yet Humphries refers to the "integrity of the group," as if there existed a cabal of fanatics sworn to the conspiracy of an academic takeover.

First, Humphries describes the "group" (let me assume here for the sake of argument that the contributors to the volume indeed form a collective) as consisting largely of "Japanese immigrants" and "defectors" from their parental "scholasticism." Unable to recall at once any immigrant member other than myself in his imaginary organization, I went back to the table of contents of *Postmodernism and Japan* in an effort to discover other alien settlers on this soil. There are four—or possibly five—Japanese-born Japanese-citizen writers (Arata Isozaki, Kojin Karatani, Kenzaburo Oe, and Akira Asada), but "immigrants"? As far as I know, they all carry their Japanese passports. There is no one else—with the possible exception of Naoki Sakai who may qualify for the "immigrant" category. But I don't know what his nationality is: it has never occurred to me to ask him. Nor do I know, I must confess, the exact definition of an "immigrant." Is a permanent resident an immigrant? Does a resident with double citizenship count as one? A regular visitor? Of course, Humphries may have meant that people with Japanese last names are all immigrants—since they all look different from him—regardless of the number of their familial generations who have settled in the United States, like Tetsuo Najita. Two problems arise at once. One, obviously Tetsuo Najita, who was born in the United States, lost two brothers in the Second World War for the United States, and is now the chair of the History—not Japanese History—Department and Robert Ingersoll Distinguished Service Professor at the University of Chicago, is no more "Japanese immigrant" than Humphries is. Two, aside from Najita and those four Japanese-Japanese who reside in Japan, plus Sakai, simply no one else has a Japanese last name. Is it possible that Humphries's paranoia about the immigrants in the United States is so acute that he cannot recognize the non-Japanese Americans who constitute an overwhelming majority in this secret organization: Harootunian, Ivy, Koschmann, Field, Wolfe, De-Bary, Stephen Melville, Michael Ryan, and Jonathan Arac (the last two were invited to and attended—that is, not excluded from—the initial work-shop, though neither gave us papers. See our acknowledgment on p. xix). That is four Japanese-Japanese, one Japanese of an uncertain nationality, one naturalized American, and ten Americans (including Najita). "A new kind of exclusivism"? "Pure ethnocentrism"? "How dare anyone who was not born Japanese pretend to encroach on the hallowed terrain?": a senti-ment which Humphries forces into the fundamental creed of this "group."

Brett DeBary is one of the scholars Humphries calls "defectors from the conservative scholasticism [sic] of their 'missionary' (literal or figurative) parents," her father being one of the "missionary" scholars at an East Coast university. Who else fits this description? All the non-Japanese-immigrant members of the secret club? Who are their "figurative" parents? Edwin O. Reischauer? In what sense—other than as a "godfather"? Does Harootu-nian descend from Reischauer's parentage? Is Marilyn Ivy his daughter? If by "figurative parents" Humphries simply means scholarly antecedents, the expression is much too inclusive to be meaningful. By this terminology, aren't we all figurative children of whoever was born earlier than us? Humphries is making an ad hominem attack on DeBary here, and in order to disguise its illegitimacy, he insinuates a category by adding "figurative." In fact, no one else in the organization is a "defector" from the conservative genealogy, missionary, occupational, or otherwise.

Since this Japanese-immigrants-dominated "group" of "theoretically-minded" "colonizers" is secret, invisible, and unidentifiable to anyone other than Humphries, and since he is not about to come forth with a specific list of individuals, I suggest a name that ought both to fit the true nature of the organization and satisfy the author of "Japan in Theory": the Nipponese Yellow Peril Scholars, or "NYPS," which will henceforth stand for Humphries's delusory immigrant takeover theorist group throughout the remainder of my response.

Before moving on to another topic, let me remind Humphries of another NYPS collection of essays, *Japan in the World* (1993), also edited by Harootunian and myself. Humphries's knowledge of Japan and Japanese studies in the United States being deplorably meager, as I will elaborate later, he fails to mention it in "Japan in Theory." Thus either he didn't know of its existence, or else knew it but was too lazy to visit his library, or possibly knew and looked at it but decided to ignore it. He should have discussed it as long as he was concerned with the NYPS, because the book's list of contributors might have added fodder to his exclusivist conspiracy charges. There is the by now familiar NYPS cadre once again, the core of Japanese last-named such as Mitsuhiro Yoshimoto (a Japanese-Japanese), Karatani (another J.-J.), Najita, Oe (still another J.-J.), Kazuo Ishiguro of *The Remains of the Day* fame (a British subject and hardly a Japanese, but Japanese last-named and Japanese-born), and myself. But then, there are Eqbal Ahmad, Perry Anderson, Bruce Cumings, Arif Dirlik, Fredric Jameson, Leslie Pincus, Miriam Silverberg, Christena Turner, and Rob Wilson as well as H. D. Harootunian, altogether ten of them. How many of them are "Japanese immigrants" or "defectors from the conservative scholasticism of the missionary . . . parents"? Exclusivist? The list seems wide open to me. In fact, as far as I know, this is *the single most* inclusive and diverse collection among all the anthologies of essays on Japan so far published in any language. Did Humphries's fearful delusion transform Ahmad, Anderson, Jameson, and others into Japanese?

I hope I have sufficiently proved the fitness of some of those adjectives listed earlier: inaccurate, irresponsible, dishonest, lazy, and sloppy, if not as yet fraudulent. Incidentally, I have never been called an "immigrant" in a scholarly—or any other—context. I am happy to be one, but isn't everyone in a settler society such as the United States an immigrant except for the Native Americans, whom we have systematically exploited and exterminated, and the African Americans, who as slaves had no choice? What makes Humphries think that he is less immigrant than Miriam Silverberg or Norma Field? Or myself?

There is another charge involved in Humphries's fantasy of NYPS exclusivism: exclusion by "academic training and specialization." I have already mentioned the presence of non-Japanologists included in *Postmod-*

ernism and Japan and *Japan in the World*, which alone should be sufficient to demolish the absurdity of Humphries's accusation. But maybe he needs to be enlightened more. Here I will limit my response to my own career. Throughout the paper Humphries insinuates that my training is in Japanese studies, and says that my first book is *Accomplices of Silence*, and my second, *As We Saw Them*. It so happens, however, that my B.A., M.A., and Ph.D. were all in English, and my first book was in Victorian literature. I taught in the English Department at Berkeley for twenty-three years before moving to San Diego nine years ago. This, I believe, is relevant here in several ways. First, when I became an assistant professor of English at Berkeley, I was probably the only Japanese-born faculty in English at any major university in the United States. The point here is: despite my unfamiliar presence, hardly anyone ever talked about my being Japanese, resident or immigrant, in connection with my scholarship. Of all the reviews of my first book, which were quite numerous for a first book, none referred to my ethnicity or nationality. Of course, this does not necessarily mean that the 1960s was a golden decade in race matters; probably the opposite was true even in Berkeley. The minorities were so successfully contained and segregated that the majority could afford to be fair to the few who strayed into their midst, unlike the 1990s when the minorities, especially the Asian Americans, are everywhere on United States campuses posing threats to some sensitive souls in the dominant group. Second, I had then little experience of having to relate my—or anybody else's—ethnicity with my scholarly practice, unlike now when identity politics consumes many academics. Humphries's unquestioned assumption that I am a Japanologist by training and specialization already says something about his deficiency in social and historical imagination. Third, Humphries insists that my criticism is "profoundly limited by [my] own position as a former Japanese, now naturalized American, in the American academy," and repeats a few pages later that "[my] critical stance cannot help being defined by [my] professional (and personal) identification with American academicism." Does he mean that all the Japanese in United States universities have an identical critical perspective? That all "former Japanese" are "profoundly limited"? I can never escape the polluted circumstances of my birth—and migration—no matter how? And Humphries from the Deep

South? A remarkable totalization even for a zealous anti-NYPS. Would he dare apply the same observation to other "immigrant" groups? To the de Mans, Bhabhas, Appiahs, Lentricchias, and Blooms?

The absence of exclusivism in the earlier stage of my career had an effect. I felt so unencumbered by segregation either by race or by specialty that I thought nothing of expanding my studies to Japanese literature. Humphries is plaintive about the membership "defined by academic training and specialization": "If a wayward presenter gets out of hand [in a conference] and says more interesting things than the length of her or his tenure in the group would allow, she or he will probably be subjected to a verbal cuffing." This does not accord with my experience. At the very early stage at least, *Accomplices of Silence* was accepted by Japanologists including the most "conservative" and "missionary" ones like Edward Seidensticker, Donald Keene, Edwin Reischauer, Earl Miner, or even Helen and William McCullough, whom Humphries cites. They all knew my training and specialization but did not object. Of course, they may well have brushed aside my Victorianism as a temporary derangement and thought of me as biologically destined to be a Japanologist. Whatever the reason, there was no disapproval of my training at first, until I began to defy the power hierarchy in Japanese studies in Berkeley and, in time, in the United States, Japan, and other places. (This is a saga in itself, involving actual students, faculty, administrators, and scholars, inside and out of the Japan field, which, however, must be told elsewhere.) My next book, *As We Saw Them*, which Humphries (who never read it) describes as recounting "the Japanese envoys' encounter . . . *in the form of a sustained narrative*" (my italics), was in history and rhetoric, rather than literature. And again, I was accepted by historians; in fact, the book was the occasion for my long-lasting association with the Chicago historians like Najita and Harootunian. More recently I wandered out again. I have been publishing on the subject of transnational economy and its impact on culture and the university, having little to do with Japan. And my "training and specialization" have not been called into question—so far.

I knew nothing about Jeff Humphries, the man, his training, or even his existence. Of course, I didn't know whether or not he was a Japan specialist. Having read "Japan in Theory," however, I became curious—because of its singular ineptitude—and spent a few hours looking up his publications and performance. But this came *after* I had read this paper and formed my judgment. My dismissal of him has nothing to do with his training, specialization, and, needless to say, immigration status. His intelligence, knowledge, and understanding—or lack thereof—alone count. Ditto with Ihab Hassan, whom Humphries calls one of the "other naturalized ones within the academic community" and "an *English* professor" (his italics). Humphries blames the NYPS for having rejected him on the basis of his race and specialization. The fact is that Hassan and I had a project together several years ago, and it soon became apparent that the man was little interested in the problems that many of us NYPS were concerned with. The article on Japan he published in *Salmagundi* and reprinted in the *International House of Japan Bulletin* flattered the Japanese on flimsy evidence, and although the piece was obviously palatable for a few academics in Japan, he did not strike me or other NYPS as adequate. His work on postmodernity as merely a style had no use for us either—unlike studies by Fredric Jameson and David Harvey. Let me reiterate here what everyone knows but Humphries: the rejection of exclusion does not mean indiscriminate inclusion. The NYPS are open to all, but exclude racists, sexists, fascists, homophobes, agents of domination, as well as simple incompetent bores.

Scholarship

One ordinarily reads before writing on a topic. What's fascinating about Humphries is his consistent indifference to this rudimentary practice. Let me take just three examples. First, his discussion of Japanese women. Challenging my description of Japanese women as oppressed by Japanese men, he argues that "categorical abstractions" such as women are unreal and untrue because "injustice and suffering are always individual." This non sequitur rejection of categories and abstractions altogether, however, is immediately forgotten when he goes on to discuss the particularities of young Japanese women (a group which, anybody else would argue, constitutes a "categorical abstraction"). Anyway, Humphries's point seems to be that young Japanese women, a category, are not victims of men, another category, because they are merely "very demanding, pleasure-oriented hyperconsumers." As against the men, a "class of clones" who do "nothing but work," the women "do everything else." We are now clearly talking "categorical abstractions," but never mind, that's not the issue anymore. Women are the dominant sex.

This observation, which goes counter to most studies on the Japanese women by either sociologists, anthropologists, or fiction/nonfiction writers, Japanese or non-Japanese, male or female—from Patricia Tsurumi, Haruko Wakita, Jennifer Robertson, Hiroko Hara, Chizuko Ueno, Masao Yamaguchi, Hideo Totsuka to the *Asahi Newspaper*, the *New York Times*—is based on a passage from *The Modern Madame Butterfly* by Karen Ma. The author is a member of the Association of Foreign Wives of Japanese and of the Association for Multicultural Families, organizations which served as her main source of information. Chatty and episodic, it is an entertaining book. The trouble is, however, that it is no more than just that. Why did Humphries choose this slight study, and not a fuller and more substantial work? The answer is that he didn't. Humphries didn't even open *The Modern Madame Butterfly*, which should be available in a neighborhood public library or at any Barnes and Noble, if not in his campus library. Instead, he found the quoted passage in a review of Ma's book. Furthermore, he found the review itself in a journal called *Mangajin*. Although its title is Japanese, the publication is no Japanese journal, but an entertainment monthly published in Atlanta, Georgia, that is aimed at English-speaking businessmen and split evenly between easy Japanese language lessons and Japanese cartoons with translated texts. The title means "Comics People." Having not achieved as yet the level of erudition of *National Lampoon*, not to say *Punch* (although its editors, I happen to know, are highly motivated), the magazine, I imagine, has never served as the basis for a scholarly argument till now. Besides, the review, Humphries's only source, calls Ma's book "in-flight magazine journalism." The question is: Is Humphries trying to pass this off as a serious book written in Japanese? How is the typical *New Literary History* reader with no Japanese supposed to react to his scholarship?

Second, to move on to Nagisa Oshima's *Merry Christmas, Mr. Lawrence*, I am not at all confident that Humphries has ever seen the film, nor am I certain that he has even read my analysis, which he disputes. So it will be futile to expect him to have done any reading and thinking about Oshima, who has been extensively discussed by non-Japanologist film theorists such as Stephen Heath, Noel Burch, and the contributors to the Oshima issue of

Wide Angle. The critics' interests are, however, in his earlier, 1960s films such as *Night and Fog in Japan*, *Death by Hanging*, *The Forgotten Imperial Army*, and *Ceremony*, rather than *In the Realm of the Senses*, which Humphries believes made the director known outside Japan. The fact is that *In the Realm of the Senses* (1976) is Oshima's first full-scale internationally produced film that became a commercial success. By the time he completed *Merry Christmas* in 1983, which was also funded and produced internationally with an international cast and crew, Oshima was fully in the export business. That does not mean that Oshima lost "purity"—a word I never use, but Humphries lies that I do—but that the critical perspective that had distinguished Oshima in the 1960s was abandoned. In *Death by Hanging*, for instance, Oshima denounces Japanese bigotry against the Koreans: the film ends by directly confronting its audience as well as the Japanese officials in the penal institution (the education officer, prosecutor, warden, doctor, and so on) with the charge of their complicity in the murder of the Korean boy. This is where the famed film voice "you, too; you, too; you, too" occurs. Having never seen the film nor read about it, Humphries inexplicably twists both Oshima's intense criticism in *Death by Hanging* and my admiration of it into something called "us-too-ism," which apparently is interchangeable with "me-too-ism," not of the film, but of the NYPS's critical doctrine!: "To enact this kind of 'me-too-ism' from within the Japanese studies community is to acquiesce in and repeat, in reactionary fashion, the assertions of the Helen McCulloughs of a previous generation, that Japanese studies are marginal, that the uniqueness and particularity of Japanese literature make it not really worthy of study, except as a quaint curiosity—not worthy, that is, as the 'great masterpieces' of Western literature are so." This is sheer hogwash. The distinction I make between the Oshima of the 1960s and the Oshima of *Merry Christmas* goes entirely unnoticed in Humphries's muddled argument.

My treatment of *Merry Christmas* is framed in the discussions of emperorism, war prison films by David Lean and Steven Spielberg, Oshima's earlier films, and *The Seed and the Sower*, a novel by a South African writer Laurens van der Post, on which *Merry Christmas* is based. It also examines van der Post's fuzzy racial mythologies, his contempt for the Koreans in particular, as expressed in the novel and in his memoir, *The Prisoner and the Bomb*. Oshima's acquiescence to van der Post's anti-Koreanism offers a sharp contrast to his earlier works like *Death by Hanging* and *The Forgotten Imperial Army*. If Humphries had read my chapter or viewed the film, even he would have avoided this outrageous misreading. But of course he doesn't read, as we know by now. Instead, he flies off with inanities: "By emphasizing universalist categories at the expense of particular circumstances," I follow Jameson's "Third-World Literature in the Era of Multinational Capitalism." And he reiterates Aijaz Ahmad's perverse accusation of Jameson. (Is he pretending not to have read anything else by Jameson, his old teacher? Come to think of it, he probably hasn't!) Oshima's new centralism and hegemonism are simplified in Humphries's hand to his "absorption of the Western gaze/text." Thus Oshima's gush over David Bowie's fair skin and blond hair is eminently laudable: after all, it is "a step beyond the old Marxian/Hegelian linear historicist worldview in which someone must always be on top, and which defines the parameters of 'political correctness.'" Oshima's infatuation with Bowie's "God-given" beauties is sadly unrequited by Bowie, but this imbalance, asymmetry, is actually symmetry, according to Humphries's mumbo-jumbo, to which I will return before I am done.

Third, the texts of most of the works Humphries criticizes are indirect, that is, unconfirmed and unexamined double quotations except for just two books, *Off Center* and *Postmodernism and Japan*. When he discusses my studies, his reference is exclusively to parts of *Off Center*; when he moves on to discuss the other NYPS in the second half of his paper, his text this time is solely and exclusively *Postmodernism and Japan* (PJ). He calls Kojin Karatani "clearly the central Japanese figure for all of the American Japanologists." And yet Karatani's long career and numerous publications on wide-ranging subjects (twenty to thirty books in the University of California Library alone, plus several journals he has edited) are dismissed out of hand. Of course, since Karatani's books are mostly in Japanese, Humphries can't possibly be expected to have read them. Still, one wonders. First, by 1996 two English translations of Karatani's books were out, so why didn't Humphries at least take a look at them before writing this essay? Second, wasn't he at least interested in finding something about what "the central Japanese figure" may have written in his own language? Third, when the sole basis of his judgment on Karatani is just one article by Karatani himself and two by Ivy and DeBary, wouldn't he be a little cautious before proceeding to make categorical statements such as *"He is the principal one to have embraced entirely the latest Western academic discourses"* (his italics), Karatani's "facile misconceptions" about the *"genbun itchi"* movement, "Karatani's eager embrace of Derrida's 'orientalist' imagination of ideographic writing," Karatani's "grasp of deconstruction is limited," and Karatani "knows nothing of the modern [Chinese?] language"? Humphries's dismissal of DeBary is based on PJ; of Najita, on PJ; *of Harootunian, on PJ*. When he attacks Sakai and defends David Pollack, one looks for a direct reading of Pollack's *The Fracture of Meaning*, but of course all one gets from Humphries is PJ, and PJ alone. Thus Harootunian's *Things Seen and Unseen* remains unopened, so does Najita's *Japan* or *Visions of Virtue*, or Sakai's *Voices of the Past*. And yet Humphries's reckless dismissal is sweeping and complete.

This sort of lackadaisical indifference to scholarship might pass unnoticed if all the sources used were equally reliable. But as we saw in Humphries's discussion of Japanese women, all sources are not equal. The notorious Derrida-Karatani-Asada conversation is another case in point. Humphries relies only on Marilyn Ivy's citation of the *Asahi jaanaru* transcription—in PJ. There is little reason to believe that anything is amiss in the process of Ivy's translation and representation of the Asahi piece, but how about the accuracy of *Asahi*'s transcription and representation of the context and tone of the conversation? One might note here that the *Asahi jaanaru*, which became extinct in 1992, was not a scholarly, but a media publication; though not for mass consumption like *Mangajin*, it was middle-brow in the sense of being tailored for the general public. Ivy vaguely warns by letting Karatani express misgivings: "[Karatani observes that] the transcript of this conversation will be consumed by the reading public within one week."[1] And, of course, the *Asahi* editors were not concerned with scholarly exactitude. Still, if Humphries had read the *Asahi jaanaru* article itself, he would have seen numerous notations of "laughter" throughout the conversation. It was a friendly and jovial *zadankai*, although they consistently talked about deconstruction. The participants made jokes and responded warmly: Karatani is marked as making everyone laugh eleven times, Asada four times, and Derrida joking eight times in a nine-page transcript. The quality of hilarity is caught in a photograph of the occasion where the usually serious Jacques Derrida is guffawing between Asada and Karatani. Karatani's remarks were made in that spirit.

Humphries, however, is not in the habit of careful reading. Textual examination—contrary to his proclaimed faith in "the close reading of individual texts"—would seem to lie beyond Humphries's interest.

Thus one is not surprised by his off-the-cuff remark about Edward Said (whom he associates with the NYPS with no explanation), although one wonders how often this sort of crude irrelevance is allowed in an academic publication: "Even 'Orientalism' is an orientalist concept: it emerged from the pen of a highly paid academic, working in New York, the world center of capitalism and one of the centers of Western academic discourse. It could not be thought outside the historico-cultural circumstances of First-World colonialism/postcolonialism." Nor does one at all wonder why Humphries's list of "Works Cited" is so short and sparse. But even among these paltry references, aside from the primary texts, one item by Roy Miller should not be there since it is not cited at all in his article. (Actually, Humphries might have gained some support from Miller's wrong-headed study of the Japanese language, had he actually consulted it instead of just padding his lean list.)

This look at Humphries's scholarship serves to justify, I believe, the use of most adjectives listed at the beginning: malicious, ignorant, inaccurate, irresponsible, dishonest, lazy, sloppy, and now, fraudulent.

"Asymmetry Is Symmetry"

According to Humphries, the NYPS are generally poor writers fascinated with "theoretico-critical jargon, all the while freely dropping neo-Marxist, poststructuralist names such as Baudrillard, Bloch, and Lefort." "A few sentences will suffice to give an idea of [Humphries's own] style":

> The mutual incomprehension described in [*As We Saw Them*], however, is not *symmetrical*. It is *mutual asymmetry*, which might be characterized as symmetry simply because it is mutual, but this points to the problem of the symmetry/asymmetry binarism: asymmetry implies inequality, nonequivalence, between two entities; it depends on difference, *but so does symmetry*: two symmetrical objects must be different before they can be symmetrical; their "likeliness" (symmetry) is a *characteristic* of their difference. The difference in the case of *asymmetry* is merely greater, not different in kind. Mutual incomprehension, in fact, as Jerzy

Kosinski's novel *Being There* demonstrates, is an extremely asymmetrical act comparable to television watching, all the more so because each side thinks that it does understand, and that it even understands what the other mistakenly thinks that it does. What Miyoshi narrates is a peculiarly ironic asymmetry: the Westerners finding the Japanese rude and prevaricating . . . and the Japanese seeing the Westerners as undecorous, clumsy, and loud, neither understanding the most basic assumptions of the other and concluding therefrom the other's self-evident inferiority (regardless of America's technological and military advantage; the Japanese always assumed that this was a temporary and remediable circumstance, and history shows they were not wrong to do so). This symmetry/asymmetry is ironic not only because it is never entirely clear which it is (symmetrical or asymmetrical) but also because it is constantly doubling back on itself, the misunderstanding which thinks it is understanding giving rise to further reciprocal (mis)understanding, and so on. This is often funny, but it is also tragic, as Miyoshi does not fail to note. Japanese-American relations, intellectual and political (the two are not, as Miyoshi rightly says, distinct), continue to be characterized by such ironic (a)symmetry.[2] (His italics.)

What is he trying to say here? No complex terms, no erudite names, nor difficult concepts, and yet Humphries thoroughly manages to befuddle his writing, producing an impenetrable blob of words where symmetry is asymmetry and mutual asymmetry is, obviously, symmetrical. Using no "theoretic-critical jargon," he succeeds in making no sense whatever.

The NYPS are all PC, he says. I have no patience here to take up Humphries on this, although he seems to believe this shop-worn word is still serviceable in a critical discussion. So instead, let me cite one more passage from his article: "The Japanese and expatriate Japanese contributors to this book find themselves in the same position as Japanese technocrats, bureaucrats, and scientists of the last century and a half, absorbing a technology from the West (in its own terms, which they have adopted, a technology which is also a commodity) which was developed and perfected in Euro-American universities, and now exported world-wide." So Humphries is at last out in the open. He racially divides the NYPS here, segregating Harootunian from me, and Sakai from his Cornell colleagues! I am in the position of the last century's Japanese technocrats and bureaucrats, but Koschmann and Ivy are exempt. The sentence contains much more. He insists that theory—which he variously identifies as "deconstructionist/postdeconstructionist," "postmodernist," "political," "the old Marxian/Hegelian linear historicist worldview," "Marxian cultural studies and Saidian (post)colonial studies," "an authentically anti-universalist discourse," "Marxist postcolonial nationalism," "feminism and cultural studies," "Western academic technology," "deconstruction and cultural/postcolonial studies," "Western cultural technology[/ies]," and so forth—is a technology (though "which is also a commodity"). And it is produced only in the West. By this argument, if the NYPS are "theoretical," they are, by tautological definition, "Westernized," that is, "technocrats" and "conformist" as well as Westcentric New-Age "Helen McCulloughs." According to Humphries, let me repeat, technology and theory are all Western, and thus any "non-Westerner" who partakes in theory and technology is inescapably an imitator and a conformist. Underlying this sophomoric assertion is an even uglier essentialism of a rare kind: anyone who does not imitate or conform in the non-West, at the same time, is incapable of technology or theory. Ah, the primitive Orientals! Ah, the copycats forever! We have not seen a remark like this for some time. It is perhaps more a product of a relaxed mind than of malice, although malice no doubt lurks near the surface of this swamp. Is this a sign of the new right-wing retrogression unfolding in parts of the United States and elsewhere?

The last paragraph of "Japan in Theory" requires a few words. According to Humphries, opposition is conformity and traditional scholarship is radical theory. Nothing surprising from someone for whom "asymmetry is symmetry," but it ought to be mentioned that this disarray of his lexicography springs from a creed against "binarism." Understood as black and white, "good" and "bad," binarism might mean nothing but reductivism and simplification, which no one would deign to endorse. The rage of antibinarism in our days of hybridity and pluralism, however, is not as innocent as Humphries presents. It needs to be examined historically in relation to the newly emerging global economy. I have written on this elsewhere,[3] so let me just point out here that the gap between the rich and the poor, what Humphries call the "downtrodden and exploited and those who are not," has been steadily widening since the 1970s rather than diminishing as he assumes. The world is on the contrary increasingly polarized into two extremes of top and bottom. And yet the job many academics assign to themselves nowadays is to legitimate and disguise this accelerating division by erasing the idea of "binarism" itself so that they may serve transborder corporatism. The Humphrieses of the world are now eager to defend and join transnational corporatism, which is radically transforming the world order. It is not just binarism in Humphries's case, but also distinction and articulation of any kind that must be altogether obliterated. Thus the poor are rich, and the downtrodden are hyperconsumers, just as asymmetry is symmetry, and opposition is conformity. At the same time, Humphries forgets his own lunatic binarism as he absolutely separates the Japanese from the non-Japanese.

Finally, the last sentence of the last paragraph, which unwittingly reveals what Humphries has been all about: "Our debates over the nature of the literary object we study may have less to do with the object itself than with where we wish to place ourselves in relation to others doing the same thing." I have been arguing this all along about Humphries's piece: it has very little to do with Japan or Japanese literature or criticism, which it purportedly examines. Its sole concern is with his "relation to others doing the same thing." In other words, where he wants to be placed in relation to the NYPS, or more to the point, how to put the NYPS in their place. I am not sure if the enterprise is worth his time, since Humphries is not at all "doing the same thing" as those NYPS, who whether Japanese or non-Japanese, take the object of their studies with dead seriousness.

In his *Losing the Text*, *The Otherness Within*, and other works on the American South and French literature, Humphries seems far more cautious about generalization. So what makes him so bold in this piece and in "The Harris and Perry Treaties and the 'Invention' of Modern Japan," which he published in the *Tamkang Review* a few years ago? Does he believe that the readers of *New Literary History* and the Taiwan publication know even less about Japan and Japanese studies than he does, and that he can therefore get away with any nonsense he cares to concoct? Or, more likely, does his contempt for the NYPS free and loosen his writing? In short, is he slumming in the "tiny ghetto" of the Japan field? Is that why Humphries is "Jeff" in Japan, and "Jefferson" in the West? As Worthing is "Ernest in town and Jack in the country" and Algernon conjures Bunbury in the Wilde territory?

Japanese studies—or any other field—should be deghettoized and opened up. It needs "outsiders" to intermix with the "insiders" so that they can eliminate the intellectual borders and all benefit from diversity. For this, however, it needs no slummers coming Bunburying; and if they saunter in, they should be exposed and identified. In this connection, I am curious about the keepers of the gate, the referees on Humphries's submission. Did they examine with care all the errors and failures I describe? How could they miss them since they are so obvious? On what ground did the "experts" in the field or general theorists give their imprimatur to this piece? In these days after the editorial fiascoes of *Social Text* and *American Poetry Review*, can we afford to be so lax and unscrupulous about what to publish? I believe that the referees should take responsibility for their opinions and thus should join this exchange of views. I fully support the symposium format of *New Literary History*, for whose health and vigor, however, their rebuttals to my discussion here are indispensable.

I have done my part; now it is their turn.

ART WITHOUT MONEY

....

documenta X

This piece, originally published in 1998 in The New Left Review, *is an assessment of* documenta, *an exhibition of modern and contemporary art that now takes place every five years in Kassel, Germany. Having traveled to Kassel and taken in the over seven hundred exhibits at* documenta X, *Miyoshi wonders what possibilities remain for the production and experience of counter-hegemonic art in the context of a globalized, commodity based economy.* —ED.

documenta X was an extraordinary event![1] From June to September last year, the exhibition mounted a fearless challenge to today's general premise and practice of art, and indeed to the entire art and culture industry. The tenth *documenta* awaits—and deserves—a sea change in the predominantly negative responses it has received. It may turn out to be a long wait, but the consequences of the 1997 exhibition could turn out to be truly important historically.

documenta was first founded in 1955 in the German city of Kassel, partly to confront Germany's catastrophic history and partly to recreate the country's links with the world of modern art, sundered by the Nazis. The exhibition attracted wide attention, and as the city's postwar reconstruction continued, the quinquennial expanded. By 1972, with *documenta* V, "The Interrogation of Reality," the hundred-day summer exhibitions held near what was then the East German border were challenging the much older Venice Biennale as the world's most prestigious contemporary art exhibition. As its fame spread, *documenta* was increasingly absorbed into the mainstream of avant-garde art. Thus *documenta* eventually became a spectacular art fest, just like any other, where tourists flock and dealers speculate. If the goal of the first *documenta* was at least partly documentation and expiation, the aims of later *documentas*—*IX* in 1992, for example—were far less definite.

When Catherine David was named as artistic director of *documenta X*, few knew what was in store. She had been a curator of contemporary art at the Pompidou Centre, and then at the Jeu de Paume. She had taught contemporary art at the Ecole du Louvre, published several books, and organized various exhibitions. Although known among curators and intellectuals, her career had been relatively short. The *documenta* advisory board's appointment of a woman born in 1954, a French national who spoke little German, was a bold move. Moreover, David was politically committed, intellectually fierce, and unblinkingly honest. She and her close-knit team moulded *documenta x*—or *dX*, with the *d* always in lower case and in its logo, ever-present in Kassel, crossed out by an orange-red *X*—to her convictions about art and politics to a degree that had not been anticipated by other curators and art historians.

The summer of 1997 saw two other large and more conventional exhibitions in Europe: the Venice Biennale and Münster's Sculpture Projects. There, objects were selected for "excellence," and arranged in national or monographic displays: the idea of artworks as pleasurable commodities for the "society of the spectacle" dominated, although there were, of course, those that went against the norms of aesthetic autonomy and sensational appeals to emotion. *dX* was sharply different. David's introduction to the exhibition's *Short Guide* precisely sets out her aim:

> While making no concessions to the commemorative trend, the last documenta of this century can hardly evade the task of elaborating a historical and critical gaze on its own history, on the recent past of the post-war period, and on everything from this now-vanished age that remains in ferment within contemporary art and culture: memory, historical reflection, decolonization and what Wolf Lepenies calls the "de-Europeanization" of the world, but also the complex processes of post-archaic, post-traditional, post-national identification at work in the "fractal societies" (Serge Gruzinski) born from the collapse of communism and the brutal imposition of the laws of the market.[2]

Thus to scrutinize the daily life of people and their art and culture against the background of global political and economic conditions over the last fifty years, dX began by reconsidering its own sites for display.

The Exhibition Route

To go beyond the walls of museums and galleries that close off art from people and people from art, dX was spread through the streets of Kassel. The route for viewing dX, called the "parcours," started at the old railroad station. Its platforms and tracks as well as a station house were refitted to house displays. The unused track was overgrown with weeds, among which the Viennese artist Lois Weinberger had planted more weeds, indistinguishable from those already there. One learned later, however, that they were of a fast-growing introduced kind, resistant to herbicides and capable of overrunning the indigenous species. For the observant, these weeds had a threatening beauty.

Once made aware, the subtlest irony and humor tuned in visitors to the complex layering of unsuspected meaning that lurked in the details of the most innocent-looking "installation" at dX. The first museum-like space on the parcours was the converted station house, where work by Steve Mc-Queen, Hans Haacke, Marc Pataut, Matthew Ngui, Lothar Baumgarten, Rem Koolhaus, Martin Walde, Ribert Adams, Michelangelo Pisoletto, and Helio Oiticica, among others, were exhibited.

The parcours then extended into the public space, descending into Kassel's much-despised pedestrian passages, a legacy of the automobile-crazed 1950s. This blight of urban decay is the background for Jeff Wall's angry *Milk* to Christine Hill's *Volksboutique*, which reproduces a used-clothes shop in Berlin, and Peter Friedl's video of a man (played by Friedl himself) who loses a coin in a cigarette machine, frantically kicks it in anger, and receives a hard kick from a panhandler he had earlier refused. In the dingy windows of a single surviving shop in the underground passage hung a poster reading "Chichi aus Paris," When I asked the store owner his feelings about dX, he denied any hostility and said, "I just keep a store" (6).

Kassel's postwar Treppenstrasse (terraced street), which retains an element of Nazi city planning in its excessive breadth and monumumentality, is also Germany's earliest urban *Marke*—space for both shopping and "hanging out," a precursor to the now globally ubiquitous shopping mall.

This commercial space descends, ironically, toward the traditional *documenta* exhibition sites of the Fridericianum and the Orangerie, both built in the early eighteenth century and restored from ruins after the 1943 bombing. The huge Friedrichsplatz dwarfs the neighboring buildings and the elegant and vast Karlsaue and the Hercules pyramid look inaccessibly distant. Next to the Ottoneum and the Staatstheather that stand at the fringe of the vacant Friedrichsplatz is the *documenta* Halle where one of the core projects of *dX*, "100 Days/100 Guests," was held at seven every evening. From its roof glared Friedl's sign KINO (Cinema), which deliberately bore no relationship to the building—a sardonic comment on urban signs in general and in the officious "Staatstheater" sign next door in particular. One was also directed toward the reconstructed antiquarian character of the plaza. At the very end of the parcours, *A House for Pigs and Men* was built by Carsten Holler and Rosemarie Trockel with a one-way mirror looking into a room housing several live hogs, lounging and sleeping. Beyond the pigsty was Martin Kippenberger's last work before his early death, *Transportable Subway Entrance*, where the entry led to a locked door of a condemned building. If his project parodied the networks of travel and communication, one realized that that the whole of *dX*, starting at the railroad station and ending at a useless, locked-up subway station, relentlessly examined a "globalized" world where people and commerce migrate and mingle.

The parcours was thus a real itinerary and a symbolic history. It was both spatial/geographical and temporal/historical. Its spatiality was grounded in the center of Kassel, once a lovely Westphalian town, demolished in the Second World War by Allied bombers because of its munitions industry and now, after reconstruction, a nondescript city of a few hundred thousand residents. Unemployment in this old industrial city hovers at around 20 percent, and its murder rate is said to be the highest of all German cites, a statistic acutely suggestive of the Kassel's relationship to the global economy. Art confined inside the architectural purlieus of the traditional gallery produces objects that are discrete, reifiable, transportable, and thus saleable and collectible; conversely, art that rejects connoisseurship and the market, commodification and isolation, aspires to free itself from the physical restrictions of place. David physically and thematically incorporated the urban environment by placing a number of exhibitions in the street and by showing many works, particularly photographs and videos, that engaged with urban life. She also challenged the frames and contours of autonomous paintings and sculpture by displaying very few of them—there were only five oil paintings shown in the entire exhibition—and by integrating artworks into an ever-expanding intellectual discourse. This was done in the arena of the "100 Days/100 Guests" project in which art, culture, politics, philosophy, and history were discussed by, among others, Edward Said, Rem Koolhaas, Etienne Balibar, Mike Davis, Andreas Huyssen, Alain Lipietz, Valentin Mudimbe, Gayatri Chakravorty Spivak, Saskia Sassen, Wole Soyinka, and Jeff Wall. Thus *dX* extended outward.

Documenting *documenta*

This integration is particularly apparent in the documentation accompanying the event. The *Short Guide*, published to provide visitors with background information about the artists—which is quite helpful—did not always correspond to the actual displays but laid out the details of their contributions to a radical culture. There was no catalogue as such. The 830-page *Politics-Poetics: documenta x—The Book*, published by Cantz in both German and English editions, is not at all a catalogue, but a huge montaged anthology of essays and images from 1945 to the present. It draws on a great variety of work—from Adorno, Artaud, and Gramsci to Guattari, Harvey, and Beckett; from Joseph Beuys and Francis Bacon to Charles Burnett and Lygia Clark—indicating a "political context for the interpretation of artistic activities at the close of the twentieth century."[3] In accordance with the stated premise of *dX*, *Politics-Poetics* contains very little art criticism or aesthetic theory, the only exception being a substantial two-part interview with Benjamin Buchloh by David and Jean-Francois Chevrier, where *dX*'s antiformalist position is fully spelled out.[4] The videotapes of the "100 Days/100 Guests" talks are available on a website until the year 2000.[5] Throughout, curatorial energy was directed towards diverting attention from being focused on individual works to an examination of their political and historical contexts. Provision was made to expand the viewers' attention from the art to the city and its history, to the current global economic and political situation, and finally, to the ways in which people place themselves in relation to this rapidly changing configuration of power.

Unlike the earlier *documentas*, which had embraced a program of discovering and promoting "cutting-edge" avant-garde artworks, *dX*, held at the close of a century and a millennium, reflected on the second half of the twentieth century, and by extension its place in human history. Obviously, it did not intend to survey human activity in every area, but concentrated on the still urgent issues around decolonization, the cold war and the consequences of its ending, de-Europeanization, economic globalization, and the "spectacularization" and "instrumentalization" of art by the culture industry.[6]

The awareness of history was not *dX*'s only prominent theme, however: another aspect of temporality was evident in the organizational principle of this exhibition. The parcours, a little less than a mile long, took at least a few hours simply to navigate. Since the exhibition was conceptual and intellectual at least as much as aesthetic and visual—although such a distinction hardly needs to be made now—each display required prolonged reflection and often required absorbing contextual information. Some works were almost like poems in the density of their references and meanings. The viewer was further slowed by videos and live art, which, of course, require time to take in. All this meant that *documenta* x could not be viewed in a casual or cursory manner if the visitor was to experience it properly, or learn anything serious from the work. Not just the size of the exhibition, but its density and dispersal, its vast referentiality, made a haphazard survey almost meaningless. One had to stop and allow all the thematic and contextual material, as well as the visual and formal, to penetrate one's mind and senses. That was, however, more easily said than done. Just imagine Gerhard Richter's *Atlas*, now expanded to six hundred panels comprising some five thousand snapshots, sketches, and newspaper clippings covering personal and public history since 1945. One felt that none of the dizzying mass of images should be missed. It would take hours, if not days, were one to shoulder the full weight of history loaded onto the expanse of *Atlas*.

Uncritical Criticism

The media rejection of the exhibition was, of course, due to the unsurprising objection of critics, teachers, and dealers deeply involved in the management of the art world to an assault on commodification and a blunt recommendation of radical politics. It was also a result of the inadequacy and unfamiliarity which professionals felt before this unyielding mass of information, resistant to producing visual pleasures. Accustomed to spectacular art and passive appreciation, and long spoiled by a surfeit of aesthetic sweets, they shied away from a confrontation with the concrete and the uncomfortable.

One did indeed have to devise a way to cope with the temporal aspect of the exhibition: to focus on some works and get a general sense of others. As one made such choices, dX reiterated the idea of the limits of historical knowledge and aesthetic experience. Selection was inevitable. Paradoxically, however, the realization of such limits was in the end emancipatory because one also realized that aesthetic understanding—or historical experience—was not generated by the encyclopedic knowledge of specific artists, works, and events, but by the depth of comprehension and the integrity of contextual links, which theories, good theories, always intend. A visitor to an ordinary exhibition walks out with a seductive memory of the celebration of sensuous forms, colors, and materials. A serious dX visitor, by contrast, left with a sense of uncertainty that grew into a desire for further probing. Out of this urge, excitement and exhilaration could explode with an unexpected power. It was a challenge. But then, rebuilt provincial Kassel was not meant to mirror the historical magnificence of Venice. Considered in this way, the temporality of the parcours precisely paralleled the historiography of dX, where the crucial periods of the last half-century of this millennium were stressed—the 1960s and 1970s.

A good deal has been said about dX's "overrepresentation" of the 1960s and 1970s, calling it nostalgic and anachronistic radicalism.[7] Some, however, rejoiced in its unflinching rejection of the art and culture that had become dominant as globalization intensified. Whatever one's view may be, a Canadian reporter's advice to "stop hankering for what's not here and get used to the good work that is" seemed eminently wise. (Jasper Johns and Rachel Whiteread, if that was what one wanted, were readily available elsewhere.) dX reached back to 1950 or even earlier, tracing and juxtaposing genealogies and individual interventions in photography, performance, installation, and videos, often criss-crossing genre boundaries. Interesting things happen to the work when a celebrated documentary photographer of the American Depression of the 1930s, Walker Evans, is seen in the same show as a contemporary Canadian photographer, Jeff Wall, who works with large, digitally constructed photographic narratives. The variety of work on display was striking: Helen Levitt, Aldo van Eyck, Maria Lassnig, Lygia Clark, Richard Hamilton, Marcel Broodthaers, Ed van der Elsken, Nancy Spero, Öyvind Fahlström, Garry Winogrand, Michaelangelo Pistoletto, Robert Adams, Hélio Oiticica, James Coleman, Gordon Matta-Clark, Susanne Lafont, William Centrifuge, Martin Walde, and many more.

Video and cybernetic devices were conspicuously plentiful at *dX*, including work by Steve McQueen, Joachim Koester, Johan Grimonprez, Stan Douglas, Mike Kelley and Tony Oursler, Reinhard Mucha, and Jordan Crandall—some amusing, and others glorious in the fullness of multiple (re)presentation. The ubiquitous presence of machines was due to a powerful fascination with technology, but at the same time the use of virtuality for the exploration of new imaginaries and theoretical possibilities was as tangible and pervasive. Other works I noted include Dorothee Golz's *Hoblwelt* (Hollow World), a plastic bubble containing objects that evade definite identification: a chair, a lamp, perhaps a figure. They are visible from all sides but Golz insists on their separateness from our external experience. "In spite of all this openness, a clear line is drawn between here and there. It represents something else."[8] This "something" is not entirely a fantasy lurking in the imaginary and unconscious, but a disturbingly unnameable presence that intervenes in our daily life. The wry double ambiguity is precise in its reference to the line (or in this case bubble) between the inside and outside itself. Her drawings, too, are peculiar externalizations of unfulfilled dreams and anticipations, suggesting a critical examination of the 1960s which she uses as the source of her images.

The preoccupation with inside/outside and with determinacy/indeterminacy was also evident in the architect Aldo van Eyck's *Arnbeim Sculpture Pavilion Ground Plan* (1965–1966). One recalls that his Amsterdam Orphanage (1957–1961), built on similar principles, was demolished a few years ago despite the protest of Herman Hertzberger. Van Eyck's display had a banner at the entrance gently soliciting the visitors to "Mourn Also for All Butterflies." The Belfast sculptor Siobhán Hapaska is also obsessed with movement. Her work *Here* (1995) is a plastic object reminiscent of a bed or tub or boat, complete with a rug and a safety belt. Is it meant to stay here or to fly, drive or sail away in? Similarly, her *Stray* (1997) is a sage bush that moves back and forth, simulating a wind-blown desert plant, except that it rolls along a rail track. It can never escape, nor can it be still. As in Yeats's poem, "The Lake Isle of Innisfree," a complex tension persists between the desire to stay or go. *Heart*, a redwood sculpture nearby, emitted the sound of waves and distant foghorns.

Rem Koolhaas's enormous talent and energy thrive at the intersection between brilliant description and cynical prescription. His *Pearl River Delta Project* is an accumulation of varied data on the present and future of the Asian city. It is a plan, an analysis, an attack, a promotion, a fairy tale, a "wet dream." This "frivolous" side is indicated by his tongue-in-cheek addiction to the copyright mark and the question mark, which incites his viewers to plunge into an excited fantasy or a sober reflection—almost at the same time. His real contributions, however, may lie elsewhere, in his actual "new urban" architecture where he has no choice but to resolve contradictions in material execution.

Only three artists who showed oil paintings appeared in this large exhibition of contemporary art: the Los Angeles–based gay painter Lari Pittman; the African American Kerry James Marshall, also from Los Angeles; and the Israeli David Reeb. Marshall's huge paintings are works in absolute black humor, portraying blacks in the most stereotypical pastoral manner that seems to refer to their unchanged status as invisible men. In Reeb's *Let's Have Another War* (1997), art is disciplined to remain at the level of newspaper illustration rather than aspire to aesthetic excellence. Documenting the Palestinian intifada, his personal political commitment and artistic will converge rather than generate a tension. As seen in these works, the general stand of *dX* against autonomous oil painting was an important full-scale polemic. When one recalls that Gerhard Richter, perhaps the most important postwar German painter, presented no painting but only his *Atlas* project, the seriousness of David's decision is indisputable. She declared war against the art industry, which is closely integrated into the global market economy and neocolonialism.

Criticisms of *documenta X* from the Left

Three charges were lodged against *dX* from the Left. First, it was claimed, the exhibition had a Western bias. One can still access the alternative website that took a determined stand against *dX* on the grounds that its representation of the third world was inadequate—"a fifth of the 100 guests come from 'non-Western' countries, and half of them have long since been living in the metropolises of the West."[9] These critics, best exemplified by Geeta Kapur of India who gave a talk at "100 Days/100 Guests," were intelligent and articulate. They pointed out that the notion of modernity evident in the exhibition's conception of the nation-state and the condition of painting did not apply to India, Asia, South America, and other parts of the world which demanded greater representation. They also attacked David's statement that token multiculturalism was an alibi for Eurocentrism. These are obviously difficult questions with which many in academia and the media have been struggling everywhere. One side insists on the principle of inclusion and diversity in representation, which alone brings about global justice. The other side believes that national and regional identities are no longer historically legitimate, for the ills of the global economy could be concealed by such mechanical geography, which may in fact be recuperating colonial exoticism and domination. Thus, for dX, the rejection of reified art—no matter where it was made—was a matter of urgency. These contradictory views are not likely to be resolved in the near future, and the two sides will have to watch their differences work themselves out in the historical process of de-Europeanization. In the meantime, however, as Kapur herself pointed out, the fact that such an argument was seriously engaged with at dX was itself a considerable achievement.

The second area of criticism was the budget. dX cost 20 million DM, of which—I was told by its organizers—8 million DM came from various state and local sources—the city of Kassel, Hessen (the province), and the Bund (the federal government). The rest, 12 million DM, was private finance raised through the main sponsors (Deutsche Bahn, Sparkasse Landesbank, and Sony) and through minor sponsors, which needed to be paid back by ticket and book sales. The presence of these sponsors was pretty evident, for instance in the full pages devoted to their names and logos in the back of the *Short Guide*. When I spoke at "100 Days/100 Guests," several people in the audience raised the issue of funding. Obviously, I could not speak for dX, nor specifically about its funding, but the question was important, especially for a project that rejected the commodification of art. My general response was as follows: First, public assistance is not necessarily purer than corporate support. Second, the rejection of all possible contamination inevitably produces quietism and inaction—distinctions must be judiciously maintained between acceptable and unacceptable subsidies. Third, an organizer must make certain that the project remains free of any interference by the funders—any advertisement must be stringently expunged. If these conditions are met, public events and institutions aided by private sources are acquitted from the charges of collusion and complicity. Being no public auditor, I had no way of ascertaining the ethical independence of the *dX* management. I did come across an article, however, in the London *Guardian*: "Ms. David ordered a Kassel cafe to remove its terrace parasols on the grounds that they interfered with her concept and carried advertising slogans, tainting her purist, anti-commercial views on art."[10] This article was not written in support of David's rejection of commercial dependence, but as a verification of her "fearsome reputation as austere and brusque, unbeholden to the commercial or critics' mafias so central to the modern art world."

The final criticism concerned David's uncompromising intellectualism. I had read, for example, that at the opening press conference at Kassel on June 19, which was attended by as many as 1,800 journalists, she dismissed most questions from the journalists as "idiotic," and called off the meeting midway as "pointless." I asked her if the report was true. She laughed and said, "I am not a politician." I persisted, and asked what she thought about the consequences of such statements. Her answer was not clearly audible in the din of the exhibition crowd. She showed, however, no signs of worry or regret. During the four days I spent in Kassel, David was generous with her time. I asked many unfocused questions, which she answered with patience and humor.

Contesting Culture

As I recall the whole experience of *documenta x*, it was absolutely clear that David and her team—one of the staff members called it a "family"—took an immense gamble. She staked her curatorial career, in fact her relationship with the art industry, on her conception of art as inescapably political. The first question David asked Edward Said on the first day of the speakers' forum was how, as a "mandarin" living in the United States, he reconciled his politics (his "militancy") with his "culture."[11] Many of us who worry about the state of art, criticism, and the world situation make many statements, oppositional and subversive to the mainstream, but we seldom take a personal professional risk. When we speak up, we generally know that whatever is being said will be unheard and therefore not injurious to our professional positions. The splendor of David's intervention is that she did willingly risk her future. One might dismiss it as an existential grandstand, an act of self-aggrandizement, or "Ego-Trip" as the German *Art: dab Kanstmagazin* (August 1997) called it, but how safe and easy that argument is to our own self-interest.

The withering responses of the mass media to *dX* were nothing unexpected. They were reacting to the notorious press conference, and earlier refusals to cooperate with the media. Most reviews written after the June press conference paid no attention to the full text of *dX*, which, it must be now recognized, was the city of Kassel itself. Consisting of all the artworks that it displayed, *dX* was not limited to them. In an age marked by the dissolution of the museum, *dX* took visitors out of the accustomed places in which art is seen to witness the urban crisis, its main theme, which formed a vital context for the art. If the city was a work of art, who then was its artist? The Faustian Catherine David, who conjured and conducted it, as was charged by some reviewers? Hardly. Like Weinberger and the "weeds," the "artist" merely bears witness. Residents and visitors together participate in the making of the city that was a "work of art," that was *dX*. In this conception, the artist—the hero of modernism—was resolutely banished, as art merged with life and emerged from life. Far from being arrogant and defiant, the maker of this "conceptual art" was ultimately self-effacing.

Art critics are deeply implicated in an integrated market with dealers. To see *dX* receive as many favorable reviews as it did—for example, from the *Frankfurter Allgemeine Zeitung*, Toronto's *Globe and Mail*, the *New York Times*, Milan's *Domus*—was surprising enough. In time, longer reviews were published that were generally sympathetic toward the exhibition—in *Archis* (August 1997), *Art in America* (October 1997), and *Third Text* (Autumn 5997). And finally, this tenth *documenta* turns out to have attracted more visitors than any that preceded it: *documenta ix* (1992) was visited by 615,000, the largest attendance to date, but *dX* surpassed that with a total of 631,000 admissions.[12] Does this say anything about the overwhelmingly negative response of the media and the art industry? The real question, however, is how David's exhibition, and her demonstration of the persistent links between culture and politics, will be assessed in the longer term. This concerns not only the future of an individual curator, but the present and future of cultural life. If the opponents of bourgeois art acquiesce over *dX*, there may not be another opportunity for a long time to fight for a culture that makes sense. *dX* was a rare, hopeful moment. Are we to let this chance slip by?

JAPAN IS NOT INTERESTING

....

First delivered as a lecture at Amherst College in 1999, in this essay Miyoshi reflects on the state of Japan drawing from conversations he had with various Japanese thinkers and artists. At stake for Miyoshi is less the need to upbraid Japan or those working and living there, than to question the category of the nation itself as the dominant unit for identity formation, and thus for any progressive collectivization.—ED.

I will begin with the title, which sounds suspect, to say the least. These four words, taken as a bare sentence, add up to a bigoted and foolish assertion. It's unqualified, totalizing, as well as vague. "Not interesting" to whom? What does "interesting" mean? What is meant by "Japan"? Is there only one "Japan"? These questions arise at once, challenging the credibility of the title. Further, perhaps, by now no nation-state can be interesting: the industrialized countries are more or less the same the world over: Coca-Cola, Microsoft, plus Disneyfied tourist icons. Only cities, parts of cities, or villages—smaller spaces—can intelligently be called interesting or uninteresting. The four words of course need elaboration.

Some people may wonder if the title has quotation marks. That is, if I am quoting this sentence from somebody else in order to criticize it as silly and misguided. Well, that would be too easy, cliché, and boringly PC. Actually, I do mean it without quotation marks in the title.

When I mentioned this title to a friend, he burst out laughing. Then a brief gasp—finally he added, "Great. You can say that." Actually, I have since told at least a dozen other people that "Japan Is Not Interesting" was going to be the title of a talk, and all of them—without exception—responded with laughter. And half of them added "You can say that," implying that they cannot. Apparently, I didn't fully realize that the title was that performative. And these responses added another dimension to this essay, to which I will return later on.

One more thing about the title for now. It is not original. In the very last essay published before his death in 1888, Matthew Arnold used the expression. Arnold as you know nearly invented the English word "culture" in his *Culture and Anarchy*, one of the most important documents in nineteenth-century imperial Europe concerning national and hegemonic culture. It was not about Japan of course, but about the United States. (The idea of Japan never occurred to the supreme Orientalist Arnold: he uses the word "Japanese" only once in his lifetime, when he lists the languages taught at the Sorbonne).[1] The essay is called "Civilization in the United States," in which he deplores the lack of "the interesting" in the nineteenth-century United States—in answer to Tocqueville's *Democracy in America* (1848). Toward the end of the essay, he says, "What really dissatisfies in American civilization is the want of the interesting, a want due chiefly to the want of those two great elements of the interesting, which are elevation and beauty."[2]

Elevation and beauty, according to him, emanate only from centralized authority and tradition. What Arnold the culturalist said about the United States is, in short, that the United States is not interesting because it is a decentralized democracy, which—as Arnold saw it—by definition stunts the growth, complexity, maturity, sophistication, elegance, and refinement. This negative view of the Protestant democratic America was inherited and espoused later by the elites of the United States itself such as T. S. Eliot, Lionel Trilling, and many other writers who dominated cultural discourse in the United States and Britain through the 1950s, 1960s, and even later.[3]

Quite obviously, this idea of a diversified American democracy as not interesting does not apply to today's Japan. If Japan lacks "the interesting' " no, it is not because Japan is a democracy, but because it is the sort of society Arnold would have liked as it discourages dissent and protest, or what he would call "Hebraism."[4] Although I am aware that this statement is susceptible to tautology—as is Arnold's ("Japan is not interesting because it discourages interesting ideas and qualities"), I should face up to the title, "Japan Is Not Interesting," with quotation marks. (The Japan I am talking about is the Japan since about 1970, certainly not the everlastingly essentialized Japan.)

I began to think of Japan in terms of "not interesting" during my visit there in 1995. I was with different kinds of people from different walks of life—writers, corporate managers, professors, editors, housewives—and spent few hours with the homeless. Most of them made remarks on Japan that can best be summarized as "Japan is not interesting" (or "Nihon wa tsumaranai," "Nihon wa dame yo"). I talked with two writers, one male and the other female, both internationally respected. The woman writer, whom I greatly admire, had just returned from France after teaching there for a year. She criticized Japan for its self-centeredness, for its contempt for minorities as well as women, for indifference to criticism, and finally for its unexamined acceptance of hierarchy. As for the male writer, he is perhaps Japan's most officially respected novelist now, who has been frequently abroad. He is a cautious man who avoids hasty remarks and bold judgments. He, too, is deeply disturbed by Japan's intellectual lethargy today. His books are not being read nowadays, the reason, often cited, that they are too "difficult." Having no readers is entirely his personal failure. For fiction, poetry, history, and "nonfiction" if they are at all serious—are unsold, unread, and undiscussed in today's Japan. My friend's point is that there is a vacuum of critical ideas in Japan today; this enervation drives him, he told me, into the same sort of intellectual stupor. He needs provocations; he needs to escape from this isolation.

The second type I met was corporate managers. (I don't mean that I go around with business tycoons. These are friends who went to school together since the seventh grade through to college, and whenever I go back to Tokyo we get together and exchange news the way Japanese schoolmates regularly do—for life.) One of the friends is the president of one of Japan's largest tourist/transportation companies. His point was simply that 10 percent of the entire population of Japan takes a trip abroad every year, while very few foreigners visit Japan for pleasure. The ratio of Japanese tourists visiting the United States versus Americans going to Japan was about 11 to 1 in 1989, and 14 to 1 in 1993, while the ratio between Japan and Australia was 13 to 1 in 1989, and 26 to 1 in 1993.[5] Even more amazing is the imbalance between the total number of the Japanese tourists visiting abroad and the foreign visitors to Japan: Japan spent more money in tourism abroad than any other country except the United States and Germany, while Japan cannot find itself among the top forty nations with the most foreign tourist arrivals. (China, Mexico, Hong Kong, Malaysia, Thailand, Macao, South Korea, Puerto Rico, Egypt, and Uruguay are all in this favored group).[6] He didn't know the reason for this disparity. Of course, Japan is expensive, but then, other expensive countries—say, Hong Kong or France, Singapore, or England—are doing very well. So why doesn't Japan attract tourists?

The other businessman friend was born in Berkeley, but educated in Japan since his high school on. Then the CEO and board chairman of a large corporation (one of *Fortune's* Global 500), he is articulate. He criticized Japan's bureaucracy and academia as unimaginative, and social relations as remnants of the past that are finally suffocating Japan's industrial, not to say intellectual, activities. His hope was a nearly complete collapse of Japan's industrial system so that it could start all over again. A radical view indeed from a businessman. (The story is more complicated, but I won't go into it for now.)

Professors as a group, as you can easily imagine, are more self-satisfied. Most of them I met were busy and happy with their jobs. There was, however, one professor of Japanese literature who was thoroughly depressed about the whole higher education in Japan, where no one studied, either students or professors. He then said that the humanities in Japan had been dead for decades. Students spend four years just having fun: between years of hellish preparation for the entrance examination and their uninterrupted lifelong drudgery after graduation, this is life's only vacation for most corporate men and their women. Knowing the hopeless future of their students, the faculty demand very little from their students—besides, he wryly added, that makes their teaching easier. Among the dozen scholars I met during that stay—and in a more recent visit—he alone insisted that the university situation in Japan was hopelessly moribund. The rest of them, according to this dispirited colleague, are a part of the cause, or at least a symptom, of Japan being intellectually stagnant. I might add here that this lone rebel professor is married to the female novelist I talked about earlier, and the two are very close in their general intellectual isolation.

The editors are the most pessimistic of all the professional groups.

Several editors I know are all in the few respected publishing firms that survive now. They were the radicals of the sixties and the books they sponsor don't sell. They continue to publish these unsaleable books to protect their prestige in the fiercely cannibalistic publishing business, while keeping their firms afloat by publishing comics, picture magazines, CD-Roms, and manuals.

I tried to talk with some homeless at Shinjuku Station. Many were in alcoholic stupor, but there were a few, full of vitality, reminding me of the sixties rebels. What impressed me especially was their organized efforts to inform the public about their precarious life. They publish pamphlets, for instance, attacking the bureaucracy for its inefficiency and indifference. One former homeless person, now a taxi driver, insisted to me that in today's Japan, the only place to stay out of the tightly structured corporate system is outdoors, that is, the domicile of the homeless. Likewise, the day laborers who live in Tokyo's slums give the impression that they are taking shelter from corporate life nearly as much as they are driven to the notorious living quarters known as the lower depths. Obviously, most are impoverished unskilled laborers, but one of them recently published a book with the title *It is a Paradise to Live from Hand to Mouth*.[7]

But even more enlightening to me were conversations with middle-aged women, housewives, now retired from work and having completed child care. They were probably the most embittered group as a whole. Several pointed to the sorry condition of women in Japan. They talked not just about job discrimination and humiliating social relations, but the self-absorption of corporate men. These men are so preoccupied with their work and corporate life that they have no time for their wives and families. The women say their social isolation is nearly unbearable. Many of them, including a relative of mine, told me that it was sheer misfortune that they were born in Japan.

In fact, I was told by several housewives about a large number of younger women who have been escaping from Japan to the United States, Europe, Southeast Asia, or Africa in the last ten years or so. The vast majority choose the United States. An anthropologist at the University of Oregon is now writing a book on this phenomenon called "The Yellow Cab."[8] "The Yellow Cab" is a self-mocking expression for the "yellow-skinned" Japanese women willing indiscriminately to pick up any men for sex, like taxis. The phrase is used for the title of a best-seller which a Japanese diasporan female published, collecting autobiographical accounts of her sister diasporans in New York and Honolulu.[9] "Office ladies" come to Manhattan and Honolulu with their life savings, looking for sexual and psychological partnerships for fulfillment. They stay as long as their money and visas last, although I am told that the number of "illegal aliens" among them is increasing. The American men they choose are overwhelmingly African American, the reason being that, for them, the white American men are more or less the same as the Japanese men, professional climbers and personal wrecks. I'm not in the least sure whether their racialism should be justified; there is an undeniable element of racist and colonialist eroticism in operation. Yet their disillusionment with their own countrymen is equally unmistakable. The anthropologist I mentioned believes that their exile makes a statement not to the American or African American men, but to the Japanese men that they had better straighten out their priorities in life.[10]

These writers, corporate executives, a professor, editors, the homeless, day laborers, and women at large make up a not negligible fraction of the Japanese population. And the fact that these significant individuals, ranging from the superelites to the lower depths, are expressing deep doubt and distrust as regards the official, dominant, corporatized Japan raises two questions. First, in any society, a critical minority coexists alongside a contented majority. Why should Japan be different? Second, as I mentioned along the way, many, though definitely not all, of these who call Japan unattractive are cultural sophisticates with a considerable experience of the metropolis, Euro-American urban society. Thus such discontent might be merely a version of elitist "Western" indifference/contempt for the peripheral, which they may have acquired in their metropolitan aspiration, rather than through sober self-criticism. I will have to deal with these two questions further before the end of this discussion. For now, however, let me revert to the question of "quotation." I started out by saying that the title has no quotation marks and yet I have cited six groups of people as having said "Japan is not interesting." Is there a contradiction here? I don't believe that is the case: these quotations are still just materials, data, from which I will have to draw out inferences at the end, which then will be, as I promised, my own enunciation.

Now to move on to the other side, the outside world. What sort of people would speak out and insist that "Japan is not interesting"? The answer is hardly anyone. That is not because everyone finds Japan to be fascinating, but simply because of the nature of the statement itself. People don't spend time talking about things that fail to interest them. If someone takes his/her time out to say something is uninteresting, the person is already interested enough to be saying that. When there is no interest at all, there can only be silence—like the case of Matthew Arnold in Victorian England. And in media as well as in general scholarship, this silence on things Japanese still prevails.

On the other hand, there are specialists in Japanology who point to Japan's culture and society as interesting—enlightening and exemplary, or odd and dangerous. The enthusiastic group was very conspicuous about ten years ago among the specialists on Japan, best represented by Ezra Vogel of Harvard, who wrote a book called *Japan as Number One*. I should mention, of course, about the same time there were nearly as many who were clamorously asserting that the Japanese were incapable of universalism and were a threat to Western capitalism and democracy, best exemplified by Chalmers Johnson, now retired from my own campus, the University of California, San Diego.[11] But these two groups—both pro and con—have been much quieter nowadays. Ever since Japan's real estate and stock market bubble burst around 1990 Japan is no longer felt to be a great threat to the American economy. Thus less support has emanated from United States in industry, hence fewer Bashers these days. On the other hand, the disappearance of the Japanese bubble means also means the disappearance of the cash flow from Japan into U.S. campuses, hence fewer Japan apologists as well. Vogel has changed his mind since, I am told: after all, he would say, the United States is Numero Uno; and Johnson has repeated himself once too often. But still, the scholars in the field of Japan who have invested a great deal of time and energy are understandably inclined to call the attention of people at large to Japan. They are eager to see modernity and postmodernity in Japan, emphasizing its up-to-date or copycat cultural state. Or its premodernity, to praise or disparage its traditionalism. But fervor and vigor are not there anymore. Outside of the language and business administration fields, little intellectual excitement is being felt in the United States today over Japan's cultural productions and social conditions; and the experts in the Japan field are as ghettoized among the generalists as ever.

Thus the question is: why is it that there is a feeling now in the United States that all that can be said about Japanese culture and society has already been said? Why is it that Japan, still the second biggest economy of the world—with its GDP at 4 trillion dollars a year, between the 6 trillion of the U.S. and the 2 trillion of the German economy—with Italy, France, and Britain, at 1 trillion each, trailing far behind—is not getting the academia and media of the industrial nations interested? Why is Japan not interesting?

I would like to concentrate on just one feature that strikes me as markedly different about Japan from the practice of other industrialized societies: an obsession with the idea of Japan among its people and its cognate development, the absence of critical discourse inside Japan.

The overwhelming majority of the Japanese place excessive importance on their collective identity, which is presented as "singular" in the sense of both single/homogeneous and unique/exceptional. In the process of nation building, all peoples ask questions about their national identities. Thus in the late eighteenth century to the nineteenth, when the modern European nation-states were constructed, national history, national culture, and national literature were formulated to cement ties among the residents within the national boundaries. At the initiative of the ruling class, who needed the idea of national solidarity for whatever capitalist and imperialist enterprises they were undertaking, "shared communities" were invented and promoted. Former colonies in the years after 1945 have sought their new identities at the time of decolonization and independence. Australia has been undergoing a similar search for some time now as it contemplates secession from the Commonwealth.

In the case of Japan, the discourse of national identity preceded the project of constructing a modern nation-state. Partly because of the insularity of the Japanese archipelago along the rim of the Asian continent, the Japanese elites seem to have always felt acutely the hegemony of Sino and Indian civilizations. Nativism was also a function of the Tokugawa policy of closure, which nearly isolated Japan from international circulation. The two centuries of this official isolation policy created a climate and ideology of Japan as an autonomous and self-sufficient space. The Meiji restoration was at least in part a result of the encroachment of Western imperialism, and consequently its program called for a policy of native imperialism as a counterforce. Japan as a potential and partial victim, and Japan as an active agent of imperialism: both roles resulted in intensifying the importance of the idea of Japan. The years leading to the Second World War were a painful period, during which the Japanese state systematically eliminated and silenced the few remaining dissidents until the end of the war briefly introduced the chance to relearn the meaning of subject positions around the controversy of individuality, identity, and subjectship. Despite the so-called era of democracy under the U.S. occupation, the Japanese fascination with the collective idea of Japan was never significantly altered. There may have been a sudden emergence of cosmopolitans and antiprovincialists; the U.S. occupation was both intensive and pervasive. And yet Japan as the frame of reference for the Japanese never disappeared. This ideology of the unitary Japan was in fact reinforced, during the six years of the U.S. occupation, by the presence of the visible dominant other in their midst. The wartime slogans of "national unity" (*kyokoku itchi*) and "one hundred million deaths for the fatherland" (*ichioku gyokusai*) were switched to the postwar "unanimous penitence" (*ichioku sozange*), preparing the public opinion for the national ideal of "economic superpower" (*keizai taikoku*)—via "peace nation" (*heiwa kokka*), "culture nation" (*bunka kokka*), and now even "atombombed nation" (*hibakukoku*) in which everyone is an atom bomb victim.

Thus the theological dogma of Japan as undifferentiated became even more entrenched in time. By this phrase I do not mean the symptom of *Nihonjinron* (or Japanism), a mental aberration of patriotic racists who insist on the genetic superiority of the Yamato race. Rather, I mean a far more prevalent habit of regarding Japan as the epistemological horizon like a Kuhnian paradigm—a grammatic addiction to preface all sentences with "we Japanese" and end them with "in Japan," and to prefix nearly all nouns with either "Japanese" or "foreign." Manufactured earlier as a public policy by the state apparatus such as the Ministries of Education, Finance, Foreign Affairs, International Trade, and Industry and cooperative media, this idea of Japan has by now turned into an automatic reflection among most of the population. Even the disenchanted types I mentioned earlier—writers, corporate executives, a professor, editors, the homeless, day laborers, and housewives and office ladies—are not free from the near absolute binarism of Japan and non-Japan. As they protest the unattractiveness of Japan, they—or a great many of them—recuperate the borders that lie between Japan and its outside.

As I read books, journals, and newspapers published in Japan, it strikes me as extraordinary that the writers and scholars of the country seem to have eschewed the opportunity to speak up, talk to each other, argue among themselves, and articulate ideas of their own. There are very few forums for the serious exchange of opinions, although many people complain about their unavailability as well as the general decline in public discourse. Many so-called journals of opinion have disappeared. What few that have managed to survive (*Sekai* and *Chuokoron*, for instance) have considerably altered their formats. The mass circulation newspapers (well over 10 to 15 million copies each—against the *New York Times*, *Los Angeles Times*, and *Washington Post*, each about 1 million) such as *Asahi*, *Mainichi*, *and Yomiuri* cater to the huge readerships by reducing the hard coverage of economic, political, and cultural events, and enlarging soft news—as if their model were *USA Today* and *Good Morning America*! An ultrasophisticated journal like *Critical Space* (*Hihyo ku kan*) should be able to fill this vacuum. But instead, it offers translations of currently fashionable names such as Žižek, Jean-Luc Nancy, or Bourdieu as well as Foucault and Derrida. I have no way of knowing how much this publication is really being read, although I am one of its advisory editors, together with Jameson, Said, and others. (My editor friends tell me that people carry it around as a brand-name accessory without ever opening it.)

The absence of disagreement and dissent in the discourse on Japan means an assumption of unanimity as to Japan's signified. The core and outline of Japan are imagined, but its precise nature is hardly discussed. Japan the signifier is what counts; Japan the signified doesn't matter. It has emptied itself of the significant—substance and content—in the discourse on itself. Form and style define whatever is assumed to be the idea of Japan. Japan is unique, because it is unique and because Japan is Japan. And in this circularity of unreferenced construction, Japan's economy continued to soar, enforcing brutal labor policies at first, imposing barest austerity budgets, erasing labor disputes, then gradually spreading out profits, and finally realizing a measure of equality in health as well as wealth.

At least until about 1990.

The last twenty-five years of Japanese history, on the other hand, have been certainly no golden age of intellectual engagement. As the memories of the Ampo conflict faded, all the disagreeable topics were put aside. Economic prosperity seems to have made all arguments superfluous, as if the purpose of intellectual exchange had all along been commodity supplies and physical comfort. Admittedly, the Japanese economy has been less inexorable than the American counterpart in the sense that the distribution of wealth is far less skewed. Although Japan is far from classless, its income disparity is infinitesimal compared with the U.S. or British equivalents. The ideology of Japan as unitary no doubt had a phenomenal success. But then, it was not without a price. By now the economic policy that subordinated nearly every other aspect of civilized life has been showing its effects. If life expectancy is the longest in the world, daily medical care is inefficient and uncomfortable. Japan's "quality of life" hardly matches its reputation of great wealth. Brand name fetishism rages without control. Worse, amidst the bourgeois satisfaction, people are ill at ease with the absence of direction and purpose, which inane abstractions like "peace," "prosperity," and "culture" cannot conceal anymore. If the economic stagnancy since 1990 had any cause in the inner workings of the public mind, it must be traced to this general malaise that permeates everywhere and everybody.

It must also be noted once and for all that Japanese society is far from homogeneous. Despite the oft-repeated official proclamations, it has minorities (the burakumin, Koreans, Chinese, other Asians, and Iranians); it discriminates against women; it is biased against gays and lesbians; there are regional gaps in wealth; and there are visible, though subtle, strata of wealth, privilege, and power. Critical discourse begins with the recognition of such differences, whereas their denial, that is to say, the ideology of homogeneity, inescapably suppresses it. In this view, as long as the dominant and the marginal "voluntarily" agree to agree, the "harmonious" totality is bound to be productive and profitable—to most sectors of society, though at the great sacrifice of a minority. And at the expense of free curiosity and open knowledge for everyone. Is this Japan's version of democracy?

Critical discourse is not the only victim of the ideology of homogeneity.

By fabricating harmonious "consensus," the privileged and empowered of Japanese society successfully manipulate the political process, concealing the actual existing differences and inequalities and substituting a monolithic appearance of unity and equality. A startlingly effective political control is in operation, in short, keeping itself invisible and passing for an unpolitical cultural essence, both communal and permanent. This is why the reference of all statements in Japan has to be directed back to Japan, the addictive formula of "we Japanese" and "in Japan."

Japanese politics thus takes the form of culturalism. Japanese culture is of utmost importance, politically. And positioned at the center of this politico-culture is the emperor system. The 1947 Constitution defines the emperor as the "symbol of the State and of the unity of the people." Although it explicitly strips the emperor of "power related to government," his exact position is far from clear. As the symbol of "unity," he urges homogeneity; as the symbol of the state, he stands somewhere outside of—above?—the law, a metalegal entity. Having no political power, he has no legal responsibility. At the same time, as a national symbol he has a powerful "cultural"—that is, political—authority. In this junction, the "symbol" as a representation is subtly transformed into the political "representation." He represents, rather than symbolizes, the people of Japan. The emperor is thus the most effective institution for converting politics into ceremony, into culture and aesthetics, and by extension, reducing social classes into a hierarchic order.

From corporations to universities, from family to community, people assume an unwritten structure of ranking. At a university seminar, for instance, the students hardly ever talk to their professors, who tower above them—although in recent days I understand the students are far more bored than awed by their uninteresting professors. The corporate systems likewise operate by a tribalistic/familial principle even today. Even the judiciary system is dictated by the concerns of the central power. There seems to be a clear understanding, too, between the media and the power structure as to what can and cannot be made public, as between academia and media, and between arts and business. This hierarchized whole is perceived as free from class conflict. All segments are expected to cohere somehow in the centrality of the whole that resembles Arnold's idea of culture.

People's abandonment of disagreement, dissent, and protest may have made daily life more pleasant and comfortable for the bourgeois majority. Trivialism and sentimentality may be more easeful than intrusive scrutiny. The banality of most media commentators is meant to reassure the readers, as it refuses to disturb them with negative criticism. Collusion for coherence, and coherence for collusion—it worked for Japan's industrial development at a crucial stage. It is, however, now unraveling Japan's critical life. It has produced this pervasive general debility among its population. The effect may well reach far beyond Japan's borders. Japanese scholarship in the humanities and its journalism have consistently failed to play a significant role in the world context. Japan's "internationalization" is being revealed as a sham—a ceremonial exchange of niceties and pleasantries without critical engagement—played by both Japanese and visiting foreign scholars and journalists for the purpose of trade. There is hardly any real encounter. When most Japanese scholars go abroad, they carry along a bit of Japan in the form of well-planned group protection. And the foreign writers have also failed to agitate their Japanese colleagues—by remaining aloof, polite, and uninterested. What is vitally problematic about Japan at the end of the twentieth century is its inability to understand the nature of its isolation from the rest of Asia, the Pacific, the Americas, Europe, and the world. Its internal coherence, water-tight adhesiveness, has inevitably resulted in severing itself from all that is "non-Japanese."

Japan's culturalism no longer works—for the elites, for the state, for the corporations, or for the unvoiced. Economically, Japan's production has been sluggish for a surprisingly long period. And those multinationals—I mean the Japanese-originated multinationals—seeking for industrial resurgence are abandoning Japan for other parts of Asia.[12] Politically, people have no trust whatever for the parliamentary system, which is unable to see its way out of the stultified inaction only marked by corruption and collusion. Culturally and intellectually, the endless regurgitation of Japan's "tradition" produces nothing that stirs any new enthusiasm. Not a single significant novel, poem, or play has been written in recent years. People cannot go on hiding their own real feelings behind the official announcements of "Japanese culture." They seem thoroughly bored with what has long been fed to them; they want to have new food, renew their vigor and restore confidence, but seem not to know where to begin.

Japan's inability to take advantage of its economic power in international politics is at least partly a consequence of this culturization of politics. It might be argued that if the Japanese are self-regarding, they should be confident as to the course of action among their neighbors. Japanese introspection, on the contrary, works differently. As they endlessly think of their own collectivity as the limit, what lies beyond becomes a blank space—except for tourism. Until the end of the cold war, Japan was completely mobilized into the side of the "Western allies." Japan served as an important logistic depot during the Korean and Vietnamese wars, and the U.S. military procurement was crucial for Japan's reconstruction. As long as the cold war lasted, the Japanese government was told what to do even after its emergence as a dominant economy. Passivity was the foreign policy of Japan. One recalls that the Peace Constitution of 1947 "forever renounced the use of armed forces." It was imposed by the victorious United States and was quietly reinterpreted, again in the interest of the United States a few years later, so that it could be read as permissive of a self-defense force. Up to the Gulf War, this contradiction between the text of the constitution and the practice of the Japanese government was more or less ignored, inasmuch as it was strategically inconspicuous and thus not worth troublesome discussion and political struggle. Peace served Japan's economic goals. All this changed abruptly. The United States demanded, mainly for economic reasons, Japan's military participation. Controversies ensued in Japan, but the arguments of the time are more interesting for their political opportunism than for their legal or intellectual substance. Between Japan's dependence on Gulf oil and its dependence on the United States, the constitution was bent and twisted in interpretation, and after a painfully long period of indecision and hesitation, the government came out with the compromise plan of buying off the participation. As some people might remember, Tokyo paid 13 billion dollars to Washington.

What is sad about the situation, as I see it, is that Japan's reluctance for military participation was more than justifiable. The Gulf War was another case of U.S. abuse of power, which even Saddam Hussein's brutal intransigence did not necessarily call for. The Japanese government could have objected to the calamitous use of military force. It could have discussed the U.S. hypocrisy in abetting Iraq during its war with Iran until the Iraqi invasion of Kuwait. Israel's defiance of the U.N. resolutions might have been compared to Iraq's invasion. Or if that is too much to ask, the Tokyo government could have persisted in its alternative—and reasonable—proposal for a diplomatic settlement, which it had initiated halfheartedly. Instead, it chose to offer money in a clumsy inarticulateness. In the history of diplomacy, there have been very few cases in which such a large amount of money ended up buying so little either in gratitude, admiration, or influence.

I began this talk with a reference to the disenchanted Japanese who voice serious criticism of their country. I also said that in almost any society, some people voice fundamental self-criticism. The problem in Japan, however, is that disenchantment is far more widespread, and yet it is as of now not articulated. The dispirited critics—across all levels of society—resign themselves before the chorus of banal and sentimental opinions that have lost credibility even to the members of the chorus themselves. Instead of rising to question and protest, the despondent majority acquiesces before the status quo. These individuals I mentioned earlier are not voicing the metropolitan, so-called Western, views out of self-doubt and self-hate. They at times also question the metropolitan center that has failed to resolve contradictions and inequities of their own. Their malaise is genuine, yet they cannot abandon their collective idea of Japan.

It is among people identified as marginal and discriminated against that signs of new creativity are more visibly emerging and serious criticism is being voiced. Nicholas D. Kristoff of the *New York Times* recently wrote about Yu Mi Ri, a Korean-Japanese writer, Ando Tadao the architect, an ex-boxer, and Beat Takeshi the outspoken entertainer—who all come from nonelite and nonconformist backgrounds—as rising "misfits."[13] I myself found a certain Eiji Otsuka, for example, who spent years as an editor of pornographic magazines, to be a critic with unusual insights. But these "interesting" Japanese are—as of now—hardly known as a serious emergence, not only outside but also inside of Japan. And those few who strive to remain free from any coercive filiative power are the ones who need our alliance.

"Japan is not interesting" is a dangerous statement. And yet there may be an even more dangerous stance that is increasingly voiced among the media and academic discourse in the United States these days. People are no longer talking about any issue outside of their own ethnic/cultural/professional/gender groups in fear of being accused of misrepresentation.

Obviously, the representation of others is hazardous, because it nearly always ends in misrepresentation. Yet one cannot forget that self-representation is not guaranteed to be right or authoritative either. Furthermore, even self-representation inevitably involves the representations of others. One should of course avoid deliberate misrepresentation of the other, which is rampant in both the media and academia. And yet the bond with all the exploited is the precondition of one's own liberation. All ethnic and social groups have internal minorities who need the support of the outside world. We cannot distort world affairs for the self-interest of totalizing and totalized tribes and families and ownerships. In fact, we need to recall that ethnic or cultural groups are not private properties or corporations. We cannot let any ethnic group privatize or monopolize its identity.[14] We need to see the others as clearly as we can, even if that goes against the interest of the dominant in minority groups, not to say against the dominant in the dominant group. As the transnationals try to "globalize" their operation, we have serious work to do—to resist and survive, and to help our neighbors also resist and survive. For the only alliance that is needed now is the alliance of all the exploited, regardless of the categories of difference.

I know that there are people in Japan who feel encouraged when they hear the sentence "Japan is not interesting," feeling aligned with those outsiders likewise concerned. And if that is true, then it should be unavoidably a concern—by a somewhat circuitous logic—for everyone in this world.

IVORY TOWER IN ESCROW

....

Ex Uno Plures

Published in boundary 2 *in 2000, this essay ties Miyoshi's concerns about globalization processes to his own home, the contemporary university. A corporate logic pervades the university structure, from its rapidly expanding administrative division and its desire to partner with business in for-profit projects, to the more subtle and even unconscious ways in which this logic informs critical thinking and basic research.—*ED.

Higher education is undergoing a rapid sea change. Everyone knows and senses it, but few try to comprehend its scope or imagine its future. This two-part essay makes some guesses by observing recent events and recalling the bygone past. Part 1 describes the quickening conversion of learning into intellectual property and of the university into the global corporation in today's research universities in the United States—and, increasingly, everywhere else. Part 2 puzzles over the failure of the humanities at this moment as a supposed agency of criticism and intervention.

1. The Conversion of Learning into Intellectual Property

Richard C. Atkinson, the president of the University of California since 1995, has repeatedly sought to identify the role of the world's largest research university. As he sees it, the goal of today's research university is to build an alliance with industries: "The program works like this. A UC researcher joins with a scientist or engineer from a private company to develop a research proposal. A panel of experts drawn from industry and academia selects the best projects for funding."[1] Thus, although university research encompasses "basic research, applied research, and development," basic research, now called "curiosity research . . . driven by a sheer interest in the phenomena," is justified only because "it may reach the stage where there is potential for application and accordingly a need for applied research."[2] Development—that is, industrial utility—is the principal objective of the research university.

In another short essay titled "Universities and the Knowledge-Based Economy," Atkinson remarks that "universities like Cambridge University and other European universities almost all take the view that university research should be divorced from any contact with the private sector." In contrast to this "culture that eschewed commercial incentives," there has always been in the United States "a tendency to build bridges between universities and industry."[3] This is the background, as he sees it, of places such as Silicon Valley and Route 128, and he proceeds to claim that one in four American biotech companies is in the vicinity of a UC campus, and that 40 percent of Californian biotech companies, including three of the world's largest, Amgen, Chiron, and Genentech, were started by UC scientists.

How does this marketized university protect its academic integrity? Atkinson is confident: "Our experience over the last 15 years or so has taught us a great deal about safeguarding the freedom to publish research findings, avoiding possible conflicts of interest and in general protecting the university's academic atmosphere and the free rein that faculty and students have to pursue what is of interest to them."[4] The issue of academic freedom—as well as the conflict of interest and commitment—is in fact complex and treacherous in today's entrepreneurial university, as we will see later. However, in this essay, written soon after he took office, Atkinson dismisses academic freedom as an already resolved negotiation between "academic atmosphere" and personal interest, and he has not touched the subject again since.

Like most university administrators today, Atkinson makes no extensive educational policy statement, not to say a full articulation of his educational views and thoughts, most announcements being scattered among truncated speeches or op-ed pieces.[5] The days of Robert M. Hutchins and Derek Bok, never mind Wilhelm von Humboldt and John Henry Newman, are long gone. It is thus perfectly understandable, if somewhat disquieting to a few, that he should give minimally short shrift to research in the humanities and social sciences in the university.

According to Atkinson, the university does have another role as "the shaper of character, a critic of values, a guardian of culture," but that is in "education and scholarship," which presumably are wholly distinct activities from serious R&D. He thus pays tributes, in his Pullias Lecture at the University of Southern California, to only one specific example each from the two divisions of human knowledge. As for the social sciences, he mentions just one book, *Habits of the Heart*, a mainstream recommendation of American core values, and asserts that the social sciences shape "our public discussion of the values that animate our society." The Humanities Research Institute, at UC Irvine, similarly, is "an important voice in the dialogue about the humanities and their contributions to our culture and our daily lives." Aside from this reference to one book and one institution, Atkinson has little else to say about the work in the humanities and in the social sciences. He then goes on to assert that the existence of research programs in the humanities and the social sciences at a university devoted to applied science is itself important.[6] Of course, it is possible that I missed some of his pronouncements, but as far as I could discover, there is no other statement concerning the humanities and the social sciences by Atkinson.[7] His listlessness to any research outside of R&D is unmistakable.

A mere generation ago, in 1963, another president of the UC system, Clark Kerr, published *The Uses of the University*, originally given as one of the Godkin Lectures at Harvard University, in which he defined the university as a service station responsive to multiple social forces rather than an autonomous site of learning.[8] These forces, in actuality, consisted mainly of national defense, agribusiness, and other corporate interests. Yet the multiversity was defined as the mediator of various and diverse expectations, however one-sided its arbitration may have been. It was still proposed to be an interventionary agent. The book was reread the following year when the UC Berkeley campus exploded with the demand for free speech by students, many of whom were fresh from the voter registration drive in the South that summer. The students and faculty who took an antimultiversity stand insisted that the university not only produced multiple skills and applications but also "enrich[ed] and enlighten[ed] the lives of its students—

informing them with the values of the intellect." Intellectual honesty, political health, and the social vision of a better future were the components of higher education for them.[9] Thus the movement for civil rights, racial equality, peace, feminism—together with free speech—found its place inside the university.

Kerr's multiversity was perhaps the first candid admission of the university as part of the corporate system by anyone in the administration of higher education. It is crucial, however, to realize that his recognition of its multiple functions was yet a far cry from Atkinson's unselfconscious idea of the university as a site dedicated to corporate R&D. Conversely, the anti-multiversity view of the students and faculty of the 1960s matter-of-factly countered Kerr's reformulation with the long-established tradition of "liberal education." In the hindsight of the 1990s, this mainstream fable of liberal education as free inquiry also requires reexamination and reformulation. We need to register here, at any rate, that today's corporatized university—which would have been an unspeakable sacrilege for many less than a generation ago—is now being embraced with hardly any complaint or criticism by the faculty, students, or society at large. What is it that has transpired between the university as the mediator and the university as the corporate partner, between the protest of the sixties and the silence of the nineties? Why this acquiescence? We need to return to the beginning of the modern university so that we may see more clearly the institutional changes alongside the unfolding of modern history.

. . . . .

The modern university was built around 1800 to fill the need for knowledge production as Europe and the United States prepared themselves for expansion overseas. Scientific and technological research was its primary program, as it was launched in the name of enlightenment and progress. Together with practical knowledge, however, what is now called the humanities and the social sciences was advanced by the emerging bourgeoisie. But the educational transformation from the ancient regime to the revolutionary bourgeois democracy was not as radical as one might suspect. On the one hand, an old-style university education was the noblesse oblige of aristocracy, and despite the self-serving devotion to the maintenance of its class position, it claimed to be antiutilitarian or useless. Erudition, learning for the sake of learning, refinement, intellectual pleasure—such privileged and elevated play constituted the goal of aristocratic education. Bourgeois revolutionary education, on the other hand, was rational, universal, secular, and enlightened. It, too, claimed to be neutral and objective rather than partisan or utilitarian. It is under these circumstances that "liberal" education continued to be a crucial idea of the modern university. There was, however, a more central agenda of founding the modern national state, which demanded the construction, information, and dissemination of the national identity by inculcating common language and centralizing history, culture, literature, and geography. The state promoted national knowledge closely aligned with practical knowledge. Despite its pretense, national knowledge was thus profoundly partisan, and liberal education and national education were often in conflict. They could be, at the same time, in agreement, too: after all, the nineteenth-century state was founded by the bourgeoisie, and it was willing to accommodate the surviving aristocracy, although it was adamant in excluding the interest of the emergent working class. Liberal education was tolerated, or even encouraged, since it promoted bourgeois class interests. It appropriated courtly arts, music, poetry, drama, and history, and, over the years, established the canon now designated as high and serious culture. Liberal education and national education contradicted and complemented each other, as the state was engaged in its principal task of expanding the market and colony by containing overseas barbarians, rivaling the neighboring nations, and suppressing the aspiring underclass. The modern university as envisioned by Johann Gottlieb Fichte, Humboldt, Newman, Charles Eliot, T. H. Huxley, Matthew Arnold, Daniel Coit Gilman, Thorstein Veblen, Hutchins, and Jacques Barzun contained such contradiction and negotiation of utilitarian nationism and antiutilitarian inquiry.

Newman had his church, and his university—a separate site—was merely to educate the "gentlemen," Lord Shaftsbury's cultured men, who were aloof to the utility of expertise and profession as well as oblivious to lives and aspirations of the lower order. Newman's heart always belonged to aristocratic Oxford, even while he was writing *The Idea of a University* for a Catholic university in Dublin.[10] Huxley's scientific research, on the other hand, was devoted to practice and utility, and, unlike the Oxbridge tradition, it was to provide expertise and profession, not Arnoldian culture and criticism. The myth of the university as a site of liberal education, that is, class-free, unrestricted, self-motivated, and unbiased learning, survives to this day. And yet academia has always been ambivalent. In the name of classless learning, it sought to mold its members in the bourgeois class identity. Emerson's "American Scholar" deployed a strategy of defining American learning as non-American or trans-American. In short, it managed to be both American and non-American at the same time, while making "American" synonymous with "universal." This hidden contradiction can readily be compared to Arnold's idea of "culture," free and spontaneous consciousness, which is supposedly free from class bias and vulgar self-interest. To safeguard this culture, however, Arnold did not hesitate to invoke the "sacred" "state," which will unflinchingly squash any working-class "anarchy and disorder," as he advocated during the second Reform Bill agitation around the late 1860s.[11]

In the United States, Abraham Lincoln signed the Morrill Act in 1862, setting "the tone for the development of American universities, both public and private."[12] This land grant movement introduced schools of agriculture, engineering, home economics, and business administration. And later, the land grant colleges and universities were required to teach a military training program, ROTC. Thus no modern university has been free from class interests, and many critical writers chose, and were often forced, to stay outside—for example, Marx, Nietzsche, Rosa Luxemburg, Bertrand Russell, Antonio Gramsci, I. F. Stone, and Frantz Fanon. But perhaps because of the as yet not completely integrated relations of money and power, the university has at times allowed some room for scholars who would transcend their immediate class interests. Such eccentrics, though not many in number, have formed an important history of their own, as we can see in our century in Jun Tosaka, Herbert Marcuse, Jean-Paul Sartre, Simone de Beauvoir, Raymond Williams, C. Wright Mills, and E. P. Thompson, all deceased now. There are others who are still active, yet the university as an institution has served Caesar and Mammon all the while manifesting its fealty to Minerva, Clio, and other Muses.

The three wars in the twentieth century—the First World War, the Second World War, and the cold war (which included the conflicts in Korea and Vietnam)—intensified the proclivity of the university to serve the interests of the state. Beginning with weapons research, such as the Manhattan Project, research extended far beyond physics and chemistry, and engineering and biology, to reach the humanities and the social sciences. Following the organization of the intelligence system (the Office of Strategic Services, or OSS), the humanities soon became far more broadly complicit with the formation of state/capitalist ideology.[13] In literature, the fetishism of irony, paradox, and complexity helped to depoliticize, that is, to conceal capitalist contradictions, by invoking the "open-minded" distantiation of bourgeois modernism.[14] The canon was devised and reinforced. In arts, abstract expressionism was promoted to counter Soviet realism,[15] and in history, progress and development were the goal toward which democracy inexorably marched. In the United States at least, the social sciences have always been directed toward policy and utility. And by compartmentalizing the world into areas, area studies has mapped out national interests in both the humanities and the social sciences.[16] Such nationalization of the university was slowly challenged after the 1960s, and by the end of the cold war, around 1990, the hegemony of the state was clearly replaced by the dominant power of the global market.

.....

What separates Atkinson from Kerr is the end of the cold war and the globalization of the economy, two events that are merely two aspects of the same capitalist development. What, then, is this event, and how does it affect the university? Globalization is certainly not new: capitalism has always looked for new markets, cheaper labor, and greater productivity everywhere, as Marx and Engels pointed out in the Manifesto of the Communist Party 150 years ago. The internationalization of trade between 1880 and the First World War was proportionately as great as the current cross-border trade.[17] This time, however, expansion is thoroughly different in its intensity and magnitude as a result of the startling technological development and sheer volume of production.

Because of the phenomenal advance in communication and transportation since the Second World War, capital, labor, production, products, and raw materials circulate with unprecedented ease and speed in search of maximum profit across nations and regions, radically diminishing along the way local and regional differences. The state has always been in service to the rich and mighty, and yet it did, from time to time, remember that it had regulatory and mediatory roles. The state was not always exclusively their agency. Now, however, with the rise of immense multinational and transnational corporations, the state, with its interventionary power, has visibly declined. It cannot deter the dominant downsizing and cost-cutting trends that often produce acute pain and suffering among the workers. It cannot restrain the immense flow of cash and investment in the world. If anything, the state supports the corporate interest, as can be seen in its repeated drives for the North American Free Trade Agreement (NAFTA) and the Multilateral Agreement on Investment (MAI).[18] Untrammeled entrepreneurship and profiteering thus grow. And the extraordinary rejection of the public sector, totality, and communitarianism in favor of privatization, individualism, and identitarianism is pervasive. This results in a fierce intensification of competition, careerism, opportunism, and, finally, the fragmentation and atomization of society.

Environmentally, the earth has reached the point of no return for the human race. There is no longer a square inch left on earth that is not contaminated by industrial pollution. Environmental degradation is now irreversible: the only thing humans can do under the capitalist system is to try to slow down the rate of decay and to attempt a little local patchwork repair.[19]

The most conspicuous social consequence of globalization, however, is the intensification of the gap between the rich and the poor. Globally, 80 percent of capital circulates among two dozen countries. Wealth is concentrated in the industrialized countries, and yet it continues to flow only in one direction, toward the North. To take just one example, Uganda's income per capita is $200 a year—compared to $39,833 of the richest country, Luxembourg. The life expectancy in Uganda is forty-two years—compared to Japan's eighty years—and one in five children there dies before the age of five. Finally, 20 percent of its population is now afflicted with HIV.[20] And yet its annual debt service is twice the government's spending on primary health. There are countries worse off than Uganda.[21] The uneven distribution of wealth is indeed pervasive in every region. Thus 225 of the world's richest individuals have assets totaling $1 trillion, equal to the collective annual income of the poorest 47 percent of the human population (2.5 billion), and these billionaires, though mostly concentrated in the North, include seventy-eight in developing countries.[22]

The national picture is no better. The inequity in wages and incomes in the United States was widely discussed from 1995 to 1997. Although we don't hear much about it nowadays, it does not mean the discrepancy is narrowing. Everyone knows the epic salary and stock options of Michael Eisner, CEO of Walt Disney Company,[23] or the assets of Bill Gates. Twenty-five years ago, in 1974, CEOs of major American corporations were paid thirty-five times the wage of an average American worker. In 1994, compensation for CEOs jumped to 187 times the pay of ordinary workers. According to a special report in *Business Week* in 1998, the average executive pay is now 326 times what a factory worker earns.[24] This gap is greater than that between Luxembourg and Uganda. Wealth is far more concentrated as the income goes up—that is, between 1979 and 1995, the income of the bottom 20 percent fell by 9 percent, while the top 20 percent gained by 26 percent.[25] From 1992 to 1995, a recent three-year period in which household net worth grew by more than $2.7 trillion, the richest 1 percent boosted their share of the total from 30.2 percent to 35.1 percent. What's more, almost all of that gain accrued to the top half of that segment, a group that saw its average net worth jump from $8 to $11.3 million. On the other hand, the bottom 90 percent of households slipped to just 31.5 percent, down from 32.9 percent.[26] Although the unemployment rate has fallen dramatically recently, many jobs are on a contingency basis—that is, part-time or temporary—with no health and retirement benefits, even in the late spring of 1999, after a long period of the so-called booming economy.[27] The state does not intervene: on the contrary, the tax structure,[28] public works programs, defense expenditures, health and welfare policies, and business deregulation are all being reorganized on behalf of the rich and the corporate. The poor are left to the paltry trickle-down or simply to their own meager resources.

Such an economy—transnational and all absorbing—obviously has effects on the university. The most structural and decisive change is the so-called technology transfer from the university to industry, accelerated with the passage of the Bayh-Dole Act of 1980. I will discuss it fully later, but let me start here with the obvious. In the specific curricula, nation-centered disciplines have been in decline, and area studies, too, has been reexamined since the end of the cold war. The studies of national literatures and histories, the cornerstone of the humanities for several generations, are visibly losing their attraction. The declining middle class sends its children to land grant public institutions that cost less, while the rich send theirs to socially elite private institutions that take pride in their rising tuition. The richer students might be more inclined to study the humanities—as they traditionally did before the Second World War—while the poorer students, who need to support themselves by working at least part-time while in school, are prone to choose practical and useful majors that might lead to careers after graduation. The ruling class always likes to remain useless, while expecting the workers to be useful. And such a political economy of student enrollment obviously affects the curriculum. The humanities suffer. Pure science—mathematics and physics, for instance—similarly languishes from diminished support. Thus academic programs are being discontinued, while disciplines in greater demand are being expanded—often regardless of their intellectual significance.[29]

The so-called job crisis in the humanities is not a consequence of an economic downturn as it was, in fact, in the 1970s, nor is it a temporary event resulting from a demographic shift. The basis of national literatures and cultures is very much hollowed out, as the nation-state declines as the hegemonic imaginary. The humanities as they are now constituted in academia are no longer desired or warranted. There is a decisive change in the academic outlook and policy to deemphasize the humanities and to shift resources to applied sciences. Culture—arts and literature—is being driven out of academia, just as in the old days, and has every sign of being reorganized into media, entertainment, and tourism—all consumer activities—that would be assigned a far more legitimate role in the emergent global economy. I will discuss this further in part 2.[30]

Aside from such vicissitudes in specific disciplines, the impact of global corporatization is clearest in the radical change in the general outlook and policy on academic productivity. The university is reexamined in terms of cost and output. Course enrollment, degree production, and Ph.D. placement are closely watched and policed, as if all such figures were industrial statistics.[31] Scholarship is measured by quantified publication and citation record. More importantly, the development office dealing with grants and endowments is one of the most active parts of the university.[32] University presses—which used to publish scholarly monographs for the sake of the autonomous academic enterprise, not for profit but for scholarship—are now reorganizing their inventories to make themselves commercially self-supporting. Once, every university press title had more than one thousand orders in a vanity press setup, where "one group wrote, one published, and one bought the books: a comfortable circuit leading to secure and tenured jobs all around." Library orders have since been radically cut, now averaging below three hundred copies per title and falling. Whole academic areas, such as "literary criticism or Latin American history," are already being eliminated from university presses.[33] The conventional trajectory of the completion of a doctoral dissertation, followed by its publication for tenure and another monograph for full professorship, is not likely to last much longer. Stanley Fish, professor of English, who also served as the director of Duke University Press, describes/prescribes that university presses "no longer think in terms of a 900 to 1,500 print run" but switch to those that "sell between 5,000 and 40,000 copies." Similarly, the director of the University of Minnesota Press ominously predicts that "in two years there will be hardly any monographs on the market."[34]

Academic downsizing is now accepted as inevitable.[35] Instead of regular faculty, contingency instructors—graduate students and temporary hires without benefits and tenure—are shouldering a major portion of undergraduate teaching.[36] Universities are making use of Internet websites for many undergraduate classes. The California Virtual University (CVU) has now been officially launched, offering hundreds of on-line courses through extension programs. The CVU involves both public and private institutions of higher education (the UC and California State University campuses, Stanford University, the University of Southern California, among others) to form a "global academic village," as one of its planners calls it. As an instructional supplement, digital programs can, of course, be helpful. But the main objective of CVU lies elsewhere. Although distance learning has yet to replace human faculty and its popularity is indeed far from guaranteed, its money-saving potential is quite obvious. Numerous virtual universities are spreading across the nation and even the world: in addition to CVU, there are New York University's profit-seeking subsidiary, Western

Governors University, Pennsylvania State University's "World Campus", and Florida State University, as well as Britain's well-tested Open University.[37] There is also a for-profit behemoth, the University of Phoenix, now the largest degree-granting private university in the United States, which employed, until a few years ago, just seven full-time faculty aided by 3,400 part-time teachers, who were paid $1,500 for teaching a course. The profit of the Apollo Group, which owns the University of Phoenix, is rising dramatically.[38] There are resistance movements among the faculty who might be replaced by the growing digital simulacra. Thus nationally, institutions such as UCLA, the University of Maine, the University of Washington, and York University in Canada are testing the strength of faculty opposition.[39]

To remain competitive in attracting students as well as grants and endowments, however, stellar professors are fiercely fought over: A dozen universities now have at least one faculty member who makes more than $750,000 in salary and benefits—very much like corporate CEOS who tower over hugely underpaid workers.[40] The policy of forging alliances with industries is firmly in place on American campuses everywhere. Fearful of the disappearance of federal support, the universities not only are in search of corporate assistance but are aggressively forming joint research centers. In southern California alone, UC Irvine is building a biomedical center to facilitate the commercialization of university science and to aid the formation of companies. UCLA and the University of Southern California each received $100 million from an entrepreneur to build a biomedical engineering center.[41] Examples are endless, as we will see below.

Such close alliance unavoidably leads to a clubby intercourse between university and industrial managers. Thus many university presidents and chancellors sit on corporate boards, including the presidents of the University of Pennsylvania (Aetna Life and Casualty Company and Electronic Data Submission Systems); Lehigh University (Parker Hannifin Corporation); Georgetown University (Walt Disney Company); UC Berkeley (Wells Fargo); Drew University (Aramark, Bell Atlantic, United HealthCare, Beneficial Corporation, Fiduciary Trust Company International, Amerada Hess Corporation); the University of Texas (Freeport McMoRan Copper and Gold Inc.); Occidental College (ARACO, IBM, Northrop Grumman Corporation); the University of California system (Consolidated Nevada Goldfields Corporation, Qualcomm Inc., and San Diego Gas and Electric/Enova Corporation); just to name a few. And many of these administrators receive sizable compensation in addition to their academic salaries (for example, the president of Penn received $200,000 in addition to her regular compensation of $514,878).[42] Finally, Robert C. Dynes, who had left Bell Laboratories after twenty-two years of service as a researcher and manager to become the vice-chancellor under Atkinson at UC San Diego, produced a booklet called "Partners in Business" after he replaced Atkinson as the chancellor. At a breakfast meeting in 1996 of the San Diego Biocommerce Association (BIOCOM), Dynes remarked that basic research is no longer being conducted by major corporations and that universities are the source of new technologies. Before this talk, he was introduced by the BIOCOM board member as the "CEO" of UC San Diego. The emcee for the occasion was a UC regent, who also served on the committee that chose Dynes for the chancellorship of UC San Diego.

Conversely, many captains of industry have for generations served on university boards of trustees and regents. Veblen complained about this intrusion of the moneyed and powerful into the academic territory years back. There are other studies of university ownership in the early twentieth century.[43] Although there may be a few exceptions, nearly all the trustees and regents of state universities are political appointments, making certain that the corporate interest be securely represented. In more recent days, the selection of the members of the governing board seems to be more blatantly corporation oriented, although systematic studies, reflecting the general apathy of scholars, are not widely available, as far as I have been able to determine.[44]

More important, the CEO has now become the only model for presidents and chancellors of universities. Harold T. Shapiro, president of Princeton University, for one, asserts that "university presidents are their institutions' CEO."[45] The age-old tradition of choosing a college president for his scholarship, vision, character, or even political or military fame is irretrievably gone for now. At least for the foreseeable future, the academic head is a corporate manager who is expected to expand the institutional and corporate base and alliance, build intellectual property, raise funds and endowments, increase labor productivity, finesse the public relations with external organizations, including various governmental agencies, and run the machinery with dexterity. The university-corporation identification cannot be much closer.[46]

. . . . .

Let me turn at this point to the issue that is central to the structural transformation of the knowledge industry, that is, today's practice of university "technology transfer." Atkinson's remarks cited at the beginning of this essay are neither exceptional nor extreme, although they are rhetorically more explicit and less guarded than most in today's academic world. Similar views are being expressed by administrators of higher education— his neighbor, Gerhard Casper, president of Stanford, for one[47]—and they accurately express the policies and practices of most research universities in the United States now.

On December 12, 1980, Senators Birch Bayh and Bob Dole passed a bipartisan bill, the Bayh-Dole Act (Public Law 96-517), the Patent and Trademark Act Amendments of 1980. This law was written in response to the prospects of an intensifying global economic competition, a feared (though not actual)[48] cutback in federal research funding, pressure toward corporate downsizing, including R&D, and the resultant greater need of academic research. During the years of the Reagan-Thatcher economy, the use of public resources for private enterprises was fast gaining respect and significance. The law, as it has been since repeatedly revised, enables universities to commercialize—that is, to own, patent, and retain title to inventions developed from federally funded research programs. Universities and research institutions could at first commercialize through nonprofit start-ups or small national companies, but later through any businesses, regardless of size or nationality. Prior to 1980, fewer than 250 patents were granted to institutions each year, whereas in FY 1996, over 2,000, and in FY 1997, over 2,740, patents (up by 26 percent) were granted. Since 1980, more than 1,500 start-up companies, including 333 in FY 1997 (up 34 percent from 246 in FY 1996), have been formed on technologies created at universities and research institutions. The revenues, in the form of licenses, equity, options, fees, and so forth, are still relatively small. Total gross license income received from licenses and options of the respondents to the Association of University Technology Managers (AUTM) in FY 1997 was only $698.5 million. (Still, it was up 18 percent from $591.7 million in FY 1996, which in turn was up 19.6 percent from $494.7 million in FY 1995. That is, there has been an "exponential" increase in technology licensing activities.) Although the direct revenues constitute merely a fraction of the total university budget, or even of the university-sponsored research expenditures (from 1 to 5 percent), these small figures belie the actual economic dynamics of university R&D.[49]

University-industry relations are far more conjoined than usually understood. First, start-up companies form a satellite R&D community, providing students and graduates, for instance, with jobs and training, while the companies receive information and technology from the universities. Also, academic licensing is said to have supported 250,000 high-paying jobs and generated $30 billion in the American economy in FY 1997 (compared to 212,500 jobs and $24.8 billion in the previous year). Second, some of the university-related labs and companies grow into corporations that then form industrial research parks such as Silicon Valley, Route 128, Research Triangle (Duke, University of North Carolina, and North Carolina State University), Princeton Corridor, Silicon Hills (Texas), the Medical Mile (Penn and Temple University), Optics Valley (University of Arizona), and the Golden Triangle (UC San Diego). These are the late twentieth-century campus landscapes that have replaced the Gothic towers of Heidelberg with their duels, songs, and romance, or Oxford and Cambridge with their chapels, pubs, and booksellers.[50]

The competition among universities for a larger share in R&D resources is fervent in search of both project grants and license incomes themselves and the prestige that comes with being among the top research universities. The UC system is by far the largest research university, with sponsored research expenditures surpassing $1.6 billion, followed by Johns Hopkins University at $942 million and MIT at $713 million in FY 1997.[51] In gross license income, too, UC leads at $67.3 million, followed by Stanford ($51.8 million), Columbia University ($50.3 million), and MIT ($21.2 million). UC is also a major recipient of federal research dollars, attracting over 10 percent of all federal funds spent on research in American universities ($12.3 billion in FY 1996).[52] It must be remembered that these federal funds generate university inventions that are then licensed or contracted to commercial developers. (The corresponding figure for industrial sources in FY 1996 is $1.5 billion, a little over one-tenth of the federal funding.) In the middle of this heightened economic activity, the university faculty ("inventors") earn from 25 to 50 percent—depending on the amount and institutions[53]—of the license royalties from the institutions in whose names the research is conducted and the patents are issued. According to Atkinson, UC is "an $11.5 billion-a-year enterprise. The State of California contributes about two billion of that $11.5 billion, which means that for every dollar the State provides we generate almost five dollars in other funds."[54] Isn't this the source of his conviction regarding the future of the research university of the United States or the world?

Concerning the transfer of federally funded research results to industry, the conversion of nonprofit scholarship to for-profit R&D might well be deemed justifiable on the grounds that inert federal funds are being used and activated by private developers for public benefits. The private sector makes profits, thereby expanding the economic base; students receive direct training, too. Thus the university is made directly serviceable to the public. The high-tech inflow may be said to result in a sharp rise in living standards and the urbanization of an area, benefiting the entire community around the university and the research park, as mentioned above.

There are, however, a number of traps and snares that enthusiastic administrators and policymakers are all too eager to ignore. First, the emphasis on patenting, that is, the conversion of knowledge into intellectual property, means the exclusion of others from sharing the knowledge. The fear of public disclosure that would nullify the commercial possibility of a patent and licensing income hampers the free flow of information that would be facilitated by the conventional means of papers in scholarly journals. Federal sponsorship ought to offer wide-open access to all discoveries and inventions created under it. Patenting delays the dissemination of information, and the principle of free inquiry is compromised. "Communication among researchers suffers, when 'the rules of business precede the rules of science'; colleagues become unwilling to share their data."[55]

Second, the real beneficiaries of academic technological inventions are not consumers and general taxpayers but corporations and entrepreneurs, who often reap enormous profits through less-than-equitable pricing. If the Bayh-Dole Act was meant to make federally funded inventions available to the public at large, such an intention is not always fulfilled. Let me cite two instances of the abuse of federal funding. One of the most notorious cases is the 1993 agreement between the Scripps Research Institute and Sandoz, an aggressive Switzerland-based biotechnology multinational corporation. In exchange for a grant of $300 million, Scripps gave Sandoz a major role in its Joint Scientific Council, access to research findings even before notifying the funding agency (the National Institutes of Health [NIH]), and licenses for marketing Scripps's entire discoveries, all funded by the federal government to the tune of $1 billion. The deal was investigated by a congressional subcommittee, and Scripps and Sandoz were eventually forced to scale down the contract. Scripps may not be strictly a university, but it is a degree-granting academic institution. A very similar agreement was made between Sandoz and the Dana-Farber Institute, a Harvard teaching hospital. For a $100 million grant, Dana-Farber gave Sandoz the rights to colon gene research that had been funded by the U.S. government.[56] Further, the agreement stipulates that anyone who accepts Sandoz money must give Sandoz licensing rights to their research findings. Corporations are saving a huge amount of money by letting universities conduct research and are reaping the profits by investing a relatively meager amount in fees and royalties. Their funding of some aspects of the research is far from ample or sufficient. Shouldn't a portion of the corporate profit be returned to the public, that is, the taxpayers?

Just as alarming as the uses made of federally funded research is the problem of conflict of interest and/or commitment—inasmuch as it involves the question of academic integrity, free intellectual inquiry, and academic freedom. A case that is not a direct instance of technology transfer and yet is closely related to the topic suggests the risks of the university-industry alliance. In April 1998, a task force was formed by Atkinson to look into the legitimacy of the active UC faculty to pursue professional interests outside the university. The dean of the College of Natural Resources, a professor of business, a professor of economics, and a professor of law, all from the UC Berkeley campus, had together formed a legal and economic consulting firm called the Legal and Economic Consulting Group (LECG). According to the official newsletter of the UC Academic Senate, the *San Francisco Chronicle* discovered that the member of the firm who earned the least stood to own $14 million in LECG stock after the initial public offering, while the member who earned the most received $33 million in stock. Academics from across the country serve as consultants for the firm, and several have significant connections in Washington, D.C. The law professor has been a senior economist on the Council of Economic Advisors, and another law professor from UC Berkeley is a major shareholder currently on leave while serving as the deputy assistant attorney general for antitrust at the Justice Department, a job the economist in the group previously held. One of the firm's principals is Laura D'Andrea Tyson, the dean of the UC Berkeley Haas School of Business. She served, one recalls, in the first Clinton administration, first as chair of the White House Council of Economic Advisers, then as national economic adviser to the president and chair of the National Economic Council. The firm has wide-ranging expertise in areas such as antitrust, environmental and natural resource economics, intellectual property, international trade and policy, and privatization, among many others. The firm's clients include not only large corporations but also the governments of such countries as Argentina, Japan, and New Zealand. The dean, Gordon Rausser, sees no conflict of interest or of commitment, while the university administration announces that "it not only accepts, but encourages outside professional work by its faculty, as such work provides two-way benefits."[57] A conflict of commitment par excellence as I see it, the case divides the jury between those who believe that what one does in one's free time is no one else's business and those who dispute the presumed divisibility of one's commitment.[58] Legally, the distribution of work in an academic employee's time schedule (company time versus private time) is nearly impossible to ascertain (don't the minds wander?), while ethically, the direct and full-scale commercialization of scholarly expertise clearly challenges the idea of a university as a site of free inquiry. In fact, tension is palpable between old-fashioned "pure" scientists and "future-oriented" entrepreneurial faculty in many research universities nowadays.

The second conflict-of-interest case—and another example of technology transfer—also concerns the division of one's interest, time, and energy between nonprofit scholarship and for-profit R&D. Gordon Rausser, the same enterprising dean of the College of Natural Resources, UC Berkeley, is involved in another case, this one concerning Sandoz, which has now merged with Ciba-Geigy and is renamed Novartis Pharmaceuticals Corporation, the world's largest biotech firm. The deal is similar to the Sandoz-Harvard partnership. A new Novartis subsidiary, the La Jolla–based Novartis Agricultural Discovery Institute, Inc., will pay $25 million to UC for research in plant genomics, housekeeping, and graduate-student stipends at the college. In exchange, Novartis will receive first rights to negotiate licenses for 30 to 40 percent of the research products. Research will be guided by a committee of three Novartis scientists and three UC Berkeley faculty members. Another committee, which will determine which projects to fund, will consist of three UC Berkeley faculty and two Novartis scientists. This is the first research agreement ever made between an entire instructional department of a university and a for-profit corporation. Is this university-industry alliance what was intended by the framers of the 1980 act? Is the public the beneficiary of the released research results? Or the Swiss multinational and the UC entrepreneurs? Is the public private, and the private public? At any rate, the cumulative effects of such research preferences will have a profound and lasting effect on the nature of university learning.

It should also be noted that genetically engineered corn produced by Novartis in Germany has cross-pollinated with nearby natural corn, stirring up a storm of protests in Europe. Future problems involving academic freedom are predictable. As if to preempt such fears of infringement, the vice-chancellor for research at UC Berkeley stated, "This research collaboration was arrived at in an open process that was highly sensitive to the public interest and to traditional campus concerns for academic freedom." The CEO of the La Jolla Novartis, on the other hand, expressed his view: "This research is, in my view, the final statement in academic freedom. It's not just the freedom to wish you could do something, it's the resources that give you the freedom to actually do it." It is quite obvious that this man doesn't know that academic freedom is a concept different from free enterprise in academia. As of this writing, a proposed $25 million lab to be provided by Novartis for UC Berkeley and the appointment of Novartis scientists to adjunct professorships at UC Berkeley are still being discussed. Since the negotiation was made public, there have been several protests, including those from graduate students of the College of Natural Resources. The faculty at large, including the Academic Senate, however, have not as yet been heard from.[59]

Universities—presumably nonprofit—are thus now engrossed with forming partnerships with business. They seek greater funds and resources that will generate marketable intellectual property, which will in turn benefit academia and business. The cycle will be repeated by the corporations that repay the universities in grants and funds. Take the example of the University of Chicago. As UC, Stanford, and Columbia compete for the leadership in licensing their technology, Chicago, which has no engineering school, saw its national rank in science funding sink over two decades from among the top ten universities to about the top twenty. To catch up, Chicago launched, in 1986, an in-house venture-capital operation. Called ARCH Development Corporation, it is a joint venture with Argonne National Laboratory to "cultivate an expanded community" of administrators, faculty, "potential CEOs, consultants, associates, and investors." The director of its biomedical operation, hired from Harvard, has replaced 50 percent of his department heads, and the place, according to him, is now staffed "with entrepreneurial people responsible both for raising funds and for turning out actual products." The head of the operation talks of "a new ethic": "I've told the faculty they have an additional responsibility to go beyond the discovery of new knowledge. . . . No longer is the job description to sit in your laboratory and think, and expect me to provide all the resources."[60]

The University of Pittsburgh and Carnegie Mellon University together have formed Innovation Works, Inc., to provide start-up funding grants to help with R&D, marketing, and other business support services.[61] UC has its own BioSTAR (Biotechnology Strategic Targets for Alliances in Research), which similarly seeks to draw private investments for biological studies. It has the MICRO program for microelectronics and the computer industry, and also has plans to establish several more system-wide programs dedicated to engineering and communication technology. Its Office of Technology Transfer, both system-wide and campus-specific, guides the practical application of the results of university research by matching them to active license seekers. "The resulting licensing income provides an incentive to University inventors and authors [i.e., faculty and researchers] to participate in the complex technology transfer process [i.e., sales], funds further University research, and supports the operation of the University technology transfer program."[62] Each campus has its own programs, such as San

Diego's Connect, which facilitates the contact and matchup between the campus and local industries. The California State University System, Stanford, University of Southern California, and the California Institute of Technology, just to mention Californian institutions, each has a project, and all these ventures show signs of a growing synergic relationship between industry and academia.[63] The bureaucracy reproduces and expands itself, as Pierre Bourdieu would observe,[64] while converting scholars into corporate employees and managers. University administration is now a steady growth industry, far outpacing the conventional scholars in every discipline. "Historically," says the director of industrial partnerships and commercialization for Lawrence Livermore National Laboratory, "we were a closed place until about five years ago. But now we are more interested in maximizing the bang for buck."[65] From the East Coast to the West, from America to Japan, from Australia to Europe, the transformation of academia is indisputable now in nearly all the institutions that are capable of attracting corporate interests.[66]

. . . . .

Not a matter of technology transfer, though certainly related, direct corporate involvement in academic research threatens to intensify the conflict of interest and jeopardize the integrity of scholarly projects and judgments. Sheldon Krimsky, professor of urban and environmental policy at Tufts University, surveyed 789 articles on biology and genetics published in 1992 in fourteen leading journals in the field. The articles were written by life scientists from nonprofit research institutions in the state of Massachusetts. Authors were defined as having a financial interest if they (1) were listed on a patent or patent application; (2) served on a scientific advisory committee of a biotech company developing a related product; or (3) served as an officer or shareholder of a company with commercial ties to the research. Krimsky's discovery was that 34 percent of the articles examined had a financial interest in the described research. Consultancies and honoraria were not included because they are impossible to trace. When these factors are considered, he believes that the percentage is likely to be much higher.[67]

The conflict-of-interest issue is far from clear-cut. Does financial involvement in itself necessarily destroy the validity of a scientific finding? Stock ownership? Should all financial activities be disclosed? There are many scientists who believe otherwise. Kenneth J. Rothman, a professor of public health at Boston University and editor of the journal *Epidemiology*, wrote in the *Journal of the American Medical Association* that "while disclosure may label someone as having a conflict of interest, it does not reveal whether there actually is a problem with the work or whether the implicit prediction is a 'false positive.'" He called it the "new McCarthyism in science."[68] Since 1992, several journals—the *Journal of the American Medical Association, Science, Lancet*, the *New England Journal of Medicine*, and the *Proceedings of the National Academy of Sciences*—have adopted a policy of financial disclosure, while others—such as *Nature*—ignore disclosure as unneeded. The last group insists that the work should be evaluated for itself, not for the author's affiliation, thus virtually erasing the idea of the perceived conflict of interest. Will this interpretation initiate a radical departure from the accustomed legal concept?

There are numerous complex cases involving at least "perceived conflict" that indeed would require minute contractual details just to be nominally accurate. A satisfactory presentation of such cases here will sidetrack this essay from its main thrust, and I would simply refer to the literature listed in the footnotes.[69] A few broad samples might suggest a general picture: a journal editor and university professor accepts and rejects articles evaluating a pharmaceutical product in which he/she is financially involved, and all the rejected pieces question the product, while the accepted ones support it; a researcher praises a drug produced by a company in which he is heavily invested; a climatologist denies global warming while not disclosing that he is paid by oil companies as well as the government of an oil-exporting country; corporate sponsors—pharmaceutical companies, for instance—insist on the rights to review, revise, and approve the research reports. Many pressures are successfully resisted, but not always. After all, the development of effective medicines is extremely costly, and since federal and public funding is not always available, industrial research funds are avidly sought. Some projects will bring huge benefits to public health, as well. Nevertheless, the eventual importance of a final product does not safeguard the project from vulnerabilities to compromise.

And while most funds are legitimate and honorable, intensified commercialization of research obviously opens more chances of jeopardy.

Finally, does high-tech corporatization benefit the public around the university? Certainly, the industry enjoys the low-cost R&D, funded by the federal taxpayers and offered by the university. The university managers who often sit on the corporate boards receive some remuneration and satisfaction. True also, a good number of start-ups—one out of four—grow into successful companies, and even those that fail can retry, and their trained employees can find positions elsewhere. But what about outside the "business community"? Science parks undoubtedly generate jobs and incomes. The inflow of high-wage researchers contributes to the growth of shops and markets, in turn creating business in service industries. On the other hand, such rapid urbanization means a steep climb in real-estate values, leading to sprawling housing developments and resulting in traffic congestion. This sets off a vicious cycle of further sprawl, traffic jams, and, above all, environmental deterioration. And the infrastructural maintenance for such a development must be entirely funded by the local and state taxpayers. Regarding the corrosive effect of Silicon Valley's indifference toward its surrounding area, an observer has this to say: "The average home price in San Mateo County is more than $400,000; in Santa Clara County, it's nearly that high. Most of the workforce that drives the high-tech engine spends hour after hour commuting to and from another valley—the Central Valley—because that's where the workers can find affordable housing. Polluted air, over-crowded schools and a yawning disparity between haves and have-nots—all are waste products of high-tech's economic internationalism."[70] Unlike some older cities—say, Pittsburgh, Pennsylvania, or Portland, Oregon—which have grown over decades and centuries, repeatedly adjusting economy and civilization to geography, the high-tech research parks lack the needed softening elements of life, such as walks, parks, landmarks, theaters, old shopping districts, plazas—the space for flaneurs. Instead, shopping malls with their sham-public spaces offer the only meeting ground to the young and to grown-ups alike. Shouldn't the university provide a place for rethinking all this before it's too late?

. . . . .

The corporatization of a university means its globalization in the current economic situation, since crucial corporations are typically transnational. Universities are networked through countless international ties. It is practically impossible, for instance, to find a scholar in any university in any industrial country who has not spent an extensive period of time in at least one foreign institution, either as a student or as a scholar. Visits, exchanges, and conferences are routines of academic life. Publications are often collaborative and transnational, and their circulation is worldwide. Third-world engineers and intellectuals are welcomed in the metropolis. Awards such as the Fields Medal and the Pritzker, Kyocera, and Nobel Prizes are, of course, global, as are, increasingly, key academic appointments. Foreign students, once pursued for geopolitical reasons, are now actively recruited for the tuition they bring from rich families in the third world. Sources of research funding—institutional funding, project support, endowment of chairs, grants, and fellowships—are often cross-border, as we have already seen. This development obviously contributes to a greater circulation of information and understanding along with capital and technology, helping to erase regional and cultural misapprehension and misrepresentation. And it indeed has salutary aspects.

One danger that cannot be ignored altogether, however, is the emergence of a global academic industry that powerfully attracts and absorbs scholars and students. The industry is far from a "village" envisioned by the administrators of the virtual university; rather, it is a deterritorialized corporation. Transnational scholars, now career professionals, organize themselves into an exclusionary body that has little to do with their fellow citizens, in their places of origin or arrival, but has everything to do with the transnational corporate structure. As it expands, Novartis is the global model swallowing up administrators, professors, researchers, and graduate students. English, the lingua franca of business, is their standard language. For generations, the goal of the humanities and the social sciences has been advertised as the investigation, interpretation, and criticism of social, cultural, and political relations. But now reality seems to have finally caught up with this façade. The huge impact of the global information and knowledge industry on academic learning that would and should be the most urgent topic of concern was hardly discussed, or even acknowledged, by scholars in the humanities or the social sciences until recent days. Once globalization discourse began, however, terms such as "globalization" and "transnational"—together with "multiculturalism"—have been spreading like any other commodity. In the process, it is being compartmentalized, sheltered, sanitized, and made tame and safe by experts, as if globalization discourse is itself a thriving cultural and intellectual activity. Although some minimal room is still left for serious inquiry and criticism in academia, such space is rapidly shrinking, and the ranks of independent eccentrics are fast thinning. This failure of professors in these "unapplied" divisions of learning to discuss and intervene in the ongoing commercialization of the university is becoming painfully glaring—at least to some observers. What are the intellectual factors that have brought about such a failure? And what are the external circumstances that have promoted this failure? The deafening silence?

2. The Failure of the Humanities as an Agency of Criticism and Intervention

Recent publications have discussed the link between the global market and the university.[71] The 1995 edition of Clark Kerr's *Uses of the University*, for instance, adds new chapters that are deeply worried about the privatization and corporatization of the university. *Academic Capitalism*, by Sheila Slaughter and Larry Leslie, published in 1998, observes that "the freedom of professors to pursue curiosity-driven research was curtailed by withdrawal of more or less autonomous funding to support this activity and by the increased targeting of R&D funds for commercial research." It even predicts that "faculty not participating in academic capitalism will become teachers rather than teacher-researchers, work on rolling contracts rather than having tenure, and will have less to say in terms of the curriculum or the direction of research universities."[72] And yet these books, solely concerned with the institutional economy, have nothing whatever to say on the humanities, as if this branch of learning had already vanished. On the other hand, books by such humanities scholars as W. B. Carnochan, David Damrosch, William V. Spanos, John Beverley, Michael Bérubé and Cary Nelson, and Neil Postman[73] have hardly anything specific to say with respect to the entrepreneurial transformation of the university and its impact on the humanities. The two sides are oblivious to each other. Slaughter and Leslie prophesy that "the concept of the university as a community of scholars will disintegrate further," but the disintegration has already taken place.[74]

In order to reflect on the circumstances around the retreat of the humanities from the line of intellectual and political resistance, I would like to draw here a thumbnail sketch of the postwar intellectual transformation, keeping a close eye on the gradual rejection of the idea of totality and universality in favor of diversity and particularity among the "progressive" humanities scholars. This ideological shift seeks to rectify enlightenment collectivism, and it is no doubt salubrious. At the same time, it must be recognized that the idea of multiplicity and difference parallels—in fact, endorses—economic globalization as described in part 1 of this essay.

To return to the 1960s, the worldwide student rebellion was obviously not a unified response to cognate historical events. Mexico City, Paris, Berkeley, and Tokyo each had different contingencies traceable to different histories. And yet there were certain circumstances that underlay most, if not all, of the campus uprisings: the pervasive effect of the independence movements in the third world; anger and guilt over colonialism and racism; a generational challenge by students born after the Second World War; an intense revulsion to cold war repression both in the East and the West; the newly aroused skepticism about dominant central power, ranging from patriarchy and sexism to statism and straight sex; the growth of the counterculture in defiance of high arts; and, finally, the rejection of Euramerican modernism and enlightenment foundationalism. Such revolts varied in configuration and consequence from society to society, but they were present in some form or other on these strife-torn campuses throughout the world. Further, in a tightening circle of globality, the regional events were interconnected and convergent.

Among the French intellectuals, the consequences of the liberation movements in Vietnam and Algeria were deep and wide, while their historical alliance with Soviet communism was being shattered by Khrushchev's revelation of Stalinism in 1956 and the Soviet intervention in Hungary that same year and Czechoslovakia later on. Marxist humanism was the first to be interrogated after the horrors of postwar discoveries began to sink in to European minds. Such skepticism called into question universality of any kind, including Eurocentricity, proposing "difference" as the cognitive framework, and "differance" as the strategy. Language was the limits beyond which "reality" was gradually banished as inaccessible. The postmodern turn thus commenced.

After the Second World War, the preeminent intellectual had been Sartre, whose Marxist commitment to humanism, universality, and collectivism was, in fact, already attenuated by his existentialist rejection of the essence and by his at least dormant structuralism. And yet for Claude Lévi-Strauss, whose ethnology replaced Sartrean existential humanism as the most hegemonic of French thoughts, it was the Saussurean linguistic model of difference that was interpreted as providing the ground for liberation egalitarianism. His perceived abandonment of totality as well as universalism, derived as it was from a profound disillusionment with collectivism, centralism, and enlightenment humanism, was instrumental in generating various schools of structuralism and poststructuralism. According to Lévi-Strauss, "Civilization implies the coexistence of cultures offering among themselves the maximum of diversity, and even consists in this very coexistence."[75] His epistemology of difference that led to the recognition and maintenance of diversity and plurality was powerfully enabling to third-worldism, Maoism (an alternative Marxism), feminism, antiracism, anti-Orientalism, and antitotalitarianism. More importantly, his challenge to totality and to Eurocentricity had an impact on every branch of learning, from anthropology and sociology, to art, literature, history, politics, and law, among the students and the now dominant poststructuralist theorists, such as Jacques Lacan, Roland Barthes, Louis Althusser, Paul de Man, Jean-François Lyotard, Gilles Deleuze, Félix Guatarri, Michel Foucault, and Jacques Derrida.

Lévi-Strauss's structuralism was a response to the rupture of the long-established tradition of Eurocentricity, and it has played an immensely important role in intellectual history not only in France but also nearly everywhere else in the world to this day. However, it also introduced problems of its own, whose culminating aftermath is now beginning to be felt in this age of the global economy. First, Lévi-Strauss's anthropology is, as the title of one of his later books indicates, "the view from afar," because to maintain the diversity of cultures, one should not/cannot intimately identify with any. The result is not only a propensity toward exoticism and superficial knowledge, but uninvolvement, laissez-faire, and indifference regarding the other. Second, diverse cultures are equally unique and autonomous in the sense that there are no common terms in which to compare them: he points out, for instance, "the absurdity of declaring one culture superior to another."[76] Does he mean that cultures, and ages, should be/are always equally desirable or undesirable? Cognitive relativism is unavoidable, and solipsism and randomness ensue. Third, in Saussurean linguistics, which is construed as based on the lexicographic system of difference, a sign is understood in its relation to other signs but not to its referent. In Lévi-Strauss's application, reference is inevitably lost, and thus "truth" is assumed to be unrepresentable. The world is now shifted to texts, and history to narratives. Fourth, every culture or age has its own unique terms and discourses, which are thus judged incommensurable across the cultural and historical borders. Fifth, to the extent that the discreteness of diverse cultures is presumed, each individual subject born into a culture is regarded as inescapably determined by it. This is an impossible contradiction to his basic premise of difference, which denies totality and collectivity (is a given culture an undifferentiated totality?); but, more significantly, the subjectship—the individual agency—is disallowed so as to make any political engagement impossible. Finally, because of this erasure of political agency, the diversity of cultures paradoxically surrenders to the hegemonic center once again—very much as in the so-called global "borderless" economy.

Obviously, this is a simplification, and it might well be called an American literary and critical interpretation of the transmigration of French structuralism/poststructuralism. Also, the rejection of universality, collectivity, reference, and agency in favor of difference, particularity, incommensurability, and structure can hardly be uniform among the poststructuralists. And yet, as seen in the context of the theorists in the United States, there is an undeniable common proclivity among them to fundamentally reject such totalizing concepts as humanity, civilization, history, and justice, and such subtotalities as a region, a nation, a locality, or even any smallest group. As if breathing together the zeitgeist of division and difference, they each believe that foundational ideas and concepts are historical and cultural constructs—as represented by Thomas Kuhn's "paradigm"[77] or Foucault's "episteme"—and that no all-inclusive judgment or causal explanation can be found. The fear of totality as inevitably totalitarian remains unabated. The theory of difference is not limited to history but extends to social and cultural relations. A totality is differentiated as a majority and minorities, then a minority into subminorities, a subminority into sub-subminorities, and so on. Differentiation and fragmentation never stop by the sheer force of its logic. Such precise identification is a beneficial calibration in the face of crude generalizations that obliterate the distinctions that exist in any category. It helps to fight marginalization and erasure. Yet if the strategy of division and fragmentation is not contained and moderated with the idea of a totality—its context—it may very well lose its initial purpose and end up paradoxically in universal marginalization.

An individual, a group, or a program requires a totality in which to position itself. Conversely, a totality is not always a monolithic system for the suppression of all differences and marginalities. Specifics and particulars negotiate at all levels with the context and with other specifics and particulars. Likewise, all concepts and ideas may be bound to a specific locale in time and place, but a specific locale in time and place does not produce uniform and identical concepts and ideas. Further, essentialism would be equally present and absent in both totality and particularity.

The contradiction, or antinomy, between totality and particularity is most clearly demonstrated in a debate between Noam Chomsky and Foucault, "Human Nature: Justice versus Power," held in 1974. Their disagreement becomes palpable in the second half of the debate, where they argue about the notion of justice. For Foucault, justice is a historical and social invention "as an instrument of a certain political and economical power or as a weapon against that power," whereas for Chomsky, it should have/has "an absolute basis . . . residing in fundamental human qualities." Foucault disagrees with Chomsky's old-fashioned enlightenment metanarrative on the grounds that it is just one discourse among many. Chomsky speaks not only as a universalist intellectual here but also as one who is committed to the struggle for the suppressed of the world. Chomsky indeed believes that truth and falsehood can be distinguished and that the individual as the subjective agent has a moral responsibility. For Foucault, such claims are merely functions of the desire for power. Chomsky, on the other hand, detects in the Foucauldian abandonment of justice and the truth a cynicism that conceals a moral and political failure behind an elaborate intellectual sophistry.[78]

The theory of difference has been far more enthusiastically embraced in the United States, Canada, and Australia than in European countries because of its long history of a settlement society par excellence, where heterogeneous races and ethnicities have "coexisted" geographically. The university rebellion of the 1960s began, as we have already seen, with the civil rights movement in the late fifties and early sixties, and with the rising protest against the war in Vietnam. Further, the United States was founded on the long history of genocide and slavery, whose effects have not yet been erased even in this late date of 2000. More recently, the global economy, as we have already seen, has vastly intensified migration and exchange, and the promise and the problem of difference have been daily encountered and accommodated. Thus multiculturalism is the urgent issue both of pedagogy and political economy in the university in the United States.

Multiculturalism that rejects the discrimination of marginal groups is a democratic improvement over the majoritarian monopoly that had long suppressed all but dominant history and culture. Under multiculturalism, all sections and factions can claim fair inclusion and representation, and there have been signs of success in several actual social programs. Affirmative action is a practical program rooted in a version of multiculturalism that has resulted in an increased participation of women and minorities in both industry and the university. The representation is still far from equitable, and yet one should remember how complete the exclusion of the peripheries was a mere generation ago. Before proceeding to celebration, however, one needs to face the problems. First, there are the revived challenges to the legality of the affirmative action laws that threaten to reduce enrollment of women and minorities once again. Though protected by the present federal laws, the future of such programs of redress is far from assured. And let me repeat once more: the equalization and inclusion of marginals are still far from adequate in any social category.

More crucially, contradictory currents that converge in the program of multiculturalism itself must be noted: the greater recognition of alterities, on the one hand, and the exclusionist reaffirmation of self-identity, on the other. The former is the official line of multiculturalism by which the world is perceived to be diverse and one's place to be within this plurality. The principles of diversity and plurality demand that one's own ethnicity or identity be deemed to be no more than just one among many. If this requirement of equal limitation and discipline were accepted by all members of the "global community," multiculturalism would make great strides toward the realization of a fair and just human community. Self-restriction, however, is seldom practiced for the betterment of general and abstract human welfare—especially when it involves material discipline and sacrifice for the parties involved.[79] Besides, multiculturalism premised on all particularities of all categories—ethnicity to class, region to development, gender to nationality, poverty to wealth, race to age—is infinitely varied, and even in this age of cross-border mobility, no one is expected to know intimately more than an infinitesimal portion of such variety. Picture the variations: aged and impoverished white lesbian women, rich Korean men who speak no English, gay middle-class Lebanese American males who are newly jobless with no families. However imaginative, sympathetic, or concerned, one is severely restricted in the ability to know and embrace others. The view is bound to be "from afar." When the difference—gap—in wealth is widening, as now, the cross-categorical understanding becomes still more difficult. And the harder the likelihood of coeval encounter proves, the louder the cry for multiculturalism rises. The abstract principle of multiculturalism, an expression of liberal open-mindedness and progressive tolerance, much too often stands in for an alibi to exonerate the existing privileges, inequities, and class differences.

Two other possible perils are inherent in the program of difference and multiplicity. First, very much like industrial globalization, multiculturalism is preoccupied with the façade of internationalism and cosmopolitanism, helping to form a league of the elite in all regions of the world, while ultimately ignoring the multitudes in hopeless economic isolation and stagnancy. Second, multiculturalism has been paradoxically aloof to the establishment of a transidentity affiliation, and this indifference directly inverts itself into the aggressive rejection of any involvement in the affairs of, for, and by the other. Thus multiculturalism amounts often to another alibi: under the pretext of eschewing the "colonialist" representation of former colonies, it abandons the natives to their "postcolonial" vacuum and disorder of authority, often a direct result of earlier colonialism itself. There are numerous examples of such developments, the most conspicuous of which are the sub-Saharan countries, where starvation, corruption, pillage, and violence relentlessly continue—while the northern nations merely stand by without offering assistance. At home, inner cities are their equivalents. Supported by the idea of postcoloniality, the positioning of colonialism as a past event, multiculturalism works nearly as a license to abandon the welfare of the unprofitable marginals and concentrate on the interests of the dominant. This is what Slavoj Žižek means when he characterizes multiculturalism as "the ideal form of ideology of this global capitalism."[80]

An oppressed and exploited group has the right and responsibility to defend itself, and it requires the firm establishment of a group identity for self-protection. Once survival and self-defense cease to be a desperate necessity, however, identity politics often turns into a policy of self-promotion, or, more exactly, a self-serving sales policy in which a history of victimization becomes a commodity that demands payment.[81] It can pervert itself into opportunism and cannibalism, be it racial, sexual, national, social, or otherwise. In the name of multiculturalism, one privileges one's own identity, while making merely a token acknowledgment of the other's—whom one proceeds to disregard when an occasion for help arrives. It is as if self-identity were an article of private property, which the group—but more likely its elite leadership—claims to own and guard exclusively. Exclusionism is destructive, whether among the rulers or the ruled. Entrepreneurial self-assertion sunders any possible political alliance with other marginal groups into uncoordinated and fragmented promotional drives, which most likely head toward a disastrous defeat in the hands of the far better organized dominant parties. In this connection, it may do well to reflect on what Tzvetan Todorov suggests as a common human feature: "The context in which human beings come into the world subjects them to multiple influences, and this context varies in time and space. What every human being has in common with all others is the ability to reject these determinations."[82] I do not believe that such freedom is given to everyone, and yet the wish occasionally to alter them, to assume the identity of another, must surely be a very common experience indeed. The borders between beings must remain passable at least in the imagining.

To return to the corporate use of multiculturalism, privatization and entrepreneurship are valorized in globalism. While the corporate system has no reason—or no profit motive—for eradicating racism and sexism, it has similarly little reason—or little profit motive—for always encouraging racism and sexism. In fact, the corporate system stands to gain under certain circumstances by promoting diversity among ethnic and gender groups as it expands its markets, insofar as it can retain class difference and uneven development—the indispensable capitalist condition for cheap labor. Here, identity politics, to which the idea of diversity often irresistibly leads, can easily be played into the hands of corporate management. Every marginal group will be as exclusive and alienated from all others, as it is led by ethnic spokespersons, each working in a self-sealed entrepreneurship, with its identity as a private investment, as capital. Transnational corporatism needs only low-cost labor, regardless of its ethnic origins and geographical roots. Which ethnicities or regions it comes from is of little consequence.[83] In the advocates of exclusionary identity politics, in fact, transnational capitalism, or neocolonialism, finds a soul mate who can stand in as the manager of the group.

. . . . .

In the context of the university's organization, identity politics is bound to create factionalism and fractionalization. But it now has the imprimatur from the philosophy of difference. The multiplicity of perspectives, specializations, and qualifications is intensified with the rage for differentiation. Agreement is ipso facto suspect and unwanted. Internecine disputation is substituted for political engagement. Thus, in a humanities department now, feminists vie with ethnic groups as well as the male of all kinds; among feminists, essentialists contest antiessentialists; assaults on the "ludic posties" become the career of "postludic" academics; post-Marxists reject orthodox Marxists; conventional disciplinary scholars hold in contempt cultural studies writers; novelists despise theorists who can't sell products; theorists look down on creative writers as ignorant and self-absorbed; empirical historians are convinced that theorists are moonstruck obscurantists; queers believe they are the best because their identities are identityless; formalists are proud of their purity, while they are the targets of derision as hopelessly out of date and out of touch according to the politically engaged; ethnics are opportunists in the eyes of the whites, whereas the whites are both mindless and heartless troglodytes as the marginals see them.

Factions disagree with each other on nearly every topic, be it the B.A. or Ph.D. requirements, recruitment and admissions preferences, promotion, tenure, or even the selection of a guest lecturer. The most difficult document to compile in any academic unit nowadays may be the general description of itself, its history and objective, in the form of a handbook or manual. Strife, however, is not the worst of possibilities: At least people are talking to each other—even if they do raise their voices. It is common today to observe a mutually icy-distant silence, which allows everyone to escape into her/his womblike cocoon, talking minimally to the fewest contacts possible. Thus, instead of open discussion and argument at a meeting, perfunctory mail ballots—likely by email—decide issues. Education of undergraduates consists of the mechanical transfer of safe packaged information unsullied by fundamentals and intricacies; graduate education is somewhat more involved, but even that is apt to be left to the students themselves. Uncontaminated as yet, graduate students expect guidance of a general nature in the humanities but often find that the best part of their education is in reading groups they form among themselves rather than in the institutional seminar rooms, where the instructors, full of anxieties over other texts and readings, tend to say nothing of significance. Indeterminacy rules, and it is a poor bargain for those graduate apprentices who must decide on their future in the few years allowed them by the production-dictated rules of their graduate administrators. The administration's pressure toward quantitative production—though no one knows the specifications— heats up the internal mechanics of academia. Nowadays, more frequently than ever, humanities departments are placed in receivership, an academic equivalence of bankruptcy, in which the unit is judged to be incapable of handling itself because of irreconcilable internal dissension.[84]

The faculty would rather do the things that might promote their professional careers. Untenured assistant professors are understandably in panic; they may not make it. Furthermore, they know that a financial downturn— real or fabricated—can legally eliminate the programs they have worked so hard to get into. But before that eventuality takes place, they must first sneak in, even if there is no guarantee of any kind for their long unfathomable future years. Yet the marginalization of the humanities and the social sciences has been terrifying not only the pretenure faculty but also the supposedly securely tenured professors. The same eventualities face them. They still have many years remaining in their careers, and during these long leftover years, they need to appear confident and attractive at least to their students (customers), if not to their colleagues (business competitors). The sad fact is that many aging professors are finding it difficult to conceal the lack of a project that fully absorbs their interest and energy, if not passion and imagination. But most choose to evade it. It is pathetic to have to witness some of those who posed as faculty rebels only a few years ago now sheepishly talking about the wisdom of ingratiating the administration—as if such demeaning mendacity could veer the indomitable march of academic corporatism by even an inch. To all but those inside, much of humanities research may well look insubstantial, precious, and irrelevant, if not useless, harmless, and humorless. Worse than the fetishism of irony, paradox, and complexity a half century ago, the cant of hybridity, nuance, and diversity now pervades the humanities faculty. Thus they are thoroughly disabled to take up the task of opposition, resistance, and confrontation, and are numbed into retreat and withdrawal as "negative intellectuals"[85]—precisely as did the older triad of new criticism. If Atkinson and many other administrators neglect to think seriously about the humanities in the corporatized universities, the fault may not be entirely theirs.

If all this is a caricature, which it is, it must nevertheless be a familiar one to most in the humanities now. It is indeed a bleak picture. I submit, however, that such demoralization and fragmentation, such loss of direction and purpose, are the cause and effect of the stunning silence, the fearful disengagement, in the face of the radical corporatization that higher education is undergoing at this time.

. . . . .

In the macromanagement picture, there is little likelihood here of a return to nation-statism, which enabled the construction of a national history, a national literature, a national culture, and a national economy during the major portions of the last two centuries. Obviously, the nation-state structure will not disappear anytime soon, but this does not mean that it is still the fecund soil for intellectual and cultural imagination now. That time is over, and it is glad tidings in several ways. At the same time, now unchecked by national and regional sectioning, control quietly made pervasive and ungraspable in the global economy is even more powerfully effective. And there is hardly any space for critical inquiry and cultural resistance in academia that might provide a base from which to launch a challenge to this seamless domination of capital. Does this mean an end to all oppositionist politics?

As long as extreme inequity in power and privilege persists, there will be discontent and resentment that can ignite at a propitious moment. The opportunity will not arrive by the call from an intellectual leader, of course. When the workers and underclass find it intolerable to live on with the uneven distribution of comfort and suffering, they will eventually rise up. The humanities as we have known it for many decades have ceased to be of use for now. Critics, however, can still discern signs among people and organize their findings into an argument and program for dissemination. The academics' work in this marketized world, then, is to learn and watch problems in as many sites as they can keep track of, not in any specific areas, nations, races, ages, genders, or cultures, but in all areas, nations, races, ages, genders, and cultures. In other words, far from abandoning the master narratives, the critics and scholars in the humanities must restore the public rigor of the metanarratives. Together with those already mentioned, there are several others whose voices I, for one, would cherish to hear. As important, we know that in every institution, there are serious minds who quietly keep toiling in their reflection and teaching, often unrewarded and unacknowledged except by their students. They may well be the ones with whom the people will share their future in large measure. What we need now is this powerfully reintegrated concept of society, where diversity does not mean a rivalry of minorities and factions, and resultant isolation. The emerging orientation of scholarship is likely to appear yet opaque and ill-defined for those accustomed to the clear dictates of the nation-state during the colonial, imperial, and cold war years. It is no mean task in these days to orient one's own scholarship in the university that is being reduced to the exclusive site for R&D. The administrators seem eager to write off the humanities—as an instrument to control minorities, or else merely as a managerial training program in metropolitan manners, style, and fashion, set aside for the socially "elite" institutions. We need a new interventional project with which to combat the corporatization of the university and the mind.

The appellation "ivory tower," a translation of "tour d'ivoire," is a cliché and is as taken for granted as the university itself. Examined closely, however, the designation reveals more than we are accustomed to seeing in it: the modern university is indeed built with ivory, a material robbed from Africa and India, where elephants are now nearly extinct, and thus ivory is contraband.[86] The greatest benefactor of the modern university, upon reflection, may indeed be King Leopold of Belgium, Queen Victoria's uncle, who may have contributed to the extinction of ten million African lives. We should perhaps never talk about the modern university without recalling Joseph Conrad's *Heart of Darkness*. The late Bill Readings's excellent book, *The University in Ruins*, is right in its discussion of the humanities.[87] In other aspects, however, today's university is immensely prosperous and opulent. No longer far from the madding crowd, the university is built increasingly among shopping malls, and shopping malls amidst the university. It is no longer selling out; it has already been sold and bought. The deed has been written and signed, and the check already signed, too. But the deed has not been registered, and the check not cashed as yet. To right the situation, to null the transaction and be just to all on earth, we may have to relearn the sense of the world, the totality, that includes all peoples in every race, class, and gender.

TURN TO THE PLANET

....

Literature and Diversity, Ecology and Totality

First presented in 2000 as a lecture about East Asian literature in Seoul, this piece—later published in Comparative Literature *in 2001—tracks shifts in literary studies, the political economy, and the university over a period of seventeen years. Besides the increased globalization of capitalism and the shifts from a formalism to a more sociohistorically oriented literary criticism, Miyoshi accounts for changes in his own scholarly and critical engagement, changes that now prioritize a rethinking of totality over the celebration of difference.—*ED.

Literary Studies in 1983

In 1983, eighteen years ago, I was in Seoul to present a paper. The occasion was a conference on East Asian literature, a topic that is not too different from the one assigned to me for another event last year in the same city.

Seventeen years may not be a long time in a normal phase of history. Between 1715 and 1732, for example, or even between 1918 and 1935, the change was certainly not trifling, but still the sense of continuation was quite solid. The difference between 1983 and 2000, however, is so immense that not only can we barely grasp the magnitude of changes and transformations between the two terminals, but the phrase like a "normal phase of history" is itself beginning to lose meaning. It looks as if we were heading toward a future where the pace of change will only accelerate and to such an extent that the trace of history may be erased as time hurries along through our everyday life. Thus, first, I'd like to recall the ideas that were crucial in 1983, or that I considered significant then, as recorded in the proceedings of the 1983 conference, and second, to set these thoughts against what seems crucial now and reflect on the intervening events. It might also reveal what has survived unchanged and suggest what may remain intact in the future. I will be of course discussing the changes and continuities inside what has been known as literature, but also those outside of it, since the two are indivisible in the long confluence of history.

By the beginning of the 1980s, the impact of Edward Said's *Orientalism*, published in 1978, had spread far beyond its immediate range of the Middle East and colonial history.[1] His Nietzschean and Foucauldian message on the genealogy of the concepts of power and learning was generalized in the discourse of modern history. Orientalism radically challenged the orthodoxy in disciplines like history, anthropology, geography, and sociology as well as literary criticism, as everyone knows. Many branches of the humanities and social sciences had been formed during the colonial period with unexamined assumptions of the centricity of European and North American civilization, and the emergent intellectuals in the just-liberated former colonized world found in Said's criticism something both revolutionary and fundamental for mapping the history and geography of the future. The term "Orientalism" was added to the vocabulary of many languages as a name for the hegemonic ideology of domination. This was to be the beginning of a new paradigm for equality and the open mind. In the context of the dominant practice of the Eurocentric formulation of knowledge, however, the anti-Orientalist criticism was looked on as a disturbing challenge. To the academic establishment, it was a movement of rebellion and resistance—at least at the initial stage.

The East Asian field (where I have been more than an occasional sojourner), had been long organized from the colonial perspective, and thus Said's criticism was not accepted at once, especially among the established scholars. Critical categories, transferred from European literature to East Asian without scrutinizing their precise applicability, were still very much in use. Genre, form, structure, periodicity (such as "modernity" and "modernization"), intentionality, affect, authorship, originality, audience, textuality, media, the plot, character, tonality, the idea of "literature" itself, and many other fundamental literary and cultural notions, the terms used in describing and analyzing European literature(s) and culture(s), were more or less randomly chosen as approximations. Even in the 1983 conference in Seoul, there were sharp divisions and disagreements among the panelists on the merit of the newly proposed transvaluation. Here I should briefly speak for myself in order to avoid misrepresenting other scholars.

As I reread my contribution, "Against the Native Grain: Reading the Japanese Novel in America," I am reminded of several events both personal and critical that took place around the time. I came to know Edward Said well, while he was finishing the final manuscript of *Orientalism* at the Center for Advanced Study in the Behavioral Sciences, Stanford, and I was in Berkeley writing my book *As We Saw Them* published in 1979.[2] I am not comparing my book to Edward's here: mine is a modest analysis of a cultural encounter, narrativized and ironic, whereas *Orientalism* is theoretical and oppositional, that is, both philosophical and political. I was stunned by the force of his opposition that fundamentally challenged the liberal tenet, from which I had not quite been able to extricate myself despite my deepening disillusionment with academic intellectualism and liberalism. Said's oppositionism was different from Foucault's in refusing to universalize power and neutralize justice. It made a deeper impact on me, furthermore, as I joined him in various programs concerning the Palestinian struggle for survival against Israel, including repeated visits to the West Bank and Tunis at his invitation in the 1980s. To the extent that I agreed with him on the matter of power and resistance, I was fully prepared to follow Said in viewing Japanese literature vis-à-vis Eurocentricity. Of course, I think I had attempted a similar project of transvaluation with *As We Saw Them*, as the title implied with its ironic coevality of "we" and "they." Except that mine was more distant, not fired with resistance and opposition in which Said was unavoidably and passionately engaged. The contribution I made in the 1983 Seoul conference was in a way my first explicit statement in an act of resistance, which has lasted to this day under changing circumstances.

In 1983 my interest was far more literary than now. The problems I saw in the novel were within the literary context in literary terms, although these problems and terms nearly always referred to the external historical developments. I chose prose narrative fiction as the crucial focus of comparison and confrontation among cultures of the world. Poetry and drama trace back to antiquity everywhere before the diverse economic and industrial developments sundered the world into haves and have-nots, while the "novel," or rather prose narrative fiction—of considerable length, printed and mass-circulated, describing the actions and events of the ordinary people—emerged after industrialization and colonialism widened the gap. (Eric Hobsbawm and David Landes agree in estimating the gap in wealth among the nations as in one digit until 1900 or later, and it widened to two digits, and then to three digits only in very recent years. The gap is far wider now between the richest and the poorest, both between nations and within nations, of which more later.)[3] As I saw it, the prose fiction form reveals this modern history's engagement with art far more clearly than poetry and drama, enabling me to avoid cultural and literary essentialism. Thus, if we place the prose narrative forms of various countries within one category of the novel, we are likely to overlook different formal features inscribed by the historical variants in development and power. Difference, in this view, was the way to illumination.

In the 1983 paper I discussed the *shosetsu*, the modern Japanese narrative form, as having features that refuse to be classified under the same headings as in the Western novel. Just to take one instance, because of the "aspect," the temporal grammatical category of the Japanese language, the perfect and imperfect rather than past, present, and future tenses as in English, the narrative sequence tends to be coeval rather than consequential, discouraging the causal linking of narrative elements. Here what Roland Barthes in *Writing Degree Zero* ascribes to the preterit or the historical past tense, that is, "the ideal instrument for every construction of a world; [which] is the unreal time of cosmogonies, myths, History and Novel," is not available.[4] The shosetsu thus tends to be paratactic instead of syntactic, resulting in weakened and loosened—or freer and open-ended—plotting. Similarly, the absence of the genesis and apocalypse myths leads to the rejection of a clear beginning and, more important, a clear ending or resolution. A narrative continues on and on, at times refusing the possibility of closure altogether. Even these broad temporal and sequential categories alone seem to indicate that the difference that lies between the novel and the shosetsu is indeed considerable.

My intention here is not to present again an eighteen-year old paper, but to suggest its position so that I can both recall and ponder the changes that have taken place in these intervening years. So let me briefly go over just one more feature that seems crucial to my over-all argument here. This difference between the novel and the shosetsu at their high modernist/ modernizing stages—from late nineteenth century to the mid-twentieth— might be explained by the marked residual features of orality in the shosetsu. I do not mean, of course, that the shosetsu is still an oral performance. It is not; it is a printed narrative just like any novel. And yet even in its printed form, the shosetsu retains many features of orality. While the modern novel is marked by invention, particularistic landscape, revision, analysis, spatiality, distance, comprehension, expansion, massive length, sculpturesque textual autonomy, and the depth and interiority in characterization, the oral narrative is characterized by memory, formulas, repetition, display, temporality, proximity and intimacy, insularity, ritualism, episodic brevity and fragmentation, contextual communality, and social roles/ relations of characters. Literacy requires the infrastructure of printing, distribution, and leisure and wealth, whereas orality depends on village or other communal space and physical places where the recitor and audience can assemble together. Such intimate sites have either vanished or been replaced by mechanical reproductions like radio or television from the literate industrial societies. So considered, it may not be greatly amiss to call literacy a central cultural marker of capitalist, metropolitan, colonial societies, while orality, that of agricultural, peripheral, colonized societies.

I hasten to add that I do not mean to differentiate literacy and orality as one capable, and the other incapable, of analytic and abstract speculation, as do Jack Goody and Ian Watt, or as one pacific and innocent and the other as violent and aggressive, as argued by Lévi-Strauss and Walter Ong.[5] Nor do I agree with Jacques Derrida, Brian Street, and Roger Chartier who insist orality and literacy are ultimately indistinguishable. A given society as a whole is always endowed with a mixture of orality and literacy (and here I agree with Derrida, Street, and Chartier), but the two *activities* are distinguishable in the manner and circumstance of communication.[6] Furthermore, the use made of literacy is different between metropolitan societies and peripheral societies. Let me repeat, however, that orality does not evolve into literacy along the axis of progress, nor is orality prelapsarian innocence doomed by literacy. They are two different speech acts, which variously develop in the manifold conditions of history. The qualitative superiority or inferiority of the two is meaningless, as are the relative merits of the novel and shosetsu forms. I was, in other words, set to prove that the critical terms that were the products of one did not fit the products of the other. This, in retrospect, was my attempt to liberate the shosetsu and other peripheral narrative forms such as the Chinese, Arab, or Urdu narratives from the metropolitan literary domination.

I liked to indulge myself by fantasying that as a written text the novel—begun in the West nearly simultaneously with the commencement of colonialism—was fit for distribution over great distances, thus particularly suitable, unlike the oral recitation, for the writer in the metropolis to send out to the colonies far away—just like an emissary or a command from the colonial office to viceroys or governors in the far-flung corners of the world. I was convinced that the novel was inescapably colonialist—even with an anticolonialist theme. Oppositionism in my literary revisionism, however, had to be considerably curtailed in considering the shosetsu form because of Japan's peculiar place in the history of colonialism. It is indisputable, on the one hand, that Japan was faced with Euro-American hegemony and adventurism since the mid-nineteenth century. Although military occupation was highly unlikely, economic and political containment of Japan in the hand of the U.S. and European powers was as comprehensive as any other Asian nations. Even more importantly, Euro-American cultural indifference to Japan was both disturbing and incomprehensible to its intellectuals in the early twentieth century, who were thoroughly familiar with proclaimed Enlightenment universalism. By the 1930s, Kuki Shuzo, Tanabe Hajime, Miki Kiyoshi, and other Japanese writers sought out Heidegger, Husserl, and Jaspers, and when they found the German philosophers were both ignorant about and indifferent to their country, their disappointment was profound. Their construction of a nationalist philosophical system that eventually served to be an apologia for Japan's aggression can be traced to such an experience of Eurocentricy. On the other hand, Japan was the first non-Western country that developed modern imperialism. Taking to heart the advice given by Bismarck and other Western leaders, the Japanese oligarchy and militarists quickly learned the realpolitik and the instrumentality of colonialism for their industrial development. After victory against imperial China and Russia around the turn of the century, Japan's swagger over their intra-Asian domination was unmistakable in the shosetsu of the time, not only thematically, but also in the narrative forms with which the writers of the time were beginning to experiment. Said was able to extend the idea of Orientalism to include political oppression and thereby to take an uncompromisingly anti-Orientalist position in dealing with the questions of Palestine and Islamic countries. My own liberationist revisionism concerning the West and the Rest, however, had to be seriously qualified. It was not allowed to focus on the historical West, but both the West *and* Japan, that is, the forces of oppression wherever they may have originated. Obviously, presenting the paper near the former colonial governor's headquarters in Seoul intensified the need to revise my Saidian anti-Orientalism. I should add, however, that I did not quite forget Euro-American oppression either.

All this was eighteen years ago.

Year 2001: Discipline on the Wane

To switch to year 2001, the kinds of literary exercise I have just described are no longer current in the literary critical scene in the United States and in many other countries. First, grammatical/formal analysis of literary products seems to interest very few scholars now, according to the programs of conferences and meetings as well as books and journals being published now. The idea of literature as composed of autonomous formal inventions survives largely within the guarded walls of few traditionalist enclaves. Gone also is the argument concerning the interrelationships of power among nation-states and national literatures. In fact, the idea of the nation-state is itself very much in decline, not in literary studies alone of course, but in intellectual discourse as a whole. If colonialism is talked about, it is often in terms of the era after the colonial rule, within the boundary of so-called *post*colonial discourse. Colonialism in this view is safely detached from today's state of affairs. Said's name is replaced by Homi Bhabha's, Stuart Hall's, and Arjun Appadurai's, a changeover signifying the replacement of political economy with culture as a central paradigm. The structure of political-economic oppression is explained as a hybrid cultural program in which the subalterns powerfully affect the oppressors' culture as they struggle for survival. By transforming the political-economical into the cultural, the suffering of the oppressed is deemphasized. It does not go so far as to convert colonialism into a benign civilizing act as yet, but history is certainly looked upon now with more leniency and latitude.

As for the decline in literature in general, one can at once point to the waning of canonic writers and works, established and mainstream scholars, conventional genres, and national literary history. White male masters were first replaced by female writers. Nearly at the same time, minority writers—first, both male and female—emerged as a new dominant, but female minority writers took the center stage. But then, fiction as a whole lost its allure for the general public—except perhaps pulp romances. Together with them are interests in foreign cultures, especially European literatures and languages, all visibly disappearing in the last decade.

One of the simplest indicators of this radical change is in the recent figures in enrollment, recruitment, and placement at the undergraduate, graduate, and faculty levels in the humanities. Down are the numbers of those enrolled in Russian, Italian, French, and German literatures and languages, conspicuous among the undergraduates but in the graduate programs as well. A sharp decline is evident in the interest in literary studies as a whole. Far fewer undergraduates take courses and major in literature, which means fewer jobs for Ph.D.s and fewer graduate students and seminars. Among the few enrolled in literature courses are social and natural science majors who want to have some "fun" in their college life— not a trivial development, since these are likely to be the students who constitute the main clientele of literary studies. There are faculty members, especially in the East Coast colleges, who are still active in specialized research in literary studies, but their classrooms are less crowded now, and fewer copies of their publications circulate.

Even among the disciplines on the wane, however, all is not lost. There are brisk departments, sections, and sectors even amidst the general decline. To begin with the most obvious, "theories" seem to have supplanted imaginative works such as the novel, poetry, and drama as the objects of study. Students and young scholars are too impatient to read an infinite number of texts that, as they see them, are mere materials for analytic statements. Skipping over novels, poems, plays, or historical documents, young—and older—scholars prefer ready-made summaries, abstractions, and analyses that are presumably provided by theorists as the end products of arduous examinations of primary documents. Novels and poems—at least the by-gone works—are no longer being read with unmediated pleasure, an activity which strikes many ambitious scholars as indulgent and inefficient. Theories are to the point, and, supposedly, endowed with universal and productive applications. Thus theories are discussed with enthusiasm. In scholarly publications, graduate seminars and, increasingly also in undergraduate lectures, the knowledge with imaginative texts is no longer presumed; or rather, the students' ignorance is the given. Theories that were born out of a desire for universalism and systematization to redress prejudicial distortion and exclusion are now as commodified as Hollywood films or designers clothes. So what is the theory to theorize, what is the subject?

As has already been mentioned, formal literary autonomy is not a subject that stirs most scholars these days. Literature is now nearly always considered in relation to extraliterary events and situations in history. Insofar as this means an attempt to broaden the space of literature, it is a matter to be celebrated. But what are the subjects around which theories abstract and construct systems of meanings? They are focused on the interrelationship of social groups: ethnic identities (minoritarian studies such as African American, Hispanic American, Asian American, etc.), gender studies (gay, lesbian, queers, and a variety of feminist studies), postcolonial studies (hegemonic/subaltern, diasporan, etc.), local/regional studies, and popular-culture studies, with emphases on the dominated and marginalized. The nation-state is much too totalizing and patriarchal a notion, and in current literary practice it is nearly always divided and subdivided into smaller units. Thus, for instance, the Association of American Studies is not about the United States as represented by the hegemonic white male elites, that is, "traditional" history and society, but has been virtually turned into a scholarly association devoted to the studies of ethnic minorities, suggesting implied contestations over the subject of history. Under the circumstances, the idea of totality is unsurprisingly taboo, avoided, distrusted, and ignored. Totality and universality, in this view, inevitably suggest repression and exclusion. The new social agenda is to recognize and insist on individual varieties, incommensurable differences. Such a development toward the principle of "difference," that is, multiculturalism, starting from universalistic centrality is no doubt salutary as long as it rejects the logic of concentrated power and authority, instanced by univocal pretensions to world hegemony, Eurocentricity, American imperialism, dictatorship, elitism, racism, patriarchy, and any other totalizing and normalizing institutionality. Multiculturalism is propelled by the democratic impulse for equality and liberation. Before further discussing this democracy of dispersal in literary and cultural scholarship, however, I would like to examine the historical process by which such a change has been enabled since the early 1980s, the time of the earlier International Conference on East Asian Literature in Seoul.

The Spirit of SUVs

To resume the discussion where I left off, Said's criticism was no doubt liberationist, and it gradually began to gain momentum in the 1980s, even in the generally conservative East Asian field. There was one development in the eighties, however, that slightly altered the course of anti-Orientalism, particularly in the Japan field. By then the net effects of the devastatingly wasteful U.S. adventurism in the 1960s and 1970s were beginning to become visible. The trade imbalance was looming larger every year, and Japan was, as it still is, accumulating a huge trade surplus. The 1985 Plaza Agreement doubled the exchange rate of yen against the dollar for the purpose of curbing Japanese exports to the United States. The U.S. strategy failed. By cutting the cost of labor and the margin of profit, Japan's industry increased its world market share throughout the eighties. The mood of protectionism intensified in the United States, and Japan was portrayed as America's greatest menace, threatening to leap from the world's second largest economy to the topmost leader in the twenty-first century. Inside Japan, the sense of confidence and arrogance grew as unaccustomed affluence replaced the humiliating poverty of the years around the Second World War. The Japanese real estate industry began, very foolishly in retrospect, to buy up American lands and buildings, driving the Americans to a frenzy of patriotism. That was the time when Ezra Vogel of Harvard wrote *Japan as Number One* ostensibly to warn the smug Americans, but as likely to flatter the Japanese industry in the hope of serving as its chief apologist—for a fee.[7] While U.S. protectionism sought to stir ugly patriotism, Japan's counter-patriotism was nearly as disturbing. Once again, my criticism of the U.S. hegemony had to be tamed by a stricture on Japan's own insular nationalism.

Alongside the Japan-U.S. international relations, there were three interconnected and far greater developments emerging in the wider context of the entire world in the eighties and nineties, which have fundamentally altered all national and international relations: first, the ascendancy of the so-called neoliberal economy; second, the end of the cold war; and, finally, the spread of desocialized individualism, or self-interest and self-indulgence as the rational choice in everyday life. These developments that can be categorized under the rubric of "globalization" also have each played a profound role in altering the course of literary studies, or even the humanities as a whole, which, however, I will discuss more fully later on. First, neoliberalism. After the elections of Margaret Thatcher in 1979 and Ronald Reagan in 1980, the United Kingdom and United States accelerated the policy of privatization: denationalization and deregulation of industries, austerity programs, tax cuts on behalf of corporations and the wealthy, and various antilabor measures. Business took steps to restructure the production process to make industry more efficient and profitable presumably to survive the intensifying competition from Japan and emergent economies. In addition to increasing productivity by downsizing, corporations transferred production, capital, and market overseas. That is, they found cheap labor abroad, and by the use of robotics and digital technology blocked the labor movements as well as lowered wages. When they needed skilled labor from abroad, on the other hand, they demanded and usually received cooperation from both home and host governments. They also transferred their operations to where the corporate taxes were lower and environmental or human rights regulations were looser, extracting concessions not only from foreign governments but also their own municipal, state, and federal governments. The corporations thus curbed the regulatory power of the states, but made use of them whenever it was to their advantage. Despite the conservative propaganda, the capitalist government did not end subsidies, but simply changed the beneficiaries from the indigent to the wealthy and corporate. Such developments were a harbinger of the soon-to-arrive post–cold war economic order, which placed the multinational and transnational corporate interest at the center stage of state policy.

Throughout the cold war the state was able to support corporations through direct military procurement that amounted to a huge proportion of the national economy (see my "A Borderless Word?").[8] In the world after 1990, where the rationale of the security state system was reduced to a defense against a handful of ramshackle rogue states, direct subsidies to corporations of vast sums in the name of defense became a little difficult to justify. The new situation required a new narrative. Hence, the state insisted that there was actually no peace. That local, civil, and tribal wars were chaotic and unpredictable, and so even more hazardous to the United States than the cold war. That religious and cultural conflicts were bound to break out. And, finally, that the Unites States and other industrial nations must remain rich and strong to defend civilization, and corporate wealth best brings prosperity to the general population. The ideology of neoliberalism was thus incubated. Left alone, corporations in service and manufacture are presumably at their most productive. Deregulation lowers the price and benefits consumers. Huge corporations are most efficient, and thus beneficial to the public. Self-dependence not only strengthens the moral fiber of citizens, but promotes production. Public programs are wasteful and corrupt. All such presumptions are more believed than documented. Taken together, at any rate, they help create an economic order that not only concentrates wealth and power among the few, but perpetuates the center against any future challenge from the fringes.

The end of the cold war was certainly not unrelated to such an economic development. Unable to keep up with the joined forces of Western capital, the Soviet Union and its satellite states collapsed around 1990. What the end of the cold war brought about was twofold: the unchallenged neoliberal economic paradigm in the world and the realignment of the third-world nations. First, the structure of the modern nation-state that had long constituted the basis for capitalism, colonialism, and social organization was abruptly found to be superfluous and out of date. While the East-West rivalry lasted, the state needed the cohesiveness of a people as a reliable military resource for protection or aggression; likewise, the rich in control of the state needed people as a dependable source of labor for greater accumulation of their wealth. The state, in short, needed the nation. Once the cold war was over and the world became a potentially seamless economic field, however, the huge multinational corporations could transfer their capital, labor, technology, factory, market, and products to any place as long as it was more efficient and profitable, as we have already seen. For corporations the national boundary was often an impediment; they needed the freedom to range over an unbounded space.

Second, for the duration of the cold war, both the Western and Eastern blocs rivaled in forming an alliance with third-world countries. One remembers the State Department strategies and CIA operations throughout the globe from Africa, the Middle East, Southeast Asia, the Far East, to South America. To keep the countries on their sides, they chose whatever means available and expedient—through foreign aid, propaganda, bribes, covert violence, manipulated elections, or dispatch of marines, naval fleets, bombers and missiles. That is, as long as the cold war lasted, the impoverished nonaligned countries could manipulate the United States and the Soviet Union to receive some handouts. Although most of the billions of dollars poured out in these years merely served to enrich dictators like Mobutu Sese Seco, Marcos, Suharto, the Saudi or Kuwait sultans, and General Pinochet—the list was endless, just as the transgression and ineptitude of the State Department and CIA were infinite—there were some trickles that eventually reached the poor in these areas. With the end of the cold war, however, even this meager beneficence stopped nearly everywhere except for the odd couple of Israel and Egypt. Private corporations have no interest whatever to help the poor: they are under fiduciary obligations to make profits. They would consider it their duty to write off sub-Sahara Africa as unprofitable and therefore useless and absent. Even when some 25 percent of the youth in these countries are dying of AIDS, the pharmaceutical companies will not make drugs affordable to them.[9] Less than 2 percent of the world capital now flows through the sub-Sahara Africa—except the Union of South Africa. Genocide draws no attention, when private corporations perpetrate it.

The gap between the rich and poor has existed throughout history. But the proportion of the difference was far smaller between nations, as has already been mentioned. The per capita GDP of the richest, Switzerland, and the poorest, Myanmar, in 1999 are $43,060 and $100 respectively, a ratio of 430 to 1.[10] And this proportion is not as sharp as the annual income of the average CEO to the blue-collar worker in the United States, 475 to 1 as of the spring 2000.[11] The point here is not just the immensity of the unequal distribution of wealth itself, nor the continuing growth of the gap, although they are both important enough. Rather the gap between the few superrich and the vast majority of humanity separates them as if they had nothing in common. That is, the rich of the world have more to share with each other across national borders, or even across the East-West or North-South divide, than with most of their fellow citizens. The world is sectioned into nations and nationalities only for those who cannot afford to move or travel beyond their home countries. For the rich, the world is indeed transnational and deterritotialized.[12]

What is most important in the world trade now is not manufactured goods, but speculative currencies, bonds, and derivatives to the tune of one trillion dollars or more a day. With digital technology, the transfer of financial capital is easy, fast, and cheap. Although it is theoretically possible to keep track of all financial transactions, there is no mechanism as of now for any state, or its central bank, or any international organization, to control, or even monitor, such an immense transnational flow.[13] As the nation-state becomes increasingly dysfunctional, those in charge of mapping the world economy are also discarding various social constructions invented for nurturing unified nation-states.

The third recent development is not a clearly definable event, but no less perceptible and pervasive than the neoliberal economy and the end of the cold war. That is, the drive for winning spreads far beyond the corporate organization into personal life. Neoliberalism or globalization is not just an operational policy of corporations and governments. The legitimation of private profit over and above public good is based on a belief in competition as the fundamental human condition, and triumph as the ultimate goal of life. That means, those in need of help are held in contempt as inept, lazy, and superfluous, while the entrepreneurial "winners" are awed as capable, quick, and intelligent. Wealth and power are considered natural rewards for such strengths; poverty and marginalization, on the other hand, are the deserts of the failures. In a situation such as this, self-interest is not only something one needs to protect from encroachment and exploitation by others, but a guiding principle, to be aggressively pursued for its own sake and with a matter-of-fact disregard for others. Opportunism is encouraged as a mark of flexibility and intelligence. The intensifying concentration of wealth and power is both the cause and effect of such social-psychological development.

Also both the cause and effect of neoliberalism is a pervasive acceptance of consumerism. Without vast and rapid consumption, the capitalist economy would just collapse. And most economists never question economic expansion as the fundamental social need. Consumption is now considered an indispensable necessity to the increase of production. Consumption for the sake of consumption via built-in obsolescence and insatiable desire—optimal waste, really—is calmly accepted and integrated by the public into everybody's daily life. The ecological consequences of untrammeled waste are vaguely felt, and some environmental protection is certainly discussed or even enforced. But it has so far not received serious consideration in economic terms—like most other public needs and programs. Without nostalgic fantasying of the past, one could readily recall merely a few decades ago when frugality even among the rich was seen as decent and commonplace, and conspicuous consumption as crude and exceptional. The change in social behaviors since has been immense in most industrial countries. Among the few rich and comfortable, everything must be big, new, and priceless. Even those moderate rich must aspire to flamboyant exhibition. The spirit of suvs infiltrates all areas of everyday life—from architecture, to urban planning, to "life style." Ostentatious displays are no longer frowned upon by tribal surveillance. Unrestrained and unregulated by any tradition or authority, self-indulgence is now nearly an unembarrassed mark of success. Furthermore, the behaviors of the affluent, unlike in the earlier days, have not so far aroused resentment among those who cannot afford them. The poor are happily persuaded that consumerism will soon become accessible to them. They are willing to wait in their dream and desire. Unless the few protests that broke out recently in cities such as Seattle, Washington, D.C., Prague, and Davos manage to gather force, the world economy seems steaming ahead in its current course toward—no one knows where.[14]

Toward an Inclusive Totality

To return to matters concerning literary studies, global neoliberalism is powerfully altering fundamental assumptions here as well. Earlier in the second half of the twentieth century, the logic of difference was a strategy of liberation. Structuralist and poststructuralist thoughts that began in the late sixties in France gained far more popularity in the United States in these twenty years. This development is in itself quite fascinating, although there is no space for a full discussion in this essay. It is in order here, however, to point out some of the issues involved in the state of comparative literary studies. The rejection of the nation-state as totalizing implies the existence of more particularistic social units. In an immigrant and multiracial country such as the United States or Australia, multiculturalism is an obvious consensual choice, each group, minority or majority, demanding its own autonomous and independent, that is, incommensurable space. Without doubt multiculturalism is preferable to the monoculturalist oppression of minorities by the dominant group. The logic of difference, however, paradoxically poses three internal difficulties that are likely to perpetuate the condition of exclusion and neglect for minorities.

First, insofar as each group's incommensurability means total uniqueness, the affairs of any given group are a matter that does not—or should not—concern the member of any other group. If this principle of noninterference is literally practiced, the minority—presumably less resourceful—groups must be left alone on their own shift. The majority group now has neither accountability nor responsibility for the minority groups. Second, the problem of totality does not vanish when a nation is divided up into ethnic or gender groups. Each group of course constitutes a smaller, but nonetheless as controlling and demanding a totality as the nation. How about, for instance, the minority called Asian American? Shouldn't that general and abstract entity be broken down into Chinese American, Korean American, Vietnamese American, and many other subgroups? But then how about the Chinese Americans? Are the mainland Chinese to be considered in the same category as the Taiwanese? The Hong Kong Chinese? Overseas Chinese? Chinese women? Gays? Lesbians? Queers? And classes? Where does the logic of difference stop? Doesn't a particular individual remain as unrepresented as a citizen of a totalized nation?

Third, among the three categories of difference (race, gender, and class), class is distinct from the other two in that class has no reason to retain its identity if liberated, whereas race and gender have no reason to lose theirs. Race and gender are thus more authentic identities than class that aspires to erase itself. In the identity politics that has consumed literary studies in recent years, this distinction among the three categories is tacitly assumed —with the result that class is seldom mentioned, unlike ethnicity and gender. Quite obviously, the ruling class welcomes this silence on class. In this respect alone, multiculturalism has every reason to be warmly embraced by transnational corporatism. Diversity at this juncture is a favored public policy, not a subversive program any longer.

If every literary and cultural system is incommensurable, the idea of "comparative" literature is an oxymoron. Incomparables cannot be compared. In fact, very little serious work is being done now in the area of comparing national or regional literatures. Such efforts are being supplanted by the studies of inner workings of a culture or literature, which presumably are different from those of another. Power as the constitutive factor, however, is nearly always introduced—with the effect of casting every ethnic or gender minority in a more or less similar light, the light, for instance, of victimology.

The problem with the logic of difference is not just classificatory. In asserting autonomy and independence, each group—whatever that may be—declares independence, rejecting commonality with others. Internal cohesiveness is then demanded, but this need for solidarity is functionally at least as disciplinarian as any national demand of loyalty and patriotism. And where does the authority of each group originate? How is the right to power and representation legitimized? Even parliamentary democracy will have to be rejected here, since elective representation requires the definition of an electorate, a totality. The minority leadership in this sense is likely to be based on self-proclamation, opening a way to opportunism and confusion. If sectionalism and secession are freely allowed, on the other hand, the social structure of a minority group will collapse to atomism. The literary discourse can also be splintered by factionalism, as recently pointed out by Nina Auerback in "Acrimony" and K. Anthony Appiah in "Battle of the Bien-Pensant" regarding feminist studies now.[15] Such a situation in fact only encourages the usurpation of power by an opportunist within the group who knows how to represent the atomized multiplicity by manipulating sympathy, loyalty, and celebrity. Also it finally serves the leaders of the dominant group, who can pursue their own interests with no regard for the minorities, just as they had always done before the days of liberation.

The disintegration of not just comparative literature but literary studies as a whole may very well be already under way. If the fractured groups are engrossed in their self-interests, outsiders have a good reason to feel repulsed by them. The general public wants to understand its place and role in the "globalized" world. There is a deep concern with the waste-based economy, too. And yet those who have traditionally intervened in such issues are preoccupied with their internecine struggles conducted in a language and references of their own. The public is excluded and unwanted, as long as it refuses to learn the jargon of partisans and become partisan. And as we have already seen, the public seems increasingly to look elsewhere for cultural interpretation and criticism. Literary productions—novels, plays, and poetry—are at present still alive, but they are no longer closely connected with the critical and analytic segments of the university.

The global economy, on the other hand, is having a profound impact on today's university everywhere, as I have described in "Ivory Tower in Escrow."[16] The corporatized university is preoccupied with the market force most conspicuously around information technology and bioengineering. Outside of applied sciences, basic research—now called "curiosity research"—is visibly being ignored. Technology transfer is the urgent agenda for administrators and managers of both business and academia. Thus learning is rapidly being transformed into intellectual property, and the free exchange of information into commerce. As "globalization" thus goes ahead full-speed, literary scholars remain absorbed in joyless self-isolation and futile infights. Under such circumstances, literary studies have little chance of competition, or even survival within the walls of the university itself.

My interest here is, however, not in recuperation or resuscitation of my professional specialization. Rather, I am concerned with restoring the sense of totality to the academic and intellectual world, both intellectually and politically. Particularity without totality is, by now we know, nonsense, deadening, and useless. Literary and cultural critics must look out at the world and interconnect all the workings of political economy and artistic and cultural productions. We must keep reminding ourselves that the "global" economy is not global at all, but an exclusionist economy. We must discover the sense of true totality that includes everyone in the world.

For this purpose, the return to the nation-state probably will not work anymore. The old power structure has proven a failure much too often in the past two centuries of its history. Perhaps we need a new organization, one that is truly global and inclusive of all. There is one such core site for inclusiveness, though entirely negative at present: that is, the future of the global environment. For the first time in human history, one single commonality involves all of the living on the planet, the environmental deterioration of the planet as a result of the human consumption of natural resources. Whether rich or poor, in the East or the West, progressive or conservative, religious or atheist, none of us can escape from the all-involving process of air pollution, ozone layer depletion, ocean contamination, toxic accumulation, and global warming. Of course, the rich will try to stay as far away as possible from the pollution, but even they cannot remain protected for long. We can start from this realization of the total commonality as we map out our world and engage in research and scholarship. Literature and literary studies now have one basis and goal: to nurture our common bonds to the planet. To replace the imaginaries of exclusionist familialism, communitarianism, nationhood, ethnic culture, regionalism, "globalization," or even humanism, with the ideal of planetarianism. Once we accept the planet-based totality, we might for once agree with humility to devise a way to share with all the rest our only true public space and resources.

What form this research on the preservation of the planet will take is not all clear now, of course. It must combine environmental engineering with economics, political science, and cultural studies so that scholars in all fields may first work out the idea of an economy that will reduce consumption without cutting employment. The reduction of waste in the first world must be simultaneous with the increase of consumption in much of the third world. They will have to devise a way to train and integrate the unused labor forces of the third world to equalize wealth. By far the most difficult task in this project is how to invent a way to persuade, not advertise, culturally as well as politically, that there is no other future for any of us. Either through schools and universities, NGOs, United Nations–affiliated organizations, media, or whatever residues of the state apparatus, we must curb our material dream and build an agreement on our unavoidable future which we will all share with an unprecedented commonality. For such a future we need to reimagine our common and universal culture, as we have never done in human history.

Of course, we may very well fail in this attempt, too. But if we do, we will not be there to see it. And perhaps we deserve to perish. On the other hand, faced with the fate of universally inescapable destruction and nullification, who knows, we may yet finally find a way to confront it together, and find the way to coexist with all others. There is at least that much promise of hope, the only hope we have been allowed to entertain together with everybody else on this planet.

A Conversation with Masao Miyoshi

NAVIGATING ISLANDS AND CONTINENTS
....
Conversations and Contestations in and around the Pacific

INTERVIEWER: Kuan-Hsing Chen, National Tsing Hua University, Taiwan
EDITOR: Steve Bradbury, National Central University, Taiwan

For anyone working in the field of Asia Pacific cultural studies, few scholars are less in need of introduction than Masao Miyoshi. But for the sake of those who may not be familiar with either the work or reputation of this formidable critic and historian, a few introductory remarks seem in order. If Edward Said can be said to have established Orientalism as a major field of cultural inquiry and political engagement, Miyoshi, in such works as *Accomplices of Silence* (1974), *As We Saw Them* (1979), and *Off Center: Power and Cultural Relations between Japan and the United States* (1991), can be credited not only with having greatly extended Said's critique of the West's representation and management of its encounter with the East into the "Far East" but with having brought a much-needed reciprocal perspective to the study of East-West relations. Like Said, with whom he shares many political convictions, critical sympathies, and years of intellectual and personal fellowship, Miyoshi is an eloquent and pugnacious émigré intellectual who began his career as a specialist of Victorian literature but wound up becoming one of the major theorists and critics of Western hegemony. In numerous articles, Miyoshi has ranged over an astonishing number of disciplines, freely discussing any topic or text he finds relevant to his ongoing critique of the Eurocentrism and disciplinary insularity of Western scholarship on Japan, East Asia, and East-West cultural relations. In recent years, in such journals as *Critical Inquiry* and *boundary 2*, Miyoshi has examined the impact that globalization has had on cultures and cultural relations at both the margin and the center. In his most recent work, he has turned his attention to the radical changes that the university, and in particular the humanities, are undergoing in the "globalized" economy. But perhaps Miyoshi's most enduring accomplishment is his having politicized, first at the University of California, Berkeley, and now at the University of California, San Diego, several generations of graduate and undergraduate students, many of whom are now among the most vigorous critics and scholars working in postcolonial and cultural studies. One of these is the interlocutor of this interview, Kuan-Hsing Chen. Author of *Stuart Hall: Critical Dialogues in Cultural Studies* (1996), *Trajectories: Inter-Asia Cultural Studies* (1995), and a number of important essays on what Chen calls a "New Internationalist Localism" of cultural studies, Chen is among the most important first-world-trained, third-world cultural studies students to return to Taiwan, where he now teaches at National Tsing Hua University and oversees much of the interventional work of the Cultural Studies Association. Chen made this interview at a time when he was much interested in the as-yet largely unwritten history of the postwar intellectual diaspora that played a crucial role in the formation and on-going critique of postcolonial and cultural studies. This interview was transcribed, edited, and introduced by Steve Bradbury.

KUAN-HSING CHEN: Here we are at Masao Miyoshi's house in Del Mar, California. It's the end of summer, about 1:30 in the afternoon. I'm interested in the intersection between theoretical and historical trajectories, and in particular, the influence that historical and social conditions have had on the development of the intellectual diaspora. I'd like you to go back to origins, if I may use the term, to see how your family and social background as well as the larger historical contexts influenced your intellectual development.

MASAO MIYOSHI: Well, I think it all revolves on the Second World War and the particular environment it created, although, at that time, I really had no clear understanding of what was going on or what it all meant. I was too young, first of all. In 1941, I was thirteen, I guess. At the same time there was a very effective system of censorship, which completely controlled the flow of information. Despite all that, there was a strange feeling of tension that I, as a growing kid, sensed at every point. One of the reasons was the influence of my brother, who was a physics major at the University of Tokyo, and very much in doubt about the war. How did he become suspicious and skeptical about the war effort? For this we must, I think, credit his roommate, who was an exchange student from China, and another Chinese friend of his, the son of the Chinese ambassador to Japan and a very articulate man. I met him once or twice through my brother. My brother was at least half-skeptical about the war. He was eight years older than me and often told me what he heard about what the Japanese were doing in China, although in a very vague outline. I began to sense that something was seriously wrong. And this is one of the most amazing things that in 1945, when the war was over, I was again very skeptical about the U.S. propaganda that came out, including the analysis of the war. The crux was the difficulty of determining what was true. In fact, in the 1970s, I had a research assistant go through all the Japanese newspapers available at Berkeley from 1931 to 1945, fifteen years of journalism in all, to determine whether or not there was any news of Japanese brutality in China, and she could not find a single piece nor any mention of it. In any case, from 1945 to around 1950, we kept wondering what had happened. And it took us a long time to figure out that this had something to do with the history of censorship during the Edo and Meiji periods. Japan is a very efficiently controlled society, then and now. And that was one of the reasons for many young intellectuals wanting to come here. Of course, this might have something to do the marginal's relationship to the center, very much like the aspiration of the colonized. I wasn't really aware of this then. But then I had been studying English, even throughout the war, which is rather curious when you come to think of it.

K: Masao, you're moving too fast. Can we backtrack a moment?

M: I thought I was moving too slow. [Laughter]

K: Could we get a little more information about you first, for instance, your class background and so forth. What sort of family did you have and in what sort of social milieu did you move? What sort of schooling did you have? Was there anything special about that?

M: I don't think I was brought up in any special way, but mine was a fairly sophisticated and privileged family. My brothers and cousins nearly all went to the University of Tokyo. And we took it for granted. That sort of thing. And they kept feeding us with "Western culture" and a great deal of news, but I don't think this news analysis constituted any serious intellectual or analytical program. Nothing like that. My family was fairly respectable, and so my identification was with the ruling class rather than the working class. The relationship between U.S. intellectuals and the working class is quite tenuous, as everyone knows. But I think the same could be said of Japanese intellectuals. Whatever political position I have come to take really started with abstraction rather than daily life. I mean I really had little if any understanding of the situation of the working class, despite efforts made by, for example, some of my teachers to enlighten me. One elementary school teacher lent me proletarian novels when I was in the fourth grade. A dangerous thing to do indeed in the late thirties. But it didn't lead to any coherent criticism.

K: What kind of daily life did you have in the early days?

M: I don't like to admit it but it was really very bourgeois. We were quite preoccupied by Western arts and literature.

K: What sort of literature were you reading?

M: Mostly European, especially the nineteenth/twentieth-century novel. I read Flaubert and Balzac, Dostoevsky and Tolstoy, Mann and Hesse, for example, when I was nine or ten.

K: In Japanese?

M: In Japanese. I read an enormous number of Western novels in Japanese translation by the time I was thirteen. And then, during the war, I began to read them in English.

K: But what about your traditional Japanese education? Did you read Japanese literature or Chinese philosophy, for example?

M: Not a thing. My reading was totally Western in its orientation. What little I know of Japanese literature came much later.

K: What sort of school did you go to?

M: I went to prestigious public schools. I went to one middle school because I desperately wanted to wear its uniform, which included a necktie and shirt. I really couldn't stand the idea of wearing the military-style outfit that you found at most public schools. You must remember that from 1931 to 1945, Japanese nationalism infused every aspect of nativist style. But, of course, I eventually had to wear a military-style uniform anyway, because the school was forced to drop the black necktie, white shirt, and navy blazer once the war heated up: it's funny but I still don't know whether wearing that necktie represented a surrender to Western colonialism or a gesture of resistance to Japanese militarism. I suppose I could say the same thing about my Western reading. I really don't know if it was a form of resistance or capitulation.

K: What was the mood during the war?

M: It's very interesting. My father was a stockbroker. He was totally against the war. Not because he thought it was wrong but he didn't think Japan would win. My mother was very much against the war, too. She was a very sophisticated and cynical woman. She didn't think anything good would come out of it. My brother was against the war as well, because he was afraid of being killed. My brother was a very important influence on my life. When he was inducted into the Japanese army, he cried at the induction ceremony in public. That was virtually unheard of. That was the kind of family I had.

K: What was it like in school?

M: In 1942 or 1943, I was persuaded that Japan would win. We were all mobilized and working in factories. I had a few friends who had come back from the United States just before Pearl Harbor. One day we were speaking in English about god knows what and we were suddenly assaulted by the entire class, forty-eight kids came and beat the two of us up. I still keep in touch with many of these classmates, who are now successful businessman, bureaucrats, professors, and the like. Whenever I go back to Japan, they throw a party for me, and sometimes we talk about that experience. But when I ask them why they beat me, they don't answer me. They have nothing to say except this inexplicable silence. There's always this peculiar alienation there.

K: If military nationalism was so strong during the war that anything foreign was opposed, you must have come over as quite an oddball.

M: Yes. This is a consistent pattern with me. One day an American airplane was shot down in our area, but the pilot managed to parachute out. When the neighbors saw him land, they all went after him with bamboo spears. I remember asking them why they were going after a man who, in his own country, was obviously a patriot. It may sound awfully corny now, but at that time I really couldn't understand why people did what they did. I must have been a real pain in the ass.

K: So you did finish college in Japan? What was your major?

M: English literature. And then I taught for a year at the Gakushuin, the college that once belonged to the Imperial Household, in which the imperial and royal families were educated but which was made into a private college after the war.

K: During this period had you already made up your mind to go to the States?

M: Yes, as I said, the colonial aspiration was there. There's no doubt about that.

K: Why the States?

M: The Fulbright Fellowship.

K: How did your family feel about your going?

M: They didn't think it was a big deal one way or the other. They simply thought I would go away for a year and then come back.

K: But then you stayed on forever, it seems.

M: I came in 1952. During the seven years after the war I had worked as an interpreter for the U.S. Army.

K: What was that like?

M: I mostly worked summers. It was a very cushy job. I didn't have much to do but sit around and read novels.

K: So that was pretty much the extent of your intellectual formation prior to coming to the States?

M: Yes. I just got a letter from an old classmate who remarked that he found it difficult to believe that I had learned much of anything in Japan as a student. Again, I'm not very certain about what I knew then except that there was, of course, the shock of hearing from the American occupation forces that much of what we had been told during the war was not true. So I suppose the one thing I learned was the uncertainty about the "truth." But it wasn't a systematic intellectual structure so much as the formation of a kind of vigilant skepticism.

K: I suppose one could, if I may, describe it as a kind of intellectual enlightenment.

M: In the eighteenth-century sense of the word, yes. But just because there was this shock of realization that so much of what we had been told during the war was false doesn't mean that I had much trust in what I was told after the war. To a certain extent, it was a continuation of the skepticism that I'd had during the war.

K: So you wouldn't describe it as an ideological break with the Japanese value system?

M: No, insofar as I had never really identified with the Japanese tradition. On the other hand, I really didn't identify with the West either. Nor did my family for that matter.

K: From there, perhaps we could move on to Yale. What happened there?

M: Actually. I was bored to death. Although I did get to know Norman Holmes Pearson pretty well. He was a very interesting man. He had been an oss operator during the war. This is the 1950s, a most ideologically repressed time period. I was thrown out of the country in 1953. 1 was married then, and my ex-wife's mother was a DAR member, Daughters of the American Revolution. This means nothing nowadays, but at the time it was still a politically influential group. She didn't like the idea of her daughter being married to a Japanese. Since I was married I worked in the library, but Fulbright students were not allowed employment. She brought my employment to the attention of the immigration authorities, and they had me arrested and thrown out of the country. This was the sort of thing that gradually altered my perceptions and drew me into politics. [Laughter]

K: Where did you go?

M: I went back to Japan, and it was about a year before I was able to return to the States.

K: How did you get back?

M: Believe it or not, I came back as a war bride. [Laughter] I still have the letter I got from the INS. It reads: "Dear Madam." [Laughter] At the time few if any Japanese men were married to American women; it was almost always the other way around, so they assumed I was a woman. Anyway, I came back, but I didn't have an academic job or anything. In fact, for a short time I found employment as a dishwasher and later as a factory worker in a steel mill. In 1953 there was, of course, the Rosenberg execution. This was just before McCarthy went into full swing. I remember I gave a speech at the factory opposing the execution. It was a fairly incoherent talk, but I remember I was very much impassioned in my defense of the Rosenbergs. Although I gradually got drawn into this kind of politics, by and large, I couldn't say my political awareness was particularly serious for at least another ten years or so, not until after the civil rights movement took off and the Vietnam War heated up.

K: Did this factory experience have much to do with your changing perceptions?

M: I'll tell you how stupid I was. I was working at a county library in Buffalo. This library was the center of the Trotskyite movement in Buffalo. They had a cell that met at the library, and it was under surveillance by the FBI, which I didn't even know about. The Trotskyites protected me by not inviting me into their cell meetings. Later on I found out who they were, but at the time I had no idea. But the library was under surveillance, and eventually I was arrested, returned to Japan, and spent another year teaching at the Gakushuin in Tokyo. I taught there when the crown prince of

Japan, the current emperor, was a student. By then, I was gradually crawling out of my innocence. It was 1955 and there was a general strike. I remember I was talking about this with the crown prince at a party. His tutor kept kicking me under the table to get me to shut up.

K: It was here that you began to be shaped into the Left? What brought you back to the States? Did you find it difficult in Japan?

M: Well, first of all, I was married to an American and, second, yes, it was difficult in Japan, and, in fact, still is.

K: For you?

M: Yes, I'm not modest enough or humble enough.

K: So where did you come back to?

M: I came first to New York City. I got a job teaching at a private school in New Jersey. It was a very small and extremely expensive school whose guiding principle was to teach kids how miserable life was, so that they would appreciate how well off they were at home. I really couldn't believe how inhuman their treatment of the kids was. Like something out of Dickens. When I tried to explain to some of the parents how their kids were being treated, I was shocked to discover that this was exactly what they expected. I remember speaking to one parent—he was the vice president of one of the country's largest publishing companies with a huge house in an exclusive suburb in New Jersey—he didn't bat an eye. He thought I was some kind of idiot. [Laughter] I must say that was some education. I even went to the New Jersey Board of Education in order to complain about the treatment of the kids in this private school, and I was told that there was nothing they could do unless the parents themselves lodged a complaint. Anyhow, after three months or so of that, I quit. That was the first time I came to understand that social evil is a legitimate part of society. [Laughter] This was 1956 or thereabouts. I started going to NYU as a graduate student in English literature. Then I got TB and was hospitalized for a whole year. After that, I started getting scholarships and fellowships.

K: Could you talk more about how the Vietnam War influenced the solidification of your politics?

M: I started at Berkeley in 1963, and the free speech movement broke out the following year. I remember that about that time I was beginning to sign statements against the war. I didn't know a great deal about the war by 1964, but at least I was already thoroughly skeptical of all official statements regarding American conduct in the war.

K: Was this Noam Chomsky's influence?

M: No, not really. This was something that went back to my experiences in the Second World War and the postwar revelations about Japanese conduct during the war. My skepticism about American conduct was no doubt bolstered by the fact that I had met a number of Vietnamese immigrants in upstate New York. In any case, by the time the Vietnam War had started, I was already a thoroughly skeptical animal. What Chomsky did was help me interpret what was going on, not just regarding the war, but many other things as well. Chomsky helped solidify my political activism, too. Although, at that point—I got to know Chomsky well when he came to Berkeley in 1967—he was known less as a political activist than as an original thinker. After Chomsky came, I proposed a demonstration against the port of Chicago—which is north of Berkeley—through which perhaps 90 percent of the war material Americans used in Vietnam was then shipped. The demonstration we staged in 1967 was actually one of the first political acts ever performed by members of the Berkeley English Department.

K: Were you active in the civil rights movement'?

M: By the time I got to Berkeley, there was some civil rights activism in the Bay Area, especially in the automobile industry. My wife was very active in this. I have to admit that I was rather equivocal at first. But, then, at that time, the passion among the Berkeley English faculty was the "Save the Bay" movement. Civil rights was regarded as little more than a form of exhibitionism. In fact, I recall one influential faculty member telling me that civil rights was simply not important—that blacks would come and go—but, once you killed the bay, nothing could be done about it. Of course, the free speech movement changed everything.

K: Were you active in the free speech movement?

M: Yes, very much so. Not that I was taken very seriously at the time. Very few Asians were, at least not until the late 1960s and early 1970s with the rise of Asian American activism.

K: Were you active in this as well?

M: I did sponsor a few Asian ethnic studies courses, but, frankly, even to this day, I don't believe in any biological animal called the Asian American. This is not to say that I don't believe that there are serious social problems among certain Asian minority groups, such as the Vietnamese and Cambodian immigrants and many other groups. But we need to maintain these distinctions among social groups and classes. We can't just lump everyone together in the name of some concoction called Asian America.

K: In 1978, you left Berkeley to go to the University of Chicago.

M: I was just a visiting professor there for a few years, but it was a very ideal situation because the University of Chicago was, at that point, a very exciting place, especially in the field of Japanese studies. By then I had begun to enjoy a friendship with Edward Said and Fredric Jameson.

K: When did you meet Jameson?

M: By then I knew Chomsky well. He introduced me to Said, who in turn invited Jameson and me, together with Hayden White and a few others, to visit the West Bank universities that were being brutalized by the Israeli occupation troops. Since then we have been together often. So, when I got to Chicago, I invited Jameson, Said, and Chomsky there. Chicago had that kind of freedom as a private university. Berkeley didn't. I couldn't do that kind of thing, at Berkeley, but once I got to Chicago, I started, with many others, to develop a kind of broad-based politics. In Berkeley, I and a number of other anti-Zionist students and faculty organized courses and political programs with a definite idea of justice but, in the end, we wound up alienating nearly everyone.

K: You never had a post in East Asian studies at Berkeley?

M: My god, I completely forgot I spent a whole year fighting with the Oriental Languages Department there. It was an amazing fight. This was in the mid-1970s. I had been teaching in the English Department but the O.L.

Department asked me to teach a course in the Japanese novel, which I did. There were quite a few students. It was an undergraduate course, but there were graduate students in the course as well. One of them, who now teaches at an Ivy League university, happened to mention that the O.L. Department at Berkeley took an awful long time to produce Ph.D.s. I suggested he apply for a grant from the student association to do a comparative study of how long the oriental languages departments at the major campuses in the U.S. took to produce their Ph.D.s. He thought that was a great idea and did it. He found out that Berkeley took the longest, something like twelve years, if I recall. Well, when the chairman of the O.L. Department found out about the study, he gave the student, who was taking one of his classes, a C on his term paper. The student was rather shocked, not only because he had never received anything but As before but because of the university rule that any Ph.D. student who received a C or less in a graduate course was out of the program. He came to me and asked me to look at the paper. It wasn't a great paper but when I compared it to the A papers he had written for the same chairman, I couldn't discover any significant difference in their quality to justify the poor grade. So I concluded that the grade was revenge for the comparative study this student had undertaken.

That started my fight with the Oriental Languages Department. I first tried to find out what the departmental requirements for graduate students were but I couldn't find anything in print. So I started writing letters to the chairman about this, and, when he didn't respond, I started writing open letters. But all they could come up with was a list of requirements drafted in pencil. As far as I was concerned requirements written in pencil could hardly be regarded as official requirements since they could always be erased. Finally, I went to the graduate dean, told him about the strange goings-on in the O.L. Department, and asked him to conduct a departmental review. Since he knew something about the department and me, or at least my work, he agreed to form a review committee.

K: Were you on the committee?

M: Certainly not, since I was the one who had instigated it. But there were quite a few established scholars on the committee, one of whom was a friend of mine who quietly passed on to me the committee reports and other paperwork. It took a hell of a long time—I don't know, maybe a year—but after an incredible number of interviews and so on, the committee eventually recommended receivership, which is where a department loses autonomy over its own affairs, which are turned over to someone appointed by the graduate dean. So I won, in other words. But then, the dean chose not to act on the committee's recommendation and simply threw the whole report into a safety deposit box somewhere. The only upshot was that the O.L. Department was told that it would come under review two years hence, which, of course, wasn't good enough for me. You cannot believe how long this fight lasted.

K: What happened to the graduate student?

M: He wasn't expelled because he was protected during the review process, but the department refused to write recommendation letters for him or to support his Ph.D. He wrote his thesis, an excellent one, but his department never recognized his existence. He had to find all of his readers outside the department. Nevertheless, he did manage to get a job at an Ivy League university, but I think that was because of the close relationship I had with a faculty member there at the time. And his case was but one of several. During the course of this review, the O.L. Department chair's wife, who was a professor in the department, wrote a letter to one of her female graduate students who had attended one of the faculty student meetings which I had organized to talk about what to do about the O.L. Department. The letter said that since she had attended this meeting, she was obviously one of my followers and therefore she could henceforth consider herself one of my students, not hers. In other words, the student could no longer expect any support from the O.L. Department. I think I directed five or six Ph.D.s by O.L. Department students writing on Japanese literature that had to look outside their own department to find readers. At times, we did this through the Comparative Literature Department. It was a hell of a fight, and I don't know whether it did anything good. Some of these students want to forget their treatment in the O.L. Department, because it is such a powerful ongoing bureaucracy upon which they depend for job placement and career advancement. I would like to think that my battle with the department had some positive repercussions among a few Japanologists in this country, but I can't say for certain that it has.

K: Has the department gotten any better?

M: Things don't change in bureaucracy. As far as I can see, it's still in a sad shape, but who knows?

K: When did you start teaching Japanese literature?

M: Pretty soon after I got tenure in English. Someone at Stanford had invited me to move there to teach Japanese literature, but I refused because I wanted to first establish myself in English. But even later on, I wasn't particularly interested in doing Japanese literature. But by then I do think I had learned a couple of things, one of which was to ignore national borders, and the other was to ignore disciplinary borders.

K: But you still have to maintain certain disciplinary responsibilities, for example, to teach Victorian literature if you're offering a Victorian literature course, don't you?

M: Not really. Even in the days when I was regularly teaching Victorian literature, I used to include twentieth-century American or nineteenth-century continental novels. And when I taught the Japanese novel, I used to include Lu Xun, Nabokov, Mansfield, and Ngugi.

K: You have this reputation, you know, of being someone who likes to throw the canonical texts on the floor.

M: Yes, I have heard this.

K: So, moving into the 1980s, what were the predominant influences in your work and life?

M: Intercultural, international, interethnic, interracial, and other intercategorical thought permeated this entire period. That is one of the reasons for my preoccupation with the outsider and things that are outside.

K: This would seem to be a consistent theme linking your academic work to your background insofar as you were a kind of outsider within Japanese culture. But then you are also an outsider within American culture.

M: You're probably right. My consistent preoccupation has been this question of borders, in both my personal and professional life: how do we make adjustments when we move across borders?

K: So would you say that by the 1980s the gap you had noticed between your political activities and your intellectual preoccupations had pretty much disappeared?

M: Yes.

K: So what kind of political activities were you involved in during the 1980s?

M: From 1980 to 1986 the Palestinian issue was the central thing. And then, through my friends at Chicago, I began to increase my activities in Japan— for example, my critique of the Japanese imperial system, which I began to write about in the Japanese press. And, of course, I continued my support for the Palestinians, at least until I came here to San Diego. Here, there's no campus-based activism on their behalf, but at least I've managed to bring in Palestinian speakers, something that the campus had not seen before. And I've been networking with scholars like Chomsky, Said, and Jameson, as well as younger people who are politically active. I became close to brilliant Chicago historians of Japan like Tetsuo Najita and Harry Harootunian. I do meet pretty often with a number of European Marxists. By networking I don't just mean getting on the telephone or fax machine, but actually getting together in various places and, more importantly, getting scholars seriously interested in cultures and localities outside their field of expertise. For example, getting Perry Anderson or Eqbal Ahmad to talk about Japan—and it's worked well I think. It's great to hear that someone like Stuart Hall is interested in China and Taiwan and so on. Of course, the number of Western scholars who have developed a serious interest in non-Western localities is still incredibly small.

K: So why did you leave Berkeley to come to San Diego? Your students must not have been very happy about that.

M: I was in the English Department at Berkeley. English departments are conservative intellectually and politically everywhere, but at Berkeley the English Department was singularly stagnant. Since I don't have a degree from a Japan-related field, many people in Japanese studies think I'm a dilettante and don't take me very seriously. Here, since I'm in a department of literature that doesn't officially care much about the nationalities of literature (though in reality, it does), I can teach pretty much anything I want. If I teach Japanese literature, African novels, or Chinese short stories, nobody bats an eye. On the other hand, while the department here is "liberal," the campus bureaucracy is quite corporate and reactionary, unlike Berkeley, which is liberal. But "liberal" can actually be worse than reactionary. At Berkeley they knew what I was doing, so they could attempt to control me, whereas here they're so committed to corporate technology that they don't even care what anyone in the humanities is doing. For example, the first scholar I invited here to speak—they have an endowed lecture series that provides quite a bit of money for this sort of thing—was Said. Then I brought Chomsky. Then Gore Vidal. I could never have invited Chomsky at Berkeley in any official and institutional capacity. Every time Chomsky came to Berkeley to talk about politics, it was at the invitation of a student organization. But here the endowed lecture series can bring in all sorts of people precisely because the university is so preoccupied with technology that they just don't care about the humanities. They don't think intellectual discourse is significant. At the same time, the department here is as fragmented as the English Department at Berkeley; people are very isolated and indifferent, but I suppose it is the same everywhere nowadays.

K: But at Berkeley you were so influential in politicizing graduate students.

M: But that is something I think I can do almost anywhere. For example, while I was at Harvard as the Edwin O. Reischauer Visiting Professor, I probably politicized a few students, although what this temporary radicalization of students actually means, especially at a place like Harvard, is very problematic. Reischauer, you know, was one of the grand policy makers of the cold war. He was the one who helped establish modernization theory and sell it as an alternative cold war model to socialists, and I felt challenged by the title. Similarly, if I did manage to do anything constructive at Berkeley, that's good, but eventually I got worn down by the conservativeness of the department. At Berkeley you can never escape from the hierarchy of structure, with its privileges and exclusions. Even the radical faculty at Berkeley have their hierarchies.

K: What about here?

M: It's less conservative, at least in my department. For example, the tenure process is open, not confidential. Of course, whether that means tolerance and plurality or simply indifference and apathy, I couldn't say.

K: So you're very happy in this department?

M: I suppose. But I have almost no close friends among the faculty. Most of my close friends with whom I network are elsewhere. That's why I'm on the phone so often and why I'm on the road so much. San Diego is for me a spiritual desert. But I console myself that a desert is better than a jungle of poison ivy. I do confess that everyone here is boringly PC, hopelessly predictable, and not seriously political. But that, too, is everywhere, I guess.

K: And students?

M: Yes, I miss the students at Berkeley. I do have quite a few great graduate students here, but at Berkeley I think I had much closer relationships with undergraduate students. That's what made teaching at Berkeley so interesting. There were always at least two or three really interesting students in each of my undergraduate classes. I taught at Chicago but I never had any undergraduates like the ones I had at Berkeley. In that regard, Berkeley is really *sui generis*.

K: So at San Diego, you have more room to maneuver to find space to do your own thing?

M: Yes. I get more institutional support here than I did at Berkeley. At Berkeley I never really knew what my role was, especially among the Japanologists, who thought I was weird, politically unacceptable, and, while they came to have some grudging acceptance of my work as a scholar and teacher, they never placed their recognition of my work in an institutional structure. To a certain extent, I also miss the intellectual culture that the city of Berkeley provides, although, in many ways, it can also be rather pompous and empty. The city of San Diego, on the other hand, is reactionary and bureaucratic, dominated by military and corporate interests. So clean and polite; so empty and desiccated; so affluent and lifeless.

K: Would you talk a little about your agenda?

M: My agenda is really very simple, I think: how do we find oppositional space around the globe? Or more specifically: how do we help the poor and the oppressed everywhere? What are the intellectual and political means to do this? At this point, I'm not really interested in anything else.

K: So far, I detect that your radicalization was very different than that experienced by other diasporic intellectuals from Japan. Your case seems very unique. Nobody else in Japan would, I think, care about Middle Eastern politics, for example.

M: Insofar as Japan is concerned, I think people there are still imaginatively and intellectually confined within their own boundaries. They are obsessed with the idea of Japan, their own identity, and very little else. I see historical reasons for that, but sincerely hope that they will get over it before too long.

K: I still can't quite understand what drove you into leftist politics. Was it your friendship with Chomsky and Said or the war in Vietnam?

M: I'm sure these friends helped me a great deal. But probably my politics goes back to the Second World War. My incomprehension of it during the war. My inability to understand it for many years after the war. Then, the eruption of anger during the Vietnam War, which was helped by Chomsky's clear understanding of the war but also was independent of it. The Second World War left me no choice but to search for some basis of fairness and justice, a modest utopian view in which one needs not be ashamed of bigotry and ignorance. You don't know how depressing it was to read the papers every morning during the 1960s. And as for my concern with the Middle East affairs, that did begin with Said tutoring me around the time he wrote *Orientalism*. But, generally speaking, my politics goes way back to the Second World War and my adolescence, even if its development was slow and tortuous. Justice is a self-evident idea, it seems to me, whether it is about the Middle East, Africa, Asia, race in America, or gender questions.

K: As far as my understanding goes, the Chinese intellectual diaspora has far more political power in their respective homelands and has far more influence in intervening politically at the local level than the Japanese intellectual diaspora. Why do you think this is the case?

M: Well, I would imagine that the answer would lie, on the one hand, with the peculiar historical relationship between Taiwan/PRC/Hong Kong and the United States and, on the other hand, with the national differences in the intellectuals' relationship to the power structure. So many more Taiwanese intellectuals and political leaders were trained in the United States than Japanese intellectuals. The social role of the intellectual is quite different from one country to another. Even between England and the United States, the differences are immense. And this changes with the political climate. For example, it seems to me that the status of the French intellectual is pretty deplorable these days. They're totally cynical and basically concerned only with themselves and little else. In England, on the other hand, at least you still have people like Stuart Hall. I think America is somewhere between England and France. At least, it seems to me that Mrs. Thatcher was far less successful than Reagan in undermining the political influence of the intellectual in their respective countries. Japanese intellectuals, diasporic or otherwise, have no influence in the political realm. Politics in Japan is conducted by a small power elite that has very few connections with the intellectual community. Japanese politics is conducted by a strangely nebulous coalition of LDP power brokers, corporate leaders in manufacturing, banking, and the underworld. What is strange is that this power structure has little formal articulation, so that it is very powerful but can never really be pinpointed. It's quite scandalous, in fact. A kind of gangsterism, largely extralegal or metalegal. With a power structure like this, the intellectuals' influence on the practical workings of the state is virtually zero. That doesn't mean that they don't have a voice in the public sphere. Japanese publishers will publish whatever dissenting intellectuals might write on practically any issue, but there are few readers. Besides, it will not have the slightest influence on the foreign or domestic conduct of the state. Intellectuals do not even have much influence in the realm of culture. The intellectuals there are basically ornamental. They provide flavor. [Laughter]

K: So you would say that the positionality of the Japanese intellectual and the particular structure of Japanese politics prevents intellectuals from intervening in politics?

M: Yes, and I don't know any way to overcome this blockage. Some time ago, Jameson, Najita, Harootunian, and I, as well as a number of Americanists like Paul Bové and Donald Pease, went to Tokyo to discuss precisely what if any kind of intellectual intervention was possible in Japan. We were very politely treated, but our trip had absolutely no repercussions of any kind. Our conversation was dutifully printed in a leading journal of opinion, but there was never a response to it. We speak, but nothing really happens. It's a lot like the problem of translation in Japan. For example, Foucault and Althusser have been translated into Japanese and various Japanese intellectuals will mention them—their names and ideas come up in the literature— but have they had any impact on the ongoing discursive conduct in Japan? My conclusion is no. They just disappear into the silence.

κ: Is there anything critical or important you want to say that might have been left out of this talk today?

M: I wanted to mention the nuclei of several ideas that preoccupy me these days. One of these is the end of the nation-state, the disappearance, almost everywhere, of the nation-state as an agency for social programs. Another is the increasing ethnic fragmentation that you see in India, Canada, the British Islands, the Balkans, Africa, and so many other places. In particular, I'm concerned with the impact that ethnic fragmentation will have on economic development. This is manifest at many levels: academically, the fragmentation of the intellectual community is tangible everywhere. It is impossible today to talk about feminism, for example, with any sense of ideological coherence. Feminism has fragmented into a host of differing ideologies and ideologues each competing for supremacy. And this is true for ethnic studies and everything else. I think the growing preoccupation with ethnic identity is particularly dangerous. People can't talk anymore to each other. It's getting kind of scary.

κ: The question that remains then is: if you stand outside of national borders wherever you stand, where do you stand?

M: You can stand anywhere and still discuss the issues that preoccupy cultural studies. Look, there's another way of looking at this. The idea of the nation-state emerges with colonialism. Before European colonialism, there was no such thing as the nation-state. As colonialism establishes national borders, the states require nationalism to legitimize national boundaries. One aspect of nationalism was the study of national literatures and cultures.

In other words, the study of national literatures emerged as part of this legitimizing process. Colonialism, imperialism, capitalism have all been traditionally defined in national terms. As we criticize colonialism, imperialism, capitalism, a reformulation of the idea of discrete national literatures is in order. The dilemma for international cultural studies is that institutional departments are still formed around national developments.

K: I wonder if I could close by arguing that much of your intellectual power derives from your diasporic experience and positioning, to the fact that, having been a cultural outsider for most of your life, you bring the outsider's perspective to bear on virtually everything you engage.

M: I have friends in Japan, the U.S., and other places—although most of my close friends are in the U.S.—but I often wind up asking myself, regardless of whether I'm in Japan or the United States or anywhere else: am I really speaking with anyone? This is a sort of uncertainty that I have to live with. And happy to live with, since my work is really becoming placeless.

K: Your position in cultural studies is rather unique in that most people in cultural studies—certainly in Australia and China—are doing "the local." But your brand of cultural studies is internationalist. I attribute your internationalist position to your internationalist politics, both of which I see emerging from your diasporic experience.

M: It's no longer diasporic in the old sense of the word, as exile from persecution, for example. The reasons for living at any particular locality are disappearing except that there are a huge majority of people who are left behind and cannot dream of leaving for any place else. They are stuck, often trapped for good. In our era of so-called globalization, globalization is reserved for the lucky few. I am obviously one of them, and so I feel an obligation to constantly think about those trapped behind with little hope. The corporations now enjoy transnational freedom of movement, and the intellectuals are active participants in this transnational freedom. But those left behind are often devastated because of this same corporate mobility. I want to acknowledge that and then devise a way to fight back.

K: Let me pose a last question. Almost all the diasporic intellectuals I've interviewed maintain certain ties with their homeland, especially the Chinese. Indeed, I think much of the Chinese intellectual diaspora, especially academics in the States, will eventually go back home because it is the moment for them to exercise their influence and power in their homeland. But that doesn't seem to be the case with you, right?

M: I've thought maybe once or twice of teaching a little back in Japan, but it's not really very important one way or the other. What is important is the willingness to go outside one's national, cultural and disciplinary borders. That's why I admire Jameson so much. He's got the right intentions.

K: In Jameson's case, I don't care about his intentions, I worry about his ability to discern what is going on at the local level.

M: Yeah, but Jameson is one of the very few scholars who actively try to learn about every region, every culture. He studies, or has studied, Chinese and Arabic; he really reads Vietnamese and Japanese writers and critics. I don't know of many scholars so willing to go out of the cultures of their expertise. I admire his curiosity, his ease at being anywhere. In fact, we should be everywhere. I told my kids that when I died they should flush my ashes down the toilet bowl and let them flow out to the Pacific. [Laughter]

K: With that, I'd like to thank you for this conversation. It's now nearly 3:30.

NOTES

....

Introduction

1. Miyoshi gives his own account of this shift in "Turn to the Planet: Literature, Diversity, and Totality," in "Globalization and the Humanities," special issue of *Comparative Literature* 53, no. 4 (fall 2001): 283–97.

2. Miyoshi, *Off Center: Power and Culture Relations between Japan and the United States* (Cambridge, Mass.: Harvard University Press, 1991), 97.

3. Ibid., 97.

4. Ibid., xv.

5. Edward Said, *Orientalism* (New York: Pantheon, 1979).

6. Karel Van Wolferen, *The Enigma of Japanese Power* (New York: Knopf, 1990); Clyde Prestowitz, *Trading Places: How We Allowed Japan to Take the Lead* (New York: Basic Books, 1988).

7. *Off Center*, 3.

8. Miyoshi and H. D. Harootunian, eds., *Postmodernism and Japan* (Durham: Duke University Press, 1989), first published as a special issue of *South Atlantic Quarterly* 87, no. 3 (summer 1988).

9. Ibid., xvi.

10. Ibid.

11. Miyoshi and H. D. Harootunian, eds., *Japan in the World* (Durham: Duke University Press, 1993), first published as a special issue of *boundary 2* 18, no. 3 (autumn 1991); *Learning Places: The Afterlives of Area Studies* (Durham: Duke University Press, 2002).

12. David Harvey, *The Condition of Postmodernity* (London: Blackwell Press, 1991); Fredric Jameson, *Postmodernism, or, The Cultural Logic of Late Capitalism* (Durham: Duke University Press, 1991).

13. *Off Center*, 3.

14. Miyoshi, "A Borderless World? From Colonialism to Transnationalism and the Decline of the Nation-State," *Critical Inquiry* 19, no. 4 (summer 1993): 751.

15. Miyoshi, "Sites of Resistance in the Global Economy," *boundary 2* 84, no. 1 (spring 1995): 61–84.

16. Miyoshi, "Modernist Agonistes," *The Nation*, May 15, 1995.

17. Miyoshi, "Outside Architecture," in *Anywise*, ed. Cynthia C. Davidson (Cambridge, Mass.: MIT Press, 1996).

18. Miyoshi, "XL in Asia: A Dialogue between Rem Koolhaas and Masao Miyoshi," *boundary 2* 24, no. 2 (summer 1997): 1–19.

19. "Outside Architecture," 47.

20. "Radical Art at *documenta X*," *New Left Review*, no. 228 (March–April 1998).

21. Unpublished interview with author, New York City, August 24, 2007.

22. "Literary Elaborations," 19.

23. Ibid., 58.

24. Ibid., 60.

25. Ibid., 62.

Literary Elaborations

I gave a talk—under the same title—that corresponds roughly to the first few pages of this essay, at a conference on Edward Said on May 25 and 26, 2007, organized by Bogazici University and Metis Publications in Istanbul. The title was inspired by Said's work *Musical Elaborations*. Although this essay does not even mention Said, my ideas about the role of the intellectual grew through many conversations between us over thirty years. He wrote several acclaimed books on the subject, but this was one topic on which I did not agree with him. One of our exchanges was publicly recorded, but only on a TV program dubbed in Japanese. *Musical Elaborations* is not as well known as his other works, but I admire it greatly. The subject is music, considered in both technical and historical aspects, and the "elaborations" extend to political problems, among many others. I would like to celebrate the memory of Edward Said here as well as acknowledge my debt. I do wish he were here to protest.

1. Even the IPCC reports have been dismissed as fraudulent not only by those in the energy industry but by the presumably progressive writer Alexander Cockburn in a series of articles in *The Nation* in the spring of 2007. His argument and documentation are mulish, unintelligent, and baseless.

2. In the spring of 2007—as much as forty years after the university reform movements of the 1960s—a special task force formed by the president of Harvard issued a report, asking the faculty to "rethink" the importance of teaching. Sara Rimer, "Harvard Task Force Calls for New Focus on Teaching and Not Just Research," *New York Times*, May 10, 2007.

3. One might remember here a more than seventy-year-old essay, "A Critic's Job of Work" (1935), by R. D. Blackmur, in *Language as Gesture: Essays in Poetry* (New York: Harcourt, Brace, 1952), 372–99. See also Edward Said's "Professionals and Amateurs," in *Representations of the Intellectual: The 1993 Reith Lectures* (New York: Pantheon Books, 1994), 65–83; and Bruce Robbins, *Secular Vocations: Intellectuals, Professionalism, Culture* (London: Verso, 1993).

4. See Kevin Robbins and Frank Webster, eds., *The Virtual University? Knowledge, Market, and Management* (Oxford: Oxford University Press, 2002).

5. See, for example, Charles Baudelaire, "Usefulness to the community has always seemed to me a most hideous thing in a man" (*My Heart Laid Bare*, 9); and Nietzsche's early book, *On the Future of Our Educational Institutions*: "How useless we were! And how proud we were of being useless! We used even to quarrel with each other as to which of us should have the glory of being the more useless." First lecture (delivered January 16, 1872), in *The Complete Works of Friedrich Nietzsche*, ed. Oscar Levy, vol. 3, *On the Future of Our Educational Institutions* [and] *Homer and Classical Philology* (New York: Russell and Russell, 1964), 32. Little read nowadays, the lectures have many sharp and sane observations on the university and culture.

6. See Masao Miyoshi and H. D. Harootunian, eds., *Learning Places: The Afterlives of Area Studies* (Durham: Duke University Press, 2002).

7. The word "culture" has had a long, complicated history of uses in English, French, and German, tracing back to the sixteenth century, or even earlier. The English Romantics used it in the sense of refinement, while Arnold borrowed it from German *Kultur* (itself a borrowing from French, first spelled *cultur*). However, the anthropological use of the word in the sense of a particular way of life is already seen in English as in E. B. Tyler's *Primitive Culture* (1871). Arnold's dual meanings of "culture" as refinement and a sociological and anthropological way of life are thus rooted in the word itself. "Hostility to the word 'culture' in English appears to date from the controversy around Arnold's views." Raymond Williams, "Culture," in *Key Words: A Vocabulary of Culture and Society* (New York: Oxford University Press, 1983), 92.

8. A century later, Bill Readings elaborates this notion of undefined and unspecified "excellence" that has become the only raison d'être of the university in *The University in Ruins* (Cambridge, Mass.: Harvard University Press, 1996).

9. Matthew Arnold, "Conclusion," *Culture and Anarchy*, ed. J. Dover Wilson (Cambridge: Cambridge University Press, 1961), 203–4.

10. There are numerous books on the sixties, but many are descriptive and not analytic enough, if at all. Further, most are limited in their scope. Even those that treat the antiwar protest movements tend to be local, national, or regional. Arthur Marwick's *The Sixties: Cultural Revolution in Britain, France, Italy, and the United States, c. 1958–c. 1974* (Oxford: Oxford University Press, 1998), for example, leaves out the unmentioned countries and regions (such as South America and Asia) despite its 903 pages. David Caute's *Sixty-Eight: The Year of the Barricades* (London: Paladio, 1988), too, fails to interlink the political, economic, social, educational, and cultural, while also failing to explain why in 1968 and why in nearly every country. The 1960s deserves further serious studies.

11. The sources of these figures are the United Nations Development Programme (UNDP), *Human Development Report 1998* (New York: Oxford University Press,

1998), 30; Lawrence Summers, "Harness Market Forces to Share Prosperity," *Financial Times*, June 24, 2007; Louisa Kroll and Allison Fass, "The World's Billionaires," www.Forbes.com, March 8, 2007. There are many studies—by the World Institute for Development Economics Research of the United Nations University, for instance, or by Thomas Piketty, Paris School of Economics, and Emmanuel Saez, University of California, Berkeley, that agree on the increasing income inequality both within the United States and in the world. See, for example, Eduardo Porter, "Study Finds Wealth Inequality Is Widening Worldwide," *New York Times*, December 6, 2006: "In 2000, the top 1 percent of the world's population—some 37 million adults with a net worth of at least $515,000—accounted for about 40 percent of the world's total net worth, according to [the World Institute for Development Economics Research]. The bottom half of the population owned merely 1.1 percent of the globe's wealth."

12. Paul Collier, *The Bottom Billion: Why the Poorest Countries Are Failing and What Can Be Done about It* (Oxford: Oxford University Press, 2007).

13. There have been three interesting books published in the last three years on the subject of the inequity in wealth distribution, each written from a different perspective: Jeffrey D. Sachs, *The End of Poverty: Economic Possibilities for Our Time* (New York: Penguin, 2005); William Easterly, *The White Man's Burden: Why the West's Efforts to Aid the Rest Have Done So Much Ill And So Little Good* (New York: Penguin, 2006); Collier, *The Bottom Billion*. In the last section of his book, Collier discusses both Sachs and Easterly, and I find myself in agreement with him. However, "What Can Ordinary People Do?"—his section title—is left unanswered on the last page.

14. There are numerous discussions questioning the validity of art—"museumized" art—by Hal Foster, Douglas Crimp, Craig Owen, Hans Haacke, and many others. There are also numerous antiart artworks and events such as *documenta X* or the site-specific San Diego Tijuana inSite project. Site-specific art is criticized in turn by Miwon Kwon in her *One Place after Another: Site-Specific Art and Locational Identity* (Cambridge, Mass.: MIT Press, 2002). See also my " 'Globalization,' the University, and the Museum."

15. As late as 2001, the year when the IPCC Third Assessment Report, *Climate Change 2001*, was issued, one in eight Americans did not believe that global warming would ever happen. There were disagreements among scientists, too, which politicians like George W. Bush (as well as his father earlier) used as an excuse for taking no action to regulate corporate practice. Soon thereafter, global warming was accepted with near unanimity among scientists. (Of course, there are exceptions. See John Tierney, " 'Feel Good' vs. 'Do Good' on Climate" about Bjorn Lomborg's money as the solution for the future, and Tierney's approval of this idea, *New York Times*, September 11, 2007. For an excellent account of the reception of the IPCC and other reports, see chap. 8, "The Discovery Confirmed," of Spencer R. Weart, *The*

Discovery of Global Warming (Cambridge, Mass.: Harvard University Press, 2003). The IPCC Fourth Assessment Report, *Climate Change 2007*, was issued in the fall of 2007 and is available online at www.ipcc.ch/ipccreports/assessments-reports.htm.

16. The performance of the U.S. government has been consistently self-destructive. After introducing the Environmental Protection Agency, the Clean Air Act, and the Clean Water Act in the 1970s, all administrations, Republican or Democratic, have deliberately failed to execute what the law stipulates. See chap. 5, "Changing the Rules," of Patrick Hossay, *Unsustainable: A Primer for Global Environmental and Social Justice* (London: Zed Books, 2006). See also note 1 above. Lawrence Summers, who now seems to be grudgingly accepting global warming as undeniable ("We Need to Bring Climate Idealism Down to Earth," *Financial Times*, April 30, 2007), was firmly convinced fifteen years ago when he was the chief economist of the World Bank that environmentalism was "external" to economics and thus inadmissible. See Herman E. Daly, *Beyond Growth: The Economics of Sustainable Development* (Boston: Beacon Press, 1996), introduction, especially 6–12.

17. I cannot dwell here on the conditions of higher education in ancient Greece, but at least let me mention an excellent history by H. I. Marrou, *A History of Education in Antiquity*, trans. George Lamb (Madison: University of Wisconsin Press, 1956). See also Pierre Hadot, *What Is Ancient Philosophy?*, trans. Michael Chase (Cambridge, Mass.: Harvard University Press, 2002).

18. Willis Rudy, *The Universities of Europe, 1100–1914: A History* (Madison, N.J.: Fairleigh Dickinson University Press, 1984), 32.

19. There is by now a vast amount of literature on the university in the Middle Ages. *A History of the University in Europe*, vol. 1, *Universities in the Middle Ages*, ed. Hilde de Ridder-Symoens (Cambridge: Cambridge University Press, 1996), is the most up-to-date and comprehensive study. See also James Bowen, *A History of Western Education*, vol. 2, *Civilization of Europe, Sixth to Sixteenth Century* (New York: St. Martin's Press, 1975). Although by now antiquated in several aspects, still delightful and useful is Charles Homer Haskins's *The Rise of Universities* (Ithaca: Cornell University Press, 1966), originally published by Henry Holt in 1923. See also Nathan Schachner, *The Medieval Universities* (New York: A. S. Barnes, 1938); Hastings Rashdall, *The Universities of Europe in the Middle Ages* (Oxford: Oxford University Press, 1895); and Lowrie J. Daly, S. J., *The Medieval University, 1200–1400* (New York: Sheed and Ward, 1961).

20. See Pearl Kibre, *Nations in the Medieval European Universities* (Cambridge, Mass.: Medieval Academy of America, 1948), Publication no. 49, which merely lists the universities in the European countries without defining the meaning of "nationality" at the time.

21. Christopher J. Lucas, *American Higher Education: A History* (New York: St. Martin's Press, 1994), 48. Although the main subject of this book is American higher education, it has a concise section on the European universities during the Middles Ages

and later. The number of the universities is not so definite, however. The status of universities is often in dispute. Jacques Verger, for instance, gives different figures in chap. 2, "Patterns," in the second volume of Ridder-Symoens, *A History of the University in Europe*, 60–65.

22. Henry Elmer Barnes, *An Intellectual and Cultural History of the Western World* (New York: Dover Publications, 1963), 1:147.

23. See Haskins, *The Rise of Universities* 52–57.

24. See C. E. McClelland, *State, Society, and University in Germany, 1700–1914* (Cambridge: Cambridge University Press, 1980), 1–98.

25. Marjorie Reeves, "The European University from Medieval Times, with Special Reference to Oxford and Cambridge," in *Higher Education: Demand and Response*, ed. W. R. Niblett (London: Tavistock Publictions, 1969), 71–72, quotation at 82.

26. Reeves, "The European University," 81.

27. Immanuel Kant, *The Conflict of the Faculties (Der Streit der Fakultaten)*, trans. Mary J. Gregor (Lincoln: University of Nebraska Press, 1979), 27–29. Unless otherwise specified, the other references in this paragraph are taken from 27–29.

28. Kant was not only a full-time professor of philosophy at the University of Königsberg, but served as the dean of the faculty of philosophy many times, and was even the rector of the university in 1786. As an administrator, however, Kant was not distinguished. He did not consider practical aspects of administration seriously enough. Manfred Kuehn, *Kant: A Biography* (Cambridge: Cambridge University Press, 2001), 314–16.

29. Thomas R. Malthus, *An Essay on the Principle of Population as It Affects the Future Improvement of Society, with Remarks on the Speculations of Mr. Godwin, M. Condorcet, and Other Writers*, Great Minds Series (a facsimile of the first edition of 1798) (Amherst: Prometheus Books, 1998), chap. 5. Malthus identifies the preventive checks with Europe, and the positive checks with non-Europe, especially China. This Orientalist view has been widely shared by demographers, but recently James Z. Lee and Wang Feng challenged it on the basis of a fascinating reexamination of materials both new and old. See their *One Quarter of Humanity: Malthusian Mythology and Chinese Realities, 1700–2000* (Cambridge, Mass.: Harvard University Press, 1999).

30. Thomas Malthus, *An Essay on the Principle of Population*, 2nd ed. (1803), ed. P. James (Cambridge: Cambridge University Press for the Royal Economic Society, 1990), 2 vols., chap 8, excerpted in the Norton Critical Edition of the *Essay*, ed. Philip Appleman (New York: W. W. Norton, 1976), 135.

31. Elie Halevy, *England in 1815*, trans. E. I. Watkin and D. A. Baker (New York: Barnes and Noble, 1961), 574–75.

32. The first British decennial census appeared in 1801. Malthus estimated the British population as seven million in the essay, but the actual figure was ten million. Thus

Malthus had to amend some of his ideas in the enlarged second edition, published in 1803.

33. The historical population figures cited here are from Massimo Livi-Bacci, *A Concise History of World Population*, 2nd ed., trans. Carl Ipsen (Oxford: Blackwell, 1997). For more recent figures, see World Bank, *Entering the 21st Century: World Development Report 1999/2000* (New York: Oxford University Press, 2000). See also the International Program Center, U.S. Bureau of the Census, www.census.gov/cgi-bin ipc/popelockw.

34. The beginning of the human species is differently calculated depending on the definition of human divergences from the other animals. However, most scholars agree as to the imperceptible growth of the population until a few centuries ago. See Livi-Bacci, *A Concise History of World Population*, passim; and Peter D. Ward and Donald Brownlee, *Rare Earth: Why Complex Life Is Uncommon in the Universe* (New York: Copernicus, 2000), 284–85.

35. Livi-Bacci, *A Concise History of World Population*, 75.

36. For the recent conditions of the world cities, see World Bank, chaps. 6 and 7, *Entering the 21st Century*, 125–55.

37. Amartya Sen, *Development as Freedom* (New York: Alfred A. Knopf, 1999); Amartya Sen with Jean Dreze, *Hunger and Public Action* (New York: Oxford University Press, 1989), and *Poverty and Famines: An Essay on Entitlement and Deprivation* (New York: Oxford University Press, 1981). Also, Worldwatch Institute, *State of the World, 2007: Our Urban Future* (New York: W. W. Norton, 2007).

38. Timothy Egan, "Near Vast Bodies of Water, Land Lies Parched," *New York Times*, August 12, 2001, 1 and 16. Malthus is wrong in another aspect: population growth levels off as living standards rise. Thus the U.N. projections are the high of 10.6 billion, the medium of 8.9 billion by 2050, and the low of 7.5 billion by 2039. Lester R. Brown, *Plan B: Rescuing a Planet under Stress and a Civilization in Trouble* (New York: W. W. Norton, 2003), 177. And yet the Malthusian fear has not completely disappeared. See, for example, Garrett Hardin, *The Ostrich Factor: Our Population Myopia* (New York: Oxford University Press, 1999).

39. Erik Assadourian, "Economic Growth Inches Up," in World Watch Institute, *Vital Signs 2003* (New York: W. W. Norton, 2003), 44–45.

40. Vanessa Friedman, "We're Entering an Age of Irrationality," *Financial Times*, May 5, 2007.

41. Samuel Eliot Morison, *The Founding of Harvard College* (Cambridge, Mass.: Harvard University Press, 1935), 95, 107.

42. Morison, *The Founding of Harvard College*, 41–46. See also Lawrence A. Cremin, *American Education: The Colonial Experience, 1607–1783* (New York: Harper and Row, 1970), 211.

43. The source of this information is *New Englands First Fruits*, a promotional pamphlet

published anonymously in London in 1643, reproduced by Lawrence A. Cremin in *American Education: The Colonal Experience, 1607–1783*, 213–16.

44. A complicated history of the founding of Columbia, or King's College, is detailed by Jurgen Herbst's *From Crisis to Crisis: American College Government, 1636–1819* (Cambridge, Mass.: Harvard University Press, 1982). Its second chapter, "Cultural Pluralism and the Great Awakening," traces the confusing story of the affiliation of King's College, but finally, the controversy was not theological, but political. Most of the parties involved in the decision seem to have been only half interested.

45. The original names of these colleges and universities were different: the Collegiate School at New Haven was renamed Yale, the College of New Jersey became Princeton, and so on. Lucas, *American Higher Education*, 105–7.

46. Quoted by Howard Zinn, *A People's History of the United States* (New York: Harper-Collins, 2005), 48. Chapter 3 of Zinn's history, "Persons of Mean and Vile Condition," is blunt and useful, providing rarely cited materials.

47. Morison, *The Founding of Harvard College*, 250, quoted by Lucas, *American Higher Education*, 104–5.

48. Lucas, *American Higher Education*, 109.

49. U.S. Department of Commerce, Bureau of Census, *The Historical Statistics of the United States, Colonial Times to 1970* (White Plains, N.Y.: Kraus International Publications, 1989), part 1, 386.

50. Christopher Jencks and David Riesman, *The Academic Revolution* (New York: Doubleday, 1968), 91.

51. These figures and the circumstances are not quite clear. See Herbst, *From Crisis to Crisis*, 1–17.

52. Martin Trow, "Comparative Perspectives on British and American Higher Education," in *The European and American University since 1800: Historical and Sociological Essays*, ed. Sheldon Rothblatt and Björn Wittrock (Cambridge: Cambridge University Press, 1993), 282 and 284ff.

53. Three Yale graduate students did research on the involvement in the slave trade by the Yale "Worthies" memorialized on Harkness Tower and elsewhere on the campus. In response to their criticism of Yale's less than straightforward representation, John H. McWhorter, author of *Losing the Race: Self-Sabotage in Black America*, argues that "it's downright inappropriate to render a moral judgment on the worth of a person's life based on moral standards which didn't exist at that time." Kate Zernike, "Slavers in Yale's Past Are Focus of Reparations Debate," *New York Times*, August 13, 2001. Henry Wiencek refutes McWhorter's defense as a case of "presentism," citing Thomas Jefferson and George Washington, who were deeply troubled by slavery in their later days. "Yale and the Price of Slavery," *New York Times*, August 18, 2001.

54. Trow, "Comparative Perspectives," 286.

55. Heidegger's relationship to the Nazis has not been resolved to everyone's satisfaction. However, on the basis of "The Self-Assertion of the German University" and "The Rectorate 1933/34: Facts and Thoughts," trans. Karsten Harries (published together in *The Review of Metaphysics: A Philosophical Quarterly* 38, no. 3 [March 1985]: 467–502), I find it nearly impossible to exonerate him of the charge of at least support of some kind. Heidegger's address exclaims that the state, if not the Nazis, is central to restoring the idea of the German university. See also Friedlich Meinecke, *The German Catastrophe: Reflections and Recollections*, trans. Sideney B. Fay (Boston: Beacon Press, 1963).

56. See note 5.

57. C. A. Bowers, who wrote a number of books on the subject, *Educating for an Ecologically Sustainable Culture: Rethinking Moral Education, Creativity, Intelligence, and Other Modern Orthodoxies* (Albany: State University of New York Press, 1994) and *The Culture of Denial: Why the Environmental Movement Needs a Strategy for Reforming Universities and Public Schools* (Albany: State University of New York Press, 1997), to take only two.

58. Spencer Weart, *The Discovery of Global Warming* (Cambridge, Mass.: Harvard University Press, 2003); David Goodstein, *Out of Gas: The End of the Age of Oil* (New York: W. W. Norton, 2004); Paul Roberts, *The End of Oil: On the Edge of a Perilous New World* (Boston: Houghton Mifflin, 2004); Ross Gelbspan, *Boiling Point: How Politicians, Big Oil and Coal, Journalists, and Activists Are Fueling the Climate Crisis— and What We Can Do to Avert Disaster* (New York: Basic Books, 2004); Mark Lynas, *High Tide: The Truth about Our Climate Crisis* (New York: Picador, 2004); Donella Meadows, Jorgen Randers, and Dennis Meadows, *Limits to Growth: The 30-Year Update* (White River Junction, Vt.: Chelsea Green Publishing, 2004); James Gustave Speth, *Red Sky at Morning: America and The Crisis of The Global Environment: A Citizen's Agenda for Action* (New Haven: Yale University Press, 2004); Paul Ehrlich and Anne Erlich, *One with Nineveh: Politics, Consumption, and the Human Future* (Washington, D.C.: Island Press, 2004). Probably I should have also included Bjorn Lomborg, ed., *Global Crises, Global Solutions* (Cambridge: Cambridge University Press), also published in 2004. But the book, like the editor's more recent publication, *Cool It* (New York: Knopf, 2007), is obstinately against the idea of anthropogenicity of climate change and so I decided it belonged to a different context of argument.

59. Martin Rees, *Our Final Hour: A Scientist's Warning: How Terror, Error, and Environmental Disaster Threaten Humankind's Future in This Century—On Earth and Beyond* (New York: Basic Books, 2003), 8.

60. James Lovelock, *The Ages of Gaia: A Biography of Our Living Earth* (1988; New York: W. W. Norton, 1995), xv.

61. Described in Alan Weisman, *The World without Us* (New York: St. Martin's Press, 2007), 241–43.

62. The IPCC Fourth Assessment Report consists of three working group reports—I, II, and III—all released in the spring of 2007, and they are now available online at www.ipcc.ch/ipccreports/assessments-reports.htm. Each of these reports has a "Summary for Policymakers," but the overall introduction AR4 [Fourth Assessment Report] Synthesis Report, scheduled to be released in November 2007, was unavailable as of this writing.

63. See John Bellamy Foster, Marx's Ecology: Materialism and Nature (New York: Monthly Review Press, 2000), and Ecology against Capitalism (New York: Monthly Review Press, 2002). The latter study is especially relevant to this essay, and instructive.

64. See my article "Sites of Resistance to the Global Economy," boundary 2 22, no. 1 (spring 1995): 61–84; reprinted in Cultural Readings of Imperialism: Edward Said and the Gravity of History, edited by Keith Ansell Pearson, Benita Parry, and Judith Squires (London: Lawrence and Wishart, 1997), 49–66.

65. There are a number of books on the subject, among them Karl Krober, Ecological Literary Criticism: Romantic Imagining and the Biology of Mind (New York: Columbia University Press, 1994); and Lawrence Buell, Writing for an Endangered World: Literature, Culture, and Environment in the U.S. and Beyond (Cambridge, Mass.: Harvard University Press, 2001).

66. Peter D. Ward and Donald Brownlees, The Life and Death of Planet Earth: How the New Science of Astrobiology Charts the Ultimate Fate of Our World (New York: Times Books, 2002).

67. David Harvey's magisterial contribution to environmental studies, Justice, Nature and the Geography of Difference (Oxford: Blackwell, 1996), rejects such an apocalyptic view as politically dangerous. I fully accept his warning—in fact we have seen examples of bourgeois political evasion in Rees and Lovelock—but I must submit that the general skepticism about ecological crisis is extremely serious. William Cronon, whom Harvey approvingly quotes often in the book, is nearly irresponsible: "In a very real sense, global warming is the ultimate example of a virtual crisis in virtual nature," although he adds a vague qualification to the statement, "which is far from saying that it is unreal. Instead, it is proof that the virtual and the natural can converge in surprising ways" (Uncommon Ground: Rethinking the Human Place in Nature [New York: W. W. Norton, 1996], 48). And, as I have discussed, no environmentalist seems to take up the issue of where to begin the environmentalist social change. I am most curious about Harvey's response to the final Fourth Assessment Report of IPCC, due in the fall of 2007.

First-Person Pronouns in Japanese Diaries

1. Fukuzawa Yukichi describes the fanatic xenophobic atmosphere after his return to Japan in his Fukuo jiden (Tokyo: Iwanami Shoten, 1954), 120. As for the circumstance of the withdrawn application, see Mori Mutsuhiko's "Tokugawa bakufu no

yogakusho no honyaku shuppan kisei," in *Rangaku to Nihon bunka*, ed. Ogata Tomio (Tokyo: Tokyo Daigaku Shuppankai, 1971), 113–20. Mori is, of course, wrong in attributing the withdrawn manuscript to a member of the 1860 Embassy.

2. The massive bibliography contained in the last volume of *Man'en gannen ken-Bei shisetsu shiryo shusei* (hereafter ss) (Collection of the historical materials of the 1860 Embassy to the United States) is indispensable to anyone interested in this event. The techniques employed in this descriptive bibliography, however, are far from ideal. Aside from several typographical errors, there are a few confusions, ambiguities, omissions, and contradictions. As far as 1 can determine, I have read every standard version of the records listed in the bibliography, except the very insignificant ones identified in it as 123, 180, and 183. There are a few publications since the ss bibliography; see my bibliography in *As We Saw Them*.

   The ss bibliography indicates that there was *Seishi suiroki* (no. 181), published in 1860 (217). But the item is merely a seven-sheet leaflet briefly describing most places visited by the Embassy, plus a few simplified maps. I am grateful to Professor Kawakita Nobuo of Keio University for providing me with a photocopy of this work. Copies of Hirose's work have survived (one of which is in the Diet Library [Kokkai Toshokan]), although a modern version is not yet published.

3. The SS bibliography lists only fourteen copies, but Numata Jiro's essay, "Tamamushi Sadayu to *Ko-Bei nichiroku*" in *Seiyo kenben shu*, ed. Numata Jiro and Matsuzawa Hiroaki (Tokyo: Iwanami Shoten, 1974), 551–64, gives the higher figure.

4. Of course, the existence of the original diary copy (entered day by day during the voyage itself) neither confirms the author's lack of interest in talking about his experience to others nor proves that no other versions remained. Kato Somo, for instance, left a day-by-day diary (item 159 in the ss bibliography), but he also revised it in several other copies (items 160 through 168) as well as told the whole story to Mizuno Masanobu, who in turn wrote it down as *Futayo gatari* (collected in SS, 3:1–130). In short, most diarists were eager storytellers about the most important experience in their lives. According to the descriptions in the ss bibliography, the works by Masuzu Hisatoshi (item 124) and Ishikawa Masataro (item 251) are definitely in the initial diary form, while the records by Namura Motonori (item 139) and Nagao Kosaku (item 221) seem to be in the raw form though not explicitly so stated.

5. Kimura Tetsuta's "Atsumegusa" and Kato Soma's *Futayo gatari* are both oral reports recorded by others.

6. The official memoranda of the Embassy, called "Shimmi Buzen-no-Kami, Muragaki Awaji-no-Kami, Oguri Bungo-no-Kami, A-ko goyodome," in six manuscript volumes, are in the Shiryo Hensanjo of the University of Tokyo. Several documents in the record have already been published in *BIGS* (*Bakumatsu ishin gaiko shiryo shusei*), ed. Maruyama Kunio, 6 vols. (Tokyo: Zeizai Gakkai, 1942–44). There are in the same library memorandum books by Muragaki and Oguri. I have checked the

former by Muragaki, a copy of the original on Gaimusho (Ministry for Foreign Affairs) stationery, which does not seem to contain any significant new material. I was told about Oguri's *Goyodome* by Professor Ishii Takashi, but I have not had a chance to examine the document itself.

7. *ss*, 7:223 (under item 198).

8. To read all these handbooks on the United States in connection with the 1860 travelogues is a fascinating exercise. Their meager substance is so similar from one to another that the reader might be able to trace the content of these geography books back to Chinese and finally to Western sources. Some of the 1860 travelogues—such as Sano Kanae's *Man'en gannen ho-Bei nikki* (The diary of the 1860 travel to America) for instance—explicitly state that they are dependent on some geography book(s) whenever they make a long comment on a city or a country. In other words, the traveler's observation is very much influence by the book(s) he has read. And even the figures and facts and data he quotes seem to have come from Japanese and Chinese reference books rather than directly from American sources. Thus, there seems to be a circular route of information: Murray's *Encyclopaedia of Geography* and Bridgeman's *Mirika gassei-koku shiryaku* to Gi Gen's *Kaikoku zushi* to the 1860 travelogues. In the last stage of this process, the travelers go back to the original source and observe America directly, as Murray presumably did at first, but much of their observation is already formed by the secondary information.

The best bibliography of the geography books during the Tokugawa period is *Sakoku jidai no Nihonjin ni jaugau chishiki*, eds. Ayuzawa Shintaro and Okubo Toshikane (Tokyo: Kangensha, 1953). See also Osatake Takeshi, *Ishin zengo ni okeru rikken-shiso* (Tokyo: Hakuyosha, 1948) and *Kinsei Nihon no kokusai kannen no hattatsu* (Tokyo: Kyoritsusha, 1932).

9. See Edwin Reischauer, *Ennin's Travels in Tang China* (New York: Ronald Press, 1955) and *Ennin's Diary* (New York: Ronald Press, 1955). Largely factual, this immense medieval record of a pilgrimage, written in Chinese, is yet fully informed with the sense of intimate knowledge of the country. Ennin's diary is also quite dramatic, that is, organized with an interpretation.

10. *ss*, 3:236–37.

11. Engelbert Kämpfer, who traveled between Nagasaki and Edo several times during his stay in Japan toward the end of the seventeenth century, calls Tokaido, the main trunk road, "more crowded, than the publick streets in any [of] the most populous town[s] in Europe." *The History of Japan* (first published London, 1726), 2:330. The Tokugawa government maintained an overall control of the nation's main highways. Their checkpoints (*sekisho*), principally established to guard the hostage system and security measures, numbered over fifty altogether throughout Japan, and survived until 1869. All travelers were required to submit for inspection their passports (*tegata*), issued by registered officials. In the case of samurai, their masters or the deputies of their masters (and in the case of commoners, village masters

[*nanushi*], landlords, parish priests, etc.) were authorized to grant passports. The fiefs had their own checkpoints (*kuchidome bansho*) along the borders. Although the strictness of control over travelers and merchandise shipments varied from fief to fief, some domains were quite reluctant to permit strangers to enter their territories. Kaempfer describes the Hakone checkpoint in *The History of Japan*, 2:59–61. See Toyoda Takeshi and Kodama Kota, eds., *Kotsu-shi* in *Taikei Nihon-shi sosho* 24 (Tokyo: Yamakawa Shuppansha) 105–233; Oshima Nobujiro, *Nihon kotsu-shi gairon* (Tokyo: Yoshikawa Kobunkan, 1964) and *Nihon kotsu-shi ronso* (Tokyo: Kokusai Kotsu Bunka Kyokai, 1939); and Hibata Setsuko, *Edo jidai no kotsu bunka* (Tokyo: Toko Shoin, 1931) and *Nihon kotsu-shi wa* (Tokyo: Yuzankaku, 1937).

12. See Toyama Shigeki, *Meiji ishin* (Tokyo: Iwanami Shoten, 1951), 73–74. This is, of course, the basis of the Meiji ideology of "family state" (*kazoku kokka*).

13. Mircea Eliade, *Patterns in Comparative Religion*, trans. Rosemary Sheed (Cleveland and New York: World, 1963), esp. chap. 10.

14. Natsume Soseki, "Danpen," in *Natsume Soseki zenshu* 13 (Tokyo: Iwanami Shoten, 1941), 23–28, dated October 1900.

15. This experience might be made clearer when compared with the experience of the European immigrant in America finding himself away from home, from civilization, his "sacred space," and in the middle of the American desert or wilderness, the Americans' "profane space." Here, too, nothing in sight seemed to hold meaning: unlike Europe, raw nature in America is innocent of history and tradition. The descendants of Euclid, Pythagoras, and Descartes, however, would not bow to any such passive documenting of their helpless situation in the world. They tend instead to push onward, aggressively searching out habitable environs for themselves, and in the process projecting the structure of their own minds onto the vast-seeming nothingness—which nature in America is. One result is the towns and cities carved out of the wilderness in which streets run in Euclidean lines crossing at clean ninety-degree angles. American spaces are a mirror image of the European mind, profane space here redeemed by the miracle of man's inner territory. No wonder America uproots or paves over its settlements as often as possible. It is important that time-suffused, history-smeared spaces be born anew from time to time, fathered by the pure interior of the human mind.

16. *Hokuyuki* is by Akiba Tomoemon and Okutani Shingoro, collected in *Kinsei Kiko bungei noto*, ed. Suzuki Tozo (Tokyo: Tokyodo Shuppan, 1974).

17. See note 8 of this essay. See chap. 2, footnote 82 in *As We Saw Them*.

18. Muragaki Awaji-no-Kami Norimasa, *Ken-Bei-shi nikki* in *Kengai shisetsu nikki sanshu* 1 (Tokyo: Nihon Shiseki Kyokai, 1928), 1:40; also available as *Kokai nikki* in *Nichibei ryokoku kankeishi* 11, ed. Yoshida Tsunekichi (Tokyo: Jijitsushinsha, 1959), 35.

19. *Ako nikki*, in *ss*, 1:45.

20. Henry Heusken, *Japan Journal 1855–1861*, trans. and ed. Jeanette C. Van der Corput and Robert A. Wilson (New Brunswick: Rutgers University Press, 1964), 124–25.

21. For studies of the literary diary tradition as a whole, see Tamai Kosuke's *Nikki bungaku no kenkyu* (Tokyo: Hanao Shobo) and Ikeda Kikan's *Nikki waka bungaku* (Tokyo: Shibundo, 1968). Also see Earl Miner's *Japanese Poetic Diaries* (Berkeley: University of California Press, 1969). For the contemporary Tokugawa travelogues, see Suzuki Tozo's *Kinsei kiko bungei noto* (Tokyo: Tokyodo Shuppan, 1974), which, however, makes no mention of the 1860 Embassy records. Numerous studies of Basho, the traveling poet, are quite helpful for reflection about the travelogue form. *Hyohaku no tamashii*, ed. Imoto Noichi (Tokyo: Kadokawa Shoten, 1973), for instance, is a convenient collection of essays on Basho and the *tabi-nikki* conventions. Although I disagree with practically everything said by Mr. Herbert Plutschow, his unpublished talk entitled "Some Characteristics of Medieval Japanese Travel Diaries," given at Berkeley on December 5, 1975, was suggestive in several ways, and I thank him for the help I found in opposing his ideas. *Kokubungaku: kaishaku to kyozai no kenkyu* 20, a special issue on the diary and travelogue, is also useful.

22. *Notes from the Japanese Legation in the United States to the Department of State, 1858– 1906.* File microcopies of records in the National Archives, no. 163, 3 rolls.

23. This passage is perhaps unintelligible to those who are unfamiliar with Japanese. In Japanese there are no pronouns equivalent to the English I/we, you/you, he-she-it/they. Instead, there are a good number of pronominal words for each of these English personal pronouns, from which selection is made in accordance with the relative or absolute social positions of the speaker, listener, and referent. It is possible to argue that the Japanese language lacks the category of personal pronoun, although what this means philosophically, or even culturally, is not at all easy to explain precisely. On the one hand, it seems quite possible that the absence in Japanese of an equivalent of the word "I" has some bearing on the Japanese concept of the self (or the lack thereof); it is also possible, on the other hand, to argue that the Japanese grammar has compensatory features (honorifics, various *joshi*, *jodoshi*, etc.) that subtly indicate the person of the narrator without the specific use of a personal pronoun. See S. Y. Kuroda's brilliant articles, "Where Epistemology, Style, and Grammar Meet: A Case Study from the Japanese" in *A Festschrift for Morris Halle*, ed. Stephen R. Anderson and Paul Kiparsky (New York: Holt, Rinehart, and Winston, 1973) and "Reflections on the Foundations of Narrative Theory" in *Pragmatics of Language and Literature*, ed. Teun A. van Dijk (Amsterdam: North Holland Publishing, 1976). Also see a series of conversations (*taidan*) that Ono Susumu had with writers in various disciplines, collected in *Taidan: Nihon-go o kangaeru* (Tokyo: Chuokoronsha, 1975). Ono appears somewhat undecided on the issue in several passages in the book that touch on this particular subject (135–37, 203–4, 214–18, 222–23). It is irrefutable, at any rate, that there are frequent cases in Japanese where the narrator of a sentence and the agent of an action described in a sentence are simply impossible to determine.

24. *SS*, 2:290–91.

25. *Kokai nichiroku*, in ss, 3:160.

26. Respectively, Kato Somo, *Futayo gatari* in *Man'en gannen kenbei shisetsu shiryo shusei* 3, (ss), ed. Nichi-Bei Shuko Tsusho Hyakunen Kinengyoji Un'eiinkai (Tokyo: Kazama Shobo, 1961), 23; Sano Kanae, *Man'en gannen ho-Bei nikki* (Kanazawa: Kanazawa Bunka Kyokai, 1946), 19; Kimura Tesuta, *Ko-Bei-ki*, ed. Matsumoto Masaaki (Kumamoto: Seichosha, 1974), 74–75; Hirose Kakuzo Hoan Kaneaki, *Kankai koro nikki*, 2, ed. Hirose Ikko and Aishin (Edo: Suharaya Mohei, 1862), 7th leaf; Tamamushi Sadayu Yasushige, *Kô-Bei nichiroku* in *Seiyô kenbun shû, Nihon shisô taikei* 66, ed. Numata Jirô and Matsuzawa Hiroaki (Tokyo: Iwanami Shoten, 1974), 47. Tamamushi's entry reads as follows: "We did not know what it was, and—as is always the case with our countrymen—[we were] frightened; but the Americans were not; seeing us [*yora*] baffled, [they said] there was nothing like this in Japan; apparently there is no phenomenon of this kind in Japan; the American name for it is 'north light.'"

27. *A-ko-ei*, in ss, 2:356.

28. Tanamushi Sadayu Yasushige, *Ko-Bei nichiroku*, ed. Yamamoto Akira (Sendai: Yamamoto Akira, 1930).

29. Fukuchi Gen'ichiro (Ochi), for instance, reminisces how severely he was criticized by Hayashi for preferring Dutch learning to Confucianism, in *Kaio jidan*, 37–39. As for the history of the Shoheiko Institute, see Wajima Yoshio, *Shoheiko to hangaku*.

30. For Tamamushi's life, see *As We Saw Them*, chap. 4, 164–67.

31. Yamamoto Akira, *Ko-Bei nichiroku*, 229–31.

32. *Ken-Bei-shi nikki*, in KSNS, 1:200–206; *Kokai nikki*, 177–80.

33. Ivan Goncharob, *The Voyage of the Frigate Pallada*, trans. and ed. N. W. Wilson (London: Henry Colburn, 1924), 156, 160.

34. Townsend Harris, *The Complete Journal of Townsend Harris*, ed. Mario Emilio Cosenza (New York: Doubleday, Doran, 1930), 362–63.

35. See, for instance, Thomas C. Smith's "Okura Nagatsune and the Technologists" in *Personality in Japanese History*, ed. Albert M. Craig and Donald H. Shively (Berkeley: University of California Press, 1970), 127–54.

36. Arai Hakuseki, *Seiyo kibun* (1715–1725), ed. Miyazaki Michio (Tokyo: Heibonsha, 1968), 16–17. Miyazaki's comments in the edition are quite helpful. Also, see Sato Shosuke, *Yogaku-shi kenkyu josetsu: Yogaku to hoken kenryoku* (Tokyo: Iwanami Shoten, 1964) and Miyazaki Michio, *Arai Hakuseki no yogaku to kaigai chishiki* (Tokyo: Yoshikawa Kobunkan, 1973).

37. *Taga Bokkyo kun ni kotaeru sho* is in the Iwanami Bunko edition of *Miura Baien shu*, ed. Saegusa Hiroto (Tokyo: Iwanami Shoten, 1955). For Miura's philosophy, see Saegusa's *Miura Baien no tetsugaku* (Tokyo: Daiichi Shobo, 1941) and Taguchi Masaharu's *Miura Baien* (Tokyo: Yoshikawa Kobunkan, 1967).

38. For the understanding of Nakae Tojo and Kumazawa Banzan, I found the collections of their works in the *Nihon shiso taikei*, 29 and 30, ed. Yamai Yu (Tokyo:

Iwanami Shoten, 1974), which include several concise discussions, most helpful. There is also an edition in the *Nihon no meicho* series. See also Bito Masahide, *Nihon hoken shiso-shi kenkyu* (Tokyo: Aoki Shoten, 1961), 136–276.

39. In addition to the studies mentioned earlier in connection with "Dutch learning," see Numata Jiro et al., eds., *Yogaku* 1; *Nihon shiso taikei* (Tokyo: Iwanami Shoten, 1976), 64 (which includes important selections from Sugita Genpaku and Shiba Kokan); Haga Tom's selection of works by Sugita Genpaku, Hiraga Gennai, and Shiba Kokan in the *Nihon no meicho* 22: *Sugita Genpaku, Hiraga Gennai, and Shiba Kokan* in the series, ed. Haga Toru (Tokyo: Chuokoronsha, 1971); Tsukatani Akihiro et al., eds., *Honda Toshiaki*; *Kaiho Seiryo, Nihon shiso taikei* (Tokyo: Iwanami Shoten, 1971), 44; Sato Shosuke et al., eds., Watanabe Kazan, *Takano Choei Sakuma Shozan, Yokoi Shonan, Hashimoto Sinai, Nihon shiso taikei,* 55 (Tokyo: Iwanami Shoten). As for monographs on individual writers, I read Katagiri Kazuo, *Sugita Genpaku* (Tokyo: Yoshikawa Kobunkan, 1971); Tatsuno Sakito, *Sakuma Shozan* (Tokyo: Shinjinbutsu Oraisha, 1975); Ohira Kimata, *Sakuma Shozan* (Tokyo: Yoshikawa Kobunkan, 1959); Matsuura Rei, *Yokoi Shozan* (Tokyo: Asahi Shinbunsha, 1976); Tamamuro Taijo, *Yokoi Shozan* (Tokyo: Yoshikawa Kobunkan, 1967); Yamaguchi Muneyuki, *Hashimoto Sanai* (Tokyo: Yoshikawa Kobunkan, 1962); Kumura Toshio, *Yoshida Shoin no shiso to kyoiku* (Tokyo: Iwanami Shoten, 1942); Kawakami Tetsutaro, *Yoshida Shoin: Bu to ju ni yoru ningenzo* (Tokyo: Bungei-Shinsha, 1971). In "Science and Confucianism in Tokugawa Japan," in *Changing Japanese Attitudes toward Modernization*, ed. Marius B. Jansen (Princeton: Princeton University Press, 1965), Albert Craig characterizes these Dutch scholars by their "eclectic syncretism" (156). As for the later development of the "Japanese soul and Western technology" attitude, see Hirakawa Sukehiro's *Wakon yosai no keifu: Uchi to soto kara no Meiji Nihon* (Tokyo: Kawade Shobo Shinsha, 1971), which discusses it in relation to Mori Ogai.

40. The text of *Gekibun* is in *Oshio Heihachiro shu*; *Sato Issai shu, Dai-Nihon shiso zenshu,* 16:470–75.

41. Various papers by Miura Meisuke are reproduced in *Minshu undo no shiso*, vol. 58 of the multivolume series *Nihon shiso taikei*, ed. Shoji Kichinosuke et al. (Tokyo: Iwanami Shoten, 1970).

42. A quite different view is expressed by Tetsuo Najita in his book *Japan* (Englewood Cliffs, N.J.: Prentice-Hall, 1974), an excellent study of the intellectual history of the country (see esp. chaps. 2 and 3, 16–68). Najita cogently analyzes the continually shifting philosophical status of categories like virtue, norm, utility, and so on, thereby revealing Tokugawa Japan as far more intellectually volatile and various than I have. His conceptualization allows him also to see in many thinkers of the time an awareness of selfhood (the "spiritual self" in Nakae Toju and Kumazawa Banzan; "personal autonomy" in Oshio Heihachiro). For myself, however, Tokugawa thinkers seem almost totally circumscribed by a hierarchic worldview, leaving

little space for recognition of a separable self. The only exceptions I could think of are Shiba Kokan (1748–1818), a painter heavily influenced by Western techniques, who wistfully talks about European countries and insists on the equality of men ("*hito to shite* hito o totomu" in *Wa-Ran tensetsu* [1795]); the antifeudal egalitarianism of Ando Shoeki (1703–1762); see E. H. Norman, *Ando Shoeki and the Anatomy of Japanese Feudalism*, *The Transactions of the Asiatic Society of Japan*, 3rd series, vol. 2 (Tokyo: Asiatic Soiety of Japan, Dec. 1949); Maruyama Masao, *Studies in the Intellectual History of Tokugawa Japan*, trans. Mikiso Hane [Princeton: Princeton University Press, 1974]; and Noguchi Takehiko, *Nihon no meicho* 19, ed. Noguchi Takehiko [Tokyo: Chuokoronsha, 1971]); and Yokoi Shonan's universalism.

Similarly, H. D. Harootunian, in his lucid and energetic book *Toward Restoration: The Growth of Political Consciousness in Tokugawa Japan* (Berkeley: University of California Press, 1970), finds in the 1867 changeover far greater "revolutionary dimensions" than I do (409). I do agree that Sakuma and Yoshida, for instance, were potentially aware both of Japan's place "among the nations of The Five Continents" (173) and of the need for a "transvaluation of values" (407). To me, however, the two men's knowledge of and interest in the West seem neither deep nor wide enough to allow them so "radical [a] break with accepted usage" (407) and with the past. In this respect I find helpful Uete Michiari's "Sakuma Shbzan ni okeru jugaku, bushi-seishin, yogaku" in *Nihon shiso taikei* 55, ed. Sato Shosuke, et al. (Tokyo: Iwanami Shoten, 1971) 652–85, and Robert N. Bellah, "Continuity and Change in Japanese Society" in *Stability and Social Change*, ed. Bernard Barber and Alex Inkles (Boston: Little, Brown, 1971), 377–404.

43. Maruyama Masao, *Nihon no shiso*, esp. 1–66.

44. See chap. 4 of *As We Saw Them*, 174.

The Tale of Genji

1. Murasaki Shikubu, *The Tale of Genji*, 2 vols., trans. Edward G. Seidensticker (New York: Alfred A. Knopf, 1977).

Who Decides, and Who Speaks?

1. Around the University of Kyoto, there were numerous ideologues and philosophers who before and during the Second World War worked to formulate and articulate the position of Japan as a political and mythical polity. Names like Nishida Kitaro, Nishitani Keijiro, Tanabe Hajime, and Watsuji Tetsuro were among the most conspicuous.

2. *New Japanese-English Dictionary*, ed. Masuda Koh, 4th ed. (1974). Shogakkan's *Nihon Kokugo Daijiten*, ed. Ichiko Sadaji et al. (1981), has a long entry for *shutaisei* that reads: "A modem philosophical term. Being an individual agent that works on the surrounding situations ethically and practically as well as being ontologically an existence in possession of a consciousness and a body. The condition of truly

realizing one's own self as one acts on one's own will. Being and existence. Generally, being self-conscious in action, on the basis of one's own will and judgment. Also, such an attitude and character" (my translation).

3. The best evidence is the records of the negotiation between the Japanese and the Americans concerning constitutional revisions. At the final confrontation between Foreign Minister Yoshida Shigeru, Minister of State Matsumoto Joji, and General Courtney Whitney in February 1946, the Japanese hope for the status quo was completely demolished. See Yoshida Shigeru, *Kaiso Junen* (Tokyo: Shinchosha, 1957), 4:170–90; also Mark Gayn, *Japan Diary* (New York: William Sloan Associates, 1948), 125–31. Some intellectuals of Japan drafted a constitution of their own, which resembled the progressive American draft that finally became the postwar Peace Constitution.

4. See the abbreviated but clear references to such efforts in the *Asahi* newspaper as early as the first half of 1945.

5. See the Miyamoto Yuriko section in chap. 8 of my book *Off Center: Power and Culture Relations between Japan and the United States* (Cambridge, Mass.: Harvard University Press, 1991; paperback edition, Harvard University Press, 1994).

6. John Livingston et al., eds., *The Japan Reader: Postwar Japan, 1945 to the Present* (New York: Pantheon, 1973), 7.

7. George Kennan, *Memoirs, 1925–1950* (New York: Pantheon, 1967), 382. See also John Curtis Perry, *Beneath the Eagle's Wings: Americans in Occupied Japan* (New York: Dodd, Mead, 1980), 47.

8. See, for example, William Appleman Williams, *The Strategy of American Diplomacy*, 2nd ed. (New York: Dell, 1972), 207. See also John Lewis Gaddis, *The United States and the Origin of the Cold War, 1941–1947* (New York: Columbia University Press, 1972); D. F. Fleming, *The Cold War and Its Origins, 1917–1960*, 2 vols. (New York: Doubleday, 1961); and Gabriel Kolko, *The Politics of War: The World and the United States Foreign Policy, 1943–45* (New York: Random House, 1968).

9. State Department Policy Planning Study 23, February 24, 1948, quoted by Noam Chomsky in *On Power and Ideology: The Managua Lectures* (Boston: South End Press, 1987), 15–16.

10. William Manchester, *American Caesar: Douglas MacArthur, 1880–1964* (Boston: Little, Brown, 1978), 184 and 441.

11. *The Japan Reader*, 116–19, and the National Security Council report, October 7, 1948.

12. Yoshida's own memoirs provide interesting materials. See *Kaiso Junen* (Tokyo: Shinchosha, 1957), 1:80–121; *Gekido no hyakunen shi* (Tokyo: Shirakawa Shoin, 1978), 154; and *Oiso Seidan* (Tokyo: Bungei Shunju Shinsha, 1956), 138–39.

13. Richard Nixon, "Douglas MacArthur and Shigeru Yoshida," in *Leaders* (New York: Warner Books, 1982), 81–132.

14. The most comprehensive Japanese study of occupation censorship is Matsuura

Sozo, *Senryoka no genron danatsu* (Tokyo: Gendai Janarizumu Shuppankai, 1969), but this book is neither systematic nor coherent. Jay Rubin, "From Wholesomeness to Decadence: The Censorship of Literature under the Allied Occupation," *Journal of Japanese Studies* 11, no. 1 (winter 1985): 71–103, is excellent in disputing Eto Jun's determined misrepresentation of the subject and in covering the Prange Collection of occupation materials at the University of Maryland's McKeldin Library. His approach, however, is largely taxonomical, failing to analyze the objectives, methods, and capabilities of the censors involved. Their inability to understand Japanese, for instance, is a significant factor that requires further study, so that the censors' incompetence—rather than malice—may be fully comprehended.

15. See the report of Higashikuni's press interview, *Asahi*, August 30, 1945. He repeated the plea in his speech to the Diet on September 5, 1945.

16. Shiina Rinzo, "Significance of Postwar Literature," *Ningen* 1, no. 3 (March 1946): 24 (my translation).

17. Kato Shuichi, "In Egoistos," originally published in *Kindai bungaku* (July 1947), reprinted in *Sengo bungaku ronso*, ed. Usui Yoshimi (Tokyo: Bancho Shobo, 1972), 1:243–47.

18. Odagiri Hideo, "Shinbungaku sozo no shutai: Atarashii dankai no tameni," Originally in *Shin-Nihon bungaku* (May–June 1946), reprinted in Yoshimi, *Sengo bungaku ronso*, 72–82.

19. Maruyama Masao, "Cho-kokkashugi no ronri to shinri," *Sekai* 1 (May 1946): 2–15.

20. Maruyama, "Cho kokka shugi no ronri to shinri," 13.

21. Maruyama Masao, *Koei no ichi kara* (Tokyo: Miraisha, 1982), 114.

22. The contemporary journals do contain articles analyzing the cold war situation (for instance, the May 1948 issue of *Chuo koron*). They do not seem to have been widely read, however. See, for instance, a 1968 *zadankai* discussing the circumstances of intellectual communities in Japan in 1948, published for the first time in a special issue of *Sekai* (July 1985): 2–53.

23. Noam Chomsky, "The Revolutionary Pacifism of A. J. Muste," in *American Power and the New Mandarins* (New York: Pantheon Books, 1967), 183.

24. Takeuchi Yoshimi's "Kindai no chokoku," originally published in November 1959, reprinted in *Nihon gendai bungaku zenshu* 93 (Tokyo: Kodansha, 1968): 360–88, is one of the few serious discussions of Japan's aggression in the context of Western hegemonism. An example of the increasingly more visible reactionary revisionist publications is Hayashi Fusao's *Dai-Toa senso kotei ron*, reprinted in *Hayashi Fusao chosakushu* 1 (Tokyo: Tsubasa Shoin, 1977).

25. Yoshimoto Takaaki, "Zen sedai no shijintachi," originally published in *Shigaku*, November 1955, reprinted in Yoshimi, *Sengo bungaku ronso*, 129–39.

26. Radhabinod Pal, dissenting opinion, in *The Tokyo War Crimes Trial*, ed. R. John Pritchard and Sonia Magbanua Zaide, vol. 21, *Separate Opinions* (New York: Garland Publishing, 1981), 983–84.

27. For further discussion of Tanizaki, see chap. 5, *Off Center*.

28. See my discussion of Kawabata in *Accomplices of Silence: The Modern Japanese Novel* (Berkeley: University of California Press, 1974), chap. 4.

29. Noma Hiroshi, "Kurai e," originally published 1946, reprinted in *Noma Hiroshi shu, Chikuma gendai bungaku taikei* 65 (Tokyo: Chikuma Shobo, 1975), 324.

30. *Shiina Rinzo shu, Chikuma gendai bungaku taikei* 66 (Tokyo: Chikuma Shobo, 1976), 362.

31. Tamura Taijiro, "Nikutai no mon," originally published 1947, reprinted in *Kitahara Takeo, Inoue Tomoichiro, Tamura Taijun shu, Nihon gendai bungaku zenshu* 94 (Tokyo: Kodansha, 1968), 332.

32. Nishikawa Nagao's book *Nihon no sengo shosetsu: haikyo no, hikari* (Tokyo: Iwanami Shoten, 1988) discusses these postwar writers and lists their references to Christ. Nishikawa is both literal and unanalytic, and his critical comments contain few interesting observations. See 246–50 and 273–74.

33. For further discussion, see my *Accomplices of Silence*, chap. 5.

34. Sakaguchi Ango, "Daraku ron," originally published April 1946, reprinted in *Sakaguchi Ango shu, Chikuma gendai bungaku taikei* 58 (Tokyo: Chikuma Shobo, 1975), 452.

35. Ibid., 191.

36. Ibid., 327.

37. Fredric Jameson, "Postmodernism, or, The Cultural Logic of Late Capitalism," *New Left Review*, no. 146 (July–August 1984): 53–92.

The Invention of English Literature in Japan

1. I was told that the Ministry of Education is in the process of discontinuing the collegiate English requirement together with the general education curriculum (*kyoyo-bu*). At the time of this writing, I have not been able to confirm this news or uncover any details of the proposal. (See, however, *Asahi shinbun*, August 28, 1991, and July 25, 1992.)

2. This paradigm of English studies is itself revealing in several ways. First, the instructive structure cannot presume any exposure to or familiarity with English life. In the United States and Europe, foreign-language teaching usually emanated either from the immigrants from the region in which the language is spoken or from those returning from missionary or colonial assignments to such a region. Either way, their knowledge and information were organized into a curriculum. Second, the English-speaking people who first helped the Japanese learn the language were missionaries or business-related personnel who were there to convert, "democratize," or otherwise "civilize" the Japanese. Thus, they enjoyed a higher status among their students than did teachers in more ordinary circumstances. Third, more recently, conversation teachers from the United States and Britain are largely adventurous, young people in search of the strong yen. They often have no

particular job qualifications except the ability to speak English, which may correlate with the low status of spoken English in Japan. Either way, the relative influence of the teacher-student relationship needs to be further studied. Equal interchange between the Japanese and the English speakers is not in evidence even now.

3. Ito Kazuo, one of the most successful English teachers in today's *yobiko* world, published *Ei-bunpo kyoshitsu* (Tokyo: Kenkyusha, 1979), in which he structurally lists phrase-clause-sentence constructions in a precise grammatical order. It assumes school grammar to be thoroughly logical, rational, and thus explainable. Brilliant in its own way, the book finally has little to do with English as it is used by English-speakers.

4. There are relatively few books that discuss the educational and cultural meaning of college entrance exams in the entrance exam–obsessed country. (The competition begins, incidentally, at the kindergarten level. A reputable kindergarten will enable its graduates to enter an elementary school that will make smooth the transfer to a junior high, which in turn. . . .) Kuroha Ryoichi's *Nyugakushiken*, Nikkei Shinsho 285 (Tokyo: Nihon Keizai Shinbunsha, 1978), offers a concise explanation of the notorious "exam hell" (*jukes jigoku*).

5. The Japanese reluctance to express feelings and opinions is often described as "shyness," a word that nearly always fails as an explanation. There may be altogether different circumstances. One sometimes forgets that the public exchange of words in the pre-Meiji days was far more formalized than it is now or than it was then elsewhere. English is likely to have been regarded as an "official" language, since a private encounter with an English-speaker was infrequent. This accounts for the publication of numerous *kaiwa-sho* (conversation books) in the very early days of English studies in Japan (1850s–1870s) and since. These books offer formulas for brief speeches designed to be chosen and used at various official occasions; examples are the "after-dinner speech" and the "wedding toast." See Sogo Masaaki, *Nihon eigaku no akebono: Bakumatsu-Meiji no Eigogaku* (Tokyo: Sotakusha, 1990), chaps. 5–9.

6. Many Japanese believe even now that British English (which they often call "King's English") is far superior ("more authentic and genuine") to American English. Moreover, there is an aesthetic difference between the two, according to them: the British version is elegant and beautiful, whereas the more plebian American tongue is vulgar and blurry. Such a phonetic judgment is of course a part of the larger cultural belief that Americans are uncultured and materialistic, while Britons are intellectual and well-mannered. This feeling, a legacy of the imperialist era, is carried over into the standard distinction between English and American literatures as well.

7. Earlier, however, "Dutch learning" had existed in defiance of Tokugawa prohibition. By the end of the Tokugawa rule, the authorities knew that any suppression of "Western studies" was not only futile but counterproductive.

8. Inoue Tetsujiro, the dean of the School of Letters then, later recalled the circumstances in *Kaikyu-roku*, 252–54, quoted in Sogo Masaaki, *Nihon no eigaku hyaku-nen*, 1:66.

9. See Gauri Viswanathan, *Masks of Conquest* (New York: Columbia University Press, 1989).

10. Tsubouchi Shoyo wrote *Shosetsu shinzui* (The Essence of the Novel) in 1885. Though this work was really only a compilation of ideas and arguments from various English magazines, encyclopedia articles, and textbooks, as well as Edo writings, Tsubouchi's urgent need to explore the nature of the novel as it relates to other literary and artistic forms, in short, the genealogy of literature, is perfectly understandable. It was an effort to discover a place for "literature" in a gradually "modernizing" Japanese society. In the book, he only rarely uses the term *bungaku*, employing mainly *bungei* (art of writing) or *bijutsu* (fine arts).

11. The history of the name and organization of the [Imperial] University of Tokyo is extremely complex, and it is difficult to summarize the logic of the changes. It is clear, however, that the binarism of the Japanese/Chinese as stagnant (*koro*), endangered, and deserving protection and the Western as attractive to the useful (*yuyo*) human resources was acutely felt. See then President Kato Hiroyuki's report to the Ministry of Education, quoted in *Tokyo Teikoku Daigaku gojunen-shi* (Tokyo: Tokyo Teikoku Daigaku, 1932), 1:685–87. See also *Kigen 2600-nen hoshuku kinen: Gakujutsu taikan* (Tokyo: Tokyo Teikoku Daigaku, 1940).

12. The one exception was Ernest Fenollosa, who taught at the university between 1878 and 1886. Fenollosa, however, mainly taught philosophy, not literature. See Sogo Masaaki, *Nihon no ei-gaku hyaku-nen*, 4 vols. (Tokyo: Kenkyusha, 1968–1969).

13. Natsume Soseki, "*Watakushi no kojin shugi*" (My Individualism), in *Soseki zenshu* (Tokyo: Iwanami Shoten, 1985), 11:440–41.

14. For a brief discussion of these "theoretical" books, see my *Accomplices of Silence: The Modern Japanese Novel* (Berkeley: University of California Press, 1974), 58–61.

15. Soseki, *Soseki zenshu*, 11:446.

16. Soseki, "Jogen" (Preface) to *Bungaku hyoron*, in *Soseki zenshu*, 10:37.

17. Soseki, letter, September 12, 1901, in *Soseki zenshu*, 14:188.

18. Soseki, "*Watakushi no kojin shugi*" (My Individualism), in *Soseki zenshu*, 11:443–46.

19. Most books being published now continue to talk about English/American authors and works as if the Anglo-American authors and the Japanese scholars were positioned together in the same space. It is never clear who the intended readers of these studies could be. I spent some time in December 1990 at the University of Tokyo and Gakushuin University browsing through their B.A. and M.A. theses in English literature, which read almost without exception as if the authors had tried their best to sound English/American/neutral. The resulting theses were no more than simplified encyclopedia entries, totally clichéd and inane. Incidentally, Pro-

fessor Kishi Tetsuo of Kyoto University voices a view vis-à-vis the International Shakespeare Congress in Tokyo that there can and should be Japanese readings of Shakespeare, in *Asahi shinbun*, August 1991. Commenting on the same congress, Stephen Greenblatt remarks, "The most exciting papers at the World Shakespeare Congress in the summer of 1991 were by Japanese Shakespeare scholars explaining the relation between Shakespeare and Noh, Kyogen, and Bunraku" ("The MLA on Trial," *Profession* 92 [New York: MLA, 1992]: 40). I hope Greenblatt will soon be able to elaborate on the grounds for his enthusiasm.

20. Hirai Masao, "Showa no Eigbungaku kenkyu," in Sogo Masaaki, *Nihon no eigaku hyakunen*, 3:79.

21. Studies of Japanese, both in language and literature, are far more advanced in the United States than in any other part of the world, yet the spread of familiarity as well as scholarship between Japan and the United States is hardly in balance. The United States is a central reference point in the minds of an overwhelming majority of Japanese; the reverse cannot be claimed for Americans.

22. See the epilogue, as well as chap. 9, of my *Off Center: Power and Culture Relations between Japan and the United States* (Cambridge, Mass.: Harvard University Press, 1991).

A Borderless World?

Many of my friends have read this essay in various stages. I am thankful to the following for detailed and insightful comments and suggestions, although errors and misinterpretations are, of course, entirely my own: Martha L. Archibald, Carlos Blanco-Aguinaga, Noam Chomsky, Arif Dirlik, Joseba Gabilondo, H. D. Harootunian, Takeo Hoshi, Stephanie McCurry, and Anders Stefanson.

1. Some examples are Aimé Césaire, *Discourse on Colonialism* (1955); C. L. R. James, *The Black Jacobins* (1938), *A History of Negro Revolt* (1938), *Beyond a Boundary* (1963), and many others; Frantz Fanon, *The Wretched of the Earth* (1961) and *A Dying Colonialism* (1961); George Lamming, *In the Castle of My Skin* (1953) and *The Pleasures of Exile* (1960).

2. During the 1960s, African American writers began to express to the white audience their anticolonialist views alongside their civil rights activism. Politically accepted by many liberal academics, they were at the same time dismissed by "respectable" critics and scholars in academic disciplines.

3. Perhaps this is more conspicuously an Anglo-American phenomenon. In South America, for instance, the discourse on colonialism started everywhere—from Mexico to Argentina—much earlier, at the latest in the 1960s.

4. Of course, there had been numerous studies in history and political science in relation to imperialism, racism, slavery, colonies, and so on, and the political activism of the 1960s and 1970s had also made contributions to the change in the

political consciousness of Western intellectuals. But before the appearance of Said's book, no text had made a serious inroad into the mainline Anglo-American disciplines of the humanities.

5. The state of colonialization is obviously much harder to define than this abbreviated argument might suggest. Any example—say, of Palestine or Hong Kong—will at once display the particular complexities of individual circumstances. It does seem undeniable, however, that while oppression and suffering continue unabated, the administrative and occupational mode of colonialism is irreversibly being replaced by an economic version—especially after the end of the cold war. To complicate the situation further, the status of the aborigines in settlement societies such as Australia, Taiwan, the United States and Canada, and the Pacific Islands, to take random examples, is far from clarified. Serious legal disputes are distinct possibilities in the near future in some of these areas, for example, in Hawaii and Australia.

6. There are six interrelated developments in post–Second World War history, none of which should/could be considered in isolation. It is indeed possible to argue that any one of these developments need to be studied in close conjunction *with every other*. They are: (1) the cold war (and its end), (2) decolonization, (3) transnational corporatism, (4) the high-tech revolution, (5) feminism, and (6) the environmental crisis. There are adjacent cultural coordinates such as postmodernism, popularization of culture, cultural studies, dedisciplinization, ethnicism, economic regionalism (tripolarism), and so on. The relationship between the two groups is neither homologic nor causal, but its exact nature requires further examination in a different context.

7. In many regions of the world, there were some improvements in general welfare. As to starvation, for instance, the rate of the chronically undernourished to the total population in the Middle East, South America, and Asia has been reduced to nearly one-half between 1970 and 1990. In Africa, however, there is hardly any change in the same period (*Sekai o yomu kii waado* [Tokyo: Iwanami Shoten, 1992], 3:82–83).

8. Basil Davidson, *The Black Man's Burden: Africa and the Curse of the Nation-State* (New York: Times Books, 1992). An Africanist journalist, Davidson may be overly influenced by his observations of Africa when he writes about the rest of the world. He is, for instance, much too pessimistic—and Orientalist!—as he predicts that aside from Japan no third-world nations would become industrialized.

9. This narrative of colonization/decolonization is obviously oversimplified and, worse, totalized. Again, the case of South America, for instance, does not apply in many important aspects. However, for an inclusive discussion of the decolonization/recolonization process, there has to be another paper with a different focus and emphasis.

10. A typically preindustrial society has about 80 percent of its population engaged in agriculture. A fully industrialized society has a very small agricultural worker

population of about 5 percent. This transformation from agriculture to manufacturing and other industries has taken most industrialized nations somewhere around two hundred years. Japan went through the process in less than a century, while the East Asian NIES are changing at the speed of less than a generation. The high cost paid for such a social change is to be expected. Industrialization and colonization converge in this development. And thus all industrialized nations are former colonizers. There is a later development of this process in industrialized societies now: as manufacturing technology improves productivity, manufacturing jobs are rapidly disappearing everywhere, and they are being replaced by service jobs. The manufacturing worker surplus urgently needs to find outlets that are nowhere visibly available. There is not even an equivalent of old colonies for these surplus workers. See Sylvia Nasar, "Clinton Job Plan in Manufacturing Meets Skepticism," *New York Times*, December 27, 1992. Also, Motoyama Yoshihiko, *Minami to kita* (Tokyo: Chikuma Library, 1991), 223–25.

11. Benedict Anderson's *Imagined Community: Reflections on the Origin and Spread of Nationalism*, 2nd ed. (London: Verso, 1991). The book does not explain *who* imagined the community, however.

12. See Paul Kennedy, *Rise and Fall of the Great Powers: Economic Change and Military Conflict from 1500 to 2000* (New York: Random House, 1987).

13. Bruce Cumings, *The Origins of the Korean War*, 2 vols. (Princeton: Princeton University Press, 1981 and 1990).

14. The figures are based on "Table B-2—Gross National Product in 1982 Dollars, 1929–87," in *The Annual Report of the Council of Economic Advisers*, in *Economic Report of the President* (Washington: D.C.: U.S. Government Printing Office, 1988), appendix.

15. President Eisenhower's farewell speech on January 17, 1961. Reproduced in *Super-State: Readings in the Military-Industrial Complex*, ed. Herbert I. Schiller and Joseph D. Phillips (Urbana: University of Illinois Press, 1972), 29–34.

16. "Institutions of Higher Education—Degrees Conferred, by Sex, 1870–1970," in U.S. Office of Education, *Biennial Survey of Education in the United States* (Washington: D.C.: U.S. Government Printing Office, 1971).

17. Seymour Melman, "Military State Capitalism," *Nation*, May 20, 1991, 649, 664–68. These quotations appears on 666 and 667. Melman's *The Demilitarized Society* (Montreal: Harvest House, 1988), *Profits without Production* (New York: Alfred A. Knopf, 1983), and *The Permanent War Economy* (New York: Simon and Schuster, 1974) are important studies on this subject.

18. During the 1960s Britain lost numerous colonies. To list a random few, Nigeria (1960), Tanzania (1964), Zanzibar (1963), Somaliland (1960), Aden (1967), Kuwait (1961), Malta (1964), Borneo (1963), and Trinidad and Tobago (1962).

19. Okumura Shigeji, *"Takokuseki kigyo to hatten tojo koku,"* in *Takokuseki kigyo to hatten tojo koku* (Tokyo: Tokyo Daigaku Shuppan Kai, 1977), 11–12.

20. The history of U.S. interventions since the Vietnam War is long and wide-ranging. To pick only the most conspicuous (overt) operations: the Dominican Republic, Lebanon, Grenada, Panama, and the Persian Gulf. In addition, there were of course numerous covert operations in Iran, Nicaragua, El Salvador, and other places.

21. These terms are used differently depending on the region and the times. In South America, for instance, the term "multinational" was not used in the 1960s and 1970s because it was felt that those giant corporations were all U.S.-based, and not "*multi*national." The term "*trans*national," on the other hand, was felt to be more accurate because it suggested the "transgressiveness" of these U.S. corporate managements. Now that there are Mexico-originated "multinational" giant corporations (such as Televisa, the biggest TV network in the world outside the United States), the term is becoming more commonly accepted (see John Sinclair, "Televisa: Mexico's Multinational," *Centro: Puerto Rican Studies Bulletin* 2, no. 8 [spring 1990]: 92–97).

    There are numerous publications treating the development of transnational corporatism. For instance, Peter F. Drucker, *The New Realities: In Government and Politics, in Economics and Business, in Sociology and World View* (New York: Harper and Row, 1990), and Kenichi Omae, *The Boderless World: Power and Strategy in the Interlinked Economy* (New York: Harper Business, 1990), 91–99. Perhaps the most important source of information, though little known, is the United Nations Center on Transnational Corporations, which publishes the biannual CTC *Reporter* as well as numerous specific reports on transnational corporate activities. The center published the *Bibliography on Transnational Corporations* in 1979.

22. See "The Logic of Global Business: An Interview with ABB's Percy Barnevik," *Harvard Business Review* 69, no. 2 (March–April 1991): 90–105. Barnevik concludes the interview by remarking, "Are we above governments? No. We answer to governments. We obey the laws in every country in which we operate, and we don't make the laws. However, we do change relations *between* countries. We function as a lubricant for worldwide economic integration. . . . We don't create the process, but we push it. We make visible the invisible hand of global competition" (105).

23. Terajima Jitsuro, *Chikyugi o te no kangaeru Amerika: 21 seiki Nichi-Bei kankei e no koso* (Tokyo: Toyo Keizai Shinposha, 1991), 78–79.

24. There are several books on this supposedly family-owned but un-Japanese enterprise, all by admiring—and commissioned?—Japanese authors. See, for instance, Itagaki Hidenori, *Yaohan: Nihon dasshutsu o hakaru tairiku-gata shoho no hasso* (Tokyo: Paru Shuppan, 1990), and Tsuchiya Takanori, *Yaohan Wada Kazuo: Inoru keiei to hito zukuri* (Tokyo: Nihon Kyobunsha, 1991). Reflecting the owner's faith, Yaohan is aggressive in evangelizing the doctrine of the Seicho-no-ie Temple among its local employees. Despite predictable conflicts with employees of other religions (e.g., Muslims in Singapore), Yaohan insists that the doctrine is the key to its success.

25. For specific comments on this aspect of TNCs, see, for instance, Raymond Vernon,

Sovereignty at Bay (Harlow, England: Longman, 1971), and Stephen Hymer, *The International Operations of National Firms* (Cambridge, Mass.: MIT Press, 1976). In this connection J. A. Hobson's foresight in his *Imperialism* (1902), esp. part 1, "The Economic of Imperialism," cannot be forgotten.

26. Amidst the fiscal crisis in the State of California, there have been rumors that the University of California, Berkeley, and University of California, Los Angeles, are being considered for privatization. Though there has been no confirmation of the rumor, there has been no official denial either.

27. Tom Petruno, "A Return to Rational Rates," *Los Angeles Times*, January 29, 1992.

28. The Japanese are very proud of this "democratic" distribution of wealth. Though it is to a large extent true and justifiable, wealth equity is not quite so real. For one thing, there is a huge sum being spent every year on executive perks such as free housing, free chauffeured car, free parking (no pittance in space-scarce Japan), plus the notorious entertainment expenses annually estimated, by one study, at $35.5 billion (Robert Neff with Joyce Barnathan, "How Much Japanese CEOs Really Make" *Business Week*, January 27, 1992), 31. The manifestation of wealth, power, and privilege obviously takes different forms from society to society.

29. After President Bush's visit to Japan in late 1991, the comparative figures of the rich and the poor in the United States attracted a good deal of media attention. These figures are assembled from the *New York Times*, March 5, 1992 (Sylvia Nasar, "The 1980s: A Very Good Time for the Very Rich") and September 4, 1992 (Robert Pear, "Ranks of U.S. Poor Reach 35.7 Million, the Most Since '64"); and the *Los Angeles Times*, January 29, 1992 (Tom Petruno, "A Return to Rational Rates"), February 7, 1992 (Tom Petruno, "Investors Seeking Voice on Execs' Pay May Get It"), and February 23, 1992 (Linda Grant, "Corporations Search for Answers on Executive Pay"); also from James E. Ellis, "Layoffs on the Line, Bonuses in the Executive Suite," *Business Week* (October 21, 1991), 34; Ann B. Fisher, "The New Debate over the Very Rich," *Fortune* 125, no. 13 (June 29, 1992), 42–55; and Louis S. Richman, "The Truth about the Rich and the Poor," *Fortune* 125, no. 16 (September 21, 1992), 134–46. See also the March 30, 1992, issue of *Business Week* (featuring "Executive Pay"), the February 24, 1992, issue of *Fortune*. 125, no. 4 (featuring "Are You Better Off?"), and the April 6, 1992, issue of *Fortune* 125, no. 7 (devoted to "CEO Pay: How to Do It Right").

30. Leslie Sklair, *Sociology of the Global System* (Baltimore: Johns Hopkins University Press, 1991), 101–2. Among numerous books on the subject, this book is singular for a social political vision that informs its economic analysis.

31. Sklair, *Sociology of the Global System*, 48–49. Also, it was said in 1973 that "of the 100 largest economic units in the world, only half are nation-states, the others multinational companies of various sorts." Harry M. Makler, Alberto Martinelli, and Neil J. Smelser, "Introduction," *The New International Economy*, eds. Makler, Martinelli, and Smelser (Beverly Hills: Sage, 1982), 25.

32. June Kinoshita, "Mapping the Mind," *New York Times*, October 18, 1992, 43, 44, 66, 75.

33. Female labor is cheaper everywhere than male labor, but especially in the third world. Thus the sexual division of labor is attracting some attention among economists. An extremely important topic, it urgently requires further studies. See Sklair, *Sociology of the Global System*, 96–101, 108–9, 233–35. Also, Maria Mies, *Patriarchy and Accumulation on a World Scale: Women in the International Division of Labor* (London: Zed, 1986), especially chaps. 3 and 4.

34. There is a good deal of literature available on this subject. See, for instance, F. Frobel, J. Heinrichs, and O. Kreye, *The New International Division of Labor: Structural Unemployment in Industrialized Countries and Industrialization in Developing Countries* (Cambridge: Cambridge University Press, 1980), and Michael J. Piore and Charles F. Sabel, *The Second Industrial Divide: Possibilities for Prosperity* (New York: Basic Books, 1984).

35. Lee A. Iacocca, the former Chrysler chairman, said little about the Nagoya Mitsubishi factory when he accompanied President Bush to Japan in 1991 to complain about the Japanese automobile imports. Stealth is entirely made in Japan except for the word "Dodge" etched in the front bumper. David E. Sanger, "A Defiant Detroit Still Depends on Japan," *New York Times*, February 27, 1992.

36. John Holusha, "International Flights, Indeed," *New York Times*, January 1, 1992; Associated Press, "'Made in America' Gets Tougher to Determine," *San Diego Union-Tribune*, February 2, 1992.

37. This does not mean that the TNCs are all capable of rationally and skillfully dealing with the complex race issues in all regions. The Japanese MNC/TNC managers in the United States, for instance, have had many serious difficulties in understanding the racial and ethnic problems, often provoking their employees of both majority and minority ethnicities to take legal actions against them. The problem as I see it, however, arises not from their informed policies but from their inexperience and ignorance in execution. The corporate managers are becoming alert enough to what is expected and demanded of them for the maintenance of their operation in alien lands.

38. Kuwahara Yasuo, *Kokkyo o koeru rodosha* (Tokyo: Iwanami Shoten, 1991), 127–43. The movements of both skilled and unskilled labor in the European Community, too, offers an economic integration model par excellence.

39. "To conclude, we know that personal income distribution is more unequal if the level of [multinational corporation] penetration is high. No empirical evidence is reported that MNCs reduce inequality in less developed countries in the course of their operation, whereas there are several hypotheses with preliminary empirical support for the contrary." Volker Bornschier, "World Economic Integration and Policy Responses: Some Developmental Impacts," in Makler, Martinelli, and Smelser, eds., *The New International Economy*, 68–69.

40. The first large-scale war after the end of the cold war, the war in the Persian Gulf requires further analysis. First-world intellectuals hardly protested, although the U.S. Congress was nearly evenly divided about the land-force invasion of Iraq before the actual event. Among several collections of essays about the war in the Gulf is Micah L. Sifry and Christopher Cerf, eds., *The Gulf War Reader: History, Documents, Opinions* (New York: Times Books, 1991). See also Christopher Norris, *Uncritical Theory: Postmodernism, Intellectuals, and the Gulf War* (London: Lawrence and Wishart, 1992).

41. David Binder and Barbara Crossette count forty-four ethnic wars in the world in their *New York Times*, February 7, 1993, article "As Ethnic Wars Multiply, U.S. Strives for a Policy."

42. Makler, Martinelli, and Smelser, eds., *The New International Economy*, 26–27.

43. Robert K. Reich, *The Work of Nations: Preparing Ourselves for. 21st-Century Capitalism* (New York: Vintage Books, 1991). See esp. chap. 12.

44. "The ratio of the overseas production totals of TNCs to the TNC sales totals is 79 percent for Switzerland, 48 percent for Britain, 33 percent for the U.S., and 12 percent for Japan. And among the top three countries, the overseas production totals were greater than the export totals. The 1981 U.S. export totals were 233.6 billion dollars, while the overseas production totals were nearly twice as much, 482.9 billion dollars. The Japanese export totals were 152 billion dollars, while its overseas production totals were merely 30 billion dollars." Motoyama Yoshihiko, *Minami to kita; Kuzureyuku daisan sekai* (Tokyo: Chikuma Library, 1991), 196–97. See also Terajima Jitsuro, *Chikyugi o te ni kangaeru Amerika: 21 seiki Nichi-Bei kankei e no koso* (Tokyo: Toyo Keizai Shimposha, 1991), 68–69, 160–62.

45. Robert Reich's comment, in conjunction with Michael Crichton's *Rising Sun*, is eloquent on this. "The purpose of having a Japanese challenge is to give us a reason to join together. That is, we seem to need Japan as we once needed the Soviet Union— as a means of defining ourselves, our interests, our obligations to one another. We should not be surprised that this wave of Japan-as-enemy books coincides exactly with the easing of cold-war tensions." *New York Times Book Review*, February 9, 1992. To quote from Leslie Sklair, protectionism "acts as a bargaining counter for the rich, and a bluff for the poor, and mainly comes to life in its use as a rhetorical device to satisfy domestic constituencies. For example, desperate politicians tend to fall back on it to appease working class voters in the United States and the United Kingdom" (*Sociology of the Global System*, 71). Among the "revisionists" are Clyde V. Prestowitz Jr., James Fallows, Karel van Wolferen, and Chalmers Johnson.

46. Chiu Yen Liang, "The Moral Politics of Industrial Conflict in Multinational Corporations Located in Hong Kong: An Anthropological Case Study," 2 vols. (Ph.D. diss., University of Chicago, 1991), discusses a strike at a Japanese TNC in Hong Kong. Although overly detailed in description and confusing in analysis, there are many interesting observations of the TNC practice.

47. "In some, though not all, export oriented zones (EOZS) the rights of workers to organize is curtailed, either formally or in practice, and . . . trade unions are either suppressed or manipulated through government-TNC collaboration." Sklair, *Sociology of the Global System*, 95.

48. Some labor unions and some Democrats, including Bill Clinton, approve NAFTA with reservations concerning worker retraining and enforcement of adequate enviromental regulations in Mexico. But the specifics are not available. As to the overall gains and losses, obviously some industrial sectors will gain, while others will lose. The question is, who gains how much as against who loses how much, and when they are going to be balanced out. As to the prospects of worker displacement, a group of researchers at the University of Michigan predicted that "as few as 15,000 to 75,000 American workers—out of a work force of 120 million—could lose their jobs over 10 years as a result of the pact" (Sylvia Nasar, "Job Loss from Pact is Called Small," *New York Times*, August 17, 1992). The details are not offered, but the prediction as reported is totally unconvincing. Nearly all in the management side agree that NAFTA will benefit everyone "in a long run." No one spells out, however, how long is "long." It remains to be proven that NAFTA will not be a disaster to the U.S. workers for a forseeable future. See also Bob Davis, "Fighting 'Nafta': Free-Trade Pact Spurs a Diverse Coalition of Grass-Roots Foes," *Wall Street Journal*, December 23, 1992.

49. Sklair, *Sociology of the Global System*, 117.

50. There are numerous works by the members of the Frankfurt school theorists on this (Adorno and Benjamin, especially). Also, Sklair, *Sociology of the Global System*, 42. See also Dean MacDonnell, *Empty Meeting Ground* (London: Routledge, 1991). Arif Dirlik in his essay, "Post-Socialism/Flexible Production: Marxism in Contemporary Radicalism," *Polygraph* 6, no. 7 (1994): 133–69, advocates a neo-Marxist localism to deal with this problem.

51. Mike Davis, *City of Quartz: Excavating the Future in Los Angeles* (London: Verso, 1990), 80–81. See also Edward W. Soja, *Postmodern Geographies: The Reassertion of Space in Critical Social Theory* (London: Verso, 1989).

52. James Risen, "Economists Watch in Quiet Fury," *Los Angeles Times*, January 8, 1993.

53. See, for example, United Nations Center on Transnational Corporations, *Environmental Aspects of the Activities of Transnational Corporations: A Survey* (New York: United Nations, 1985).

54. For recent studies, see, for instance, Lance E. Davis and Robert A. Huttenback's *Mammon and the Pursuit of Empire: The Economics of British Imperialism* (Cambridge: Cambridge University Press, 1988). They argue that the elite members of British society were the gainers economically, and the middle-class British tax payers were the financial losers during the nation's imperial expansion.

55. See Kuwahara, *Kokkyo o koeru rodosha*.

56. See Noam Chomsky's book, *Year 501: The Conquest Continues* (Boston: South End Press, 1993), esp. chaps. 3 and 4.

57. To name a few, Anthony Appiah, "Is the Post- in Postmodernism the Post- in Postcolonial?" *Critical Inquiry* 17 (winter 1991): 336–57; Homi Bhabha, "Of Mimicry and Man: The Ambivalence of Colonial Discourse," *October* 28 (spring 1984): 125–33; Sara Suleri, "Woman Skin Deep: Feminism and the Postcolonial Condition," *Critical Inquiry* 18 (summer 1991): 759; Dipesh Chakrabarty, "Postcoloniality and the Article of History: Who Speaks for 'Indian' Pasts?" *Representations* (winter 1992): 1–26. And most important, *Social Text* 31–32, which addresses the question of postcolonialism and the third world; I like some of the essays collected in this special issue, Anne McClintock's "The Angel of Progress: Pitfalls of the Term 'Post-Colonialism,'" for example. None of the articles, however, directly discusses the TNC development.

Outside Architecture

1. Philip Shenon, "Either Filthy and Free or Clean and Mean," *New York Times*, February 5, 1995 ("Week in Review" section).
2. Rem Koolhaus, *Delirious New York* (New York: Monacelli Press, 1994).
3. See my "A Borderless World? From Colonialism to Transnationalism and the Demise of the Nation-State," *Critical Inquiry* 19, no. 4.(summer 1993): 726–51, and "Sites of Resistance in the Global Economy," *boundary 2*, no. 1 (spring 1995): 61–84.
4. Richard J. Barnet, "Lords of the Global Economy," *The Nation*, December 19, 1994, 754–57.
5. Saskia Sassen, *The Global City: New York, London, Tokyo* (Princeton: Princeton University Press, 1991).
6. Manual Castells, *The Informational City: Information Technology, Economic Restructuring, and the Urban Regional Process* (Oxford: Blackwell, 1989).
7. Aaron Betsky, "Future World with Vegas as a Model—Really!—Our Cities Might Not Be So Grim after All," *Los Angeles Times*, December 12, 1993.
8. Herbert Muschamp, "A Flare for Fantasy: 'Miami Vice' Meets 42nd Street," *New York Times*, May 21, 1995 ("Arts and Leisure" section).
9. "Peter Eisenman: An Architectural Design Interview by Charles Jencks," in *Deconstruction in Architecture*, ed. Andreas C. Papadakis (London: Architectural Design, 1988), 49–62.
10. Manfredo Tafuri, *The Sphere and the Labyrinth: Avant-Gardes and Architecture from Piranesi to the 1970s* (Cambridge, Mass.: MIT Press, 1987), 302.

"Bunburying" in the Japan Field

1. Marilyn Ivy, "Critical Texts, Mass Artifacts: The Consumption of Knowledge in Postmodern Japan," in *Postmodernism and Japan*, ed. Masao Miyoshi and H. D. Harootunian (Durham: Duke University Press, 1989), 42.
2. Jeff Humphries, "Japan in Theory," *New Literary History* 28, no. 3 (summer 1997): 618.

3. Masao Miyoshi, "A Borderless World?" *Critical Inquiry* 19 (1993): 726–51; and "Sites of Resistance in the Global Economy," *boundary 2* 22 (1995): 61–84.

Art without Money: *documenta X*

1. A version of this essay appeared earlier as "Letter from *documenta X*," in "How the Critic Sees," a special issue of *Any* 21 (1997): 6–9. I am grateful to Cynthia Davidson, Paul Henninger, Marri Archibald, and Fredric Jameson for their comments.

2. Catherine David, "Introduction," in *documenta X: Short Guide* (Ostfildern-Ruit: Verlag Gerd Hatje, 1997), 9.

3. Catherine David and Jean-François Chevrier, "Editors' Introduction," in *Politics-Poetics: documenta X—The Book*, ed. Catherine David and Jean-François Chevrier (Ostfildern-Ruit: Cantz Verlag, 1997), 24. *Politics-Poetics* is being widely read despite its price (£55/$85). According to its U.S. distributor, 33,500 copies were sold as of January 1998.

4. "The Political Potential of Art," in David and Chevrier, *Politics-Poetics*, 174–97, 624–43.

5. The address is www.mediaweb-tv.de.

6. See David, "Introduction," *Short Guide*, 7–13.

7. For a symptomatic example, which crudely relates these characteristics of the exhibition to David's age, see Matthew Higgs, "Vive les Sixties," *Art Monthly*, no. 209 (September 1997): 1–4.

8. David, *Short Guide*, 72.

9. The address is www.kulturbox.de/univers/doc/english/html. [Website no longer accessible.]

10. *Guardian*, June 21, 1997.

11. Catherine David during her interview, available at the website identified in note 5.

12. For the *documenta ix* figure, see Ken Johnson, "A Post-Retinal Documenta," *Art in America*, October 1997, 88. The total of *dX* admissions comes from officials in Kassel.

Japan Is Not Interesting

An earlier version of this essay was presented as the Inaugural Tagliabue Lecture at Amherst College in October 1996. I am grateful to John Solt, its organizer, for his comments.

1. Matthew Arnold, "Superior or University Instruction in France," in *The Complete Prose Works of Matthew Arnold*, ed. R. H. Super, vol. 4, *Schools and Universities on the Continent* (Ann Arbor: University of Michigan Press, 1963), 137.

2. Matthew Arnold,, "Civilization in the United States," in vol. 15 of ibid., 368.

3. T. S. Eliot, *The Idea of a Christian Society* (London: Faber and Faber, 1939) and *Notes toward a Definition of a Culture* (London: Faber and Faber, 1948).

4. Matthew Arnold, "Culture and Anarchy," in *The Complete Prose Works of Matthew Arnold*, chap. 4 and passim.

5. The number of Japanese tourists to the United States in 1989 was 2,773,000; in 1993, 3,067,000; while the number of U.S. tourists visiting Japan in 1989 was 247,000; in 1993, 214,000. The Japanese visiting Australia in 1989 were 262,000; in 1993, 594,000; while Australian tourists to Japan in 1989 numbered 20,000 and in 1993, 23,000 (*Facts and Figures of Japan*, 1996, 106–7). See also *Balance of Payments Monthly*, no. 364 (11/1996: 101), where comparable figures in travelers' expenditures are given.

6. *The Economist Pocket World in Figures 1997* (London: Profile Books, 1997).

7. The *Asahi Evening News* (June 6, 1997) reports the publication of *Sono hi gurashi wa paradaisu* (It's a Paradise to Live from Hand to Mouth) by Mizuno Ashura, a day worker in Kamagasaki, Osaka, Japan's largest "doya gai" or slum. According to Itakura Kimie, the reporter, Mizuno insists, "I love being here. Many other places are neat and clean, but they seem a bit cold and exclusive to me." Itakura adds that Mizuno spends time helping non-Japanese workers as a counselor. See Edward Fowler, *San'ya Blues: Laboring Life in Contemporary Tokyo* (Ithaca: Cornell University Press, 1996); and Carolyn S. Stevens, *On the Margins of Japanese Society: Volunteers and the Welfare of the Urban Underclass* (London: Routledge, 1997).

8. Karen Kelsky, "Flirting with the Foreign: Interracial Sex in Japan's 'International' Age," in *Global/Local: Cultural Production and the Transnational Imaginary*, ed. Rob Wilson and Wimal Dissanayake (Durham: Duke University Press, 1996).

9. Ieda Shoko, *Iero kabbu* (Yellow Cab) (Tokyo: Koyo Shuppansha, 1991).

10. There was a controversy as to where the term "yellow cab" originated. There was even a meeting in New York in protest of the characterization of the Japanese women residents in the city. See also Karen Ma, *The Modern Madame Butterfly: Fantasy and Reality in Japanese Cross-Cultural Relationships* (Rutland, Vt.: Charles E. Tuttle, 1996), chap. 3.

11. Masao Miyoshi, *Off Center: Power and Cultural Relations between Japan and the United States* (Cambridge, Mass.: Harvard University Press, 1991), chap. 3.

12. Michael Hirsh and E. Keith Henry, "The Unraveling of Japan Inc.: Multinationals as Agents of Change," *Foreign Affairs* 76, no. 2 (March–April 1997): 11–16. The authors, of course, say nothing about the pain and price this transfer of capital, labor, and technology overseas is likely to cause among the Japanese.

13. Nicholas Kristoff, "Where Conformity Rules, Misfits Thrive," *New York Times*, May 18, 1997.

14. I am in debt to Bernard S. Silberman for some of these observations made during the 1996 workshop on Area Studies, Cultural Studies, and Identity Politics held at the University of California, San Diego.

I have presented this essay in various stages at the following institutions and conferences: the conference "Critical Theories: China and the West," at the Chinese Academy of Social Sciences and the Human Normal University; the Border Studies Research Circle, the University of Wisconsin, Madison; the Inter-Asia Cultural Studies Conference, the National Tsing Hua University, Taipei; the conference "Aesthetics and Difference: Cultural Diversity, Literature, and the Arts," at UC Riverside; the Center for the Study of Race and Ethnicity and the Department of Ethnic Studies, UC San Diego; the Critical Theory Institute, UC Irvine; the Institute for Global Studies, the University of Minnesota; and the Freeman Lecture Series in Oregon. I am in debt to the organizers and audiences for their responses. Many friends and colleagues have read the manuscript also in various versions, and I am grateful for their comments and critiques: Marti Archibald, Paul Bové, Chen Kuan-Hsing, Eric Cazdyn, Noam Chomsky, Rey Chow, Arif Dirlik, H. D. Harootunian, Gerald Iguchi, Fredric Jameson, Mary Layoun, Meaghan Morris, Richard Okada, Edward Said, Rosaura Sanchez, Ulrike Schaede, Don Wayne, Wang Fengzhen, and Rob Wilson. I would like to thank especially Allen Paau, the director of the Office of Technology Transfer, UC San Diego, who spent a generous amount of time with me on this essay.

1. Richard C. Atkinson and Edward E. Penhoet (president and CEO of Chiron Corp.), "Town and Gown Join Forces to Boost State," *Los Angeles Times*, December 31, 1996.

2. Richard C. Atkinson, "The Role of Research in the University of the Future," paper presented at the United Nations University, Tokyo, Japan, November 4, 1997, available at www.ucop.edu/ucophome/pres/comments/role.html.

3. Richard C. Atkinson, "Universities and the Knowledge-Based Economy," paper presented at the California State Senate Fiscal Retreat, 3 February 1996, available at www.ucop.edu/ucophome/pres/comments/senate.html. Actually, Cambridge has been forming an alliance with business by, for instance, developing a science park since the 1960s and forming an internal incubator corporation, Cambridge University Technical Services, Ltd. Though a late starter, Oxford University is also catching up with its Isis Innovation. See Sarah Gracie, "Dreaming Spires Wake Up to Business," *Sunday Times* (London), June 6, 1999.

4. Richard C. Atkinson, "High Stakes for Knowledge," *Los Angeles Times*, April 28, 1996.

5. While chancellor at UC San Diego, Atkinson, with Donald Tuzin, a professor in the Department of Anthropology, authored an article titled "Equilibrium in the Research University," *Change: The Magazine of Higher Learning* (May–June 1992): 21–31. It is a general statement regarding the missions of the university, of teaching, of general education, and so forth, but, even here, Atkinson and Tuzin barely touch the intellectual issues faced by the humanities and the social sciences.

6. Richard C. Atkinson, "Visions and Values: The Research University in Transition,"

19th Annual Pullias Lecture, delivered at University of Southern California, March 1, 1997, available at www.ucop.edu/ucophome/pres/comments/pulli.html. Atkinson's writing is not always clear. My sentence is a paraphrase of the following: "In each case the fact that these activities unfolded in an institution with research as a central mission has been essential to their nature and impact."

7. Atkinson has another op-ed piece, "It Takes Cash to Keep Ideas Flowing," *Los Angeles Times*, September 25, 1998, which, as the unselfconscious title suggests, repeats what he has been expressing all along. I am grateful to the UC Office of the President for its generous cooperation with my inquiries.

8. Clark Kerr, *The Uses of the University*, 4th ed. (Cambridge, Mass.: Harvard University Press, 1995).

9. Sheldon S. Wolin and John H. Schaar, "Berkeley and the Fate of the Multiversity," *New York Review of Books* 4, no. 3 (March 11, 1965): 17.

10. John Henry Newman, *The Idea of a University*, ed. Frank M. Turner (New Haven, Conn.: Yale University Press, 1996).

11. Matthew Arnold, "Conclusion," in *Culture and Anarchy*, ed. J. Dover Wilson (Cambridge: Cambridge University Press, 1932), 202–12.

12. Kerr, *Uses of the University*, 35.

13. See Robin W. Winks, *Cloak and Gown: Scholars in the Secret War, 1939–1961* (New York: William Morrow, 1987). On the academic mobilization during the cold war, see Noam Chomsky et al., *The Cold War and the University: Toward an Intellectual History of the Postwar Years* (New York: New Press, 1997).

14. See Franco Moretti, "The Spell of Indecision," in *Marxism and the Interpretation of Culture*, ed. Cary Nelson and Lawrence Grossberg (Urbana: University of Illinois Press, 1988), 339–46.

15. Serge Guilbaut, *How New York Stole the Idea of Modern Art: Abstract Expressionism, Freedom, and the Cold War*, trans. Arthur Goldhammer (Chicago: University of Chicago Press, 1983).

16. See Bruce Cumings, "Boundary Displacement: Area Studies and International Studies during and after the Cold War," *Bulletin of Concerned Asian Scholars* 29, no. 1 (January–March 1997): 6–26.

17. "One measure of the extent to which product markets are integrated is the ratio of trade to output. This has increased sharply in most countries since 1950. But by this measure Britain and France are only slightly more open to trade today than they were in 1913, while Japan is less open now than then" (see "One World?," *Economist*, October 18, 1997, 79–80).

18. Among the former colonies, nationalism and statism play considerably different roles. For a succinct discussion, see Neil Lazarus, "Transnationalism and the Alleged Death of the Nation-State," in *Cultural Readings of Imperialism: Edward Said and the Gravity of History*, ed. Keith Ansell-Pearson, Benita Parry, and Judith Squires (London: Lawrence and Wishart, 1997), 28–48.

19. For a recent concise survey, see Bill McKibben, "A Special Moment in History," *Atlantic Monthly*, May 1998, 55–78. For a full-scale study of environmental issues, see David Harvey, *Justice, Nature, and Geography of Difference* (Oxford: Blackwell, 1996).

20. Michael Specter, "Urgency Tempers Ethics Concerns in Uganda Trial of AIDS Vaccine," *New York Times*, October 1, 1998. According to Donald G. McNeil ("AIDS Stalking Africa's Struggling Economies," *New York Times*, November 15, 1998), 9.51 percent of Ugandan adults are infected with AIDS.

21. Mark Weisbrot, research director at the Preamble Center, Washington, D.C., provided the data on Uganda's annual debt service in a recent telephone conversation, September 29, 1999. As for the poorer countries, examples are, in gross national product per capita, Malawi ($144), Ethiopia ($130), Afghanistan ($111), Tanzania ($85), Mozambique ($80), Somalia ($74), and Sudan ($63) (*The Economist Pocket World in Figures 1997* [London: Profile Books, 1997]). As for the debt–export ratio, Guinea-Bissau is over seven times, São Tomé and Príncipe over six times, and Burundi over five times ("Helping the Third World," *Economist*, 26 June 1999).

22. The United Nations Development Programme (UNDP), *Human Development Report 1998* (New York: Oxford University Press, 1998), 30.

23. Eisner's salary was raised by 23 percent to $10.65 million in 1997 (from staff and wire reports, *Los Angeles Times*, December 20, 1997), while he exercised his stock options of $565 million, according to James Bates, *Los Angeles Times*, December 4, 1997.

24. See the special report on executive pay, "The Good, the Bad, the Ugly of CEO Salaries Scoreboard: Executive Compensation," *Business Week*, April 20, 1998, 64–110, with contributions by Jennifer Reingold, Richard A. Melcher, Gary McWilliams, and other bureau reports. The figures for 1974 and 1994 are taken from the website of the House Democratic Policy Committee. What is interesting about this phenomenon is that the raise and option have very little to do with the performance of the companies the executives manage. See Adam Bryant, "Stock Options That Raise Investors' Ire," *New York Times*, March 27, 1998; Adam Bryant, "Flying High on the Option Express," *New York Times*, April 5, 1998; and Adam Bryant, "Executive Cash Machine," *New York Times*, November 8, 1998.

25. David E. Sanger, "A Last Liberal (Almost) Leaves Town," *New York Times*, January 9, 1997.

26. Gene Koretz, "Where Wealth Surged in the 90s," *Business Week*, August 25, 1997, 32. See also Jeff Madrick, "In the Shadows of Prosperity," *New York Review of Books*, August 14, 1997, 40–44.

27. Robert B. Reich, "Despite the U.S. Boom, Free Trade Is Off Track," *Los Angeles Times*, June 18, 1999.

28. "The Disappearing Taxpayer," *Economist*, May 31–June 6, 1997, 15, 21–23; and

David Cay Johnston, "Tax Cuts Help the Wealthy in the Strong Economy," *New York Times*, October 5, 1997.

29. The closure of departments is no longer episodic. See my "'Globalization,' Culture, and the University," in *The Cultures of Globalization*, ed. Fredric Jameson and Masao Miyoshi (Durham: Duke University Press, 1998), 247–70.

30. In the fall of 1998, the Modern Language Association of America (MLA) published *Profession 1998*, a booklet "covering a range of topics of professional concern." It is, however, hopelessly out of touch with the changing conditions of the profession and the global culture around it. Its last essay, "Bob's Job: Campus Crises and 'Adjunct' Education," by former president Sandra M. Gilbert, personalizes the historical transformation of today's American culture into a memory of her friend Bob J. Griffin. Profoundly saddening, Bob's death, however, demands a far more clear-headed analysis of the political economy of the United States in the 1990s than the episode of a man with a Ph.D. in English from UC Berkeley who died in his mid-sixties as a part-time composition teacher earning $15,000 without health insurance. The MLA seems committed to evading the real historical situation, thereby perhaps duplicating similar cases in the future as it keeps its operation. As another erstwhile friend of Bob's, I feel the urgency of the need to face honestly the academic-professional situation today.

31. Placement statistics are, of course, indispensable. The question is, what to do with these figures? A recent MLA report finds that of the 7,598 who earned Ph.D.s in English and foreign languages between 1990 and 1995, 4,188—55 percent—failed to find a tenure-track job in the year the degree was awarded. The report then compares the job crisis to earlier crises and to those in other disciplines. The report readily recognizes the "pedagogical and professional—indeed, cultural—crises of great magnitude." It then points out that the current graduate program is mainly "aimed at the major research institution rather than a future in the community colleges, junior colleges, and small sectarian schools that now provide our profession with so large a proportion of its work." Its subsequent recommendations—to cut the size of the graduate program, for instance—should be taken seriously. Yet the report hardly considers the changing nature of the humanities program, or rather of the university itself, which is at the root of this change in higher education. Even if all the funding crises were solved today, the crisis in the intellectual content of learning and teaching in higher education in the United States, or perhaps any other place, would not change. Suppose all the Ph.D.s in the humanities were able to secure tenure-track positions this year. Would this solve the crisis of the content of the humanities teaching? See *Final Report: MLA Committee on Professional Employment* (New York: MLA, 1997). Reproduced in *PMLA* 113, no. 5 (October 1998): 1154–77.

32. "Harvard, with a $12.8 billion endowment, is in the middle of raising $2.1 billion

more." An economist asks if the university really needs $15 billion. An endowment, like any other property accumulation, turns into a "habit," whether or not it is needed, and to whatever end. See Karen W. Arenson, "Modest Proposal," *New York Times*, August 2, 1998. In "Ballooning Endowments Prompt Rich Universities to Loosen Their Belts," *New York Times*, October 21, 1998, Arenson argues that Harvard, Texas, Yale University, and other universities are now spending their soaring endowments in building, maintenance, and financial aid. In a closer look, however, the expenditures seem to be more like an investment for the future: the faculty positions created at these now richer universities are all in biomedical engineering.

33. Phil Pochoda, "Universities Press On," *Nation*, December 29, 1997, 11–16. See also Mark Crispin Miller, "The Crushing Power of Big Publishing," *Nation*, March 17, 1997, 11–18: "Meanwhile, the academic houses are now pressed by cost-conscious university administrators to make it on their own, without institutional subsidies. Thus those houses too are giving in to market pressure, dumping recondite monographs in favor of trendier academic fare or, better yet, whatever sells at Borders— which, presumably, means few footnotes. Those publishers are so hard pressed there's talk in the academy of changing tenure rules, because it's next to impossible to get an arcane study published—a dark development indeed" (17–18).

34. Judith Shulevitz, "Keepers of the Tenure Track," University Presses supplement, *New York Times*, October 29, 1995. The decline of monograph publication is widely noted. Some efforts are being made to reverse this trend by substituting electronic publication, as by the American Historical Association and some university presses. See Robert Darnton, "The New Age of the Book," *New York Review of Books*, March 18, 1999; and Dinitia Smith, "Hoping the Web Will Rescue Young Professors," *New York Times*, June 12, 1999.

35. George Dennis O'Brien, *All the Essential Half-Truths about Higher Education* (Chicago: University of Chicago Press, 1997), quoted in James Shapiro, "Beyond the Culture Wars," *New York Times Book Review*, January 4, 1998. See also William H. Honan, "The Ivory Tower under Siege: Everyone Else Is Downsized; Why Not the Academy?" Education Life supplement, *New York Times* (spring 1998): 33, 44, 46; and Randy Martin, ed., *Chalk Lines: The Politics of Work in the Managed University* (Durham: Duke University Press, 1998).

36. "In the Ph.D.-granting [English] departments, graduate student instructors taught 63 percent of the first-year writing sections, part-timers 19 percent, and full-time non-tenure-track faculty members 14 percent, on average." The corresponding figures in foreign-language departments are 68, 7, and 15 percent. See MLA, *Final Report*, 8. A large number of Ph.D.s from literature departments remain jobless, and for them even such temporary lecturerships are highly desirable. See also Seth Mydans, "Part-Time College Teaching Rises, as Do Worries," *New York Times*, January 4, 1995; and Joseph Berger, "After Her Ph.D., a Scavenger's Life: A Temp Professor among Thousands," *New York Times*, March 8, 1998.

37. Such commercial ventures, however, have not proven an immediate success. As of the fall of 1998, most universities—Penn State, the State University of New York, the University of Illinois, and UC Berkeley—have attracted fewer than five thousand students. To remedy the difficulties, New York University is planning to use a for-profit subsidiary to build its Internet capacity. In "N.Y.U. Sees Profits in Virtual Classes," *New York Times*, October 7, 1998, Karen W. Arenson writes, "Non-profit universities like N.Y.U. have increasingly turned to profit-making ventures to capitalize on their professors' research." See also the same reporter's article, "More Colleges Plunging into Uncharted Waters of On-Line Courses," *New York Times*, November 2, 1998.

38. Lawrence Solely, "Higher Education . . . or Higher Profits? For-Profit Universities Sell Free Enterprise Education," *In These Times* 22, no. 21 (September 20, 1998): 14–17. "Because of questions raised by accreditors, the university increased the size of its fulltime faculty—it now has 45 full-times on board" (16). The Apollo Group, Phoenix's parent corporation, has increased its revenues more than three times in five years from $124,720,000 in FY1994 to $391,082,000 in FY1998. See also Apollo's website, www.apollogrp.edu.

39. See "California's 'Virtual University' Aims to Be a Digital Center for Higher Education," *Notice: A Publication of the Academic Senate, University of California* 22, no. 3 (December 1997): 1, 3; and "Notes from the Chair: Course Articulation," *Notice: A Publication of the Academic Senate, University of California* 22, no. 7 (May 1998): 5. See also Kenneth R. Weiss, "A Wary Academia on Edge of Cyberspace" and "State Won't Oversee Virtual University," *Los Angeles Times*, March 31, 1998, and July 30, 1998, respectively. As for faculty opposition to the administrative downsizing via digitalization, see David Noble, *The Religion of Technology: The Divinity of Man and the Spirit of Invention* (New York: Penguin, 1999).

40. Victoria Griffith, "High Pay in Ivory Towers: Star Professors Are Subject of Concern," *Financial Times*, June 6, 1998.

41. James Flanigan, "Southland's Tech Prowess Is in Partnerships," *Los Angeles Times*, March 8, 1998.

42. Kit Lively, "What They Earned in 1996–97: A Survey of Private Colleges' Pay and Benefits: The Presidents of Rockefeller, Vanderbilt, and U. of Pennsylvania Top $500,000," *Chronicle of Higher Education*, October 23, 1998. See also Karen W. Arenson, "For University Presidents, Higher Compensation Made It a 'Gilded' Year," *New York Times*, October 18, 1998.

43. Thorstein Veblen, *The Higher Learning in America: A Memorandum on the Conduct of Universities by Business Men*, American Century Edition (New York: Hill and Wang, 1969). See also Clyde W. Barrow, *Universities and the Capitalist State: Corporate Liberalism and the Reconstruction of American Higher Education, 1894–1928* (Madison: University of Wisconsin Press, 1990).

44. Charles L. Schwartz, professor emeritus of physics at UC Berkeley, single-handedly

studied the conduct of the UC regents over many years, but after a score of detailed reports, he recently gave up his efforts, partly, at least, as a result of lack of support and encouragement.

45. Harold T. Shapiro, "University Presidents—Then and Now," paper presented at the Princeton Conference on Higher Education, March 1996, the 250th Anniversary of Princeton University, included in *Universities and Their Leadership*, ed. William G. Bowen and Harold T. Shapiro (Princeton: Princeton University Press, 1998).

46. San Diego Biocommerce Association On-Line, available at www.biocom.org/index.html.

47. Gerhard Casper, "The Advantage of the Research-Intensive University: The University of the Twenty-first Century," paper presented May 3, 1998, Peking University, available at www.stanford.edu/dept/pres-provost/president/speeches/980503peking.html. Testifying before the Subcommittee on Technology, the House Committee on Science, during a session entitled "Defining Successful Partnerships and Collaborations in Scientific Research" (March 11, 1998), MIT President Charles M. Vest stated, "Universities should work synergistically with industry; they must not be industry" (available at www.house.gov/science/vest_03-11.htm).

48. At least in the context of university research. The research expenditures by federal government sources steadily increased from $8,119,977,073 in FY1991 to $12,317,829,551 in FY1996, and $13,040,581,674 in FY1997. See Association of University Technology Managers, Inc., AUTM *Licensing Survey, Fiscal Year 1996: A Survey Summary of Technology Licensing (and Related) Performance for U.S. and Canadian Academic and Nonprofit Institutions and Patent Management Firms* (Norwalk, Conn.: AUTM, 1997), and its FY1997 version (1998).

49. See the Council on Governmental Relations (COGR) brochure, *The Bayh-Dole Act: A Guide to the Law and Implementing Regulations*, November 30, 1993, available at www.tmc.tulane.edu/techdev/Bayh.html.

50. See, however, note 3 above.

51. AUTM Licensing Survey, FY1997. See also Richard C. Atkinson, "The Future of the University of California," September 1998, available at www.ucop.edu. The three universities are followed by the University of Washington, the University of Michigan, Stanford, the University of Wisconsin, Madison, SUNY, Texas A&M, Harvard, and Penn in total sponsored research expenditures in FY1997.

52. Atkinson, "Future of the University of California."

53. The distribution of license revenues varies from university to university. The University of Michigan gives to the inventor(s): 50 percent up to $200,000, 33.33 percent above $200,000 (University of Michigan Technology Management Office, "Working with Faculty and Staff" [unpublished document]). The University of California rate is more flexible (UC Office of Technology Transfer, "UC Equity Policy," February 16, 1996, available at www.ucop.edu/ott/equi-pol.html).

54. Atkinson, "Future of the University of California."

55. Seth Shulman, *Owning the Future* (Boston: Houghton Mifflin, 1999), 51. The inside quotation is from an article by Steven Rosenberg in the *New England Journal of Medicine*.

56. Lawrence C. Soley, *Leasing the Ivory Tower: The Corporate Takeover of Academia* (Boston: South End, 1995), 41–42. I became aware of the book late in my writing of this essay. Like Soley's virtual university article, the book has good episodic information concerning aspects of the corporatization of the university. Kristi Coale's article, "The $50 Million Question," *Salon Magazine*, October 15, 1998, updates the Scripps deal, reporting that the agreement was detected by the National Institutes of Health and that Scripps was forced to scale it back to $20 million annually for five years.

57. *Notice: A Publication of the Academic Senate, University of California* 22, no. 7 (May 1998): 1, 3, 4.

58. "Some universities state that the 'academic year salary' covers 80% of the faculty member's time during the nine months of the academic year. Faculty are free to consult 'up to 20% of the time' (usually understood to be one day per week) during the academic year. Payment for the 'summer months' is often under a separate arrangement." See Council on Governmental Relations, "University Technology Transfer: Questions and Answers," November 30, 1993, available at www.cogr.edu/ qu.htm.

59. The preceding two paragraphs are based on the following reports: Coale, "The $50 Million Question"; Peter Rosset and Monica Moore, "Research Alliance Debated: Deal Benefits Business, Ignores uc's Mission," *San Francisco Chronicle*, October 23, 1998; Joseph Cerny, "uc Research Alliance," letters to the editor, *San Francisco Chronicle*, November 7, 1998; James Carter, "Concerns over Corporation Alliance with uc College of Natural Resources, *Berkeley Voice*, November 19, 1998; Michelle Locke, "Berkeley Celebrates $25 Million Novartis Grant, but Some Have Questions," Associated Press, November 23, 1998, available at www.sfgate.com; "Bay Area Datelines," *San Francisco Examiner*, November 24, 1998; Charles Burress, "uc Finalizes Pioneering Research Deal with Biotech Firm: Pie Tossers Leave Taste of Protest," *San Francisco Chronicle*, November 24, 1998; Arielle Levine and Susan West, Students for Responsible Research, Department of Environmental Science, Policy and Management, College of Natural Resources, uc Berkeley, letters to the editor, *San Francisco Chronicle*, November 26, 1998.

60. arch Development Corporation, the University of Chicago, "About arch," available at www.arch.uchicago.edu. See also Richard Melcher, "An Old University Hits the High-Tech Road," *Business Week*, August 24–31, 1998, 94–96.

61. See the article in the University of Pittsburgh faculty and staff newspaper, "Pitt, cmu Form New Non-profit Corporation, Innovation Works, Inc.," *University Times* 31, no. 7, November 25, 1998, available at www.pitt.edu/utimes/issues/112598/ 06.html.

62. UC Office of Technology Transfer, "UC Equity Policy."

63. Kenneth R. Weiss and Paul Jacobs, "Caltech Joins Rush to Foster Biotech Spinoff Companies," *Los Angeles Times*, September 16, 1998.

64. See Pierre Bourdieu, *The Inheritors: French Students and Their Relations to Culture*, trans. Richard Nice (Chicago: University of Chicago Press, 1977); *Homo Academicus*, trans. Peter Collier (Stanford: Stanford University Press, 1988); and, with Jean-Claude Passeron, *Reproduction in Education, Society, and Culture*, trans. Richard Nice (Newbury Park, Calif.: Sage, 1990).

65. Alex Gove, "Ivory Towers for Sale," *Red Herring*, August 1995, available at www.her ring.com/mag/issue22/tech1.html.

66. Sheila Slaughter and Larry L. Leslie, *Academic Capitalism: Politics, Policies, and the Entrepreneurial University* (Baltimore, Md.: Johns Hopkins University Press, 1997), is a systematic study on the corporatization of the university in Australia, the United Kingdom, Canada, and the United States. The book is not concerned with intellectually substantial issues, such as the humanities, the social sciences, academic freedom, and political responsibility, although they surface from time to time despite the book's scheme. See also Jan Currie and Lesley Vidovich, "The Ascent toward Corporate Managerialism in American and Australian Universities," in Martin, ed., *Chalk Lines*, 112–44. Technology transfer is ordinarily from a university to a corporation. President John R. Silber of Boston University reverses this direction by investing in a corporation, Seragen, for its pharmaceutical research. The university as a capital investor, however, may not be as successful as the other way around: Boston University reportedly invested $84 million over thirteen years, and its value now stands at $8.4 million. See David Barboza, "Loving a Stock, Not Wisely but Too Well," *New York Times*, September 20, 1998.

67. Karen Young Kreeger, "Studies Call Attention to Ethics of Industry Support," *Scientist* 11, no. 7 (March 31, 1997): 1, 4–5; available at www.the-scientist.library.upenn .edu/; Sheldon Krimsky, *Biotechnics and Society: The Rise of Industrial Genetics* (New York: Praeger, 1991); and Roger J. Porter and Thomas E. Malone, eds., *Biomedical Research: Collaboration and Conflict of Interest* (Baltimore, Md.: Johns Hopkins University Press, 1992).

68. Cited by Kreeger, "Studies Call Attention." See Kenneth J. Rothman, "Conflict of Interest: The New McCarthyism in Science," *JAMA—The Journal of the American Medical Association* 269, no. 21 (June 2, 1993): 2782–84.

69. In addition to those listed in note 56, see David Blumenthal, E. G. Campbell, and K. S. Louis et al., "Participation of Life-Science Faculty in Research Relationships with Industry," *New England Journal of Medicine* 335 (1996): 1734–39; Edgar Haber, "Industry and the University," *Nature Biotechnology* 14 (1996): 441–42; Sheldon Krimsky, L. S. Rothenberg, P. Scott, and G. Kyle, "Financial Interests of Authors in Scientific Journals: A Pilot Study of 14 Publications," *Science and Engineering Ethics* 2 (1996): 396–410; Rothman, "Conflict of Interest"; and Daniel Zalewski, "Ties

That Bind: Do Corporate Dollars Strangle Scientific Research?" *Lingua Franca* 7, no. 6 (June/July 1997): 51–59.

70. Steve Scott, "Silicon Valley's Political Myopia," *Los Angeles Times*, July 4, 1999.

71. Sheila Slaughter and Philip G. Althach, eds., *The Higher Learning and High Technology: Dynamics of Higher Education Policy Formation (Frontiers in Education)* (Albany: State University of New York Press, 1990); Howard Dickman, ed., *The Imperiled Academy* (New Brunswick, N.J.: Transaction Publishers, 1993); Arthur Levine, ed., *Higher Learning in America, 1980–2000* (Baltimore, Md.: Johns Hopkins University Press, 1993); Ronald G. Ehrenberg, ed., *The American University: National Treasure or Endangered Species?* (Ithaca: Cornell University Press, 1997); Hugh Davis Graham and Nancy Diamond, *The Rise of American Research Universities: Elites and Challengers in the Postwar Era* (Baltimore, Md.: Johns Hopkins University Press, 1997); Donald Kennedy, *Academic Duty* (Cambridge, Mass.: Harvard University Press, 1997); William G. Tierney, ed., *The Responsive University: Restructuring for High Performance* (Baltimore, Md.: Johns Hopkins University Press, 1997); Roger G. Noll, ed., *Challenges to Research Universities* (Washington, D.C.: Brookings Institution Press, 1998). Although Hanna H. Gray, the former president of the University of Chicago, talks about the crisis in the humanities, her interest is mainly in restoring traditional humanistic scholarship ("Prospects for the Humanities," Ehrenberg, *American University*, 115–27). Donald Kennedy, the former president of Stanford, has a great deal to say about university management, especially technology transfer, but hardly anything to say about the humanities. By no means exhaustive, the list still convincingly indicates the general indifference to the problems of the humanities in the corporatized university.

72. Slaughter and Leslie, *Academic Capitalism*, 211.

73. W. B. Carnochan, *The Battleground of the Curriculum: Liberal Education and American Experience* (Stanford: Stanford University Press, 1993); David Damrosch, *We Scholars: Changing the Culture of the University* (Cambridge, Mass.: Harvard University Press, 1995); William V. Spanos, *The End of Education: Toward Posthumanism* (Minneapolis: University of Minnesota Press, 1993); John Beverley, *Against Literature* (Minneapolis: University of Minnesota Press, 1993); Michael Bérubé and Cary Nelson, *Higher Education under Fire: Politics, Economics, and the Crisis of the Humanities* (London: Routledge, 1995); and Neil Postman, *The End of Education: Redefining the Value of School* (New York: Vintage, 1998).

74. Slaughter and Leslie, *Academic Capitalism*, 243.

75. Claude Lévi-Strauss, *Structural Anthropology*, trans. Monique Layton, vol. 2 (New York: Basic Books, 1976), 358.

76. Lévi-Strauss, *Structural Anthropology*, 354.

77. See Steven Weinberg, "The Revolution That Didn't Happen," *New York Review of Books*, October 8, 1998, 48–52.

78. Fons Elders, ed., *Reflexive Water: The Basic Concerns of Mankind* (London: Souvenir

Press, 1974), 133–97. This important debate deserves to be read and discussed extensively. Edward Said's well-known essay, "Traveling Theory," was the earliest I know to discuss it (in *The World, the Text, and the Critic* [Cambridge, Mass.: Harvard University Press, 1983], 244–47), followed much later by Christopher Norris's *Uncritical Theory: Postmodernism, Intellectuals, and the Gulf War* (Amherst: University of Massachusetts Press, 1992), esp. "Chomsky versus Foucault," "The Political Economy of Truth," and "Reversing the Drift: Reality Regained," 100–125. Norris's related works, such as *What's Wrong with Postmodernism: Critical Theory and the Ends of Philosophy* (Baltimore, Md.: Johns Hopkins University Press, 1990*); *Deconstruction: Theory and Practice*, rev. ed. (London: Routledge, 1991); *The Truth about Postmodernism* (Oxford: Blackwell, 1993); and *Reclaiming Truth: Contribution to a Critique of Cultural Relativism* (Durham: Duke University Press, 1996), examine Richard Rorty, Stanley Fish, Jean Baudrillard, and other pragmatic postmodernists, as well as Foucault.

79. Terry Eagleton, "Defending the Free World," in *The Eagleton Reader*, ed. Stephen Regan (Oxford: Blackwell, 1998), 285–93, is suggestive on this point.

80. Slavoj Žižek, "Multiculturalism, or, the Cultural Logic of Multinational Capitalism," *New Left Review* 225 (September/October 1997): 44. The title is abbreviated on the cover of the issue as "Multiculturalism—A New Racism?"

81. Žižek's *New Left Review* essay is translated into Japanese by Wada Tadashi in *Hihyo kukan*, which has several additional pages that have no counterpart in the English version. In this portion, Žižek makes a very similar point about the victimological use of identity politics. See *Hihyo kukan* 2, no. 18 (1998): 79.

82. Tzvetan Todorov, *On Human Diversity: Nationalism, Racism, and Exoticism in French Thought*, trans. Catherine Porter (Cambridge, Mass.: Harvard University Press, 1993), 390; his emphasis.

83. On September 24, 1989, the House approved a measure aimed at bringing nearly 150,000 skilled foreign workers into the United States. The high-tech industry claims that there is an acute shortage of qualified workers, but the claim is contested by the Institute of Electrical and Electronic Engineers–USA. The applications have no ethnic, national, or regional restrictions. See Jube Shiver Jr., "House Lifts Visa Cap for High-Tech Workers," *Los Angeles Times*, September 25, 1998.

84. See Charlotte Allen, "As Bad as It Gets: Three Dark Tales from the Annals of Academic Receivership," *Lingua Franca* 8, no. 2 (March 1998): 52–59. See also Janny Scott, "Star Professors, as a Team, Fail Chemistry: Once a Model, English Department at Duke Dissolves in Anger," *New York Times*, November 21, 1998.

85. Pierre Bourdieu, "The Negative Intellectual," in *Acts of Resistance: Against the Tyranny of the Market*, trans. Richard Nice (New York: New Press, 1998), 91–93.

86. "Ivory tower" is a translation of *tour d'ivoire*, which was first used in 1837 by Charles-Augustin Sainte-Beuve (according to *A Supplement to the Oxford English Dictionary*, vol. 3), and in 1869 (according to Webster's *Third New International*

Dictionary). The English phrase first appeared (according to the OED Supplement) in 1911, in Henri Bergson's *Laughter: An Essay on the Meaning of the Comic*, trans. Cloudesley Brereton and Fred Rothwell (New York: Macmillan Company, 1911), iii, 135. No explanation is given for the choice of ivory for indicating seclusion from the world or shelter from harsh realities. The fact that no one—as far as I know—has ever detected in the phrase the connection between academia and ivory, the university and colonialism, might reaffirm the devastatingly accurate denunciation implanted in the phrase.

87. Bill Readings, *The University in Ruins* (Cambridge, Mass.: Harvard University Press, 1996).

Turn to the Planet

1. Edward Said, *Orientalism* (New York: Pantheon, 1978).
2. Masao Miyoshi, *As We Saw Them: The First Japanese Embassy to the United States (1860)* (Berkeley: University of California Press, 1979).
3. Eric Hobsbawm, *The Age of Empire, 1875–1914* (New York: Pantheon Books, 1987), 15; and David S. Landes, *The Wealth and Poverty of Nations: Why Some Are So Rich and Some So Poor* (New York: W. W. Norton, 1998), xx.
4. Roland Barthes, *Writing Degree Zero*, trans. Annette Lavers and Colin Smith (New York: Hill and Wang, 1967), 30–31.
5. Jack Goody and Ian Watt, "The Consequences of Literacy," in *Literacy in Traditional Societies*, ed. Jack Goody (Cambridge: Cambridge University Press, 1968), 27–68; Claude Lévi-Strauss, "A Writing Lesson," in *Tristes Tropiques*, trans. John Russell (New York: Atheneum, 1972), 286–97; Walter Ong, *Orality and Literacy: The Technologizing of the Word* (London: Methuen, 1982).
6. Jacques Derrida, *Of Grammatology*, trans. Gayatri Chakravorty Spivak (Baltimore, Md.: Johns Hopkins University Press, 1976); BrianStreet, *Literacy in Theory and Practice* (Cambridge: Cambridge University Press, 1984); Roger Chartier, *The Cultural Uses of Print in Early Modern France*, trans. Lydia G. Cochrane (Princeton: Princeton University Press, 1987).
7. Ezra F. Vogel, *Japan as Number One: Lessons for America* (Cambridge, Mass.: Harvard University Press, 1979).
8. Masao Miyoshi, "A Borderless World? From Colonialism to Transnationalism and the Decline of the Nation-State," *Critical Inquiry* 19, no. 4 (1993): 726–51.
9. On February 7, 2000, the *New York Times* reported that an Indian generic drug manufacturer, Cipla Ltd. of Bombay, together with companies in Brazil, Thailand, and so on, are offering to sell their products at a far lower price to African countries. Of course, major patent-holders in the United States, Britain, and Germany "can be expected to wage a hard fight against the distribution of generic versions of their drugs" Donald G. McNeil Jr., "Indian Company Offers to Supply AIDS Drugs at Low Cost in Africa," *New York Times*, February 7, 2000, A1.

10. *The Economist Pocket World in Figures, 2000* (London: Profile Books, 2000).

11. Kevin Phillips, "The Wealth Effect," *Los Angeles Times* April 16, 2000, M1.

12. One of the most concise and forceful arguments on the subject is found in Jeff Faux and Larry Mishel, "Inequality and the Global Economy" in *Global Capitalism*, ed. Will Hutton and Anthony Giddens (New York: The New Press, 2000), 93–111.

13. Manuel Castells, "Information Technology and Global Capitalism," in *Global Capitalism*, ed. Will Hutton and Anthony Giddens (New York: New Press, 2000), 52–74.

14. Studies of neoliberalism and globalization are by now numerous. Some of the most helpful books are David Held et al., *Global Transformations: Politics, Economics, and Culture* (Stanford: Stanford University Press, 1999); William Greider, *One World, Ready or Not: The Manic Logic of Global Capitalism* (New York: Simon and Schuster, 1998); John Gray, *False Dawn: The Delusions of Global Capitalism* (New York: W. W. Norton, 1998); Thomas Frank, *One Market under God: Extreme Capitalism, Market Populism, and the End of Economic Democracy* (New York: Doubleday, 2000); Juliet B. Schor and Douglas B. Holt, *The Consumer Society Reader* (New York: The New Press, 2000).

15. Nina Auerback, "Acrimony," *London Review of Books*, July 6, 2000, 6–8; K. Anthony Appiah, "Battle of the Bien-Pensant," *New York Review of Books*, April 27, 2000, 42–44.

16. Masao Miyoshi, "Ivory Tower in Escrow," *boundary 2* 27, no. 1 (2000): 7–50.

SELECTED WORKS BY MASAO MIYOSHI

....

Books

Accomplices of Silence: The Modern Japanese Novel. Berkeley: University of California Press, 1974. 2nd ed., University of California Press, 1983; 3rd ed., Center for Japanese Studies, University of Michigan, 1996.

As We Saw Them: The First Japanese Embassy to the United States (1860). Berkeley: University of California Press, 1979. 2nd ed., New York: Kodansha International, 1994.

The Cultures of Globalization. Coedited with Fredric Jameson. Durham: Duke University Press, 1998.

The Divided Self: A Perspective on the Literature of the Victorians. New York: New York University Press; London: London University Press, 1969.

"Japan." A special issue, edited by Miyoshi, of *Manoa: A Pacific Journal of International Writing*. Honolulu: University of Hawaii Press, 1991.

Japan in the World. Coedited with H. D. Harootunian. Durham: Duke University Press, 1993.

Learning Places: The Afterlives of Area Studies. Coedited with H. D. Harootunian. Durham: Duke University Press, 2002.

Off Center: Power and Culture Relations between Japan and the United States. Cambridge, Mass.: Harvard University Press, 1991. Paperback ed., Harvard University Press, 1994.

Postmodernism and Japan. Coedited with H. D. Harootunian. Durham: Duke University Press, 1989.

Teiko no ba e [To the Sites of Resistance: Interviews]. Translated into Japanese and edited by Mitsuhiro Yoshimoto. Kyoto: Rakuhoku Shuppan, 2007.

this is not here: Selected Photographs by Masao Miyoshi. Los Angeles: highmoonoon, 2009.

Articles

"A Borderless World? From Colonialism to Transnationalism and the Decline of the Nation-State." *Critical Inquiry* 19, no. 4 (summer 1993): 726–51.

"'Bunburying' in the Japan Field: A Reply to Jeff Humphries." *New Literary History* 28, no. 3 (summer 1997): 625–38.

"Architecture in a Reconfigured Body Politics." In *Anybody*, edited by Cynthia C. Davidson. Cambridge, Mass.: MIT Press, 1997. 78–85.

"Do the Americans Know How to Tell Time?—Some Do, Some Don't." *Journal of the Association of Teachers of Japanese* 10, nos. 2 and 3 (September 1975): 209–16.

"Empty Museums." In a not-yet-titled volume edited by Gabriele Schwab. New York: Columbia University Press, forthcoming.

"'Globalization,' Culture, and the University." In *The Cultures of Globalization*, coedited with Fredric Jameson. Durham: Duke University Press, 1998. 247–70.

"Gurobaru Ekonomi to Dokuritsu Gyosei Hojin." In *Gekishin! Kokuritsu Daigaku*, edited by Iwasaki Minoru and Ozawa Miroaki. Tokyo: Miraisha, 1999. 48–58.

"The Invention of English Literature in Japan." In *Japan in the World*, edited by Masao Miyoshi and H. D. Harootunian. Durham: Duke University Press, 1993. 271–87.

"Ivory Tower in Escrow: Ex Uno Plures." In "University," a special issue of *boundary 2* 27, no. 1 (spring 2000): 8–50.

"Japan Is Not Interesting." In *Re-Mapping Japanese Culture: Papers of the 10th Biennial Conference of the Japanese Studies Association of Australia*. Monash, Australia: Monash Asia Institute Press, 2000. 11–25.

"Mill and 'Pauline': The Myth and Some Facts." *Victorian Studies* 9, no. 2 (1965): 154–63.

"Modernist Agonistes," *The Nation*, May 15, 1995.

"Outside Architecture." In *Anywise*, edited by Cynthia C. Davidson. Cambridge, Mass.: MIT Press, 1996. 40–47.

"Radical Art at *documenta X*." *New Left Review* 228 (March–April 1998): 151–61.

"Sites of Resistance in the Global Economy." *boundary 2* 22, no. 1 (spring 1995): 61–84. Reprinted in *Cultural Readings of Imperialism: Edward Said and the Gravity of History*, edited by Keith Ansell Pearson, Benita Parry, and Judith Squires. London: Lawrence and Wishart, 1997. 49–66.

"Thinking Aloud in Japan." *Raritan* 9, no. 2 (fall 1989): 29–44.

"Translation as Interpretation." *Journal of Asian Studies* 38, no. 2 (February 1979): 299–302.

"Turn to the Planet: Literature and Diversity, Ecology and Totality." In "Globalization and the Humanities," a special issue of *Comparative Literature* 53, no. 4 (fall 2001): 283–97.

"The University and the Global Economy: The Cases of the United States and Japan." *South Atlantic Quarterly* 99, no. 4 (fall 2000): 669–96. "XL in Asia: A Dialogue between Rem Koolhaas and Masao Miyoshi." *boundary 2* 24, no. 2 (summer 1997): 1–19.

INDEX

....

academic freedom, 18, 87, 326 n. 66; conflict of interest and, 206, 221, 223

Adorno, Theodor, xii, 10

Ahmad, Eqbal, 162, 277

Alcock, Rutherford, 52, 74

Anderson, Perry, 162, 277

Anglican Church of England, 20, 30

anti-intellectualism, xii. *See also* intellectuals

anti-Orientalism, 244, 248–49, 252. See also *Orientalism* (Said)

Arai Hakuseki, 60, 72–73

Ara Masahito, 92

architecture: discourse, 152–53; Koolhaas and, xxviii, 183; Las Vegas, 155–56; postmodernism and, 154–56; Taipei and Tokyo, 151–52, 156–57; utopianism and, 153–54

"area studies," xxv, 8–9, 211, 213–14

Aristotelian philosophy, 16, 18, 79

Arnold, Matthew, 195, 287 n. 7; *Culture and Anarchy*, 9–11, 13, 190, 200, 209–10

art: anti, 14, 288 n. 14; contemporary, 175–76, 183; feelings and, 93; at *documenta X*, xxviii–xxix, 177–87; high art, 10, 12; modern history and, 246; postmodern, xxvii–xxviii

Asada Akira, 169

Asea Brown Bovari, 137

Association of Southeast Asian Nations (ASEAN), 129, 136

Atkinson, Richard C., 205, 217, 239; compared to Kerr, 208, 211; on technology transfer, 218, 220, 221; "Universities and the Knowledge-Based Economy," 206–7

Atlas (Richter), 180, 183

Barthes, Roland, 153, 231; *Writing Degree Zero*, 246

Basho, 52, 59, 106, 298 n. 21

Bayh-Dole Act (1980), 213, 218, 220–21

Benjamin, Walter, 10; "The Destructive Character," xii

binarism: Humphries on, 170, 172–73; of Japan, 198, 306 n. 11

Brecht, Bertolt, xiii

Brownlees, Donald, 44

bungaku, 117–18, 306 n. 10

Bush-Cheney administration, 37, 40, 43, 47, 138

Calvin, John, 19–20

Cambridge University: history of, 17, 19–20, 22, 29–30, 40; research, 206

capitalism: academic, 229, 240; democracy and, 195; ecology and, 44–45; economic crash of 1929 and, xvi; economics and, 45; global, 154–55, 211–

Davidson, Basil, 129, 308 n. 8

Dazai Osamu, 101, 106; *The Setting Sun*, 102, 104

Death by Hanging (Oshima), 167–68

DeBary, Brett, 161, 168–69

decolonization process, 11, 196, 308 n. 9; history of, 128–29, 134; as theme at *documenta X*, 176, 180

democracy: American, 38, 97, 190; bourgeois, 100, 208; in Japan, 195, 197, 199

Derrida, Jacques, 123, 169, 198, 247

Descartes, René, 21, 74–75, 297 n. 15

Dixon, James Main, 119

documenta X (Kassel, Germany): artists and works, 182–83; attendance, 186; criticisms of, 180–81, 183–86; the curator Catherine David, xxviii, 176, 178, 183–86; documentation and programs, 179–80; history of, 175–78, 181–82; "100 Days / 100 Guests" project, 178–79, 184; parcours (viewing route), 177–78; visitor impressions of, 181

Dostoyevsky, Fyodor, 15, 92, 266

Dynes, Robert C., 217

East Asian newly industrialized economies (NIES), 129, 136, 139, 146, 309 n. 10

East Asian studies, xix, 273. *See also* Japanese studies

economy: as Eros, 155; Japan, 196, 198–99, 202; national, 143, 145, 239, 253; neoliberal, 253, 256; new economics, 44–45; transnational, 146, 164; U.S., 133–34, 195, 219. *See also* global economy

egoism, 92

Ehrlich, Anne, 38

Ehrlich, Paul, 38

Eisenman, Peter, xxviii, 156

Eliade, Mircea, 54–55

Eliot, T. S., 123, 190

Emmanuel College, Cambridge, 29

energy, 36–37

English literature studies (in Japan): during U.S. occupation, 122–23; early history of, 115–19; foreign teachers, 115–16; institutions, 112–15; Japanese books published in English, 121–22; leading scholars of, 119–21, 124–25; Miyoshi's background in, 268, 271

environmentalism, 14–15, 46; Lovelock's Gaia theory, 39–41

environmental justice studies, xxxi, 2, 14, 35–36, 43

environmental protection, xxx, 15, 139, 257

ethnicity (or ethnicism), 163, 234; neo-ethnicism, 142–43, 146

European Economic Community (EEC), 134–35, 136

exile, xi, 194

expansionism: colonial, 117, 127, 131; economic, 5, 108–9, 256; industrial, 40, 118, 134; production and, 208, 211

extinction: human, xii, xxx–xxxi, 35–36, 46–47; Rees on, 38; the planet's history of, 44

Fanon, Frantz, 94, 127, 130, 210

feminism: criticism of, 123, 282; labor, 139, 312 n. 33; studies of, xxx, 7, 251, 259

Fenollosa, Ernest, 122, 306 n. 12

Fish, Stanley, 215

foreign investment, 134–35

foreign language teaching, 112–13, 304 n. 2

Foucault, Michel, 123, 198, 282; Chomsky debate (1974) and, 233 free trade, 144; North American Free Trade Agreement (NAFTA), 145, 212, 314 n. 48

Fukuzawa Yukichi, 51, 74, 294 n. 1

Gaia theory (Lovelock), 39–41

Gelbspan, Ross, 37

gender: the corporate system and, 236–37; in the humanities, 7, 240, 241; nation and, 235, 258–59; studies, 44, 251. *See also* feminism

Genji monogatari, xiii, 81, Seidensticker's translation of, 77–80, 82

German "rationality," 94

Germany: culture, 9, 287 n. 7; economy, 196; philosophers, 34, 248; population growth (1750–1850), 27; Second World War, 34, 94, 129; Thirty Years War, 20; tourism, 192; universities, 18–19, 22, 34, 293 n. 35. See also *documenta X*

global economy: impact on migration, 234; the nation-state and, xxv, 6, 239–40; the university and, xxix, 5–6, 211, 228–30, 260; world resources and, 154

globalization: capitalism and, 109, 154, 211, 236; corporatization and, 205, 214; culture and, xxvi, 181, 264, 283; discourse, xxv–xxvi, 229; the humanities and, 5, 253; industrial, 235; inequality and, xxix, 154; intellectuals of, xi; wealth distribution and, 212. *See also* global economy

global warming, 36, 261, 294 n. 67; denial of, 226, 288 n. 15. *See also* climate change

Goodstein, David, 36

Gulf War, 142, 148, 202

Hall, Stuart, 10, 277, 281

Harootunian, Harry: friendship with Miyoshi, 277, 281; *Postmodernism and Japan*, xxiv–xxv; Humphries's critique of, 161–62, 169, 171

Harris, Townsend, xx, 52, 57, 61–62, 71–72

Harvard University: Dana Farber Institute and Sandoz partnership, 221, 223; endowments, 321–22 n. 32; history of, 29–32

Harvey, David, xxv, 165, 294 n. 67

Hassan, Ihab, 165

Hayashi Fukusai, 68–69

Hayashi Fusao, 97

Hearn, Lafcadio, 116, 119

Hegelian theory, 34, 96, 168, 172

hegemonism: criticisms of, 86, 97, 252; culture and, 190, 232; economics and, 136; ideology, 150, 244; Japanese literature and, xxiv, 97, 107, 125

Heian period: *Genji* tale of, 79, 82; travelogues from, 52, 56

Heidegger, Martin, 34, 248, 293 n. 55

Heusken, Henry, 52, 56–58, 61

Higashikuni Naruhiko, 90, 93

high culture, 10, 12, 13

Hirohito, 97–98

Hirose Kakuzo Kaneaki, 49, 64, 66

Hobson, J. A., 127, 147

humanism: egoism as a form of, 92; global or world, xiii, 261; Marxist, 230–31; neo-, 17–19

humanities: alternative, 7; Atkinson on, 206–7, 239, 318 n. 5; bourgeois advancement of, 208–9; critics and theorists of, xvi, 147, 240–41; decline of discipline, 1–2, 7–9, 214, 229–30; departments or faculties, 237–39, 250, 321 n. 31; environmental studies as an alternative to, xxx, 15, 35, 36;

globalization and, xxvi, 5, 228–29, 253, 264; Humanities Research Institute (UC, Irvine), 149, 207; Japanese scholarship in, 192, 201; scholars of, 230; university management of, 278, 327 n. 71; utilitarianism of, 6–7

Humboldt, Wilhelm von, 34, 206, 209

Humphries, Jefferson: Miyoshi's reply to "Japan in Theory," 159–74

identity politics, xxi, xxvii, 7, 163, 236–37

identity studies, 8–9, 258

imperialism, 8, 24, 283; *Culture and Imperialism* (Said), 127; Japanese, 94, 108, 197, 248; Western, 94, 96, 197

income gap: disparity between U.S. and Japan, 138, 199; tax rates, 138; Uganda and Luxembourg ratio, 212–13; in the U.S. from 1995–97, 213; world's richest individuals, 13, 212–13; worldwide rich and poor ratios, 138, 154, 255

Inns of Court (London), 21

intellectuals: academic, xii, 5, 21, 245; Japanese, 91, 108, 109, 248, 280–83; "negative," 239; public, 3, 6; role in transnational corporatism, 141; U.S. or Western, 244, 266

intellectual property, 217, 220, 222, 224, 260

Intergovernmental Panel on Climate Change (IPCC), 36, 41, 42, 286 n. 1, 288 n. 15

Ivy, Marilyn, 161, 168–69, 172

Jameson, Fredric, 162, 165, 168; on the death of the subject, 109; friendship with Miyoshi, xx, 273, 277, 281, 284; on postmodernism, xxv

Japan: ambassadors, 63; censorship, 90, 96–97; deference to the West, 98–99; dissent in discourse on, 196, 198, 201; domestic privacy, 88; economic power, 96, 109, 198–99, 202; emperor system, 94; exports, 135, 252, 313 n. 44; feudalism, 53–54; general strike (1947), 88; individualism, 108; intellectualism, 91, 107–8, 248, 280–83; liberation, 129–30; military participation, 202; minorities, 199; national identity, 196–97; non-communication policy, 72; nonfiction writing/writers, xxii, 103, 166, 191, 198; postwar fiction and I-fiction, 99–106; postwar journals, 89–93; self-criticism, 109, 203; tourist visits to America, 191–92; travelers (1860), xx–xxi, 59, 62, 70; U.S. occupation of, 85–89, 96–97, 197, 248; war crimes, 90, 96–98; Western travelers to, 63; written language, 62–64, 116–17. *See also* Japanese culture; Tokugawa period

Japanese culture, xix, 74, 118, 201; differences with England, 116; Japanese books in English on, 121; Japanology specialists on, 195; lack of homogeneity in, 199; and politics, 200; Western influence on, 98–99

Japanese literature: definition and history of *bungaku*, 117–18, 306 n. 10; Edo *gesaku* writers, 102; Eurocentricity and, 245; identity and, 7; Miyoshi as a teacher of, 276; postwar fiction and I-fiction (*shishosetu*), 99–107; postwar journals and periodicals, 89–93. See also *shosetsu*; travelogues

Japanese prose narrative. See *shosetsu*

Japanese studies: Japanologists or "colonizers" of, 160–64, 167–68, 173–74,

Japanese studies (*cont.*)
307 n. 21; Miyoshi's background in, xxii–xxiii, 163–64, 273, 278; scholars, 123–24, 201, 306 n. 19
Japanism (*Nihonjinron*), 197

Kant, Immanuel, 26, 96, 290 n. 28; *The Conflict of the Faculties*, 22–24
Karatani Kojin, 160, 162, 168–69
Kato Shuichi, 92
Kato Somo, 50, 64, 66, 295 n. 4
Kawabata Yasunari, 99–100
Kennan, George, 86
Kennedy administration, 10–11, 134
Kennedy, Paul, 132
Kerr, Clark, 208, 211; *The Uses of the University*, 207, 229
Kimura Settsu-no-Kami Yoshitake, 67
Kimura Tetsuta, 50, 64, 66
Koolhaas, Rem, xxviii, 153, 177, 179, 183
Korean War, 10, 133, 202
Krimsky, Sheldon, 225
Kuan-Hsing Chen: interview with Miyoshi, 264–84

labor: cheap, 5, 135, 237, 252–54; female, 139, 312 n. 33; movements, 88; policies, 198; strikes, 88, 132, 271; unions, xxvii, 136, 145, 314 n. 48; unskilled, 141, 193, 312 n. 38; wage inequality, 148
Las Vegas, 155–56
Leslie, Larry, 229–30
Lévi-Strauss, Claude, 231–32, 247
"liberal education," 19, 208–10
liberation, 11, 90, 97, 128, 230–31, 252; Japanese, 129–30; Odagiri on, 93; sexual, 102
literature: classical, 18; comparative, 258–59; culture and, 13, 244; decline in academia, 1, 7, 250; ecology and, 44; Miyoshi and, 266, 278; national, 125, 196, 214, 239, 249, 282–83; planetarianism and, 261; in relation to extra-literary events, 251. *See also* English literature studies; Japanese literature
Locke, John, 31, 127
Lovelock, James, 39–42
Lutheranism, 20–21; Lutheran Church 30
Lyna, Mark, 37

MacArthur, General Douglas, 85–89, 95
Ma, Karen, 166
Malthus, Thomas, 41, 290–91 n. 32, 291 n. 38; *An Essay on the Principle of Population*, 24–26, 28, 290 n. 29
markets: in academia, 7, 32, 34, 206, 229, 260; art and, 178, 183, 186; colonialism and, 131; global or world, 134, 211, 229; Japanese, 195, 252; products, 155, 319 n. 17; U.S., 135–36
Marshall, George, 86
Marshall, Kerry James, 183
Maruyama Masao, 75, 93–95, 109
Marxist thought: Hegelian linear worldview and, 168, 172; humanism and, 230–31; in the humanities, 237; neo-Marxist thought, 170; in *shutaisei* discourse, 91, 95; writers inspired by, 100, 101, 123
Marx, Karl, 143, 211
McCullough, Helen, 164, 167, 172
medieval university: eleventh to fourteenth century Europe, 16–18; fifteenth to eighteenth century Europe, 18–24; first North American institutions, 29–32
Merry Christmas, Mr. Lawrence (Oshima), 166–68

religion: Anglican Church of England, 20, 30; freedom of, 85; Lutheranism and Catholicism, 20–21; in universities, 15, 29–30

Richter, Gerhard, 180, 183

Roberts, Paul, 36–37

Roman Catholic Church, 20–21, 30

Rothman, Kenneth J., 226

Said, Edward: anti-Orientalism and, 244, 248–49, 252; *Culture and Imperialism*, 127; friendship with Miyoshi, xx, 263, 273, 277–78, 280; at "100 Days/100 Guests" forum, 185; *Orientalism*, xix, xxi, 123, 128, 244–45, 170, 263

Sakaguchi Ango, 101, 104–7

samurai, 53–55, 115

Sano Kanae, 55–56, 64, 296 n. 8

Sartre, Jean-Paul, 231

Sassen, Saskia, 154, 179

Saussurean linguistics, 231, 232

Scripps Research Institute: partnership with Sandoz, 221, 325 n. 56

Second World War: Allied Powers, 84–86, 142; decolonization following, 129–30; General MacArthur, 85–89; German nationalism, 34; influence on Miyoshi's life, xvii–xviii, 264; Japanese dissidents, 197; Japanese postwar fiction, 99–107; Japanese postwar journals and periodicals, 89–93; New World Order, 129; Potsdam Declaration, 84, 85, 90; Soviet Union, 84–87, 89, 129; U.S. occupation of Japan, 85–89, 96–97, 197, 248; war crimes 90, 96–98

Seidensticker, Edward G., 164; *The Tale of Genji*, 77–80, 82

Shaw, George Bernard, 151

Shiina Rinzo, 100, 106–7; "Significance of Postwar Literature", 91–92, 101

Shimmi Buzen-no-Kami, 50–51, 68, 295 n. 6

shosetsu (Japanese prose narrative), xxiii–xxiv; 245–48; "accidental fiction" (*guzen shosetsu*), 103

shutaisei (subjectivity): consumerism as, 109; definition of, 83, 301 n. 2; in I-fiction (*shishosetu*), 106–7; in Japanese political thought, 84, 89–91, 94; in postwar writing, 88, 91–92, 101, 103–5; as a universal value, 107–8; war responsibility and, 95, 96

Sklair, Leslie, 138, 145, 313 n. 45

Slaughter, Sheila, 229–30

social justice, 14, 46. *See also* environmental justice studies

Soseki Natsume, 116, 117–18, 124; as an English scholar, 118–22; essay on the sea, 54–55

Soviet Union: Cold War, 108, 142, 254–55; communism, 230; disharmony with the U.S., 84–87, 89; Toshiba Machine Corporation scandal and, xxii

student rebellions, 11, 230

Summers, Lawrence, 13, 147, 289 n. 16

Supreme Commander of the Allied Powers (SCAP), 85, 90

Taipei, Taiwan, 151–52

Tale of Genji. See *Genji monogatari*

Tamagami Takuya, 79

Tamamushi Sadayu Yasushige, 51, 55, 66, 68–70, 299 n. 26

Tamura Taijiro, 101–2, 106–7

Tanizaki Junichiro, 99

Thatcher, Margaret, 25, 218, 253, 281

third-world nations: alliances among, 131; consumption in, 261; literature

Climate Change, 37; occupation of Japan, 85–89, 96–97 197, 248; privatization, 137–38, 218, 253; protectionism, 144, 252, 313 n. 45; tourists to Japan, 191, 317 n. 5; Soviet Union relations and, 84–87, 89; in Vietnam, xx, 10–11, 133–34, 210 n. 20; wealth, 138, 199, 213

university: academic downsizing, 215; academic salaries, 216–17, 325 n. 58; administrators, xxv, 8, 206–7, 240; American and European differences in, 32–33; "area studies," xxv, 8–9, 211, 213–14; arts faculty, 16; careerism in, xxx, 4–6, 14, 212; conflict of interest cases, 221–23, 225–26; corporate alliances or partnerships, 216–17, 221–29; criticism of the contemporary, xii, xxxii; degree production, 4, 214; early American institutions, 29–32; empirical science in, 21; environmental justice studies, xxxi, 2, 14, 35–36, 43; financial disclosure, 226; funding, 33, 34, 221; global economy and, xxix, 5–6, 211, 228–30, 260; graduate and undergraduate education, 4–6, 16, 215, 238, 250, 321 n. 31; identity politics, 237; Kant's criticism of, 22–24; library funding, 215; medieval history of, 15–22; modern university, 208–10, 241; multiculturalism, 234; multiversity, 207–8; neoliberalism and, 6–7; Nietzsche's view on, 34; presses, 215; public respect for, 3; public vs. private institutions, 214; religious conflict in early, 15, 29–30; research and development, 205–7, 219–24, 227, 229; role of professor, 2, 4, 238–39; student rebellions, 11, 230; technology transfer,

218, 220, 221, 225, 260, 326 n. 66; traditional disciplines, xxx, 35; weapons research and, 211; virtual universities, 215–16. *See also under specific university name*; English literature studies; humanities; Japanese studies

University of California, Berkeley: "Beyond 'Orientalism'" conference, 148; enrolment, 323 n. 37; Haas School of Business, 222; Legal and Economic Consulting Group (LECG), 221; Miyoshi's time at, xx, 163, 272–75, 277–78; Novartis Pharmaceuticals Corporation partnership, 222–23, 228; student rebellions, 230. *See also* Atkinson, Richard C.

University of California, San Diego: Dynes of, 217; Miyoshi's time at, xxi–xxii, 279

University of Tokyo, xvii, 115, 118–19, 306 n. 11

Ury, Marian, 77–78, 80

utilitarianism, 6–7, 209

Victorian literature, xviii, 276

Vietnam War: influence on Miyoshi, xx, 83, 271–72, 280; protests, 234; U.S. involvement in, 10–11, 133–34, 148

virtual universities, 215–16

Waley, Arthur, 77–78, 81

Wall, Jeff, 177, 179, 181–82

Walt Disney Corporation, 156, 213

war crimes, 90, 96; Tokyo tribunal, 97–98

Ward, Peter D., 44

Weart, Spencer, 36

Western hegemonism. *See* hegemonism

Western imperialism, 94, 96, 197

Williams, Raymond, 10, 210

Woodstock concert (1969), 12

Woolf, Virginia, 81–82

World Bank, 131, 139; Summers involvement with, 147, 289 n. 16

World War II. *See* Second World War

MASAO MIYOSHI (1928–2009) was the Hajime Mori Distinguished Professor Emeritus of Japanese, English, and Comparative Literature at the University of California, San Diego. His books include *Off Center: Power and Culture Relations between Japan and the United States* (1994), *As We Saw Them: The First Japanese Embassy to the United States* (1979, reprint 1994), *Accomplices of Silence: The Modern Japanese Novel* (1974, reprint 1996), and *The Divided Self: A Perspective on the Literature of the Victorians* (1969). He edited (with H. D. Harootunian) *Learning Places* (2002), *Japan in the World* (1993), and *Postmodernism and Japan* (1989), as well as *The Cultures of Globalization* (with Fredric Jameson, 1997). Miyoshi's book of photography, *this is not here*, was published in 2009 by highmoonnoon.

FREDRIC JAMESON is the William A. Lane Professor in the Program in Literature and Romance Studies at Duke University. His books include *Valences of the Dialectic* (2009), *Jameson on Jameson* (2007), *The Cultural Turn* (1998), *The Seeds of Time* (1994), *Postmodernism, or, The Cultural Logic of Late Capitalism* (1991), *The Political Unconscious* (1981), and *Marxism and Form* (1971). In 2008, he received the Holberg International Memorial Prize.

ERIC CAZDYN is professor of comparative literature and East Asian studies at the University of Toronto. He edited a volume of *South Atlantic Quarterly* in 2007 on the philosophical and political problem of disaster and has completed a book manuscript on illness and time entitled *The Already Dead*. His book *The Flash of Capital: Film and Geopolitics in Japan* was published by Duke University Press in 2002.

Library of Congress Cataloging-in-Publication Data
Miyoshi, Masao.
Trespasses : selected writings / Masao Miyoshi ; edited and with an
introduction by Eric Cazdyn ; foreword by Fredric Jameson.
p. cm.—(Post-contemporary interventions)
Includes bibliographical references and index.
ISBN 978-0-8223-4626-5 (cloth : alk. paper)
ISBN 978-0-8223-4637-1 (pbk. : alk. paper)
1. Literature, Comparative—Western and Japanese. 2. Literature, Comparative—
Japanese and Western. 3. Comparative civilization. 4. Cultural relations.
5. Politics and literature. I. Cazdyn, Eric M. II. Jameson, Fredric. III. Title.
IV. Series: Post-contemporary interventions.
P879.J3M59 2010
952.04—dc22   2009043378